MAKING FAMILY HEIRLOOMS

MAKING FAMILY HEIRLOOMS

Jack Hill

With 16 pages of colour photographs
149 line drawings and parts' lists
and 209 black-and-white photographs

ST. MARTIN'S PRESS
New York

 For information, address St. Martin's Press, 175 Fifth Avenue, New York, N.Y. 10010.

ISBN 0-312-50678-3

Library of Congress Catalog Card Number: 84-52538

First published in Great Britain in 1985 by David & Charles (Publishers) Limited.

First U.S. Edition.

CONTENTS

Acknowledgements

I acknowledge with gratitude the help which I have received from earlier generations of craftsmen and also those of my contemporaries who follow in their footsteps, too.

As the variety of items covered in this book extends beyond my own range of skills, I enlisted the active participation of a number of craftsmen colleagues in the production of several of the pieces described and illustrated. To each of them I owe a debt of gratitude, not only for their expertise but also for their willingness to be involved.

To Ian Massey, Keith Riley, Spock Morgan, Judith Wrightson, John Woods, Sid Cooke and Bernard Yaffe, who also gave photographic help and advice, my sincere thanks.

Most of the items made were commissioned and subsequently purchased by a number of discerning people and to these I also give my thanks.

I acknowledge the help and patience of my publishers, David & Charles, with whom the idea for the book originated.

Finally, I thank Michael and Sally for keeping a low profile; Marion for typing the manuscript and God for the trees we have all used.

Introduction

Family heirlooms are no longer the prerogative of the titled or the very rich. Town houses, city flats and country cottages are as likely to contain at least one cherished piece of furniture or other artefact from an earlier generation as are the drawing-rooms of both public and private stately homes. Many have their favourite heirloom, often handed down through the family or between friends, while, in addition, the busy antique trade is witness to the fact that more people still wish to have their own classical piece, irrespective of its origins. Each seeks to possess or acquire a part of their heritage – a tangible and often usable piece of the past.

And it is no coincidence, I feel, that such pieces blend so well with much of our modern ideas on interior design, for durability was a major criterion of their construction and a timeless elegance the hallmark of their design.

Within these pages I have sought to create a real heritage in wood. Unimpressed by the quality and standard of workmanship of much of the so-called reproduction furniture available today, and with a genuine regard for the high level of craftsmanship to be found in so many of the genuine antique pieces which have come down to us from earlier generations, I have brought together a useful collection of 'make-it-yourself' projects for the concerned craftsman and collector.

Each project describes the step-by-step construction of a classical piece of furniture or other object with informative and, I trust, interesting discussion on how the work might be carried out using traditional methods and materials. Each piece of furniture is based upon a style from an earlier period, some strictly so and unashamedly traditional. Others, however, reflect the influence of good contemporary design without being too modern or in any way 'trendy'.

The text is supported throughout with clear working drawings, measured diagrams and photographs where appropriate. In some cases the alternative use of more modern techniques is discussed, but only where such usage does not debase the finished work.

Each piece has been made by myself or by a craftsman colleague or friend with whom I am closely associated. Some items were made for personal use, others to clients' commissions, while others were primarily made for exhibition purposes. None should be outside the ability of the average woodworker who seriously wishes to produce a quality piece of furniture worthy of becoming a desirable family heirloom.

Publisher's note on the use of British and American terms in the text

Wherever British and American terms differ from each other, the British version is used first and the American equivalent is placed after it in brackets [ ].

PART I
BACKGROUND

1

Furniture Styles and Periods

The furniture made in the past is often divided, sometimes confusingly, into a number of styles, periods or ages. Early furniture is usually associated with the ruling royal household of the period, eg Tudor; at other times, more specifically, with the name of the particular monarch, eg Queen Anne, and sometimes by the recognised historical period, eg Renaissance. Then there is the French connection with Louis XIV and Rococo. Later, it is additionally identified with the name of the most influential designer of the time, eg Chippendale. Superimposed upon all this the whole history of furniture style can be divided into ages, the Age of the Carpenter, the Age of the Designer, etc, or according to the wood commonly in use, eg the Age of Walnut, and so on.

Plate 1 Fifteenth-century oak chest (*Victoria & Albert Museum*)

Although the type of wood available at any time, because of its structural properties, influenced general style, proportion and finish of furniture made from it, it is well to remember that there was considerable overlap and simultaneous usage. But it is as good a way as any to begin with.

Thus we have first the Age of Oak, characterised by simple, solid construction. In use in England right through to the second half of the seventeenth century, throughout the Medieval, Tudor, Jacobean and Cromwellian periods, oak was used for all forms of woodwork, not just furniture.

The simple tools of medieval times made woodworking difficult. The oak furniture of the day was therefore plain and unpretentious, its designs architectural, and ornamentation, such as it was, basic and Gothic. There was little domestic furniture apart from simple benches and trestle tables and, of course, the oak chest with its solid

DIAGRAM ONE

A selection of furniture styles from about 1650 to 1720

slab sides secured with iron nails or wooden pegs. And there were no specialist furniture makers for this was also the Age of the Carpenter.

European influence – the Renaissance – is seen in furniture of the Tudor period (1485–1603). Frame-and-panel construction was introduced, and tables and stools, now 'joyned' with mortice-and-tenon joints, had lathe-turned legs with low stretcher rails. During Elizabeth I's reign the court cupboard made its appearance as did the four-poster bed. Chairs came into more widespread use – hitherto they had been throne-like and few in number and reserved for the most important person in the house, hence the still used title of chairman. Furniture continued to be of massive proportion with turned work bulbous and heavy. Carved ornamentation became more elaborate and inlay was used.

The Jacobean period (1603–88) covers the reigns of James I and Charles I, embraces Cromwell's Commonwealth and goes on to include the Restoration of Charles II.

Early Jacobean furniture became smaller, turnings less bulbous and carving more simple in style. There was a marked accent on comfort with upholstered seats and padded arms on chairs. The gate-leg table was introduced for occasional use together with the 'Farthingale chair' designed to suit the voluminous hooped skirts worn by fashionable ladies of the day.

The Civil War brought a restraint on decoration and comfort. During Cromwell's time, along with dress and the general way of life, furniture became severely simple. Ornamentation was reduced to a bare minimum, with plain turnings and simplified applied carvings of geometric designs, while leather and heavy studding replaced the rich velvet and brocade upholstery of the earlier period.

The Restoration of Charles II (1660) brought with it a new opulence of European elegance and luxury. New designs, following the Louis XIV baroque style were introduced; curved forms, spiral turnings and ornate carving, often gilded, predominated. Veneer was increasingly used as was inlay and marquetry. Walnut became the popular wood; it turned well, could be delicately carved and gave a fine finish, and its close, even grain and fine texture made possible lighter and more graceful pieces of furniture. Cane chairs became very popular as did the lacquered or japanned work of the Far East. It was during this period, too, that some specialisation in furniture making began; the general carpenter could no longer adequately cope with the demand for high-quality work and so the end of the late-Jacobean or Carolean period marks the beginning of the Age of the Cabinet Maker as well as the Age of Walnut.

The reign of William and Mary (1689–1702) brought a strong Dutch influence to domestic furniture. Owing partly to an influx of continental craftsmen and partly to the fresh ideas of the cabinet makers, many new pieces of furniture appeared, often reflecting the social changes of the time. Chests of drawers, card tables, small bureaux and cabinets of all types were popular. Scroll legs, octagonal legs, inverted cup turnery, serpentine underframing and bracket feet, together with a move towards more curvilinear forms, are all features of this period.

The Queen Anne period (1702–14) heralded the development of a truly English furniture style. The desire for improved domestic comfort led to furniture being well constructed on more simple, more graceful, curved lines. The cabriole leg, introduced earlier, became a well-known feature of this period. It did not need underframing or stretchers and as a result chair and table designs became much more elegant. The hooped-back chair with its solid curved back splat and cabriole legs is a fine example of this. Some furniture became taller, composite pieces such as bureau-bookcases, the cabinet on chest or tallboy, each raised on bracket feet and often surmounted by a heavy pediment. Carved ornamentation and inlay was kept to a minimum with more emphasis on the use of beautifully matched walnut veneers ornamented with cross-bandings of similar or other veneers. This period also saw the introduction of the easy chair and sofa, upholstered in fine fabrics.

(*opposite*)
Plate 2 Early-eighteenth-century bureau-bookcase (*Victoria & Albert Museum*)

Plate 3 Late-eighteenth-century Chippendale writing table (*Victoria & Albert Museum*)

The so-called golden age of English furniture making and makers came with the Georges, I, II and III, spanning the years 1714–1820. Early Georgian furniture was similar to Queen Anne in style, but the increased use of another timber, mahogany, in turn brought about a number of significant changes. Mahogany had been known since Elizabethan times, but it was not until a tax on timber imports was abolished in 1733 that it came into regular use for furniture making. As the properties of the new wood came to be appreciated so designs changed. Its interlocking grain gave it considerable strength and its availability in large pieces free from twisting and shrinkage enabled it to be used in wide boards in table tops, etc. Early work tended to be rather heavy and architectural, but later extensive pierced decoration was used to advantage. So began the Age of Mahogany.

Additionally, throughout the accepted Georgian period, a number of famous names became linked with the furniture made at that time, Chippendale, Adam, Hepplewhite and Sheraton being prominent among them. As the demand for good furniture increased, these, and others, filled the growing need for new designs by producing books of drawings which were in turn freely copied by contemporary craftsmen. Thus, all Chippendale chairs, for example, were not made by Chippendale himself; all we can be sure of is that they are in a Chippendale style. So the second half of the eighteenth century is also known as the Age of the Designer.

Thomas Chippendale's best work is characterised by strong, graceful lines and good proportion, although some is a little too heavy and rather over-ornate. Many of his later designs were eclectic, details borrowed or modified from earlier styles, Gothic, French and Chinese. He is perhaps best known for his chair designs, eg his ribbon back and pierced ladder backs, and for his fretted lattice work (Chinese Chippendale) and the use of both modified cabriole legs and straight, square-section legs.

Robert Adam was one of a family of architects whose names are associated with the style known as Neo-Classicism – designs based upon classical Greek and Roman forms. Complete harmony between buildings and interiors, including furniture and fittings, was his forte and, better known perhaps for his fireplaces, he is credited with designing a number of distinctive furniture details including fluted tapered legs, upholstered round- and oval-backed chairs and his applied decorative details, rosettes, urns, garlands, etc.

Influenced by both Chippendale and Adam, George Hepplewhite, active between 1760 and 1786, is best known for the shield-back chair design which bears his name. Other designs – all published two years after his death – include the small bow-fronted sideboard and a Pembroke table. His designs are distinguished by their delicacy and elegance, unencumbered by unnecessary ornamentation.

Sheraton Card Table

The last of the famous eighteenth-century designers was Thomas Sheraton. Following Hepplewhite, he pursued the same ideas of lightness and elegance taking them on even further, and, combining this with improved construction, he achieved a high standard of excellence. His designs covered all articles of furniture, many of which incorporated ingenious mechanical devices which operated folding flaps, hidden compartments, and the like. His chair backs were lower and more substantial than others of the same period, with vertical splats or diamond-shaped lattice work. The legs of small tables and chairs were tapered and had spade feet.

Plate 4 Early-nineteenth-century Windsor chair (*Victoria & Albert Museum*)

These eighteenth-century designs were by now being made in a variety of woods, not just mahogany. Walnut was still in use mainly as a veneer, while others, such as rosewood, satinwood and tulipwood, all imported from abroad, were in popular demand by the wealthy classes. Native hardwoods and some imported softwoods were often used as groundwork for veneering. It should be noted that much of the foregoing was centred on London; elsewhere, native hardwoods, such as oak, ash, beech, sycamore and elm, were in use for locally

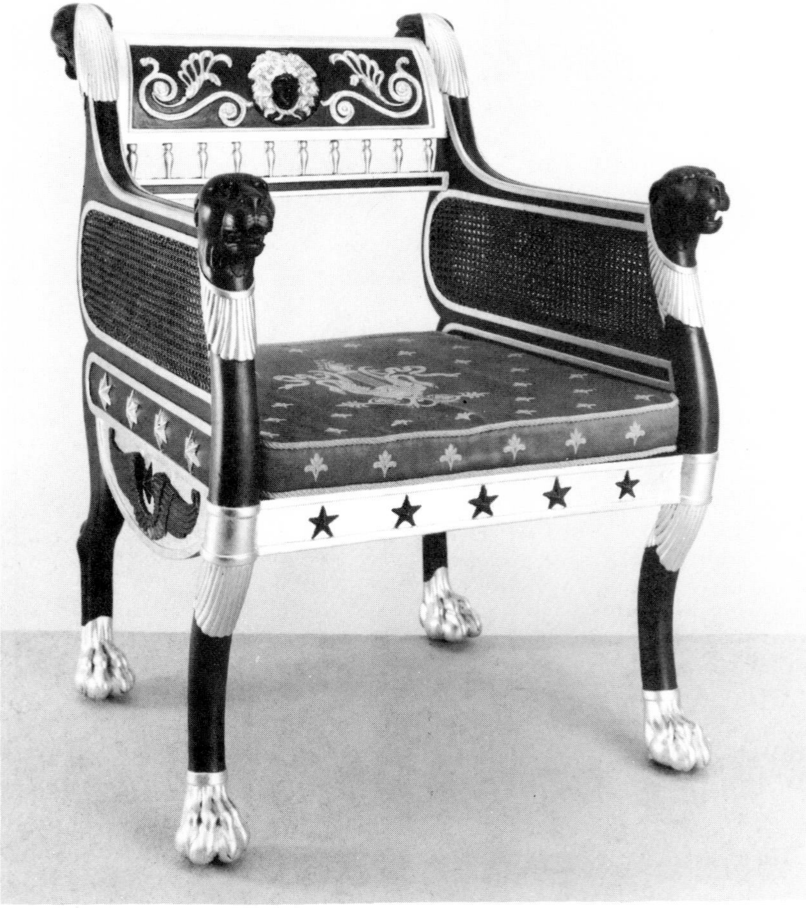

Plate 5 Early-nineteenth-century Regency chair (*Victoria & Albert Museum*)

made domestic furniture. Sturdy tables, settles, ladderback chairs with rush seats, stools and stick-back chairs, kitchen dressers, corner cupboards – all were made by local craftsmen to meet a local demand. A number of interesting regional designs evolved, eg the Welsh dresser and the Windsor chair, but later, owing to the influence of the city stylists and increasing demand, much of the charm of country furniture was to be lost.

At about the same time – the first quarter of the nineteenth century – there was a marked change in the quality of design and construction of furniture. The period, known as the Empire or Regency period, owes much to the influence of the French Empire style. This style, which reached England during the regency of the Prince of Wales, before he became George IV in 1820, was a conglomeration of earlier classical styles together with a mixture of Oriental and Egyptian. Furniture became stiff, heavy and over-ornate, completely at odds with the design developments of the previous century.

This situation continued into the new age of the Victorian period, a time of considerable social transition and upheaval. A growing population, the emergence of a wealthy middle class and the introduction of machinery into furniture making, all contributed to this new age – the Age of the Machine. There was never a definite Victorian 'style', but rather a series of attempts to revive earlier styles using machinery to mass-produce articles in sufficient quantity to meet a growing demand. Poor taste, poor design and poor materials seem to have gone hand in hand. An overwhelming desire to show off resulted in useless and sometimes vulgar over-ornamentation often consisting of applied mouldings produced by machines. Architects were the leaders of design; furniture generally became cumbersome and heavy. Big tables supported by massive legs were fashionable, as were side tables on which to display collections of bric-à-brac; huge Gothic wardrobes overpowered the bedroom alongside the ubiquitous marble-top wash-stand and dressing-table; sofas and armchairs, horse-hair padded to excess, fought for space in the over-furnished parlour together with the balloon-back chairs, chiffonier, upright piano and bamboo whatnot. Dark, heavy curtaining, covers and fringes on everything, sombre wallpaper, pictures and china ornaments only added to the feeling of overbearing.

A wide range of woods were used; mahogany remained popular as did walnut, but beech was often stained to imitate both. An imported softwood, pitch pine, was used extensively. In later work, veneer was often employed to cover up poor groundwork of inferior wood. Papier mâché, usually lacquered and painted, was used on wooden and sometimes iron frames for some types of furniture.

Not all Victorian furniture is regarded now as vulgar or inferior; indeed, certain small pieces are still much sought after and copied, too. The less elaborate display cabinets, small sets of drawers and some of the balloon-back chairs fall into this category. And the various types of Windsor

Plate 6 Victorian drawing-room from a sepia photograph (*BBC Hulton Picture Library*)

chair are essentially products of the 'Victorian' period, many of them factory made, although it is worth noting that these were originally the work of the country craftsman and not the cabinet maker/ designers.

Towards the close of the nineteenth century a move towards rationality was seen in the work of the disciples of the Art and Crafts Movement founded in the 1860s by William Morris. Its followers abhorred machinery and believed that the way forward was to go backward – to the hand craftsmanship of the medieval craftsman. Considerable interest was shown in traditional country furniture which had not been influenced by changing styles. The Barnsley brothers, Ernest and Sidney, and Ernest Gimson were prominent among those who pursued this theme and, later, designers like Ambrose Heal and Gordon Russell succeeded in blending good craftsmanship with machine working.

Between the two world wars, 1914–18 and 1939–45, 'period furniture' became popular, mainly poor reproductions of Tudor and Jacobean styles mostly dark stained and heavily varnished. Mass-produced, cheap furniture continued to be made and there was a demand for it. Plywood was now available in quantity and a great deal of furniture was made from this, veneered and varnished. Furniture became simple and of plain construction with smooth flat or curved surfaces with the wood grain often used as the main element of decoration.

Simplicity reached its zenith in the 'Utility' furniture of the 1940s, furniture carefully designed to be cheaply made using the minimum of materials and labour, both then in short supply. But Utility came to mean shoddy and when timber [lumber] supplies

A Utility dressing table

improved towards the end of the decade most furniture manufacturers returned to their pre-war designs.

Various innovations in furniture design and manufacture have followed, most being in and out of vogue as fast as fashions change. Scandinavian design dominated the 1960s, smaller homes brought an increase in built-in unit furniture, and tubular steel, laminates, glass and plastics brought even newer dimensions in design. And while the work of a new wave of contemporary designers is to be seen at all angles alongside a continuing demand for reproduction period styles and a minority interest in good-quality hand-made furniture, a majority of all new furniture bought today must surely be of the pack-flat, put-it-together-yourself variety with chipboard, veneered or melamined, the most obvious material of the present Age.

CHRONOLOGY OF ENGLISH FURNITURE

Date	Period	Monarch	Age (of the)	Age (wood)
1100–1399	Medieval			Oak
1399–1461		Henry IV, V, VI	Carpenter	
1461–85		Edward IV, V, Richard III		
1485–1547	Tudor, Renaissance	Henry VII, VIII		
1547–58		Edward VI, Mary I		
1558–1603		Elizabeth I		
1603–49	Jacobean, early Stuart	James I, Charles I		
1649–60		(Cromwell)		
1660–85	Restoration	Charles II		Walnut
1685–8	Carolean or late Jacobean	James II		
1689–1702	William & Mary	William & Mary	Cabinet Maker	
1702–14	Queen Anne	Anne		
1714–27	Georgian (early) (Louis XIV, Baroque)	George I		Mahogany
1727–60	(Louis XV, Rococo)	George II	Designer (Chippendale) (Adam)	
1760–1811		George III	(Hepplewhite) (Sheraton)	
1811–20	Regency or Empire	(Regency)		
1820–30	Georgian (late)	George IV		(Various)
1830–7		William IV		
1837–1901	Victorian	Victoria	Machine	
1901–10	Edwardian	Edward VII		
1910–52		George V, VI		
1952–		Elizabeth II		?

2
Materials

Wood, as everyone knows, comes from trees, and trees, as plants, are divided into two main classes or groups. These are the Conifereae (conifers) and the Dicotyledoneae (dicotyledons). Each of these is further divided into families – trees which are related, each of these into genera and each of these into species. Therefore, to identify any tree correctly it is necessary to know its family, genus and species. For example, among the dicotyledons is the family Fagaceae, a huge family embracing the beeches, oaks and sweet chestnuts. Northern beeches have the generic name Fagus, the most common European species being *Fagus sylvatica*, while an American species is *Fagus grandiflora*. Oaks have the generic name Quercus, three specific examples being *Quercus robur*, *Quercus rubra* and *Quercus mongolica*.

Don't worry about the taxonomy too much when buying wood, however. The timber trade rarely use these botanical names. The last three above will simply be English, American and Japanese oak respectively. The important thing is to be aware that from a workability point of view the different types, the different species, in spite of their family relationships, have often quite different characteristics.

The main difference between types of wood is that between softwood and hardwood. The distinction relates to the division between conifers, the cone-bearing trees with needle-like and mainly evergreen leaves, and the dicotyledons, the broad-leaved, usually deciduous trees which shed their leaves in winter. Softwoods come from conifers, hardwoods from the deciduous trees.

The terms are not entirely accurate, however. The distinction is a botanical classification concerned with foliage, seed formation

Plate 1 A typical timber-merchant's hardwood store

and with the cell structure of the wood. Some softwoods are quite hard: yew, for example, is a 'hard' softwood, while the very soft balsa is actually a hardwood. And while it is often said that hardwoods are more difficult to work than softwoods, this too can be misleading. Some hardwoods, sycamore, ash, Japanese oak, are easier to work and are 'kinder' than, for example, a knotty pine or a piece of old yew.

Buying wood suitable for furniture making can be problematic not only for the amateur but also for the small professional. Many large timber or lumber merchants seem to be interested only in large quantity buyers, while most small retailers tend only to stock softwood and this too often of doubtful quality and kept mainly for the DIY enthusiasts. Fortunately, there are still a few saw mills around where it is still a pleasure to do business and, most pleasingly, certain of the larger timber [lumber] yards, recognising the potential of this side of timber marketing, are now offering facilities for choosing and buying both softwood and hardwood in small quantities.

It helps everyone if, when you go to buy materials, you have a clear understanding of what you want, how much will be needed and how to order it most economically. And, if you are able to examine the wood in stock – and this is how it ought to be done – to know what to choose.

Softwood can be bought either sawn or planed. Sawn softwood usually costs a little less. Planed softwood is designated PAR [4S] – planed all round, ie both sides and both edges – or PBS [2S], planed both sides only. Sizes quoted by the seller are usually for sawn timber [lumber], so beware that the actual or finished size of planed wood will be less by a factor of about ⅛in on each planed surface, eg 3 × 1in sawn will be closer to 2¾ × ¾in PAR [4S]. Standard or stock sizes are shown in the chart.

Some of the larger merchants quote prices in terms of cubic measure, eg cubic feet or cubic metres of a specified thickness with widths and lengths random. (Cubic measure is explained under hardwoods, below.) For smaller quantities it is more usual to give prices as per foot or per metre for a given section.

The most common softwood in use in the UK is pine, generally Scots pine, *Pinus silvestris*, but known under several different names in the English timber trade including Scandinavian or Russian redwood, red deal, etc. Other pine species include *P. strobus*, yellow pine or Eastern white pine in the USA and *P. ponderosa*, Columbian or Western pine. Parana pine is not a pine at all but a South American softwood, *Araucaria angustifolia*.

Plate 2 Self-selection facilities with hardwoods priced 'by-the-piece'

In Britain softwoods are graded from Prime, which is top quality, down through Seconds, FAS (Firsts and Seconds) and FAQ (Fair Average Quality). The category U/S, meaning unsorted, means you get a mix of all grades. American grading is from Selects and Better (the top grade), through Selects (mainly top grade) to Shop grade and three descending grades of Common.

Hardwoods are the true furniture woods. They are more expensive than softwoods – although the price difference of some species is not all that considerable – but they are more durable, usually more stable and often much more decorative. Timber merchants specialising in hardwoods usually stock both native and imported species; some country saw mills deal only with home-grown trees.

An important characteristic in Britain is

that home-grown timber is normally offered for sale as sawn through and through (T & T) and waney edged. This means that the tree has been sawn through its length to produce boards of a specified thickness having sapwood and bark on both edges. It may be designated as one sawn edge (1/SE), ie one edge sawn square, one with its bark intact. It will also be seen as square edged both sides (S/E) or as squares. Imported hardwoods are almost always square edged; the bark, being a potential breeding ground for insects and decay, is usually removed at source. Occasionally, timber [lumber] which has been quarter sawn is obtainable and this has numerous advantages (see Diagrams One and Two).

Hardwood in Britain is usually graded as either First Quality or Second Quality while in the USA grading runs through FAS(Firsts and Seconds), Selects and two grades of Common.

Standard thicknesses of sawn hardwoods are ¾in, ⅞in, 1in, 1¼in, 1½in, 2in, 3in and 4in. Widths are random and vary with diameter of tree but some imported timbers are sawn to 6in, 7in, 8in and 9in widths. Widths of waney-edged boards vary according to the diameter of the tree, of course. Here, too, a dual measuring system exists with inches and fractions used more often and more easily by most than those minute millimetres.

British prices are usually quoted in cubic measure for each specified thickness, ie 1 cubic foot of 1in beech, and so on. A cubic foot is the volume of a cube measuring 12 × 12 × 12in. In more practical terms, 1 cubic foot of 1in beech could be a board of 1in thickness, 12in wide and 144in (12ft) long; if the 1in board were only 6in wide you would get 24ft, and so on. The metric unit is a cubic metre, equal to approximately 10 cubic feet. Hardwoods are also sold by the square foot or square metre of a given thickness. American lumber yards mainly use board feet as a basis for measurement, one board foot containing a quantity of wood equal to 1in thick, 12in wide and 12in long.

Sometimes you will find hardwoods – and occasionally softwoods – priced 'by the piece'; individual boards labelled with a selling price for that board. This is an easy way to buy small quantities, but it is not particularly good for larger amounts. Ideally, all the wood used in a piece of

THICKNESS IN INCHES ↓ / WIDTH IN INCHES →	¾	1	1½	2	3	4	5	6	7	8
½	O	O	O	O		*				
⅝	O	O	O	O		*				
¾	O	O	O	O	*	*	*			
⅞					*	*	*			
1		(*)	*	(*)	(*)	(*)	(*)	(*)	*	*
1¼					*	*	*			
1½		*			*	*	*			
1¾					*	*				
2		(*)		(*)	*	*	*	*	*	*
2½						*				
3		*				*	*	*	*	*
4		*				*		*		*

CHART SHOWING MOST COMMON STOCK SIZES OF SOFTWOOD GENERALLY AVAILABLE IN THE BRITISH ISLES

* STANDARD SAWN SIZE

O " PLANED (P.A.R)

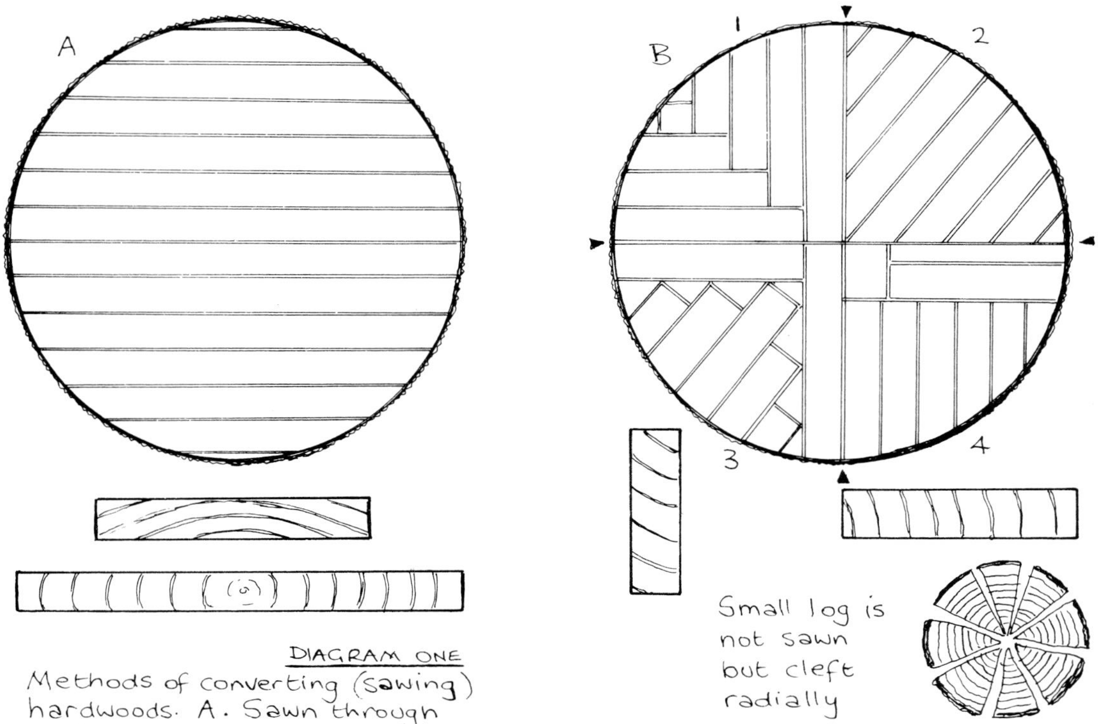

DIAGRAM ONE

Methods of converting (sawing) hardwoods. A. Sawn through and through ~ normal method. B. Four different methods of quarter sawing.

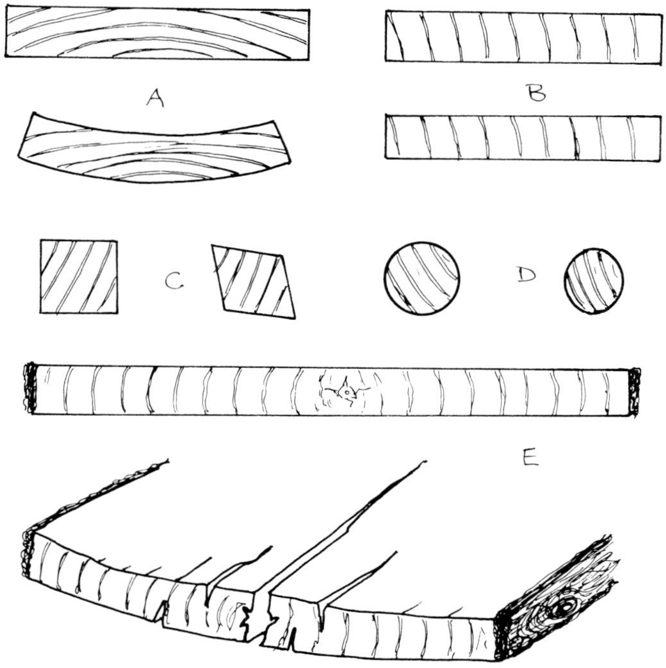

DIAGRAM TWO

Some defects caused by movement of timber during seasoning.

A. Board sawn through and through will shrink in width and is liable to distortion as shown.

B. Quarter sawn board less liable to distortion and shrinks only a little in thickness.

C. Squares tend to go diamond shape in section.

D. Rounds tend to go oval in section

E. A wide central board sawn through and through liable to splitting (heart shake) at ends but yields good boards on either side

furniture should be from the one source, ie the same board or similar boards from the same tree.

When ordering, make some allowance for waste. Ends of boards may be unsuitable and defects may have to be avoided – for both of these a good supplier will often make an allowance anyway. But wood will also be lost in sawing and planing to size and on the occasions when we make a mistake and waste a piece.

For good work wood must be properly and thoroughly seasoned. The term seasoning refers to the reduction of the moisure contained in wood, a newly felled tree being saturated with watery sap which, for use in furniture making, needs to be reduced for furniture used in moderately heated rooms in a temperate climate to a moisture content (mc) of around 12 per cent or preferably less. Seasoning makes wood lighter but stronger, and less liable to shrinkage and distortion resulting in warping and splitting during subsequent use.

The two most usual ways of seasoning wood are by air drying or kiln drying. Air drying, or natural seasoning, is the old, much liked method where sawn timber is stacked in the open or in opensided sheds to dry naturally over a period of years, while kiln drying uses a combination of hot air and steam on sawn wood in an enclosed space to dry it out in just a matter of weeks. The moisture content of air-dried wood is that of the ambient humidity – averaging between 15 and 20 per cent in temperate regions – and so requires further gentle drying in a warm, dry workshop or store before use. Kiln-dried wood, on the other hand, is usually taken down to about 10–12 per cent [7–10 per cent] mc. It should be noted, however, that kiln-dried timber stored in an unheated space will gradually take up atmospheric moisture and revert to the ambient 15–20 per cent.

Shrinkage during seasoning may be quite considerable, resulting in distortion (warping) and splitting, the latter often most troublesome at the ends of boards (see Diagram Two). Further movement may take place after seasoning. After purchase, both shrinkage and swelling may occur, and it is for this reason that all wood used should be at or very close to the correct mc for the situation in which it is to be used. Certain constructional methods such as loose panels in framed-up work are practised with possible movement in mind. Purchase timber [lumber] well in advance of working it and store in conditions similar to subsequent use. Centrally heated homes can play havoc with furniture – even antiques.

3
Joints

Woodworking joints, to serve their purposes efficiently, must be strong enough to withstand the stresses to which they are subjected. To achieve this they should be well proportioned, ie one part should not be made oversize for apparent strength if this unduly weakens its mating part. Additionally, the joint used must be that which is most suitable for the task it has to do. Parts need to be marked out and cut accurately so that they fit together properly and have a neat appearance.

The proportions and purposes of most joints have been arrived at by the process of trial and error over a long period of time and have proved satisfactory ways of solving the problems associated with joining wood together. Dovetail joints are designed to withstand tension in one direction and are ideal as corner joints for drawers; mortice-and-tenon joints make strong end-to-side edge joints, are load bearing and, when provided with a haunch, resist twisting, making them most suitable for rigid framing and carcase construction. Housing or dado joints are load bearing, too, and give a neat appearance in applications such as shelving.

The making of all these and some other joints is described here, together with some of their variations. All are used in one or other of the projects which come later.

One of the simplest joints, but not necessarily the easiest to make, is that used to join two or more narrow boards edge-to-edge to make up a wide surface of solid wood. There are several ways, the most common being the rubbed joint in which two edges are planed true and joined with glue. When well made this is a strong joint, its glue line so neat as to be almost invisible. It is suitable for softwoods and most hardwoods up to 1in in thickness. Extra strength and additional gluing area may be provided by inserting a loose tongue in grooves or rebates cut in each mating edge. The tongue is usually of ply so that there is cross-grain at the joint. For boards greater than 1in in thickness the joint is usually dowelled.

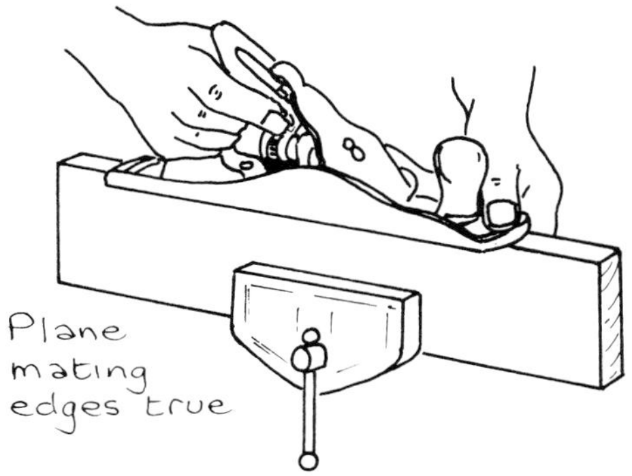
Plane
mating
edges true

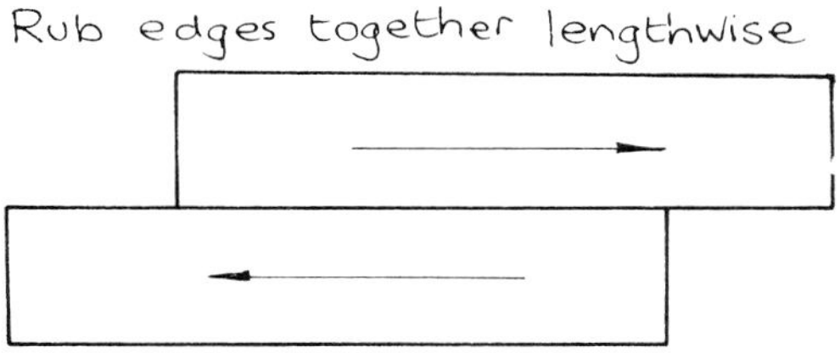
Rub edges together lengthwise

DIAGRAM ONE

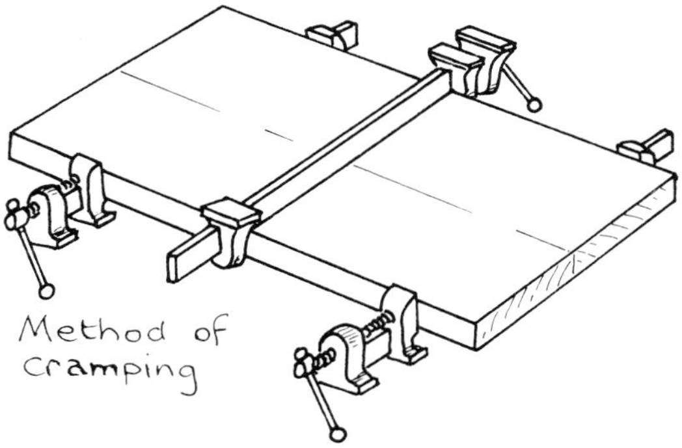
Method of
cramping

DIAGRAM TWO

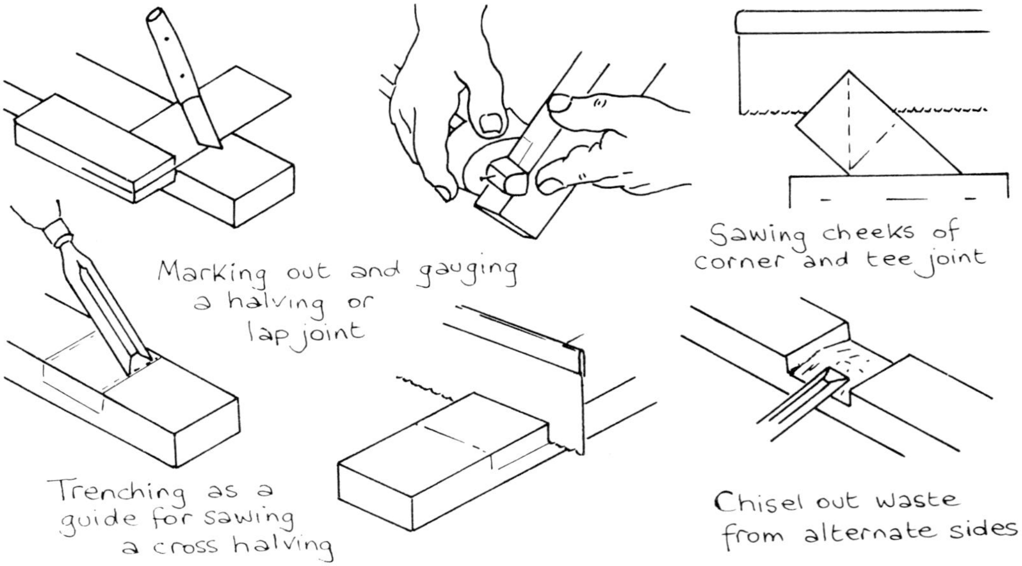
Sawing cheeks of corner and tee joint
Marking out and gauging a halving or lap joint
Trenching as a guide for sawing a cross halving
Chisel out waste from alternate sides

Plane the edges of the boards using, for trueness, the longest plane you have. Avoid the tendency to plane more off at each end by trying to plane more off in the middle. Check mating edges for perfect squareness by holding one board on edge against the edge of the other. They should not rock, neither should there be light visible between the two edges. Some advocate planing two edges together at the same time as a way to greater accuracy.

When satisfied that the edges are true, set up a pair of sash cramps [clamps] on the bench, open to just over the required width and have a third one near by. Put glue on both or all mating edges and rub the edges together lengthwise. This removes surplus glue and any air from the joint. Check for alignment as the two cramps [clamps] are lightly tightened; place the third cramp [clamp] over the work as shown in Diagram One and tighten this top cramp [clamp], ensuring that the surfaces of the boards are even. Finally, tighten the two outer cramps [clamps] and wipe off surplus glue with a damp cloth. For long boards use more cramps [clamps]. When the glue is set, clean up with plane or scraper.

For joining two pieces that meet or need to cross at right angles the halving or lap joint, in its various forms, provides the simplest solution (Diagram Two). Although these

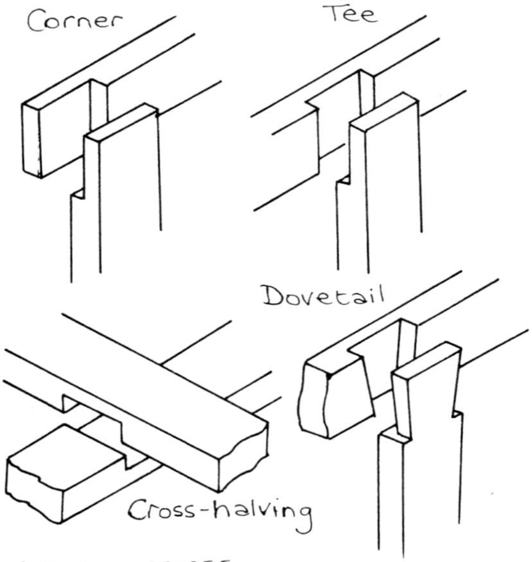
Corner
Tee
Dovetail
Cross-halving

DIAGRAM THREE

lack the strength and rigidity of, say, the mortice and tenon, they are particularly suitable when fitting cross rails flush into carcase frames, etc, which are to be panelled.

The corner, tee, and cross joints are the most common in use (Diagram Three). For marking out, where both mating pieces are of equal thickness, a marking gauge is first set to half their thickness and, when the position of the joint is marked out with a marking knife and squared across, both pieces are gauged between the lines working from the face side in each case. Diagram Two shows how the half lap or cheek of both the corner and tee joints are sawn. With the wood held in the vice in this way it is easier to start the saw and to see the gauge line. Saw in the waste side, work from both sides and finish to the gauge line with the wood held upright.

In cutting out cross-halving joints, greater accuracy and cleaner edges result when the shoulders are lightly trenched on the waste side as shown before sawing. Place the tenon saw in the trench and saw very carefully down to the gauged line at each side. Make one or two additional cuts in the waste as an aid to its removal. Then chisel from alternate sides, gradually working down to the gauge line at both sides and finally finishing flat across the full width (see Diagram Two).

For additional strength the dovetail halving joint is a useful alternative (see Diagram Three). Begin by cutting the cheek as for the normal tee joint, then mark the tail slope (1 in 6 for softwood, 1 in 8 for hardwood) and saw the tail shoulders. Remove the waste by chiselling down to the saw cuts each side. Now mark the housing from the tail and saw and chisel out the waste as in the cross-lap housing.

The dado or housing joint is the best means of joining a board end on to an upright. As a load-bearing joint it is most suitable for fixing shelves, etc, within carcase frames. There are two main types – the through joint and the stopped joint – and there is a dovetail variation of both of these. To make the plain through joint, first mark the thickness of the shelf square across the upright using a marking knife. Continue the marking a little way down on both edges of the upright. Set a marking gauge to one-third the thickness of the upright and mark the housing depth from the inside face. Light trenching on the waste side is an aid to the next stage which is sawing with a tenon saw down to the gauge line. The waste is removed by careful chiselling from both sides. The cut is levelled with a hand router if you have one. The whole operation may be done much more quickly using a machine router and suitable cutter (Diagram Four).

The stopped version gives a neater appearance and will give an unbroken vertical line to the front edge of, say, a book shelf. Leave this front edge unmarked when marking out and instead work the stopped end (about 1in from the front edge is sufficient) with a marking gauge. Clean a space for the point of the saw to move in by chiselling or drilling

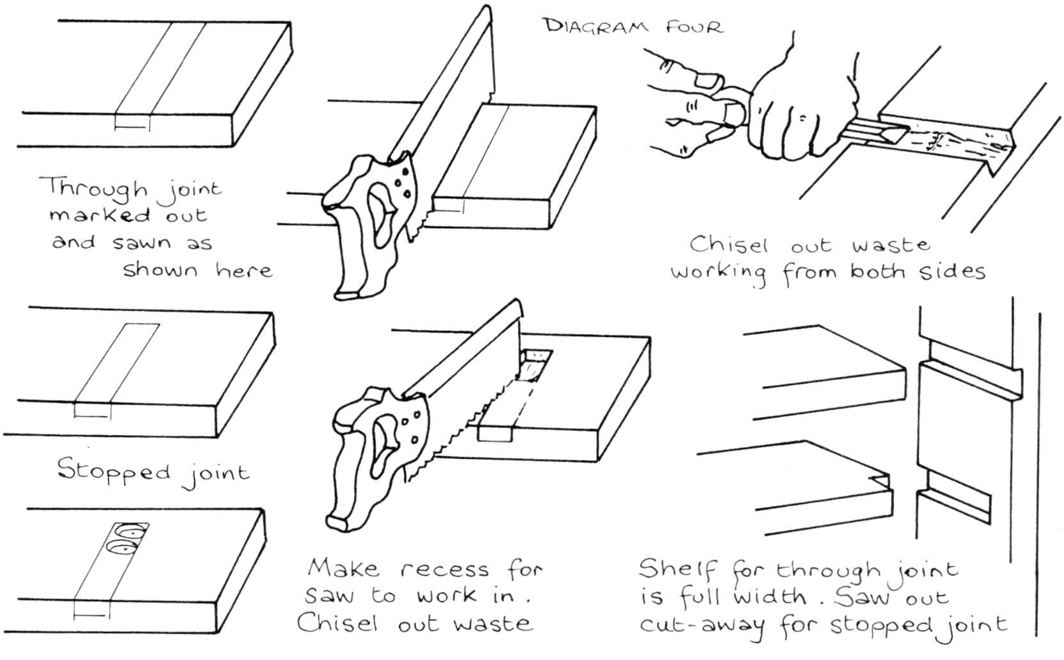

DIAGRAM FOUR
Through joint marked out and sawn as shown here
Chisel out waste working from both sides
Stopped joint
Make recess for saw to work in. Chisel out waste
Shelf for through joint is full width. Saw out cut-away for stopped joint

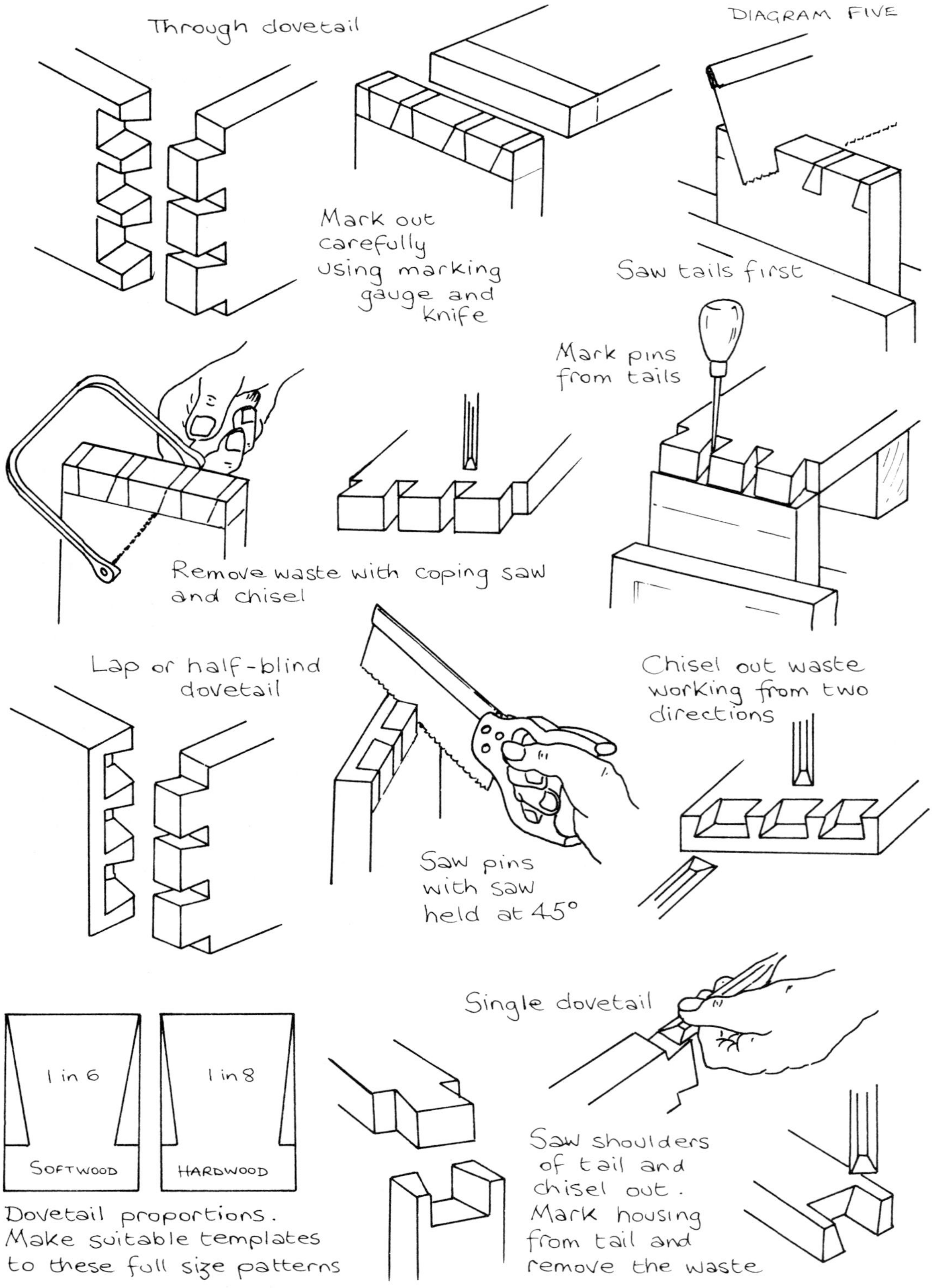
DIAGRAM FIVE
Through dovetail
Mark out carefully using marking gauge and knife
Saw tails first
Mark pins from tails
Remove waste with coping saw and chisel
Lap or half-blind dovetail
Chisel out waste working from two directions
Saw pins with saw held at 45°
Single dovetail
1 in 6
SOFTWOOD
1 in 8
HARDWOOD
Saw shoulders of tail and chisel out. Mark housing from tail and remove the waste
Dovetail proportions. Make suitable templates to these full size patterns

out a recess just behind this mark. After sawing, the waste is chiselled out as before. On the shelf mark the depth of the housing and the length of the cut-out from the front edge and saw away the waste.

Dovetails are the strongest corner joints, decorative when well made and useful for joining wide boards in box construction. The strength of these joints lies in the increased gluing area and in the shape of the dovetails and pins which can only be pulled apart in one direction. This makes them particularly suitable for drawer making (Diagram Five).

There are several types and variations of dovetails, the two most useful being the through or common dovetail and the lapped dovetail. In the through joint end grain tails and pins are visible on both sides. These are used mainly for box construction and the backs of drawers. End grain tails are concealed in the lapped version which is used mainly on drawer fronts. A useful third type is the single dovetail which is a through version of the dovetail halving joint mentioned earlier.

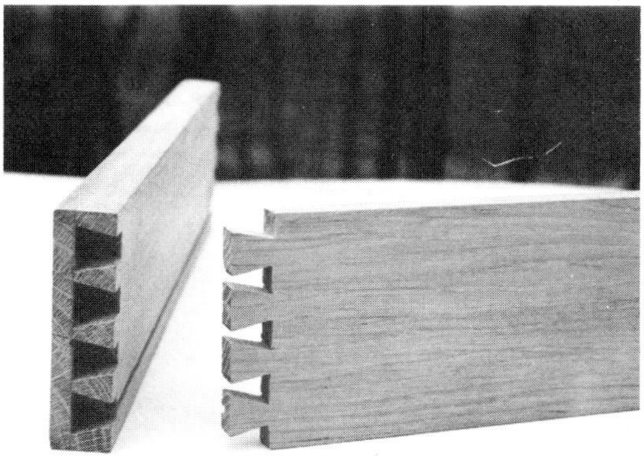

Plate 1 Lapped dovetail

A sliding bevel may be used for marking out, but a dovetail template is a useful aid – make one in strong card or, preferably, thin metal. As a general guide mark out and cut tails first, then mark sockets between pins from the tails and cut these last. In drawer construction the tails are cut on the side pieces of the drawers.

For a through dovetail, set a marking gauge to the thickness of the wood and mark the ends all round. This is the depth line of the joint. Mark out the tails, evenly spaced, and square the lines across the ends. Saw in the waste, down the tails with a dovetail or small tenon saw and remove the bulk of the waste with a coping saw. Finish, from both sides, with a sharp bevel-edge chisel. To mark out the pins, place that piece upright in the vice and rest the tails on the end using a block to support its length. Align the tails on the end and mark through with a fine scriber. Square these down to the depth line. Clean out any waste as described above and test the joint for fit.

The lap of the lapped or half-blind dovetail is usually one-quarter to one-third the thickness of the wood and what remains should be the setting for the marking gauge. Gauge all round the tail piece and cut as described for a through dovetail. Mark out the joining piece, first on the end with the marking gauge set as above, then on the inside face to the thickness of the tail piece. Place the tails over the end and mark the sockets and pins and square down to the inside line. With the wood upright in the vice saw in the waste at 45° down to the gauged lines; then, with the work clamped flat on the bench top, remove the waste by careful chiselling across the grain. Make sure that the inside corners are clean.

A much simplified joint for use at corners is the rebate or rabbet-and-groove joint. These lack the strength of the well-made dovetail, but they are easy and quick to make. Mark out the plain rebate to the thickness of the wood and make the lap one-third the thickness. Two versions of the rebate-and-groove joint are shown in Diagram Six.

In one of its many forms, the mortice-and-tenon joint is probably the strongest end-to-side joint used. The basic form of the joint is the through mortice and tenon consisting of a slot or mortice cut into, usually, an upright member and a matching tenon cut on the end of a joining member, for example, a rail, which sockets into it. The tenon is normally one-third the thickness of the wood (Diagram Seven).

To make the joint, first mark in pencil the width of the rail all round on the upright and the width of the upright all round on the rail using a marking knife. Set the twin spurs of the mortice gauge to the width of the chisel to be used to chop out the mortice and centre the points from the face side of the work. Mark both mortice and tenon at this setting. Cut the mortice either entirely by chiselling or by removing most of the waste by drilling first and then finishing with a chisel. Work from both sides of the wood when doing this. A morticing machine or attachment to a drill may also be used.

The tenon is sawn, on the waste side of the lines, as shown, taking care to keep the shoulders square. Final fitting is achieved by careful paring with a chisel. Wedges can be used to secure these joints (see Diagram Seven).

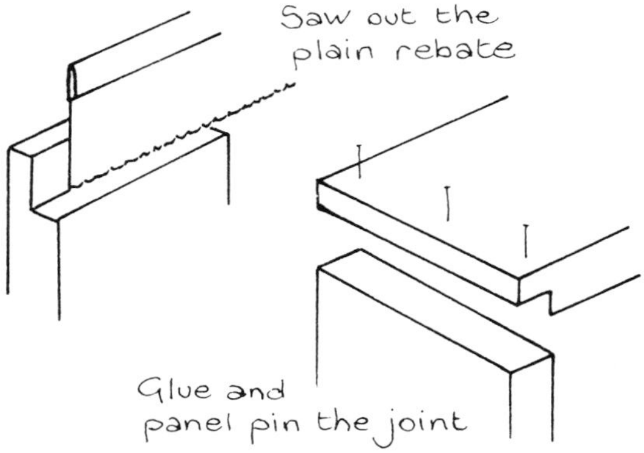
Saw out the plain rebate
Glue and panel pin the joint

DIAGRAM SIX

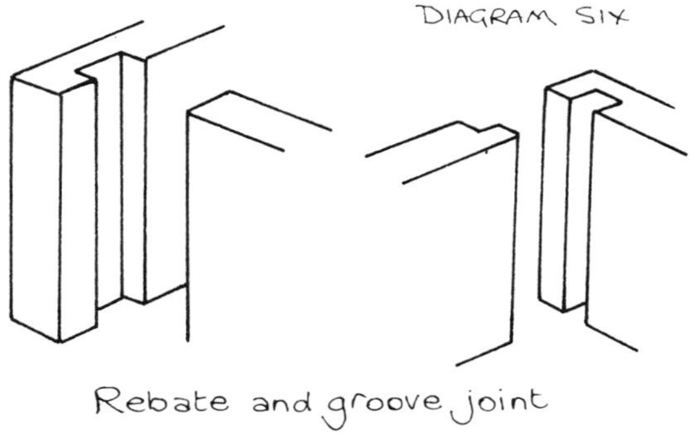
Rebate and groove joint

Plate 2 Chiselling out a mortice

Plate 3 Light paring to finish a tenon

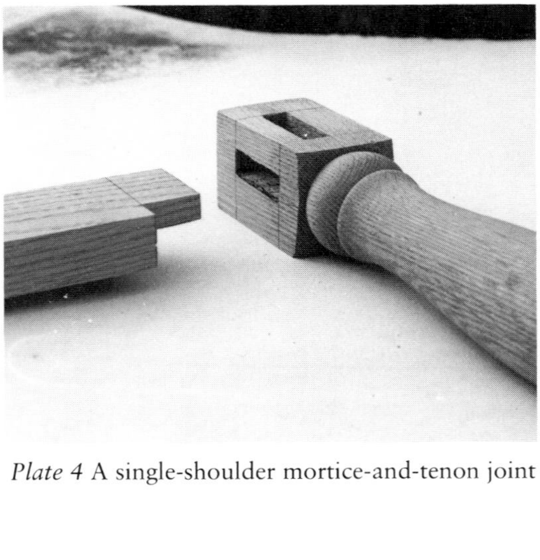

Plate 4 A single-shoulder mortice-and-tenon joint

DIAGRAM SEVEN

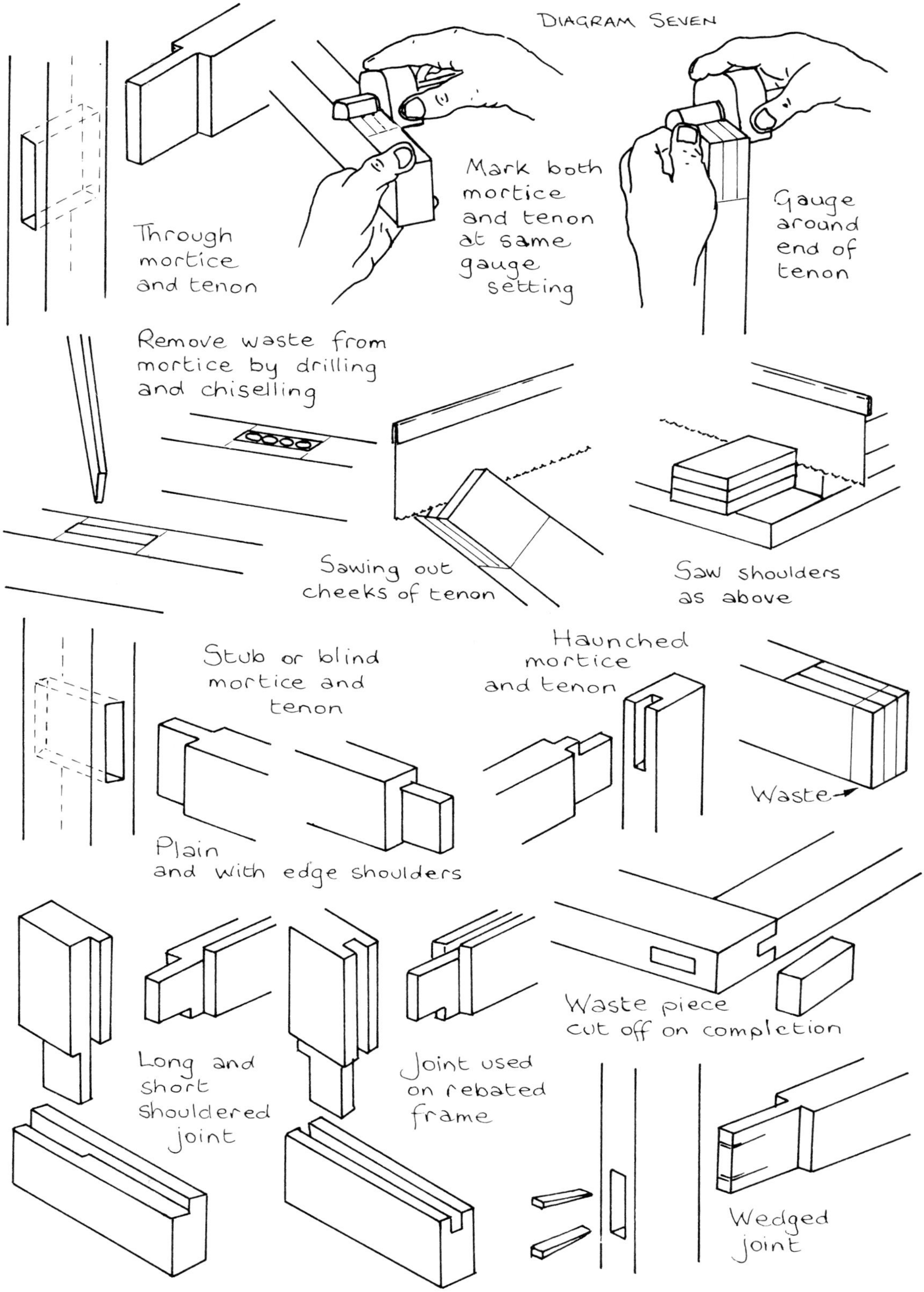

Through mortice and tenon
Mark both mortice and tenon at same gauge setting
Gauge around end of tenon
Remove waste from mortice by drilling and chiselling
Sawing out cheeks of tenon
Saw shoulders as above
Stub or blind mortice and tenon
Plain and with edge shoulders
Haunched mortice and tenon
Waste
Waste piece cut off on completion
Long and short shouldered joint
Joint used on rebated frame
Wedged joint

To conceal the end grain of the tenon, visible in the through joint, a stub mortice and tenon may be used. This has a tenon length shorter than the width of its joining piece and a mortice hole which is blind, ie does not go right through. Cut the mortice a little deeper than the length of the tenon. In this, and in the through tenon, shoulders all round the tenon make a neater job.

For corner joints in carcase work the haunched mortice and tenon is used. In this the width of the tenon is reduced on one side except for a short portion near the shoulder. This forms the haunch which helps resist twisting and allows for some wood to be left above the mortice slot. It is accommodated in a groove extending from the mortice. When making this joint leave at least ½in waste on the end of the mortice piece; this prevents splitting when cutting the joint. It is sawn off on completion. When a thin rail and a thicker upright are to join flush on one side the bare-faced joint is used. The single shoulder of the tenon allows for making the mortice away from the edge.

Of the many other variations on this joint, that used on rebated frames, the long and

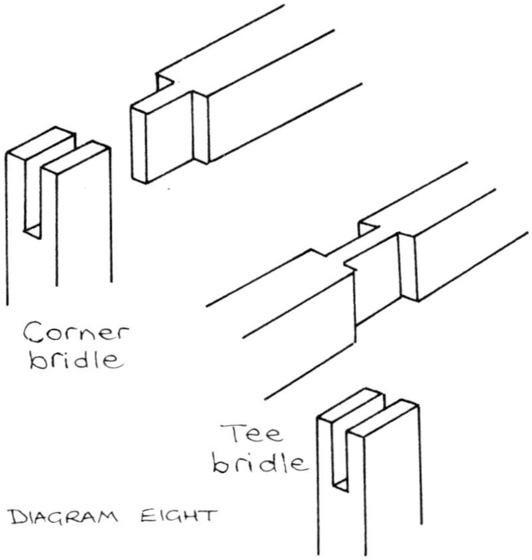
Corner bridle
Tee bridle

DIAGRAM EIGHT

DIAGRAM NINE

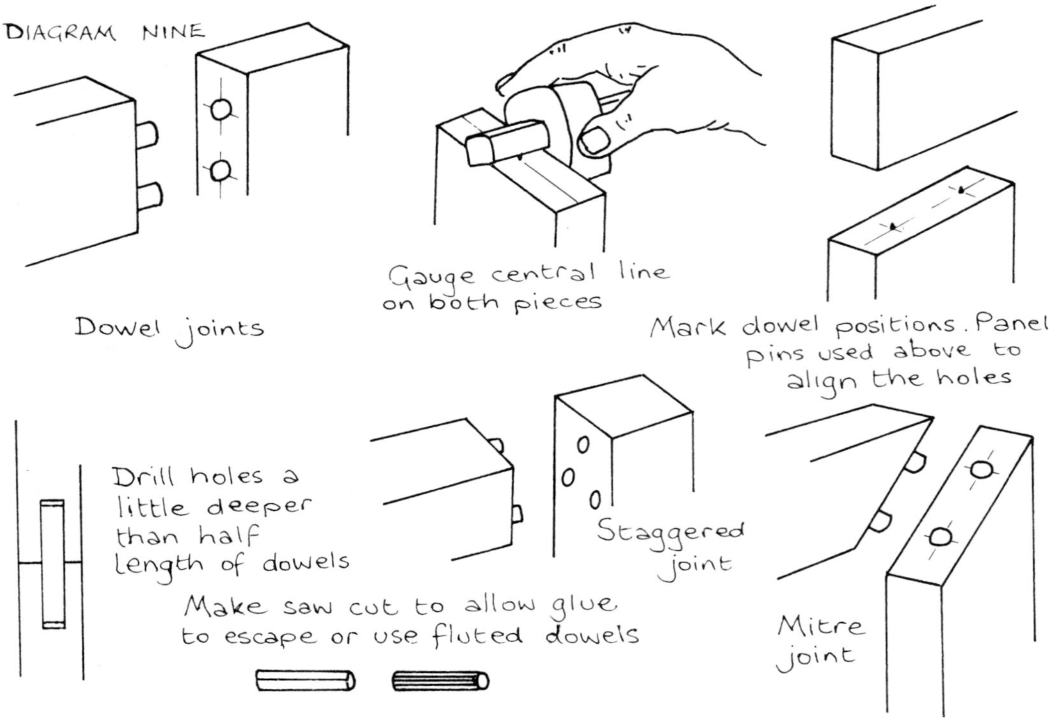
Dowel joints
Gauge central line on both pieces
Mark dowel positions. Panel pins used above to align the holes
Drill holes a little deeper than half length of dowels
Staggered joint
Make saw cut to allow glue to escape or use fluted dowels
Mitre joint

short shoulder joint, and the one used when frames are grooved to take plywood or solid wood panels are shown in Diagram Seven. The corner bridle joint is a kind of open-ended mortice and tenon while a second type is in part similar to the half-lap tee joint. They are marked out like a mortice and tenon with a mortice gauge set at one-third the thickness of the wood. In both joints saw down on the waste side of the cut-out section and remove the waste at the bottom with a coping saw and chisel; cut the tenon of the corner joint as you would a normal tenon and for the tee joint use the lap-joint method of waste removal on both sides (Diagram Eight).

Dowel joints (see Diagram Nine) are regarded by some as an inferior substitute for the mortice and tenon, but are undeniably easier to make and almost as strong. They may also be used in mitre joints and in strengthening edge-to-edge joints in wide boards. In making dowel joints the holes bored for the dowels must be accurately aligned in both mating pieces which must also be square and true. There are various dowelling jigs on the market which aid this

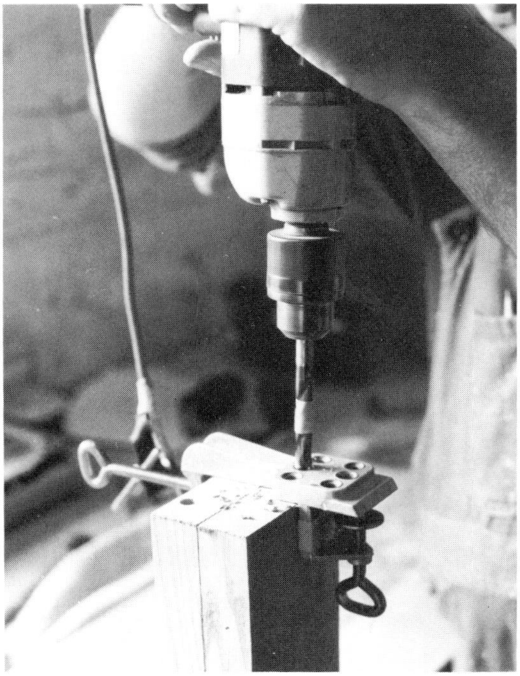

Plate 5 Drilling a dowel joint using a simple jig

Plate 6 Putting fluted dowels in place

Plate 7 Assembling a dowel joint

work, but a simple method is to mark up one piece, knock in panel pins at the dowel positions, cut off their heads and, with the mating piece held squarely in place, tap it down on to the pins. Remove the pins and drill at all the marked positions, pin holes and their opposite impressions. All drilled holes must be at right angles to the mating surfaces and should each be a little deeper than half the length of the dowel. Countersinking dowel holes prevents any rough edges interfering with the close fitting of the joint. Put glue in the dowel holes, insert the dowels and cramp [clamp] up the joint until set.

4

Methods

CARCASE CONSTRUCTION

In all cabinet work a number of construction features are shared by a range of furniture. A common denominator is the basic framework of the piece – the carcase as it is generally known – and into which may be fitted drawers, hinged or sliding doors, etc, depending upon the design and function of the finished work.

In most mass-production cabinet work carcases are machine made and assembled by different operatives from those who assemble and finish drawers and cupboard doors. A third operative is often involved in bringing these components together – nowadays, with furniture in kit form – sometimes the purchaser himself. Final assembly is only achieved by allowing so much tolerance in dimensions to take account of any inaccuracies in manufacure or by utilising suspect construction methods that the end result is often far from satisfactory. Drawers, for example, to quote a trade saying, can virtually be thrown into their holes. Fitting false drawer fronts is one way of hiding the gaps which would otherwise be in full view. There is a market for this type of work, but it can hardly be called quality cabinet making.

There are two main types of carcase construction – one which uses solid ends and one in which the ends are framed and panelled. Because of the high cost and scarcity of good-quality, well-seasoned timber [wood] I accept that solid construction will be prohibitive to many people, but the technique is worth knowing about and understanding, and anyway, there are ways and means of overcoming the high cost/scarcity problem.

Common to both types of construction are the allowances made for movement in the wood used. Wood has a nasty habit of shrinking across the grain; therefore it 'moves' and, in addition, growth rings tend towards straightening, thus causing cupping, especially across wide boards. Early planked chests, made from solid, wide boards, nailed, dowelled or perhaps dovetailed together, split front and back because the vertical grain of the end boards resisted the movement of back and front boards. Frame and panel construction was developed to prevent this happening by allowing for this movement in the wood, the panels, slotted loose into grooves in the frame members, being able to move independently of the frame itself.

Some of the problems of solid construction are overcome by gluing narrow boards side edge-to-edge so that movement in one is counterbalanced by the next. Wide panels of solid wood used in frame and panel work may be made up by this same method (see Diagram Three). The more recent use of manufactured board, ie ply, block and chipboard, etc, has made a significant difference in attitudes towards movement problems and has brought about important changes in carcase construction techniques, although not always for the best.

A typical form of solid construction is shown in Diagram One. The ends are made up of edge-joined boards (details of edge jointing are given on p25), the boards finished to about ¾in or ⅞in in thickness. This is an extremely strong form of construction with due care taken to minimise problems of subsequent movement. Lapped dovetails are used at the corners, the triangular fillets (x) dowelled to front and/or back rails providing extra strength. The solid top in this particular case would be mounted on to the top rails of the carcase and fixed by means of buttons or pocket screwing (Diagram Three).

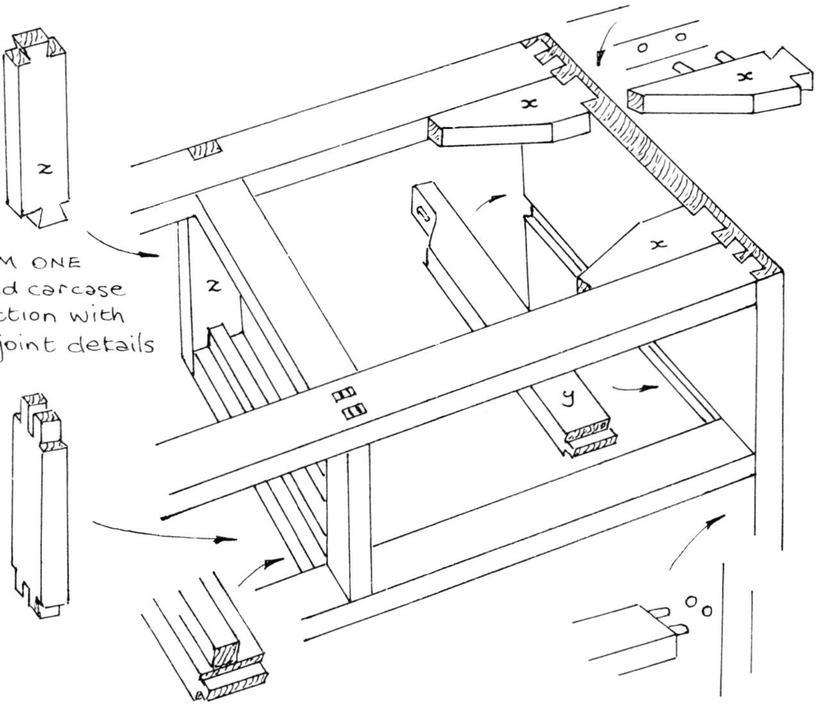

DIAGRAM ONE
Solid end carcase construction with typical joint details

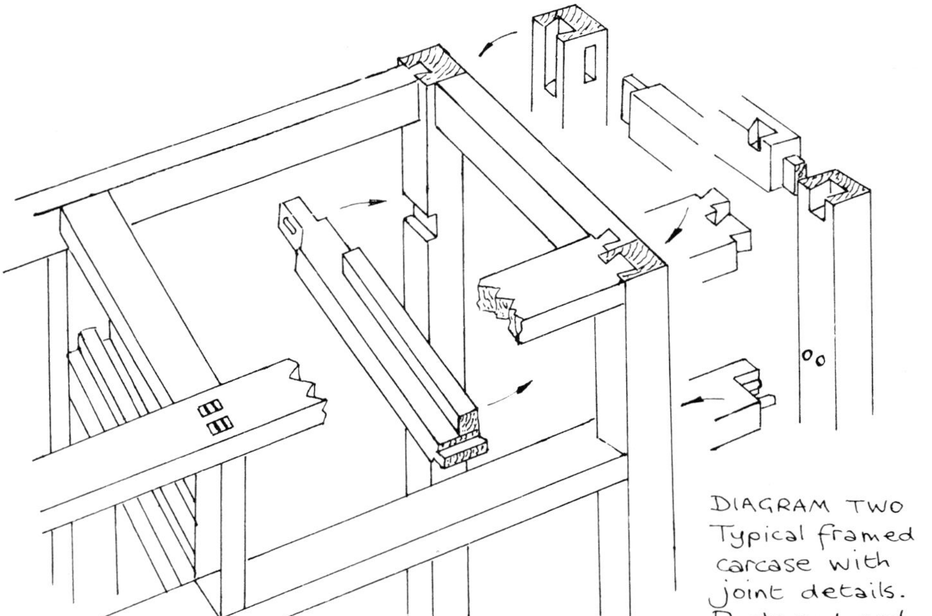

DIAGRAM TWO
Typical framed carcase with joint details. Posts and end rails slotted to take panels

DIAGRAM THREE

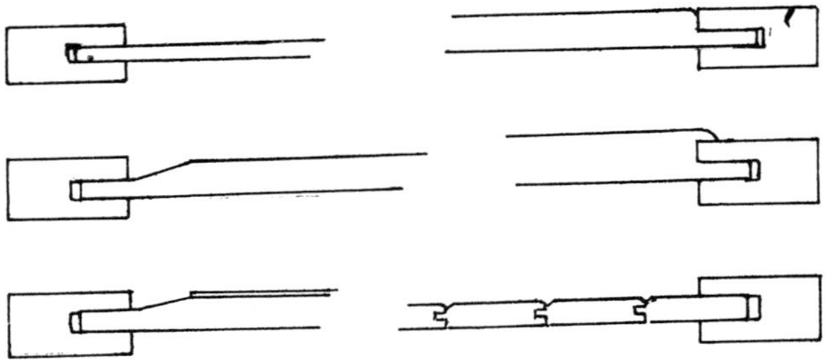

FRAME & PANEL CONSTRUCTION
A haunched mortice and tenon is used for the frame. Groove usually one third of thickness

PANEL VARIATIONS. Types a) and b) may be of ply or chipboard. Others normally of solidwood. Note end gap

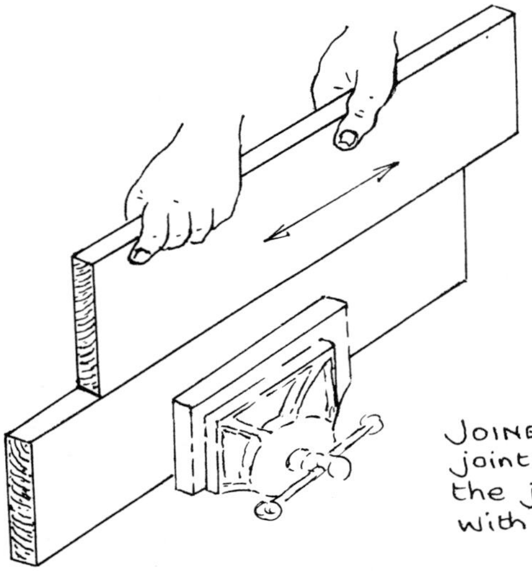

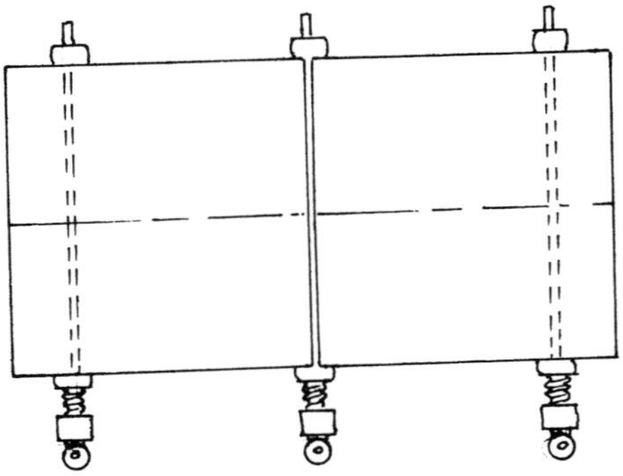

JOINED WIDE BOARDS. Similar to the rubbed joint, two edges are planed true, glued and the joint 'rubbed' as shown, left. Cramp-up with sash cramps, tightening centre first

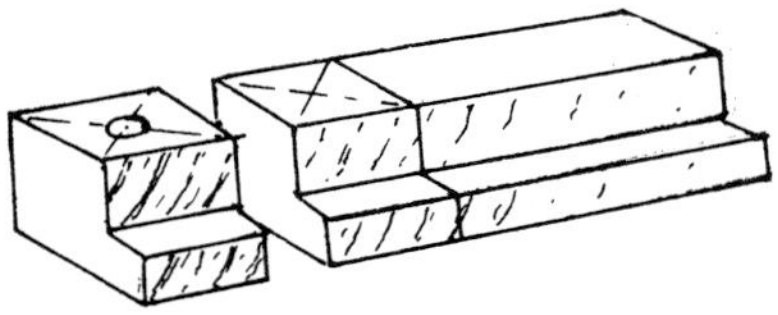

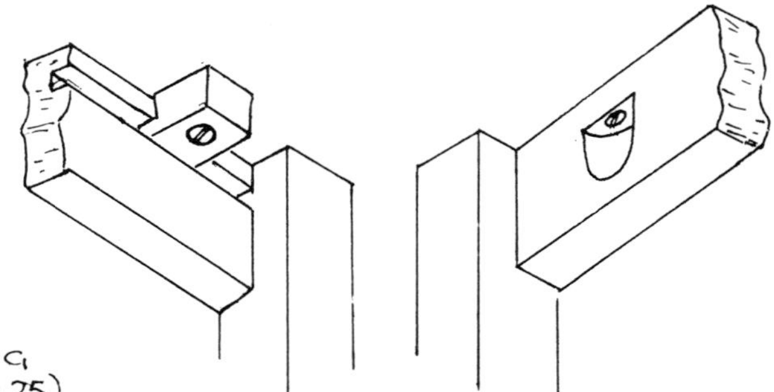

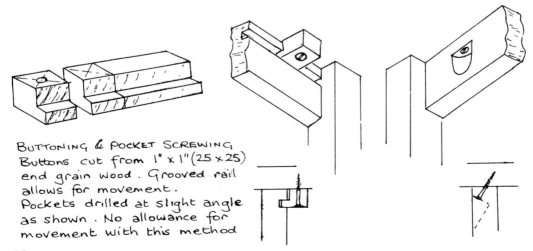

BUTTONING & POCKET SCREWING
Buttons cut from 1" x 1" (25 x 25) end grain wood. Grooved rail allows for movement.
Pockets drilled at slight angle as shown. No allowance for movement with this method

A well-made framed-up carcase is shown in Diagram Two. Stout end posts with lighter side rails secured by mortice-and-tenon joints make up the end frame which is grooved all round to accept a panel. The front rail has a double dovetail, one into the front post, the other into the side rail. The back rail may be tenoned into the post on edge as shown, or dovetailed (see p35). Triangular fillets may be added for extra strength as shown earlier.

In a solid carcase, drawer rails may be grooved along their back edge to enable dustboards to be fixed under the drawers. This same groove can house the stub tenon at the front of the drawer runners (y); where dustboards are not used a mortice is cut for the tenon in the normal way. Runners are also grooved and fitted into stopped housings in the solid ends without glue. At the back the runner is cut away and slot screwed. This method ensures that any movement of the solid end is not restricted by the cross-grain of the runner. Dustboards, where fitted, are slid in from the back. Where centre or perhaps intermediate runners are fitted these are stub tenoned into the front drawer rail and into a groove in a purposely placed upright at the back (z). Where this is not possible a hanger must be dovetailed into the top back rail and to the runner. Drawer guides are screwed to the top of these runners.

In the traditional frame and panel carcase, front drawer rails are dowelled into the front posts and, being wider than the post, are cut round them at the back. Their back edges are grooved as described above. Side runners are stub tenoned into these at the front and, housed in grooves, are screwed into the back post. Guide rails must be screwed to the runners to fill the space between the posts and the panel. Do not glue runners or guides to the back of the panel.

To prevent drawers from tipping forward when opened, pieces known as kickers are fitted between the top rails. These can be secured to carcase ends with wood screws and no glue; intermediate kickers are stub tenoned. Where a solid top is dovetailed to the ends, kickers are omitted – the top itself prevents the drawers from tipping.

Particular attention should be given to all inside surfaces against which drawers will run. No matter how well made the drawer, if contact surfaces within the carcase are unsatisfactory drawer fitting will be troublesome. Runners, etc, must be planed true to start with for this cannot be done properly after the carcase is assembled and at assembly check thoroughly that the carcase is square and not in wind. Do this before the glue has set – later adjustments will be impossible without breaking a joint somewhere. Align cramps [clamps] properly when cramping up and avoid uneven pull on components. A little pushing and pulling will usually bring a carcase square; if badly out, the components, especially shoulders of joints, are probably not fitting properly square.

Strength is added to any carcase when a back is fitted, for this does much more than just fill a gap. Early work had backs of thin tongue and groove boards, and some fine country furniture is still made using this same method today. Top-quality cabinets have a frame and panel back. A common practice is to use a ¼in ply panel screwed, but not glued, into rebates cut into the back edge of the carcase.

In solid work where a back is not to be fitted, ie open book shelves and similar structures likely to be submitted to heavy loading, a slightly different approach is necessary. Strong, well-fitted corner joints are required to ensure rigidity and lapped dovetails are the usual choice of joint, double lap at top, single lap at bottom. Fixed shelves further increase strength, the usual method of fixing these being to use housing joints, preferably stopped at the front edge to improve appearance. Stub tenons or dowels within the housing give further strength. The addition of full-width side rails increases rigidity considerably, even if only fitted as plinth rails inset below the bottom shelf.

DRAWER MAKING

The process of making well-fitting drawers and cupboard doors begins with the carcase before and during assembly. To receive drawers, etc, properly the carcase must be square, especially the openings into which these will fit. The third to last paragraph of the previous section is worth reading again before starting to make drawers.

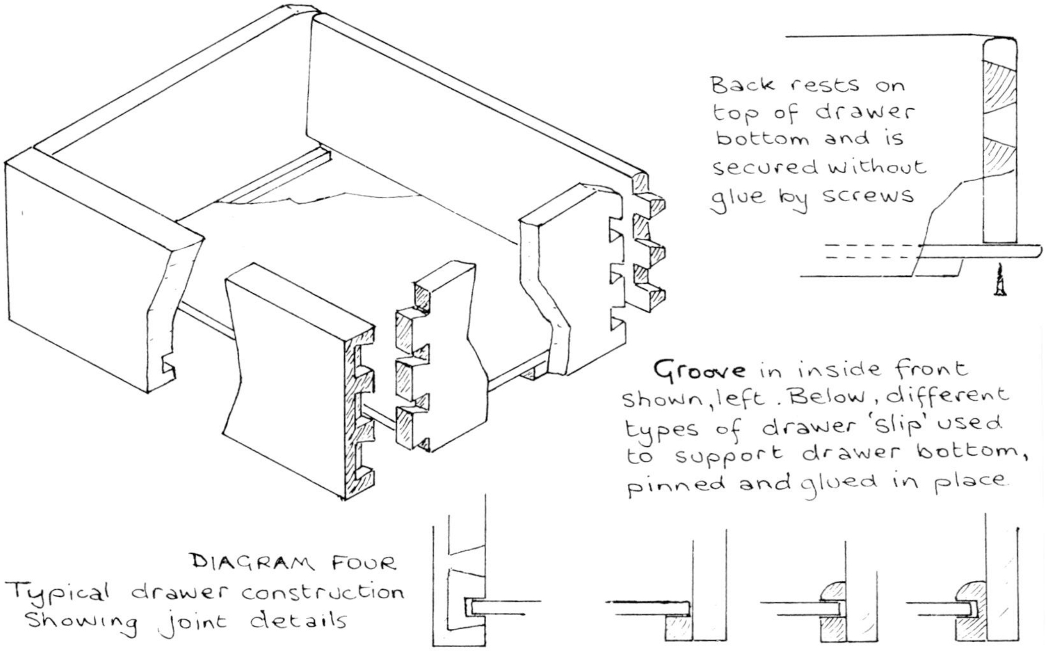

Back rests on top of drawer bottom and is secured without glue by screws
Groove in inside front shown, left. Below, different types of drawer 'slip' used to support drawer bottom, pinned and glued in place
DIAGRAM FOUR
Typical drawer construction
Showing joint details

In drawer construction dovetail joints give the best results, first because they resist any tendency of the front or back to pull away from the sides each time the drawer is pulled or pushed, and secondly because the joint spreads any strain owing to shrinkage over the full width of the drawer side. The back is through or open dovetailed to the sides, the front normally being lap dovetailed so that no joint is visible from the front. A good craftsman takes great pride in the neat appearance of drawer dovetails even though they remain concealed most of the time.

Make each drawer to fit its own opening in the carcase – forget that nonsense about a sign of good workmanship is that drawers should be interchangeable. Cut the drawer front from $\frac{3}{4}$in or $\frac{7}{8}$in material and plane its edges carefully to fit its opening. The front inside is grooved to take the drawer bottom and this groove must come above the bottom pin of the dovetail and be contained in the bottom socket, otherwise it will show. If the sides are thick enough, these too should be grooved to accept the bottom, but where they are too thin – and in top quality work they should be – a grooved moulding [a drawer slip] is screwed and glued to the lower edge of the drawer side. Check that the sides are of equal length. The back, cut to size a fraction shorter than the front, should reach down to the top of the groove, or the moulding so that, when the drawer is assembled the back rests on the bottom.

Dovetails are cut as shown on p28, pins on front and back, tails on sides. When joints are cleaned up and checked for fitting, mark mating corners AA, BB, and so on. To assemble a drawer the front is gripped vertically in the vice, inside face towards you, ie sockets outward, and two or three inches above the vice edge. Glue the correct mating side into place, using enough glue so that a little squeezes out – this way you know you do not have a dry joint. Light taps with a hammer, using a piece of scrap wood across the full width of the drawer, may be used to drive the joint home. Wipe off surplus glue.

Remove the drawer front from the vice and replace it with the opposite end uppermost. Follow the procedure described above. On completion, remove from the vice and place the now U-shaped box on one of its sides on the bench. The sides should be firmly held and should not flop. Do not worry if at this stage the sides are not parallel; ideally, it should be necessary to spring them lightly apart when fitting in the back. Put glue on the pins first and gently spring apart the uppermost drawer side to just allow the pins to engage in their sockets. With the batten in place on top carefully hammer down to close the joints. Wipe off surplus glue.

Check that the joints are closed up all round and that the drawer is square and true. When dry, clean up the joints. Then put the bottom in place without glue and fit the drawer into its opening in the carcase. It should fit; any tight spots will show as shiny marks on the surface of the wood. Remove these by taking thin shavings with a sharp plane. When the drawer is a good fit, fix the drawer bottom into place, glued into the front groove only, screwed or pinned at the back.

A point to note about drawer bottoms: 1/4in ply is now usually used, but solid wood is preferable. The grain of this should run from side to side, not front to back – the other way round and shrinkage would cause the bottom to move away from the sides, losing support and leaving ugly gaps. An allowance for shrinkage back to front is made by allowing the bottom to pass under the back and leaving a surplus overhang. This also explains why the bottom is not glued in all round.

Wide drawers (those over 2ft) have a two-piece bottom and a centre rail or muntin. This is grooved along its two long edges to take the drawer bottoms and dovetailed or tenoned into the drawer front. At the back it is notched out and screwed into place.

5

Woodbending and Chairs

Certain pieces of furniture incorporate curved or bent components in their construction. Chairs in particular are a good example. Some curved parts can be sawn to shape but this method has its limitations; the curve has to be of fairly large radii and with the grain as much as possible. Cross-grain introduces structural weaknesses in components produced this way. An old method of creating gentle curves was to make a series of saw cuts in the inside or concave surface of the wood to be bent. Close spaced and cut to within about 3/16in of the outer or convex surface, this technique was once quite popular but of limited application.

There are two methods by which wood can be physically and permanently bent, without loss of strength: by laminating and by steam bending. In the first method thin pieces of wood veneers are glued together, one on another, to build up the necessary thickness. This is done on a former of the required shape and all is held in place under pressure until the glue has set. In the second method selected solid wood is heat treated until pliable, bent on a former and held under pressure to set to shape.

Laminated bands built up as described will retain their shape because each layer is concentric to and of a slightly different radius from its neighbour. The adhesive used effectively bonds together the various layers and they cannot therefore revert to their former flat state.

Ordinary furniture veneers may be used for this purpose, but as these are normally rather thin (1/32in) they take more time to build up and require more glue. Incidentally, this makes them stiffer but heavier. Thicker laminae [laminates] known as constructional veneers, are used commercially and these, at 1/10in in thickness, are best if obtainable. The glue used should be a synthetic resin type such as Aerolite or Cascamite.

Formers [forms] should be carefully made and of two parts to ensure close fitting to and even pressure on the laminae [laminates]. A wooden former [form] with a metal strap with a means of bringing the strap under pressure and in close contact with the built-up laminae [laminates] is sometimes used and proprietary [commercial] metal strapping is available for this purpose. Alternatively, and specifically when making complex bends, two-part wooden formers [forms], ie with male and female parts, are required (see Diagram One).

An organised approach is required for

Plate 1 Everything ready for laminating

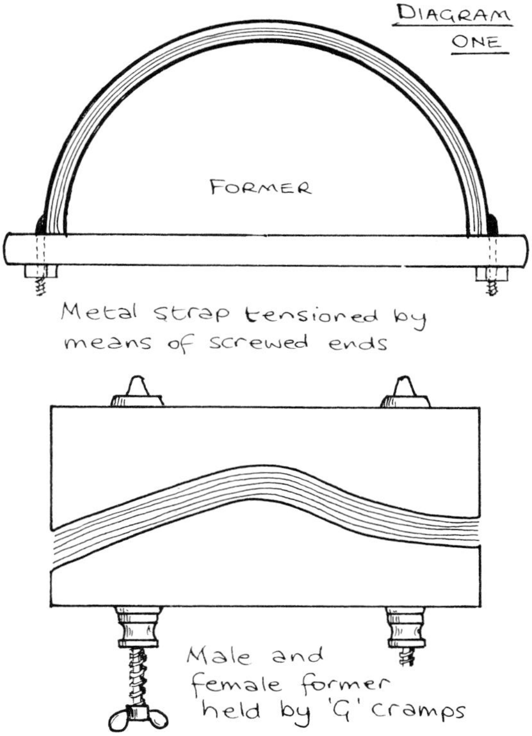

laminating, for success lies in being well prepared before beginning to build up a laminated component. Have everything ready to hand before starting, the right number of laminae [laminates] cut to size, sufficient glue and the space and the means to spread it on evenly, enough cramps [clamps] close by, and so on. The process of making a laminated bend is described in some detail in Chapter 13 on making a small, half-round hall table.

Steam bent, solid wood is the preferred method of bending wood, especially for use in traditional chair making. Most types of hardwood can be bent in this way; ash, beech, chestnut, oak, elm and hickory are all eminently suitable, as are the fruit woods, apple and pear. Yew is also suitable, although botanically it is a softwood. The wood for bending should be selected for straight grain and be knot free. Unseasoned wood bends most successfully; partly air-dried wood bends with moderate success, but kiln dried hardly at all.

DIAGRAM TWO
Suspension method for vertical steamers
The horizontal steam box is more efficient. This is made from ½ in. marine ply. The boiler used is a metal bucket into which is put a 2½ kw electric kettle element
Two types of vertical steamer and two ways of raising steam

The wood is first rendered pliable by heating, most usually using saturated steam at atmospheric pressure. Simple apparatus for

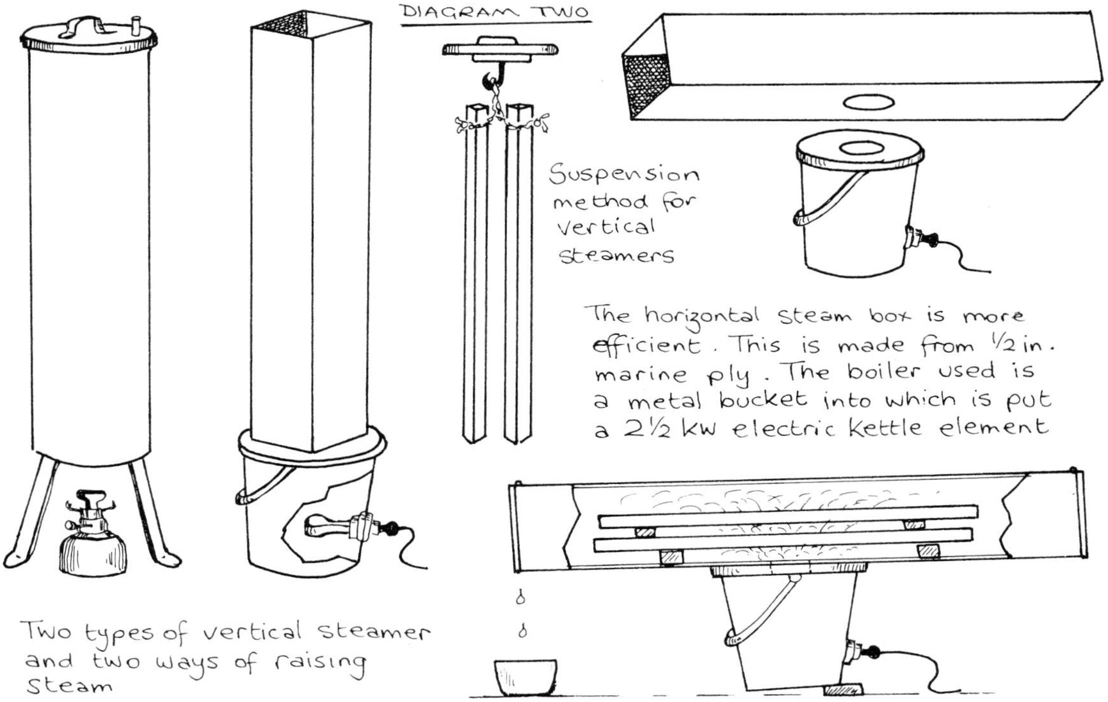

doing this are shown in Diagram Two. Approximately one hour per inch of thickness is sufficient to bring the wood to the right condition for bending.

Immediately the wood is ready it is placed on a prepared former [form] and quickly bent to the shape before the wood has time to cool. It is held there until 'set', the actual time taken depending on the size of the bent section, workshop temperature, etc. On average about one week should be sufficient for chair bends not exceeding 1½ × 1½in section.

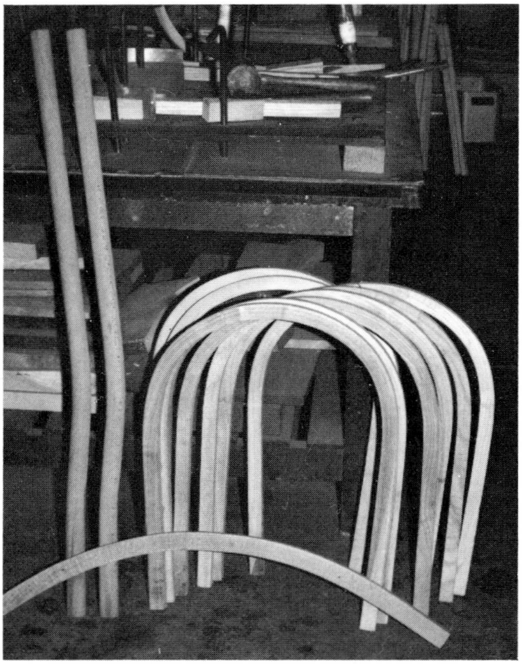

Plate 2 Steam-bent components ready for use

Traditional methods of chair back and bow bending involved the use of a simple bending board with wedges and pegs. A former [form] was bolted to the board and the bend was pulled into place against it and held, starting at the top centre, with wedges and pegs as shown in Diagram Three. After a while the two ends would be tied off with stout cord and the bend, removed from the former [form], hung up to dry out. This method served well enough once the knack was learned, but for improved results the use of supporting straps and close-fitting end-

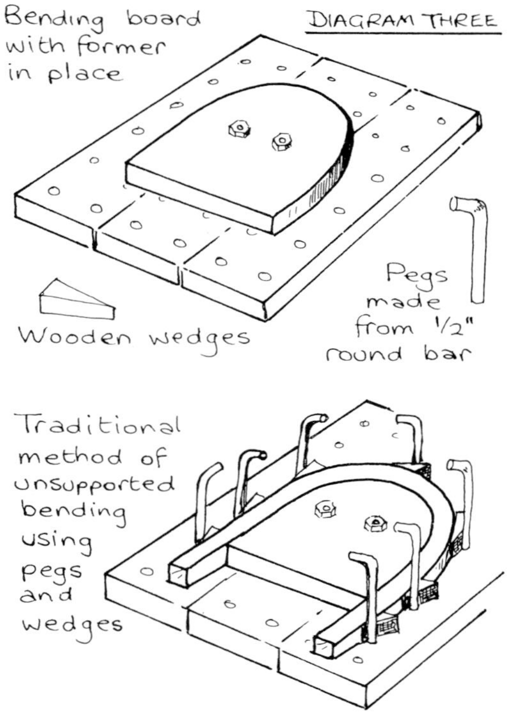

stops is advocated. During bending, wood is subjected to two induced stresses which place fibres on the convex or outward side of a bend under tension and cause them to be stretched, while those on the concave or inside are compressed and so shortened. It is the first of these stresses which causes most failures in steam bending. The supporting strap and end-stops is a means of reducing this problem. Details are given in Diagram Four.

In practice, the supporting strap and end-stops restrict the stretching movement of the wood fibres, while the back plates help reduce any tendency towards twisting under pressure. The detachable handles provide extra leverage for bending.

The shaped back uprights of ladderback and similar chairs are bent in pairs over the simple former shown in the diagram. A method for bending chair combs and ladder-back rails is also illustrated. Flat rails of up to ⅜in in thickness may be bent together, one inside the other, as shown.

Failures are not uncommon when bending wood and, like so much else, experience is the best teacher and the surest way to success.

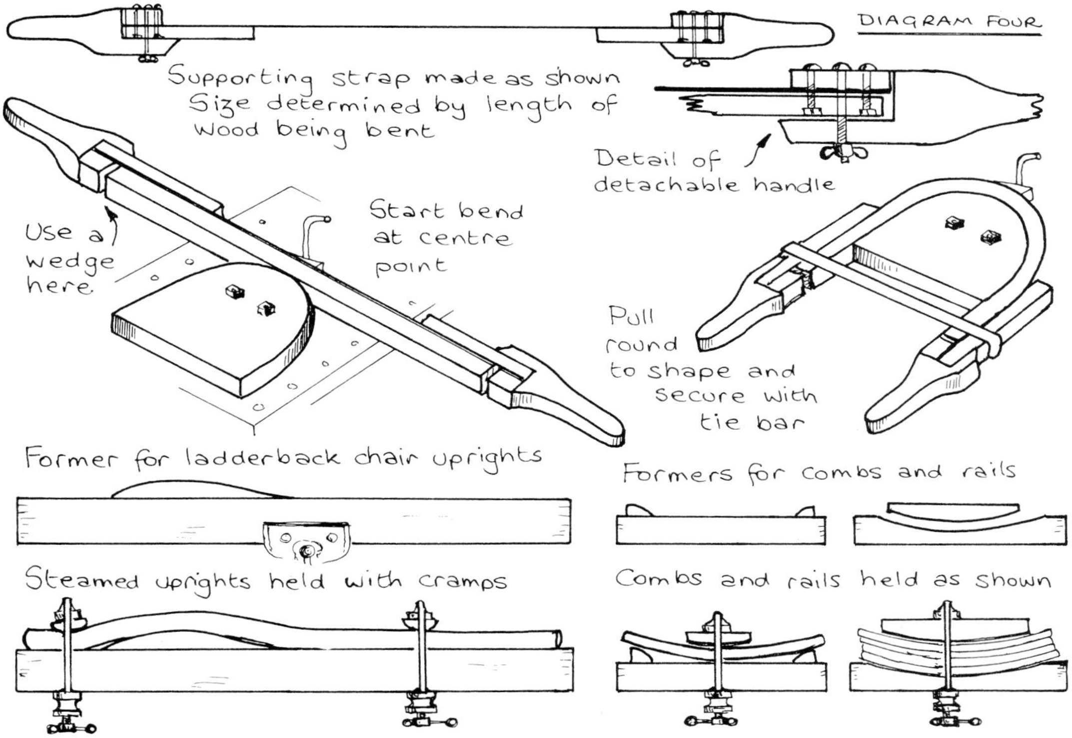
DIAGRAM FOUR
Supporting strap made as shown
Size determined by length of
wood being bent
Detail of
detachable handle
Use a
wedge
here
Start bend
at centre
point
Pull
round
to shape and
secure with
tie bar
Former for ladderback chair uprights
Formers for combs and rails
Steamed uprights held with cramps
Combs and rails held as shown

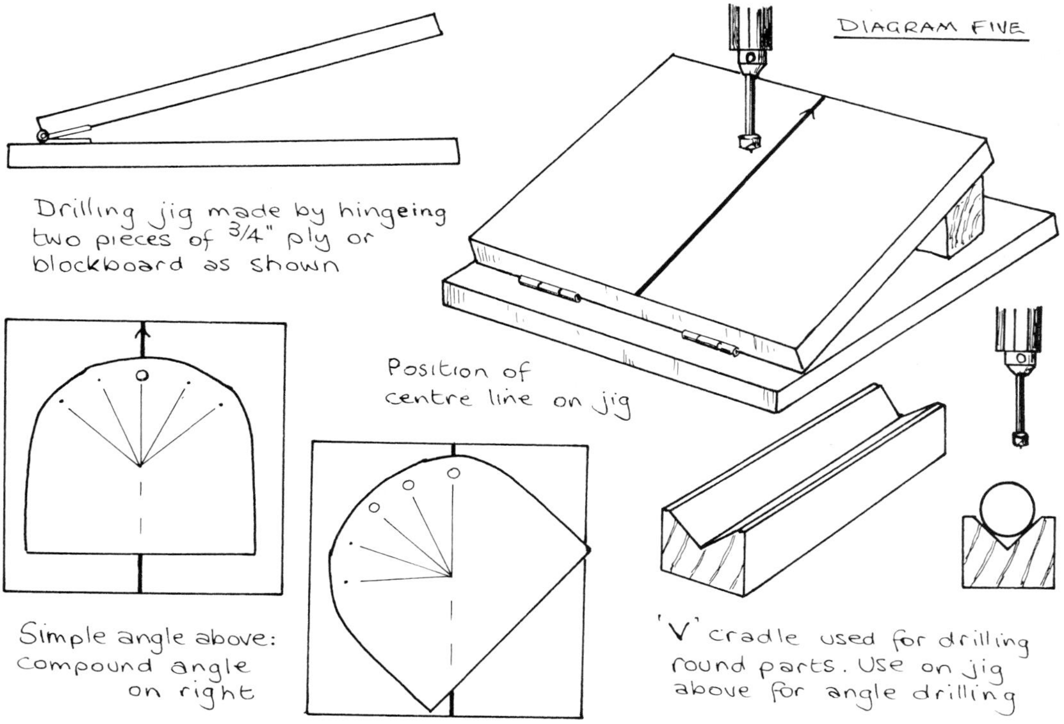
DIAGRAM FIVE
Drilling jig made by hingeing
two pieces of 3/4" ply or
blockboard as shown
Position of
centre line on jig
Simple angle above:
compound angle
on right
'V' cradle used for drilling
round parts. Use on jig
above for angle drilling

Some types of chair, in addition to their requirements for curved and bent parts, also need to have many of these parts fitted together at angles other than 90°. This often means drilling holes at these angles and sometimes into components round in section. Additionally, some parts, legs for example, have an outward 'splay', which means that their sockets have to be drilled at a compound angle. Such drilling can present problems but the use of simple jigs as shown in Diagram Five can help minimise these. They are intended for use with a pillar drill or an electric hand drill in a pillar attachment – both provide accurate, vertical drilling and all other angles are drilled with reference to this.

The drilling jig or sloping table can be adjusted to give a required simple angle, while orientation of the work piece about the centre line marked on the table provides for compound angles. For this, 'sight lines' are marked on the work where possible and aligned with this centre line for accuracy, the centre line itself being always positioned directly below the point of the drill.

The jig could be elaborated by having a screwed adjustment and a graduated scale, but a protractor or sliding bevel to set the angle and a block of wood placed under the hinged part to keep it at the correct angle suffice.

For accurate drilling of round parts, ie legs, stretchers, etc, the engineer's V-block principle is a useful method. A simple V-cradle as shown is satisfactory for most work, but for certain applications the jig shown in the chapter on making a ladder-back chair (p125) is more suitable and dual purpose.

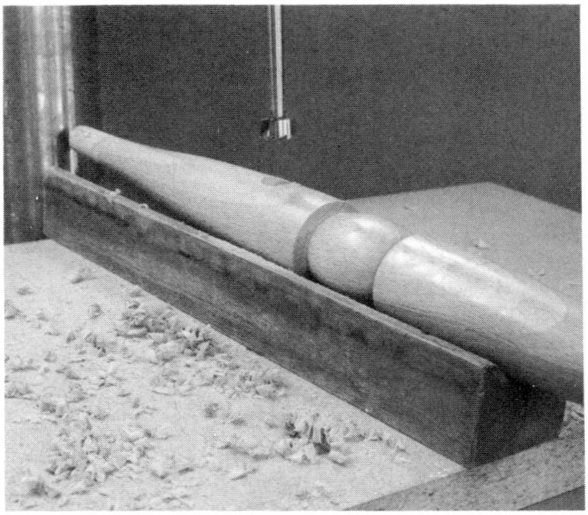

Plate 3 V-cradle in use on a drilling jig

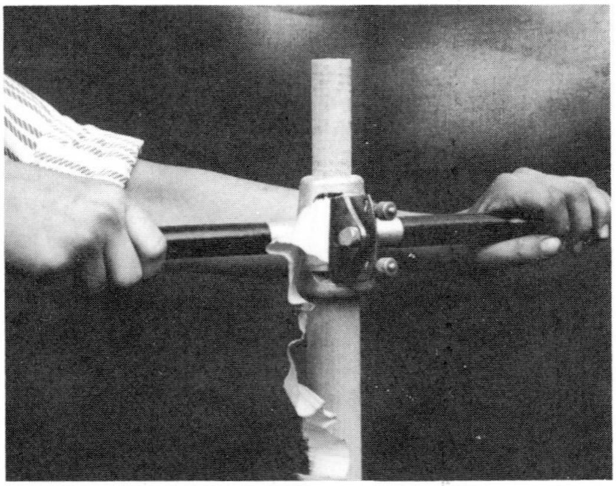

Plate 4 Using the rotary plane or rounder

In the chairmaking projects which follow occasional reference is made to making components round in section using tools known as Rotary or Rounding Planes, or more simply, Rounders. These traditional tools were originally made with wooden stocks and fitted with individually forged steel blades, or cutting irons, as they were known. In more recent times these were updated and made with cast aluminium bodies fitted with adjustable blades identical to those fitted to modern steel spokeshaves. These were developed and made by a friend of mine, Fred Lambert of Worcester, and for some years he has instructed teachers, craftsmen and would-be craftsmen, and women, in their use and manufacture.

At one period they were made commercially, intended mainly for use in schools and colleges and were included in an educational catalogue. To my knowledge, they have never been distributed through the tool trade. However, numerous tools in various sizes have found their way into many school and college workshops and into those of individual craftsmen and women. Very occasionally one may see them on offer at auction or you may find them advertised in the small advertisements columns of woodworking magazines.

6

Carved Decoration

The surface decoration of wood is one of the most ancient of art forms. It has its beginnings in the distant past when carved symbols played an important role in the superstition and ceremonial beliefs of many primitive peoples in many separate parts of the world. Early carvers had few tools at their disposal and their work reflects this, being largely of simple stylised or geometric shapes. Known now as chip carving, it is work of this kind which is still to be seen as decoration on much extant medieval furniture.

The carver's craft reached a peak during the sixteenth-century Renaissance. Italian influence on design, the availability of the greater range of tools and the realisation that wood could be carved in more delicate detail than was ever possible in stone gave the craftsmen of the period a golden opportunity to display their skills. First it was in the decoration of the great cathedrals, and then, during the seventeenth century, the large houses and ornate furniture of the wealthy. A room or a piece of furniture was considered lacking if it did not have a proliferation of foliage and fruit, allegorical beasts, trailing vines and acanthus leaves and a Cupid or two. The work of Grinling Gibbons is typical of this period.

In time things changed; carved decoration on furniture became much more restrained, except perhaps during the Regency period. During Queen Victoria's reign, however, it was revived with a vengeance. The huge pieces of furniture of the period lent themselves well to the carving of great narrative scenes and a great deal of mock-Gothic decoration. The later reaction against Victorian taste and the decline in large furniture brought about the demise of interest in carved work and it has played little part in the decoration of contemporary furniture. However, some carved decoration, perhaps as a single motif on a panel or as a repeating pattern along an edge or rail can, if properly done, add that little extra something to a piece of hand-made furniture.

The range of wood-carving tools now available is immense; the catalogue of a well-known English manufacturer lists over 300 different sizes and types; straight, bent and back-bent chisels, spade chisels, left- and right-hand skews, front-bent, back-bent and fishtail gouges; fluters, veiners and parting tools; fluteroni, macaroni and backeroni; spoons and doglegs. Each kind comes in a range of sizes from 1/16in up to 1in and above.

The amateur carver need not have all of them; ten or a dozen are ample to start with. And to acquire some skill with these tools there is no better place to start than with the ancient art of chip carving. Only two basic tools are needed for this: a straight chisel to make rectangular and triangular pockets and

Plate 1 Carving a chair-back motif using a chip-carving technique

Plate 2 Finished carving. Note the effect of light and shadow on this type of carved decoration

a straight gouge to produce thumb-nail notches and curved patterns.

Work on a flat piece of 'soft' hardwood – lime is ideal, sycamore good, mahogany quite good. Pencil parallel lines on its surface, the space between being equal to the width of the chisel to be used. Mark lines at right angles to form squares. Then, with the straight chisel, make near-vertical cuts on the lines and sloping cuts at an angle to meet them and remove a wedge-shaped chip. If one corner of the chisel is dug in deeper, triangular chips are removed to make three-sided shapes. Work with the gouge is basically the same, the second cut usually made towards the convex side of the first.

Work in which a surface is carved with shapes and the wood between removed so that the shape is raised is called relief carving. This can be shallow or deeply cut, the distinction being described by the terms low and high relief. For this the outline of the design is marked on the surface and the wood in the spaces between cut away. Discreet modelling of the raised surfaces sometimes combined with subtle undercutting in some areas gives a three-dimensional effect. Fully three-dimensional work or carving in the round is rarely used as furniture decoration.

In relief carving the design is first drawn on paper then transferred to the wood using carbon paper. The initial cuts are vertical ones made just away from the drawn lines in the waste wood area. Use a chisel or gouge which in size and shape corresponds closely to the drawn outline – it helps to design shapes that relate to the shape of the tools you have. This process is known as setting in.

Now, with a medium-sized gouge held at about 45°, make cuts towards the vertical cuts from the waste side. Do this all round to establish the raised shapes, then remove the rest of the waste where necessary. Try to keep the ground, ie the space or background between the raised shapes, attractive, either smooth or with nice, crisp gouge markings. Failing this, the ground may later be uniformly treated with a matting punch. With some woods this will often enhance the relief.

Modelling of the raised shape is now carried out. In low-relief work this must of necessity remain somewhat flat; high relief gives more scope for sculptural effects. In some designs it may be necessary to make further vertical cuts to set-in sections which need to appear to be above or below the general level of the shape. A variety of different tools are now used: bent gouges for hollows, skew chisels for undercutting, and so on. The main outline may now be cut back to the drawn line and the aim should be to leave everything crisp and sharp from the cutting tools. It goes without saying that the cutting tools should be sharp.

Plate 3 Work in progress on carving initials – incised lettering

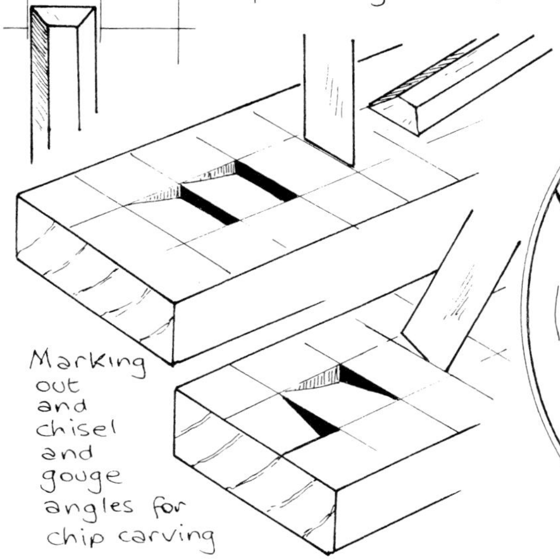

Marking out and chisel and gouge angles for chip carving

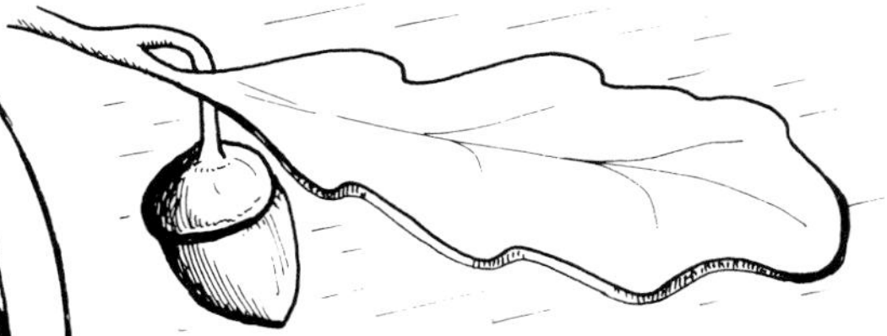

DIAGRAM ONE

Examples of chip and relief carving, showing tool angles and including some of the designs used in the furniture projects which follow

Carved lettering, which may be appropriate on some furniture in the form of initials or a date on commemorative pieces, may be either in the manner of relief carving or it may be incised, ie the individual letters cut into the wood as in stone carving. Again, the letters are drawn first on paper and transferred to the wood. Lettering in relief follows the method already outlined above, but for incised lettering the technique is slightly different. The first cut is vertical but on the centre line of each letter. For straight letters, such as A and E, etc, a straight chisel is used. It should be about ¼in shorter than the full height of the letter, ie for 1in letters use a ¾in chisel. Place it vertically on the centre line, away from the ends of the letter and give it a tap with the mallet. Then place the same chisel on one of the adjacent lines at an angle of about 30° and cut in towards the vertical cut. Repeat from the other side to make a clean V-shaped groove. Curved letters, such as C, D and O, require a gouge which matches the radius of the letter curve for the first cut and a shallower shape for subsequent cuts.

Serifs, the curved thickenings on the ends of letters, are made with a small spade or fishtail chisel. Two downward cuts angled out from the centre line to the corners of the letter, the chisel tilted so the cuts are deepest where they meet, followed by a cut each side to remove a triangular piece from the end of the letter, and this terminal feature is completed. Chip carving is good practice for this.

Plate 4 Completed initials with the carving tools used to do the work. (The initials are an enlarged version of my own 'craftsman's mark' carved into each piece of furniture which I make. It incorporates the initials J. H. with a subtle sign of the cross – the mark of the one who provides the trees)

7

Fixings and Fittings

The earliest furniture, like chests and so on, had fittings such as handles and hinges of wrought iron. Hand-made by a local blacksmith, some were quite crude but functional while others were highly decorative – fine examples of the blacksmith's craft. They were fixed on by means of hand-made, wrought-iron nails, driven through and clenched rather like a rivet, for screws were a later development. Furniture was often nailed together using similar nails or it might have been secured with wooden pegs – tree-nails as they were known.

As methods of constructing furniture improved and as furniture styles changed, the metalwork or hardware used altered accordingly. Brass came into general use during the seventeenth century for hinges, handles, etc, many early examples continuing to be hand made, as were the first screws made both in steel and in brass.

With the introduction of screw-cutting machinery and small forges producing hinges, handles, castors, catches and locks, etc, the range of furniture fixings and fittings gradually became fairly standardised and it is often possible to date old furniture by the type of hinges or handles, etc, fitted to it.

Today, the variety of furniture hardware available is considerable. Mass-production techniques and the popularity of 'knock-down' furniture and DIY has resulted in the development of many new types of hinges and other furniture fittings easier to fit and more suitable for the man-made sheet material being widely used. Traditional fixtures and fittings are still available, however, both in steel and in brass and so, too, are many fine examples of reproduction antique brassware, specially made for quality cabinet work. Screws for use in assembly and for fixing hardware are readily available in a variety of metals and/or finishes and a range of sizes (see Diagram One). Screws are ordered by giving the length in inches and the required gauge, thickness or diameter, which increases in size over a range of numbers from 1 to 20.

The traditional butt hinge continues to be the hinge type most frequently used for quality work, brass being the most popular choice of material. They are of two types, the solid drawn or extruded kind being preferred to the pressed or folded variety. Take care when buying that they are brass and not brassed – these are steel, brass plated. The same applies also to brassed screws.

Butt hinges are recessed into the door frame and into the edge of the door stile either equally, or unequally to allow the stile to clear the edge of the frame immediately it

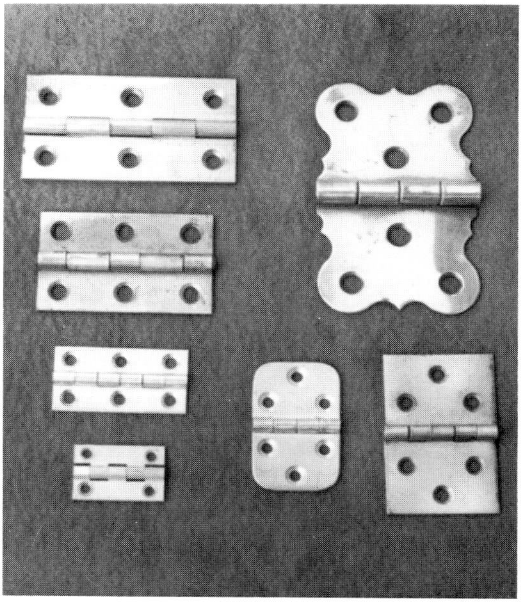

Plate 1 Some examples of solid-drawn brass hinges

DIAGRAM ONE

Types and sizes of woodscrews in general use

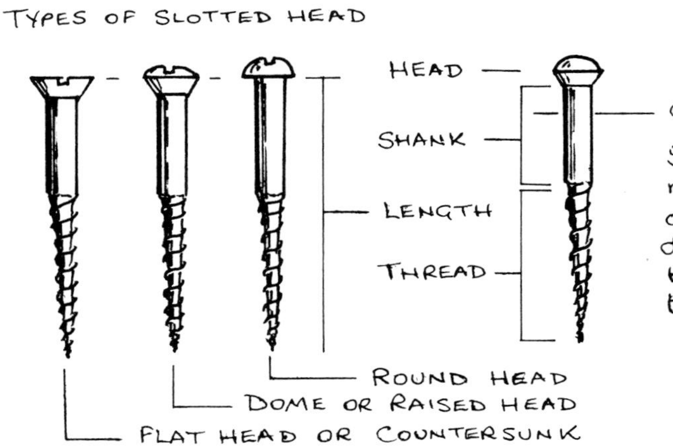

Specific to screws, the gauge number indicates the diameter of the parallel shank. To find drill size to suit screw, add 3 to gauge number to give size to nearest 1/64 th of an inch

GAUGE NUMBER	1	2	3	4	5	6	7	8	9	10
HEAD										
LENGTH IN INCHES										
1/4	*	* *		*						
3/8	*	* *	*	* * *		* *		*		
1/2		*	* *	* * *	* *	* * *	*	* *		*
5/8			*	* * *		* * *	* *	* *		* *
3/4			*	* * *	* * *	* * *	* *	* * *	*	* *
7/8				*		*	*	*		
1			*	* * *	*	* * *	* *	* * *	*	* * *
1 1/8						*		*		* * *
1 1/4				*		* * *	*	* * *		* * *
1 1/2				*		* * *	*	* * *	*	* * *
1 3/4						*	*	* *		* * *
2						* *	*	* * *		* * *

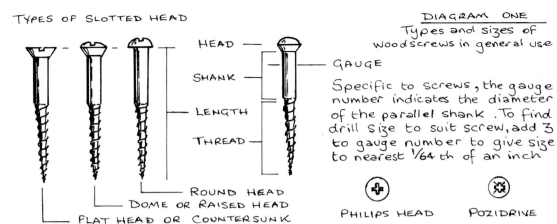

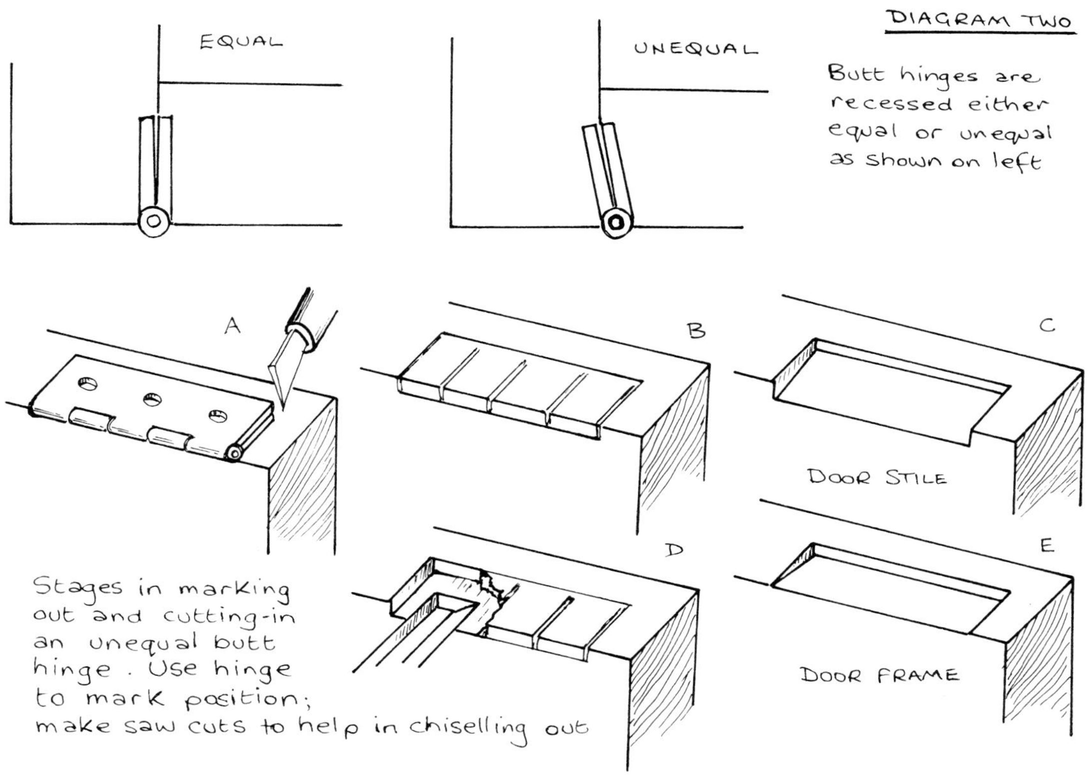
DIAGRAM TWO
EQUAL
UNEQUAL
Butt hinges are recessed either equal or unequal as shown on left
A
B
C
DOOR STILE
D
E
DOOR FRAME
Stages in marking out and cutting-in an unequal butt hinge. Use hinge to mark position; make saw cuts to help in chiselling out

begins to open (see Diagram Two). To set a hinge unequally, knife mark its position and square these marks across both door frame and door. Set a marking gauge to the full thickness of the hinge at the knuckle and mark this on the front of the door stile. Reset the gauge to the width of the hinge, ie from its edge to the centre of the knuckle pin and mark this on the edge of both the stile and the door frame. Chisel out these marked areas, tapering the recesses on the stile from the full thickness to the thickness of one flap at the back, and on the door frame from nothing on the face to the thickness of one flap at the back. Screw the hinge into position first to the door then to the frame, using the centre screws only at first to check the fit. Other hinges which require recessing include counter-flap and rule-joint hinges, all of which have their own special applications.

Surface-fitting hinges are much easier to fit, some of these being purposely decorative and intended to fit to and make a feature on the front of the cabinet and cupboard doors, (Diagram Three). For supporting long lengths, such as some box and piano lids, the piano hinge is available in lengths of up to 6ft long suitable for cutting to individual requirements.

Handles come in a variety of designs, frequently related to recognised furniture periods and there is currently a wide range of reproduction brassware available. All those shown in Diagram Three are fixed in the same way, by means of threaded spindles inserted through holes bored in drawer fronts or cupboard-door stiles and secured with washers and nuts on the inside. During the nineteenth century turned wooden knobs were used on some types of furniture and these continue to be popular even today. Early ones had a thread worked on them with a tool known as a screw box and this fitted into a similarly threaded hole. Reproduction wooden knobs usually have a plain dowel for gluing in or may be fitted by means of a single steel or brass screw from inside the drawer or cupboard.

Locks were once fitted to almost everything and they were generally of good

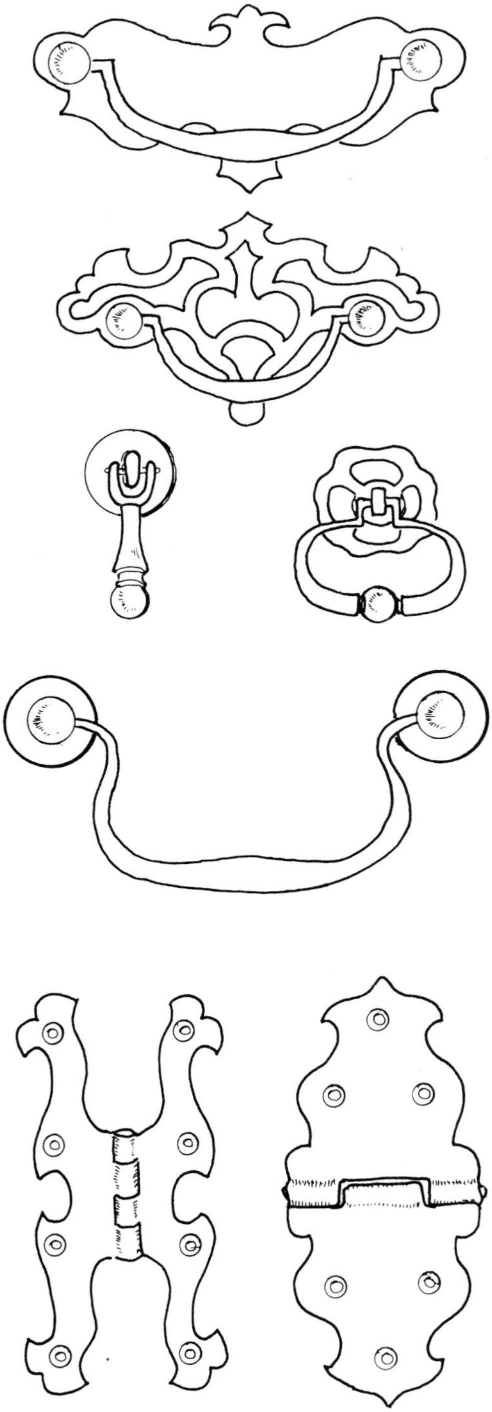

DIAGRAM THREE
Decorative brass handles and hinges

quality. Modern furniture makers either dispense with them altogether and fit catches instead or, if locks are fitted, they are often of a poor pattern and provide little or no security. If locks are to be fitted they should be the best of their type. Solid brass, multi-lever locks should be used and not the folded brass or steel single-lever type.

Types of lock vary according to their specialist application. The most common types are the straight-cupboard lock, the cut-cupboard and the cut-drawer lock and mortice-lock versions of these. The straight lock is usually suitable for either left- or right-hand fixing as its bolt moves through the lock to both left and right; it is easily fitted, too, being simply screwed to the surface of the work. Cut locks and mortice locks, however, must be bought 'handed', ie either for left- or right-handed fixing as the bolt can only move one way; also, they must be recessed into place.

Fitting the cut lock is described in stages in Diagram Four. The face plate dimensions are lightly set out where the lock is to be fitted and this recess cut out, inside the line for now as shown in A and B. Next, the position of the case is marked and cut out as in C. This is cut out so that the case is an easy fit. The lock is placed in position, and the face plate recess checked and trimmed as required. With the lock back in position scribe round the back plate, remove and cut out this shallow recess to finish as in E. With the lock back in position again a gentle tap will register the mark of the protruding key pin. With a small drill, bore through at this point, and then, working from the front of the cupboard or drawer, the keyhole is cut to size and the lock fitted. Alternatively, some like to cut the keyhole first, marking its position either by careful measuring and gauging or with the help of a cardboard template. Mortice locks fit into the thickness of the door or drawer front and a suitable mortice must be cut to accommodate the lock case.

To mark the position of the slot into which the bolt engages for all these lock types a little paint or grease smeared on the end of the lock bolt will leave a mark when the key is turned. Cut the slot at this point and fit the striking plate. Locks for special purposes include the box lock, which incorporates a striking plate with two projecting tabs which enter the lock case and are held by a sideways-moving bolt, and the bird's-beak lock made specifically for roll-top desks but now often seen on television cabinets. This lock has twin hooked bolts which move upward and outward to engage in the striking plate.

To protect the wood around the keyhole, escutcheons or key plates are fitted. Usually of brass, these may be of the press-fit type or held with pins (escutcheon pins) or small screws. They may be quite plain or decorative and, in addition to brass, may be made from ivory or bone.

Where the security of a lock is not required, catches are used to keep doors closed. Brass ball and double-ball catches are old favourites and can be very useful in keeping closed a door which has warped slightly if fitted at the top and bottom. Normally small to medium-sized doors require only one catch fitted centrally. Magnetic catches are a modern innovation which work well.

Double doors require a means of holding one door fixed and this is usually achieved by means of a sliding bolt. The most common type is the surface-fitting barrel bolt available either straight or cranked for rebated doors, and there are various types of flush bolts which recess neatly into the door frame.

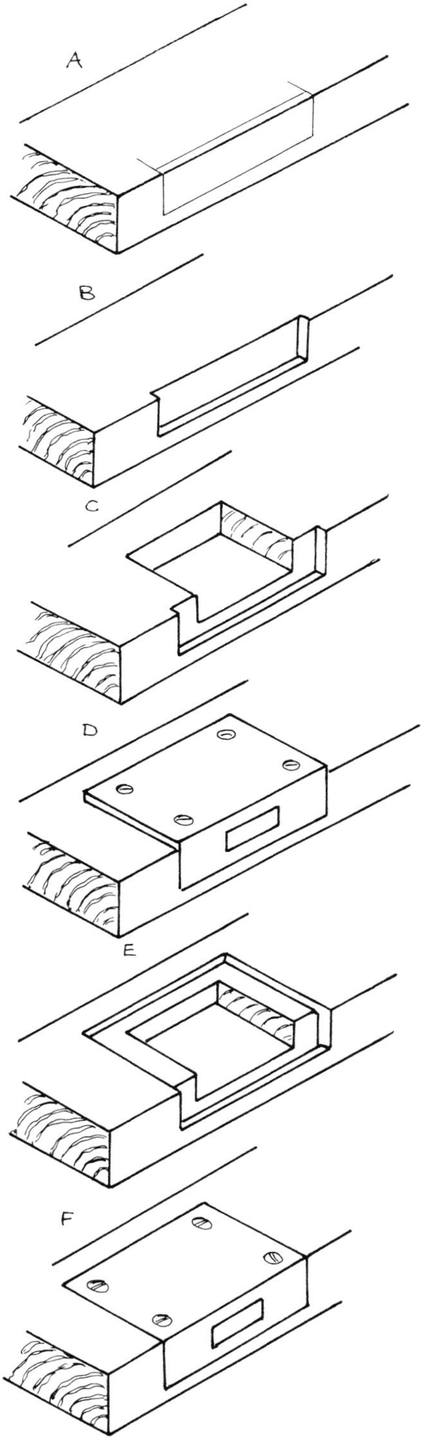

DIAGRAM FOUR

Stages in marking out and cutting-in a typical cut cupboard or drawer lock

8
Finishings

The wood used in making a piece of furniture must be given some kind of surface finish on completion. This seals the pores and helps resist the effects of use and misuse, ie general soiling due to handling, grease, spilt liquids, etc. Moreover, where a transparent finish is applied the natural beauty of the wood's grain and figure is often considerably enhanced.

Choosing the right finish from the many possibilities depends upon how and where the piece of furniture is to be used and, to some extent, upon the nature of the material used in its construction. Sometimes the wood grain needs to be filled; sometimes a high-gloss polish is preferable to a semi-matt surface, or perhaps heat resistance is a prime consideration. In some cases it is necessary to stain the wood before polishing it. Whatever finish is required it is as well to remember that polishing and staining is specialised work and separate from cabinet making; what follows can therefore only be a brief general outline.

Before applying any finish the wood must be thoroughly prepared and clean, ie the surface scraped or sanded smooth and all pencil marks and finger marks, etc removed. Most polishing processes and all staining tends to emphasise rather than conceal

Plate 1 A selection of types of wood-finishing materials

Plate 2 Applying teak oil to a piece of furniture

surface marks and defects. It is true to say, in fact, that the first step in finishing is actually part of the last step in the construction part of the job, ie the smoothing and sanding of the wood.

The earliest polishes used on wood were probably vegetable oils and one of these, linseed oil, has continued in use. Properly applied this will give a high gloss with moderate heat and water resistance. Its disadvantage is that it must have many coats – up to twelve are advocated – applied at intervals of at least one week, each coat being allowed to dry by oxidisation. Raw or boiled linseed oil may be used – the latter is less sticky and slightly quicker drying. The addition of 5 per cent white spirit and 5 per cent terebene eases working and assists drying.

Oils incorporating rapid oxidising agents are now widely used. These include teak oil and Danish oil; they are easy to apply and will give sufficient buildup in two or, at most, three coats. They enhance the natural grain of most dark-coloured hardwoods but do not produce as glossy or as durable a finish as the older process using linseed oil.

One of the oldest, most attractive and simplest methods of preserving and polishing wood is to use wax polish. Pure beeswax is difficult to apply in its semi-solid form, although it and Carnuba wax (Brazilian palm wax) both work well used as friction waxes on lathe work. A well-tried formula is to cover shredded beeswax with turpentine (1lb beeswax to approximately ½pt turpentine). This will combine to a waxy paste if left overnight, although heating is often advocated to speed up this process. The addition of a little Carnuba wax gives some extra hardness and shine while an old recipe lists oil of roses or lavender as a perfumatory ingredient. Apply the wax paste to the wood using a soft cloth or brush along the grain, allow to dry, then rub hard and burnish with a soft cloth. Several applications are needed over a period of time to build up a good finish. On carved surfaces burnish with a brush of the shoe-cleaning variety.

An alternative and recommended method is to first seal the pores of the wood with a suitable sanding sealer – or thinned polyurethane 'varnish' may be used instead. Rub this down lightly with flour-grade garnet paper and apply two coats of wax polish to the surface, the first on 0000 wire wool (fine grade) and buffed with a cloth or brush, the second on a soft cloth and finally burnished with a soft dry cloth. Proprietary [commercial] wax polishes are available but most are unsuitable for bare wood.

Wax gives a soft shine and enhances the figure of wood beautifully, but it offers no resistance to heat and very little to moisture; it marks easily and tends to hold dust, which, unless the pores are sealed, can become embedded in the wood. However, as with oil finishes, the great virtue of a wax finish is that it can be easily renovated by further application.

French polish, introduced in the early nineteenth century, consists basically of shellac dissolved in methylated spirits [alcohol]. Its proper use is a highly specialised craft and I would not presume to describe here its application in detail. The aim is to build up a film of polish by the application of numerous thin coats, each allowed to dry before the next is applied. Each new coat partially dissolves the previous one and amalgamates with it; the number of coats given, generally speaking, determines the degree of gloss. French polish is difficult to work with and most amateur attempts end up looking like a cheap varnish or treacle finish, but when correctly done it produces one of the finest finishes. There are proprietary [commercial] brands of French polish, some incorporating ingredients for quick drying, quick buildup, ease of application, etc, and even some for use in spray guns, but none are as good as the real thing.

A number of lacquers – some confusingly called varnish by some manufacturers – are now widely used in the furniture industry. Many are for spray-gun application but some may be brushed. These include certain nitro-cellulose and acid-catalysed lacquers and polyurethane. This last, perhaps most familiar as a transparent wood finish, may be applied by brush and produces a hard surface with good moisture and heat-resistant qualities. It is available in matt, semi-matt and full-gloss finishes; it can also be coloured by use of spirit stains. Nitrocellulose lacquer, or just cellulose, has the advantage of being very quick drying, useful where dust in the air may be a problem. Acid-catalyst lacquers have generally been in two-part form, lacquer and separate catalyst to induce hardening, but a pre-catalysed version is now available.

Transparent polyurethane and pre-catalysed lacquer are both eminently suitable for coffee-table and dining-table tops. Polyurethane dries more slowly than pre-catalysed lacquer which cures very rapidly. Both set by polymerisation, ie a chemical change, and should not be allowed to set glass hard between coats otherwise buildup will be as separate layers. Both should be lightly sanded between coats to remove the orange-peel surface or dust nibs; several thin layers are preferable to one or two thick coats. Final coats may be wire-woolled and waxed, as was described earlier in discussing wax polishing.

Although these materials may produce similar finishes they are not compatible and should never be mixed or one type applied on top of another. A true varnish, incidentally, is composed of natural gums and resins mixed with natural oils, eg linseed and turpentine; polyurethane is made with synthetic resins.

Wood fillers are frequently referred to in some textbooks on furniture finishing. Most are based on chalk or plaster of Paris mixed with a solvent such as water or linseed oil to produce a paste. This is applied to wood to fill the grain pores and when dry it is sanded smooth. Its objective is to level the surface and prevent undue absorption of whatever polish is subsequently applied. Proprietary [commercial] brands of sanding sealer are much easier to use, and those which have ethnol [alcohol] as their solvent are very quick drying to give an easily sanded surface.

Wood may be stained to darken it to a uniform colour or to intensify the natural figure and sometimes, regrettably, in order to imitate another wood. There are three main groups: water stains, oil stains and spirit stains. The first are now mainly pigments or dyes dissolved in water to produce a wide range of intermixable colours quite cheaply. Certain chemicals when mixed in water can

Plate 3 Using stain to darken the wood used in making a stool frame

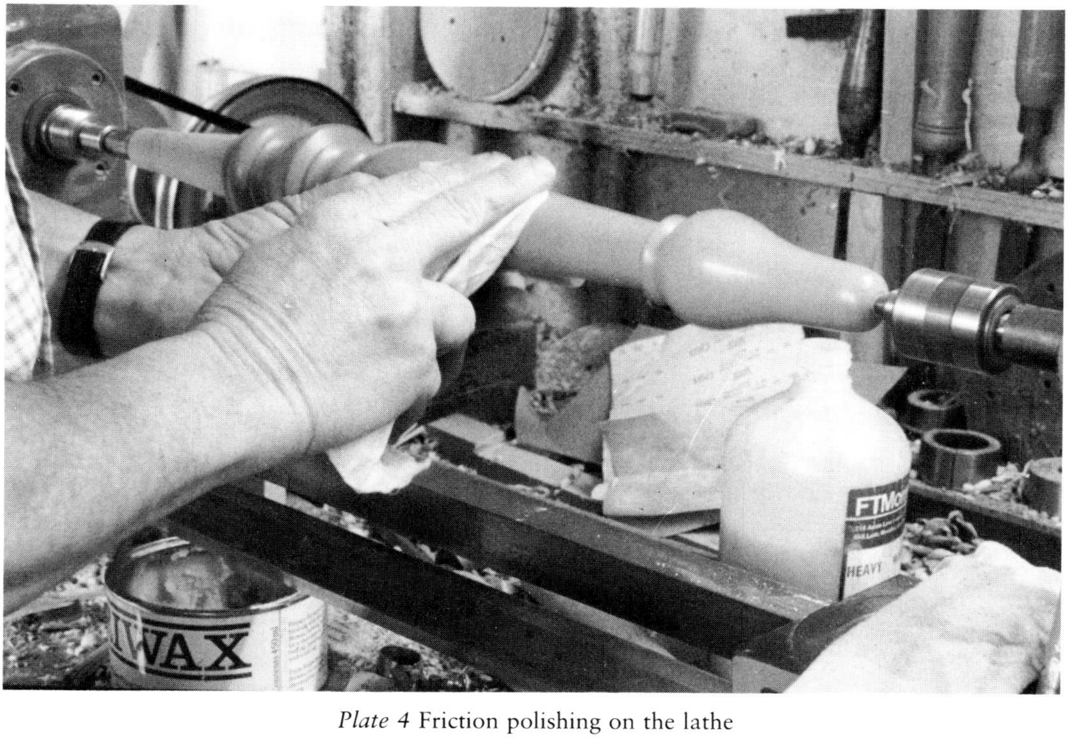

Plate 4 Friction polishing on the lathe

be used to stain wood also. Water stains tend to raise the grain and so it is advisable to wet the surface first with clean water, and when dry sand smooth before staining.

Oil stains are colours dissolved in turpentine, or something similar. They are not as penetrating as water stains and do not raise the grain, but they are more expensive to use.

Spirit stains consist of dry pigment powders in methylated spirits [alcohol]. They dry rapidly on contact with the wood surface and can be difficult to apply evenly over large areas. The colours also have a tendency to fade.

All proprietary [commercial] brands of these stains are most commonly named according to the timber they are supposed to imitate, ie dark oak, walnut, rosewood, and so on. They are also available as transparent colours, ie red, green, etc. All stains should be allowed to dry thoroughly before applying polish and polish must be applied over stains as in themselves they do not afford any protection to the wood surface.

Finally, turned pieces of work may be clear polished while the piece is revolved in the lathe. This is known as friction polishing and takes advantage of the heat generated through friction. Sealer and various waxes may be applied on a cloth in this way, but proprietary polishes specifically made for this purpose are best. Take care not to have a trailing end of cloth which could get caught up in moving parts.

PART II
PROJECTS

1

Shelves and Boxes

Illustrated on page 65

Heirlooms in wood do not need to be big; as in so many other cases, small can be beautiful. By way of an introduction to this section, therefore, we will begin by describing the making of several of the smaller items. Each can be completed in the course of two or three evenings or a weekend's work, while the amount of wood required in each case is relatively small. Additionally, some of the work entailed provides excellent practice for the later, larger projects.

Almost every household at one time had its set of shelves, a kind of supplement to the mantelpiece, on which to display favourite knick-knacks, small ornaments, books, plants, and other such items. Well-made shelves are pleasing in appearance and simple in construction and can be made as decorative or as plain as takes the fancy of the maker. Pine is a suitable wood, but it must be good quality and well seasoned or it will warp and spoil the finished job. Use a hardwood if available but avoid plywood or chipboard.

Three examples are given here. The first, shown in Diagram One, was made in pine, from easily obtainable 7in-wide boards, ¾in in thickness. The pieces are first cut to length (see Materials Requirement List, p69) and both ends of the three shelves are made square. The joint used to fix shelves to end pieces is the concealed housing or dado joint; a through joint is easier to make, but is not as neat in appearance. The shelves are shown evenly spaced, but this is quite arbitrary as is the shaping of the end pieces. You may wish to follow exactly the drawing as given or to make changes to suit your own requirements. Remember, though, to keep the maximum width of any end piece shaping to coincide with each shelf position.

Shaping can be done by hand, with a coping saw or bow saw, or mechanically on a band saw. Clean up with a spokeshave,

DIAGRAM ONE

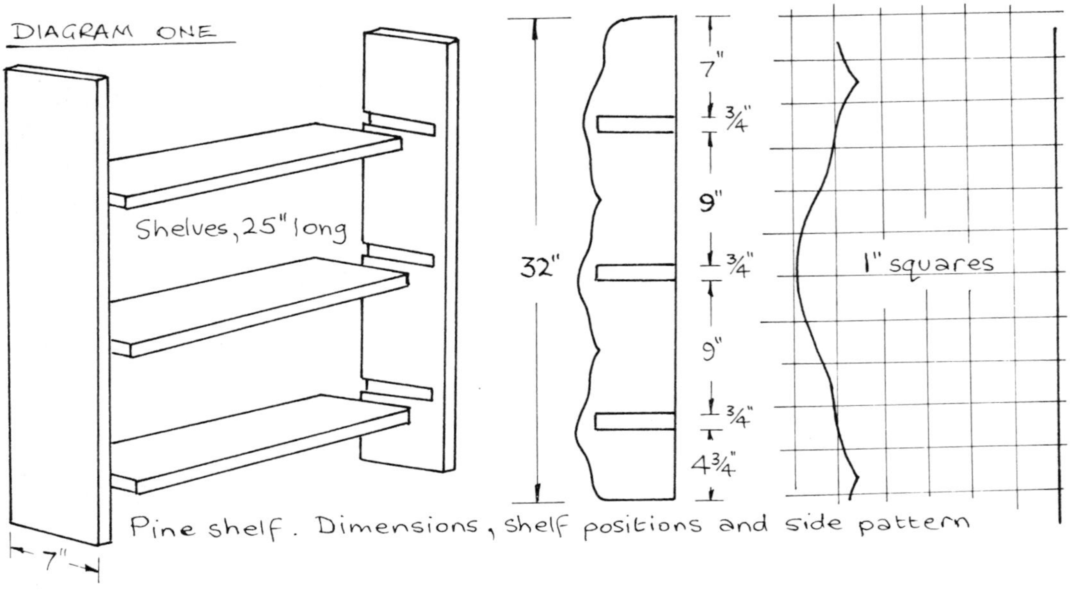

Pine shelf. Dimensions, shelf positions and side pattern

Plate 1 Cleaning up a shaped shelf with a spokeshave

scraper and glass-paper [sandpaper]. After checking that all joints are a nice fit and that everything goes together 'square', prepare for gluing up. Adjust sash cramps [clamps] to a ready fit and have softwood blocks available. Glue up the joints, assemble the shelves in place and cramp [clamp] up, checking for squareness as you do so. Where suitable cramps [clamps] are not available, satisfactory assembly may be carried out, provided the joints are tight, by gluing and panel pinning, the pin heads being punched below the surface and later filled. Wipe off surplus glue with a damp cloth immediately and leave overnight.

When the glue has set, clean up the set of shelves ready for finishing. That shown was left natural and wax polished after sealing the grain (see Finishing, p55). It could have been stained and polished.

The second set of shelves is smaller in overall appearance but just a little more complicated. To obtain the greater width of wood used, it may be necessary to edge joint two narrower boards together. In this case the wood used was oak but again, good-quality pine would be suitable. As the Materials Requirement List shows (p69), the wood was initially 8in wide and ¾in in thickness. All the pieces are cut to length and planed, and, making sure that the ends of the three shelves are square, marked out ready for jointing. Again, the concealed housing or dado joint is used to join the shelves to the two shaped end pieces. The shaped top piece, if made a good tight fit between the two end pieces (do this after assembly), may simply be glued and panel pinned into place, or it may be omitted altogether (Diagram Two).

It will also be seen that a drawer has been fitted in the completed example shown. This is optional; it gives some early practice in drawer making if anyone should feel like tackling this now, or it can always be added later. Think about it, anyway. Both these sets of shelves may be fixed to a wall by means of mirror plates. These are screwed first to the

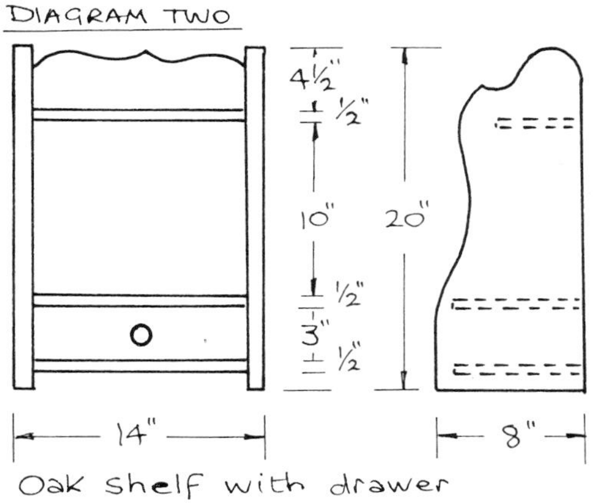

back of the shelves themselves and then, after drilling and plugging the wall, placed into position on the wall.

The third example is a simple corner shelf, which is not difficult to make (later you can make a much more desirable but more difficult corner cupboard). Corner furniture – shelves, cupboards, cabinets, chairs – always seems to add that little extra something to a room, a new dimension, a different focal point. Whatever it is, most people, lighthouse-keepers excepted, like something to occupy their corners.

Room corners are always assumed to be close to 90° and corner furniture is made accordingly. Working wood to fit this angle is no problem – other angles may pose difficulties but are outside our discussion here.

To obtain the wide boards needed it may be necessary to edge joint narrower boards again. Wide boards – up to 12in – of pine are available and this is what was used here. Note that one of the side pieces is narrower than the other, by the thickness of the wood used, so that when they are joined together the inside dimension of both is the same. The shelves are cut from a board as shown in Plate 3; make sure that each corner is square, ie at 90° and that the front radius is constant.

Because the back is to the wall and thus always concealed, it is quite acceptable to assemble the corner shelf by means of screws and glue. The shelves could be accommodated in housings as in the previous items if required. Mark out shelf positions, using a set square, and drill two holes through each side piece to support each shelf. Drill holes to join the two side pieces to each other and countersink all drilled holes. Use screws which go through and into the shelves by at least ¾in. The shelves may go in any position to suit the individual's choice; finishing, too, is a matter of choice. The corner shelves shown in Diagram Three were antique stained and polished to the client's requirements.

Small boxes served a variety of purposes in the home. My grandmother always kept a lidded box hanging close to the hob of the open fire on which she did most of her cook-

Plate 2 Parts for a corner shelf

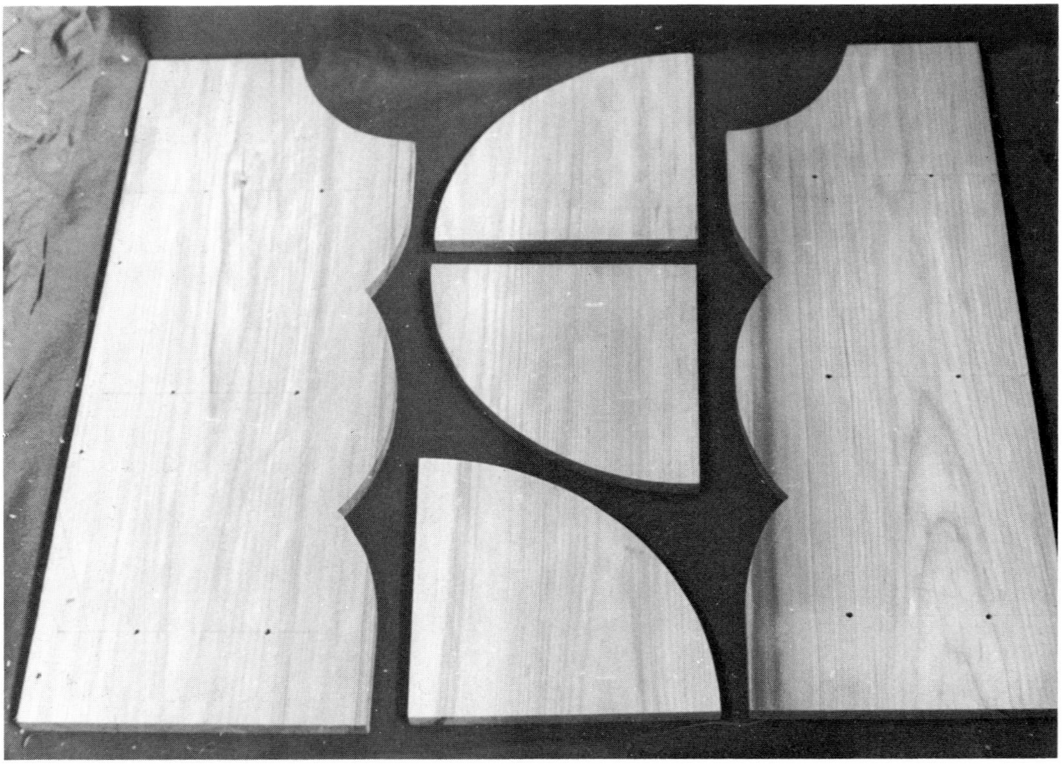

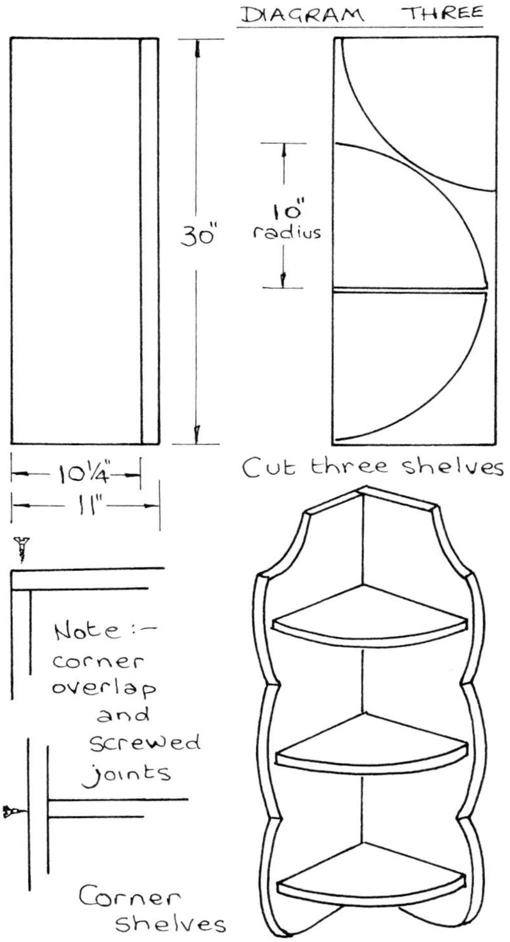

ing. In it she kept salt and it was never damp. Kitchen utensils were kept handy in an open box and her knife box – which contained forks and spoons as well in separate compartments – had a handle so it could be carried about when 'laying the table'. Jewellery, letters or family papers were kept in boxes, some plain, others with carved lids, while pride of place must surely go to those rather special boxes known as writing slopes, secretariats, etc, some exquisitely fitted inside and many with secret compartments.

Wall boxes, like grandma's salt box, were made in all shapes and sizes and held all manner of things and they still have their uses today. Some were made with dovetailed or comb-jointed corners, while others made use of the simpler half-lap joint or rebated joint. Glued and pinned joints are also quite

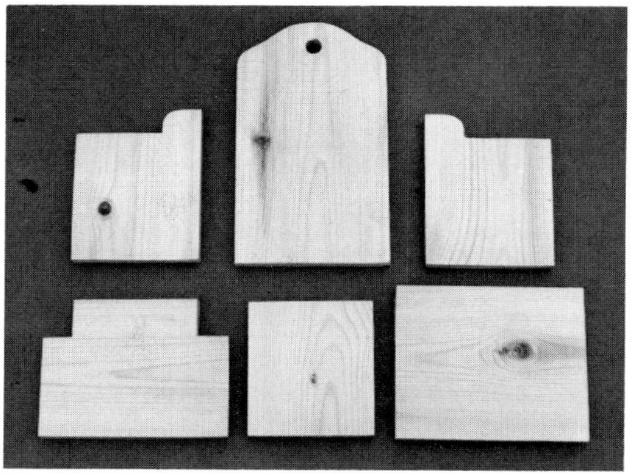

Plate 3 Parts for a salt box

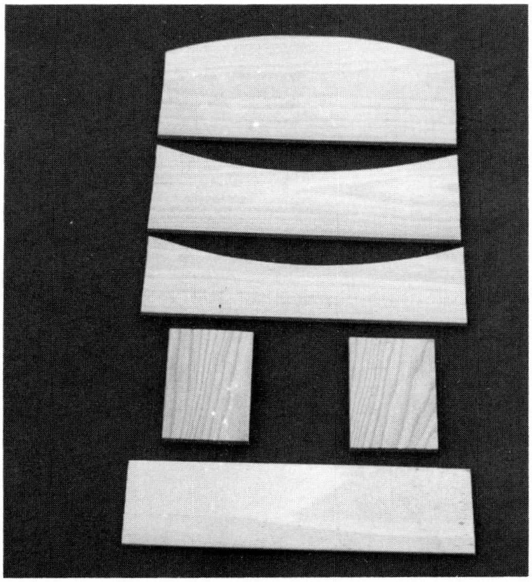

Plate 4 Parts for a letter rack

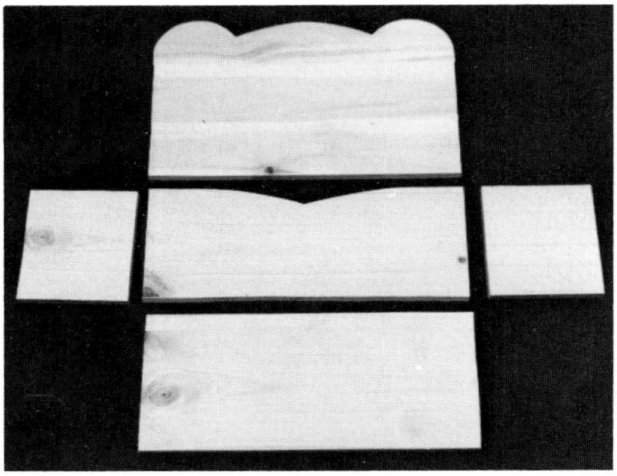

Plate 5 Parts for a wall box

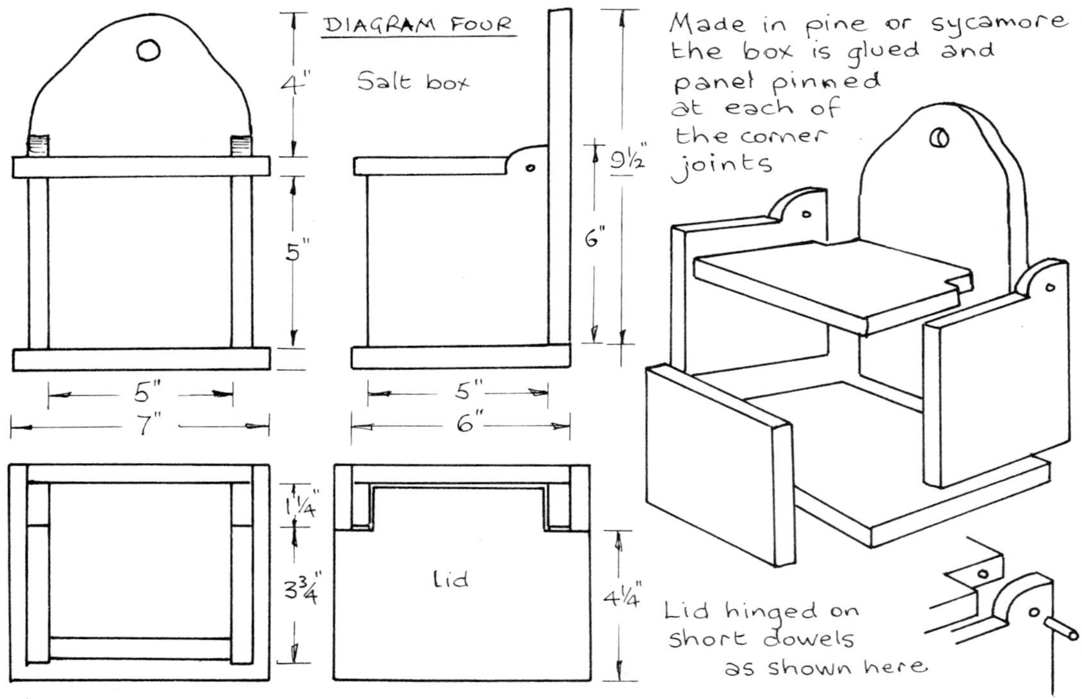
DIAGRAM FOUR
Salt box
Made in pine or sycamore the box is glued and panel pinned at each of the corner joints
4"
5"
9½"
6"
5"
7"
5"
6"
1¼"
3¾"
Lid
4¼"
Lid hinged on short dowels as shown here

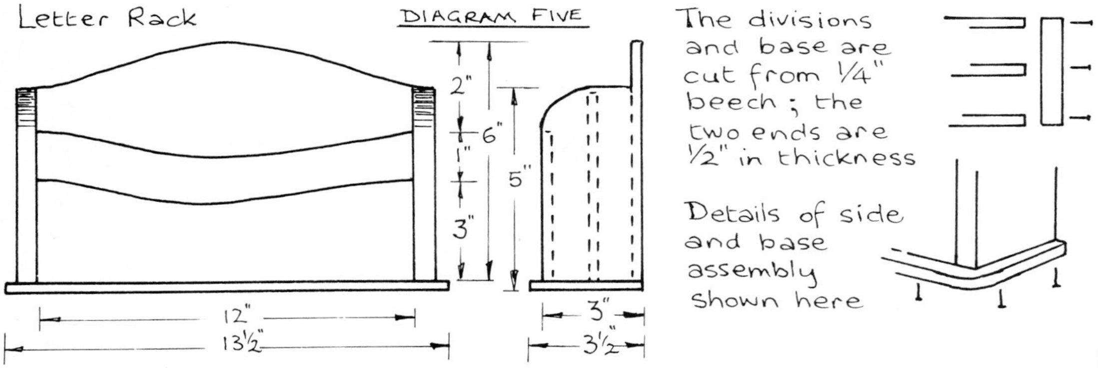
Letter Rack
DIAGRAM FIVE
The divisions and base are cut from ¼" beech; the two ends are ½" in thickness
2"
6"
1"
5"
3"
12"
13½"
3"
3½"
Details of side and base assembly shown here

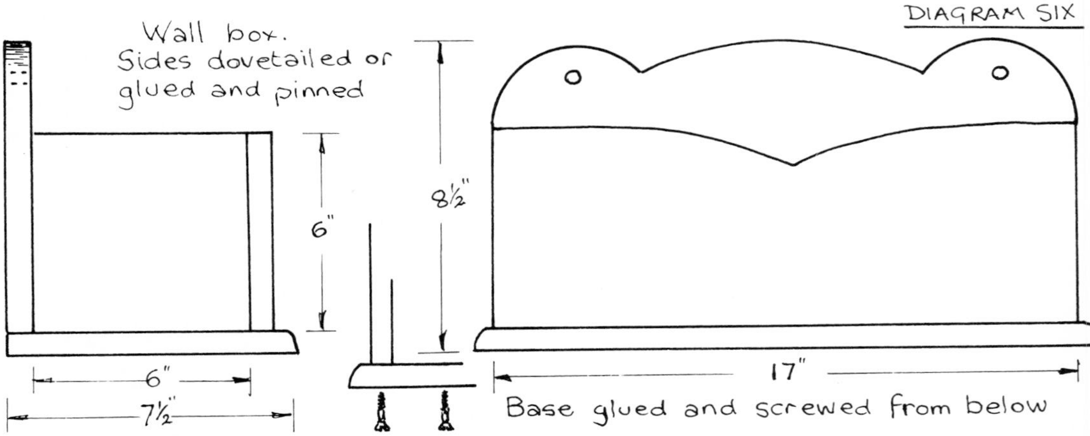
Wall box.
Sides dovetailed or glued and pinned
DIAGRAM SIX
6"
8½"
6"
7½"
17"
Base glued and screwed from below

Plate 6 Assembling a salt box in the workshop

adequate. The wall box shown in Diagram Four uses this latter method. Made in pine, this has been in use in my own kitchen as a salt box for over three years. An alternative design without a lid and shown in Diagram Five is made in beech and is used as a letter rack. The open box in Diagram Six, based on a wall box once used to hold a ready supply of candles, may be used as a stylish plant container. In each instance the planed wood – it may be pine or a suitable hardwood – is cut to size and the ends made square. Appropriate joints are cut and tested for fit. Ideally, bases should be inset into grooves just up inside the box, but adequate results may be obtained by using either of the two alternative methods shown in Diagrams Five and Six.

Glue and, where required, panel pin the box components together. Small boxes may be held under pressure in the vice or with G-cramps [C-clamps] and corner blocks. Use a waterproof glue on boxes to be used in the kitchen or bathroom. Note that the salt box

(*opposite*) Back row: joyned stool; second row down, left to right: elm bench, trestle stool; third row down, left to right: square stool, woven-seat stool; front row: round stool (*see pp71–80*)

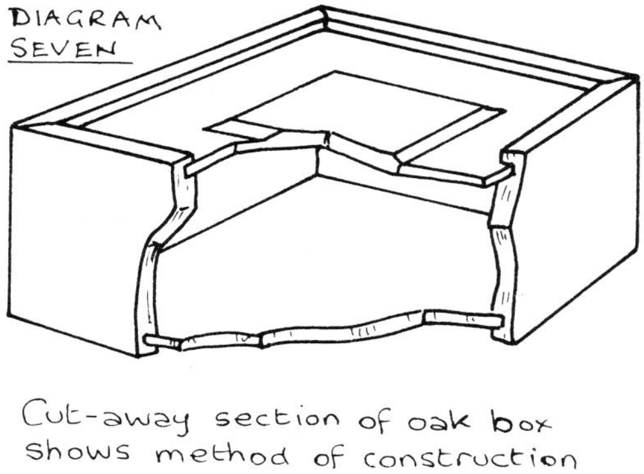
DIAGRAM SEVEN
Cut-away section of oak box shows method of construction

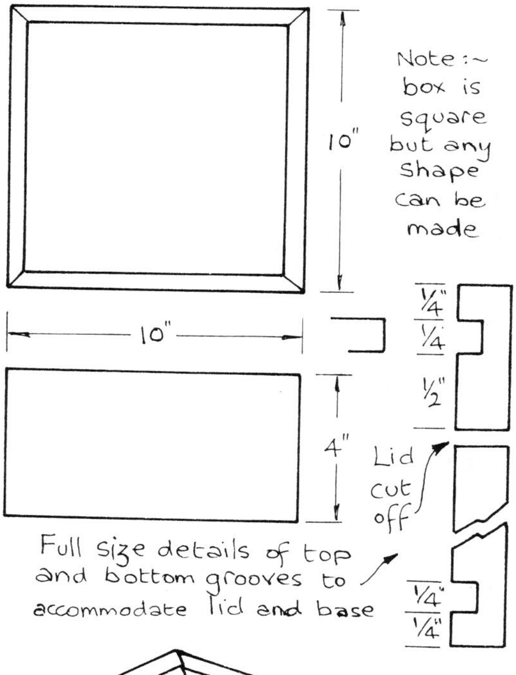
10"
Note :~ box is square but any shape can be made
10"
4"
¼"
¼"
½"
Lid cut off
Full size details of top and bottom grooves to accommodate lid and base
¼"
¼"

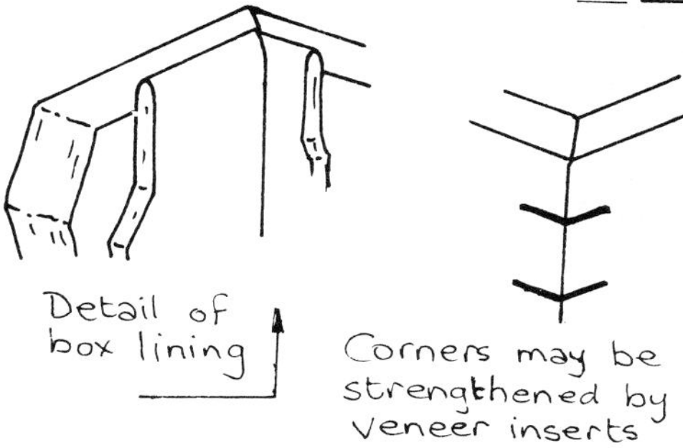
Detail of box lining
Corners may be strengthened by veneer inserts

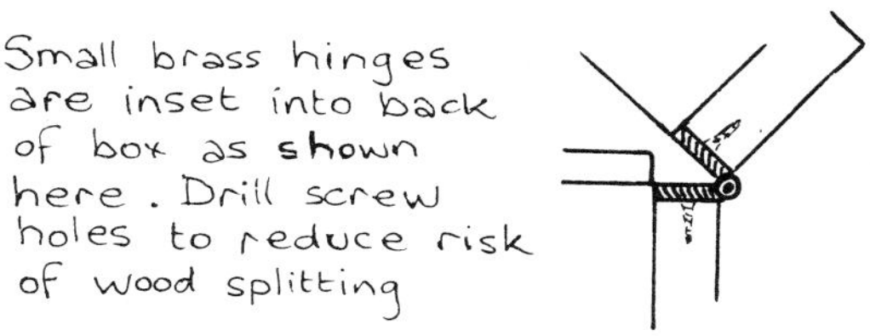
Small brass hinges are inset into back of box as shown here . Drill screw holes to reduce risk of wood splitting

does not have conventional hinges but uses wooden dowels instead. If a box whose lid has metal hinges is used to store salt ensure that they are solid brass and not steel or brassed steel which will corrode.

The type of finish to be applied is left entirely to the maker or the user. Salt boxes may be left entirely unfinished or the outside only given a finish to seal the grain. Boxes for other uses may be stained if required, sealed and wax polished.

The type of lidded box shown in Diagram Seven is best made all in one piece, the lid portion being carefully sawn from the box itself to ensure a snug and matching fit on completion. The corners could be dovetailed, but these were neatly mitred and glued to give an adequate joint. This type of joint is often further strengthened by the insertion of pieces of veneer across the corners. Made in oak, the lid has an optional carved motif in its centre.

First, all the 3/8in material is planed and cut to length. Then the corners are mitred and, as both top and bottom are to be inset, two 1/4in grooves are cut into each piece to accommodate these as shown in the diagram. Note that the top shown is thicker than the bottom and is fielded into its groove in the manner of a fielded panel as used in later projects. Alternatively, top and bottom can be of identical thickness. Check that top

Plate 7 Cutting the lid from an oak box

Plate 8 The lid separated from an oak box

and bottom pieces lie nicely in these grooves; make their length and width just a fraction smaller than needed so that they do not prevent the mitred corners coming correctly together. Place two or three spots of glue in the grooves to hold top and bottom in place. With cramps [clamps] at the ready apply glue to the mitres, assemble all together and apply pressure, checking that the box is square before leaving to dry.

When dry, mark with a continuous double line the position of the lid and carefully saw through between the lines to separate the lid from its box. The sawn edges will require cleaning up by careful planing with a sharp plane set fine. Planing inwards from the corners will eliminate the problem of splintering off at these points.

The box section is lined with thin strips of oak – or a contrasting wood could be used – to give a raised lip all round the inside edge of the box. This ensures a snug fit for the lid. The corners of this lining are mitred to give a tight fit within the box and its upper edges are rounded over. Small brass hinges are used to fix the lid to the box and a small catch or lock may be fitted if required.

The carved top makes a pleasing personal touch; it can be to the design shown or any other, or it could be in the form of initials, a date or a family crest. If carving is to be done, it is best carried out before the box components are assembled so that the top panel can be held solid to the workbench. Finish by wax polishing.

MATERIALS REQUIREMENT LIST (CUTTING LIST IN INCHES)

Nº	PURPOSE	MATERIAL	INITIAL SIZES		
	PINE SHELF				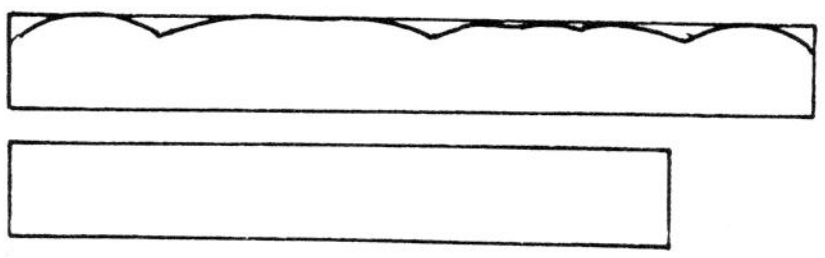
2	END PIECES	PINE	32 × 7 × 3/4		
3	SHELVES		25 × 7 × 3/4		
	OAK SHELF – with drawer				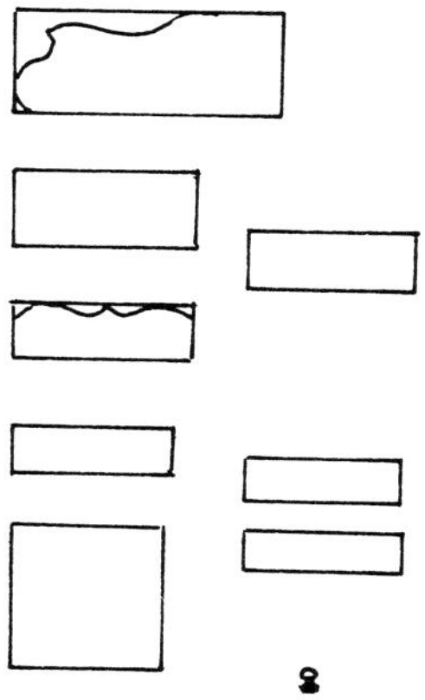
2	SIDE PIECES	OAK	20 × 8 × 3/4	SHAPED	
2	SHELVES		13 × 7½ × ½		
1	SHELF		13 × 4 × ½		
1	TOP PIECE		12½ × 4 × ½	SHAPED	
	~ for drawer				
1	FRONT		12½ × 3 × 3/4	DOVETAILED	
2	SIDES		7 × 3 × ½		
1	BACK		12 × 2½ × ½		
1	BOTTOM	PLY	12¼ × 7⅛ × ⅛		
1	TURNED KNOB				
	CORNER SHELF				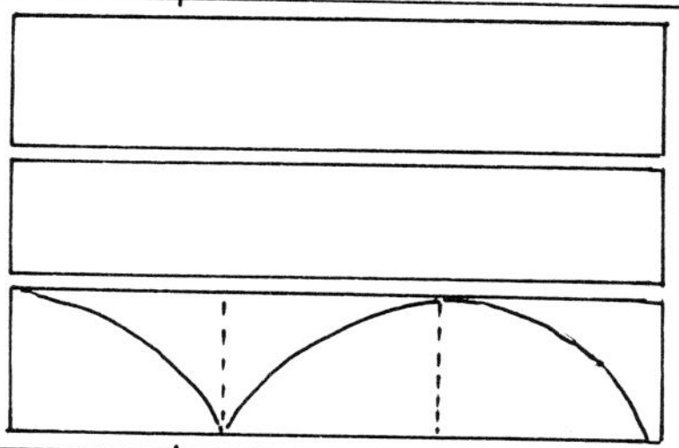
1	SIDE PIECE	PINE	30 × 11 × 3/4		
1	SIDE PIECE		30 × 10¼ × 3/4		
3	SHELVES		30 × 11 × 3/4		
	SALT BOX				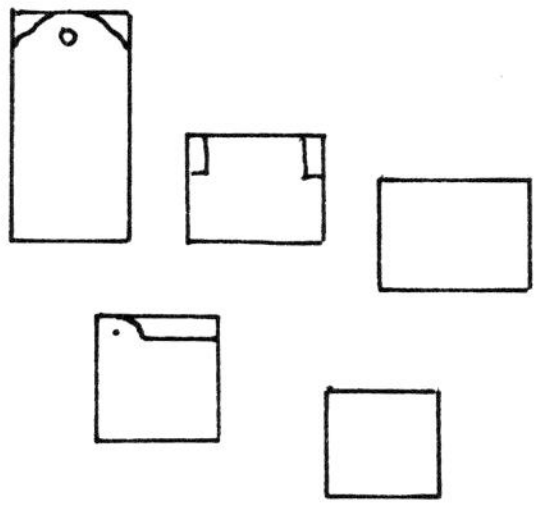
1	BACK	PINE	9½ × 6 × ½	SHAPED	
1	LID		7 × 6 × ½		
1	BASE		7 × 6 × ½		
2	SIDES		6 × 5 × ½	SHAPED	
1	FRONT.		5 × 5 × ½		
	LETTER RACK				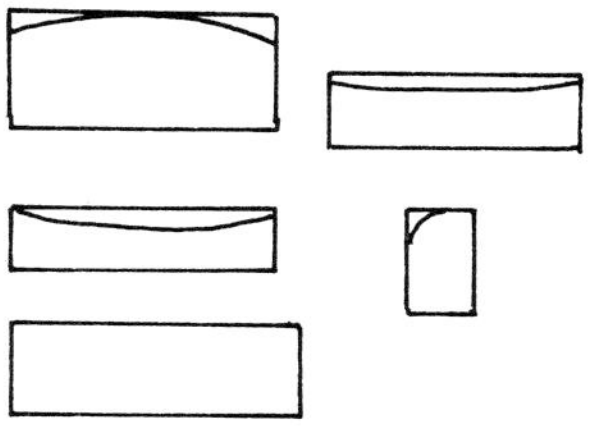
1	BACK PIECE	BEECH	12 × 6 × ¼	SHAPED	
1	CENTRE		12 × 4 × ¼		
1	FRONT		12 × 3 × ¼		
2	END PIECES		5 × 3 × ½		
1	BASE		13½ × 3½ × ¼		

MATERIALS REQUIREMENT LIST. (CUTTING LIST IN INCHES)

Nº	PURPOSE	MATERIAL	INITIAL SIZES		
	PLANT BOX				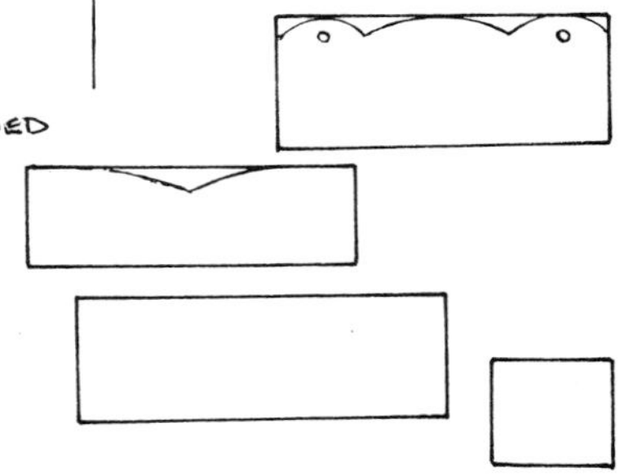
1	BACK	ASH	17 × 8½ × ½	PLANED	
1	FRONT		17 × 6 × ½		
1	BASE		18 × 7½ × ½		
2	ENDS		6 × 6 × ½		
	CARVED BOX				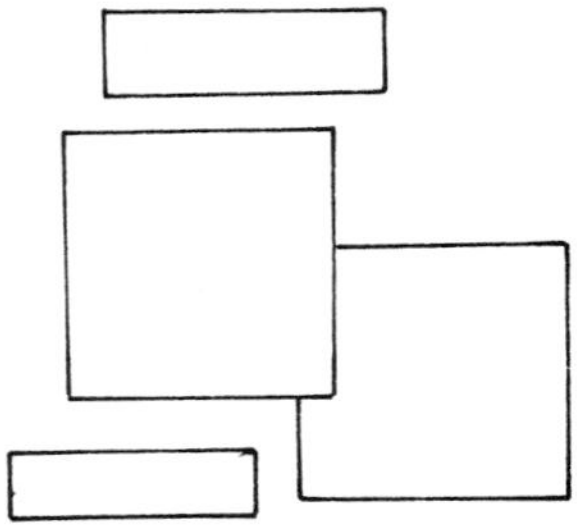
4	SIDE PIECES	OAK	10 × 4½ × 3/8	PLANED	
1	TOP		9½ × 9½ × ½		
1	BOTTOM		9½ × 9½ × ¼		
4	LINING PIECES		9¼ × 3¾ × 3/16		

2

Stools

Illustrated on page 66

Small stools were always handy around the house, especially for small children sitting near the fire. Not so popular for this purpose today now that central heating and thick pile carpets make sitting on the floor even handier, stools still have their uses, some, if not for seats, as small tables placed close to other more comfortable seats. Such stools come in a variety of styles from the plain pine trestle or box stool – known in the USA as the five-board stool – to the Tudor-style 'joyned' stool, the simple woven seat stool and the even older three- and four-legged turned stick or 'peg-leg' stool.

In the first, the plain board top is supported by two solid ends linked by two cross members close up under the top – hence, five boards while the joyned stool had a solid board seat with a mortice-and-tenoned underframe. Later examples had an upholstered seat. The woven seat stool has a more lightly constructed open framework, its seat being woven or matted with a variety of materials. The turned stool consists of a circular or rectangular top into which splayed, turned legs are dowelled, usually right through the top, where they are wedged for security. This last type of stool is the acknowledged ancestor of the various forms of Windsor chair and their construction affords excellent practice for making that type of chair.

First to the trestle stool (Diagram One). A wide, dry board of pine is ideal for this and a total board length of 5ft will yield all that is needed. Cut square across to the sizes given in the Materials Requirement List, p80, and cut one of the 18in pieces down its length to make the two side members. Carry out the shaping of these next and then mark their position on each side of the two 'legs'. Mark these to the thickness of the wood and cut out at each place to form the housings. The two ends or legs are shaped by sawing into a drilled hole as shown in Plate 1.

Many of these stools were painted and

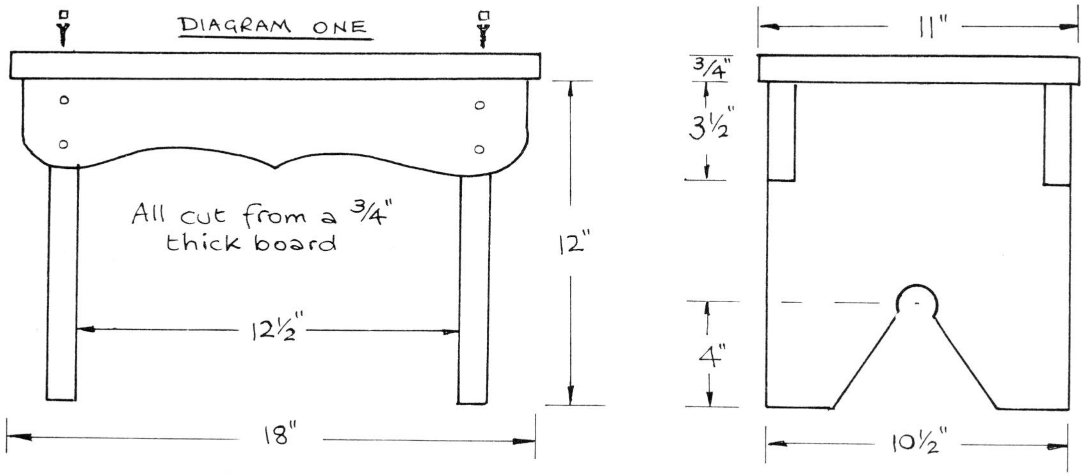

Five board trestle stool. The parts are cut to shape and glued and screwed together. Screw holes are plugged

Plate 1 Trestle stool parts marked out for cutting

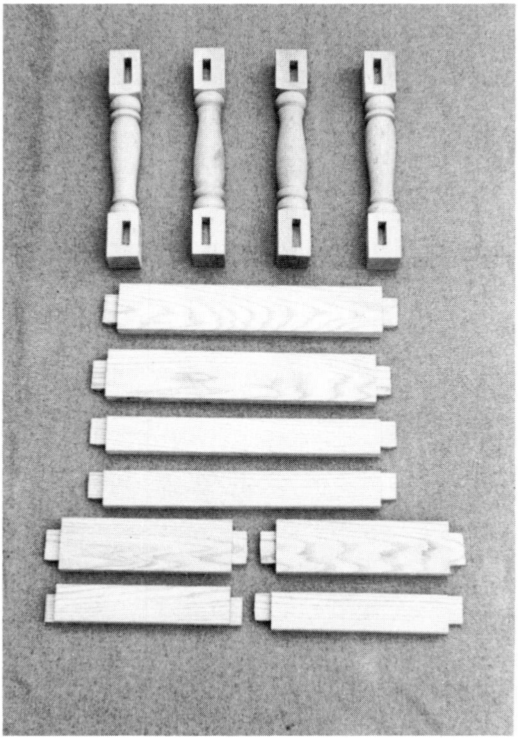

Plate 2 Parts for a joyned stool

were simply nailed together, the nails being punched below the surface and filled before painting – an adequate, quick job. Gluing and screwing makes a better job, the screws being recessed in counterbored holes and filled with wooden plugs. Such stools may then be naturally polished or stained and polished, or painted.

The 'joyned' stool – so called because it was joined together by using mortice-and-tenon joints – is made, in contrast, with an upholstered seat (Diagram Two). Oak, the wood traditional for this style of furniture, was used, everything cut from a 2in thick board. First the legs are turned, the two ends being left square for morticing, and the eight side rails prepared to overall size. The tenons at each end of these are marked out and cut, followed by the mortices to receive them in the legs. Have a dry run to check that everything fits, then glue up. It is an advantage, especially if cramps [clamps] are scarce, to assemble the two ends first, cramp [clamp] up and let these dry and then connect together with the other cross members, thus completing the assembly in two stages.

The upholstered seat is a drop-in type made as shown in the diagram. The upholstery may be made traditionally on a wooden frame using a webbing foundation and fibre stuffing or by the modern upholsterer's less skilled method of foam padding on a plywood base.

The woven seat stool was popular in some country districts where it was made entirely from locally grown natural materials. The frame consisted simply of four square or turned legs with eight rails, four upper seat rails and four lower stretchers, joining them at right angles. Legs similar to those used in the 'joyned' stool may be used, joined by square rails, morticed and tenoned into the legs. However, the original country stool had plain square or round legs joined by round rails, each having a round tenon jointed into a matching socket hole. The stool described here has square legs as this simplifies the socket hole drilling. It was made under instruction by a partially handicapped teenager. The slight staggering of the socket holes bored into each leg is done to retain strength. Bore the upper holes in each leg and assemble the two ends, ie a pair of legs joined by a pair of rails (Diagram Three).

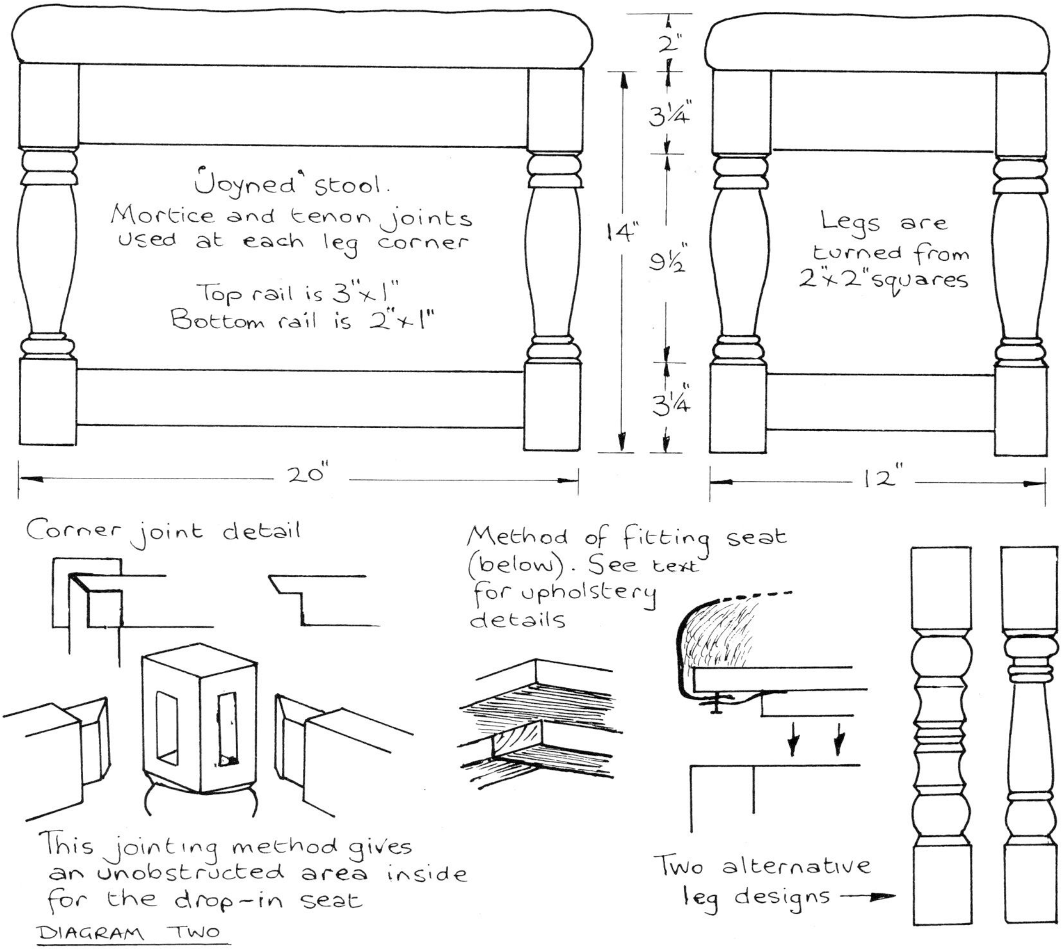
2"
3¼"
14"
9½"
3¼"
20"
12"
'Joyned' stool.
Mortice and tenon joints used at each leg corner
Top rail is 3"×1"
Bottom rail is 2"×1"
Legs are turned from 2"×2" squares
Corner joint detail
Method of fitting seat (below). See text for upholstery details
This jointing method gives an unobstructed area inside for the drop-in seat
Two alternative leg designs
DIAGRAM TWO

Plate 3 A joyned stool glued up and cramped

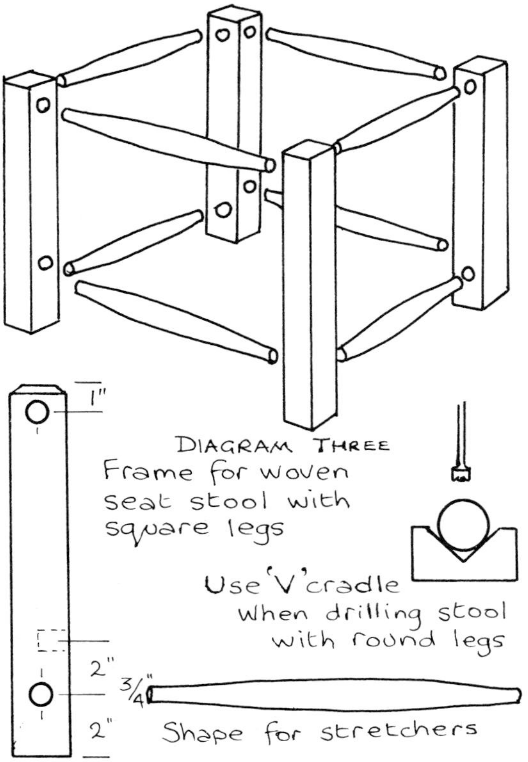
1"
DIAGRAM THREE
Frame for woven seat stool with square legs
Use 'V' cradle when drilling stool with round legs
2"
3/4"
2"
Shape for stretchers

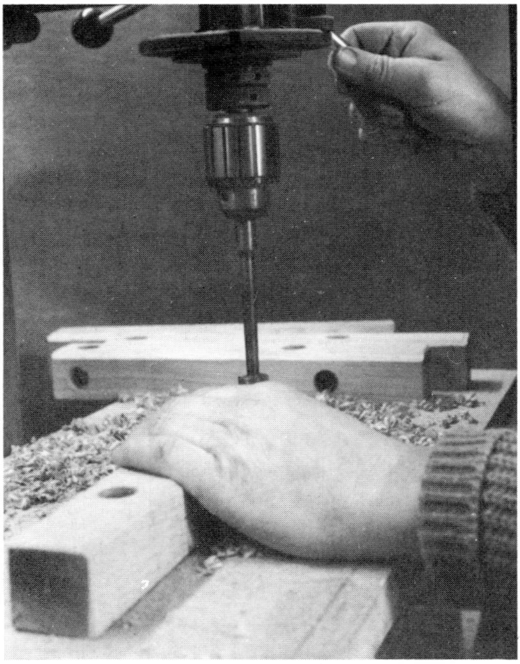

Plate 4 Drilling socket holes for a woven seat stool

Round legs and rails may be turned or made with the rotary planes described earlier. Turned legs should be kept the same diameter along their length or they may taper slightly below the bottom rails. Each leg has a rounded top. The rails all have ¾in tenons turned on their ends to fit the matching socket holes. Use the V-shaped cradle to support turned legs when boring these sockets and a saw-tooth Forstner-type bit to give flat bottom holes. For accuracy in drilling the use of a bench or pillar drill [drill press] is advocated (see Chairs, p44).

First, mark the position of the upper holes on the 'centre' line as shown and bore these out to the correct depth – set this on the drill stop. Then check the side rails for fit and assemble two ends. Now mark the position of the lower holes relative to the rails already fitted and, by holding each assembled end section horizontally while drilling vertically down into the marked positions, holes at right angles to those already bored will be produced. Check that cross rails are a good fit and assemble the complete stool.

When gluing up, put the glue into the socket holes and not on to the rail tenons, following the procedure of making up two end sections first; glue and cramp [clamp] these up until the glue is dry, then add the cross rails and recramp [reclamp]. A suitable finish is sanding sealer, rubbed down, followed by wax polish.

The stool is now ready to have its seat woven. Traditionally, this would have been done in native green rush, *Cripus lacustria*, or, later, perhaps an imported variety from Holland. If rush is unobtainable the instructions given may be followed using other materials such as sea-grass cord. There are two points of difference: rush, sold dry in bundles called bolts, must be moistened before use and worked in a damp condition to avoid breakage; sea-grass cord is used dry. Also, as the sea-grass is already twisted, the remarks on twisting rush should be ignored. And a word of advice – rush is the correct material, but sea-grass cord is easier to use.

Basically, rush bottoming or matting is done by taking two rushes of similar size, placing them alongside each other (butt to tip) and twisting them together to form a strong smooth coil of even thickness. This rush coil is woven over and around the frame

Plate 5 Woven seat stool frame ready for weaving

of the chair. The twisting or coiling, which is all-important, takes place as the work proceeds and is done only on the top of the seat and around the framework where it will show; underneath, the rush is not twisted.

The start is made by tying the first ends of the rush tightly together with string. For a square or rectangular seat the string is then tied to the inside of the left-hand rail of the chair frame about halfway along. The rushes, brought over the top of the front rail, are held in the left hand (of a right-handed person), while the right hand begins the twisting, the twist being made away from the corner. The coil goes below the front rail, up behind it on the inside of the frame and, twisted again, to the left, over itself and over and under the left-hand rail. Then, without twisting, it comes up on the inside again and goes across to the opposite front corner where, twisted again, it goes over the right-hand rail and the whole process is repeated. The rush is pulled quite tightly across. Care has to be taken to ensure that the cross-over, which forms at the corners as the work proceeds, is kept 'square' (Diagram Four).

New rushes are joined on as old ones run out by tying in with a reef knot, or an extra one can be added to one that has become too thin by means of a half-hitch. Joins are made underneath and clear of the corners. Some professional bottomers work with pairs of rushes of uneven length and simply twist in a

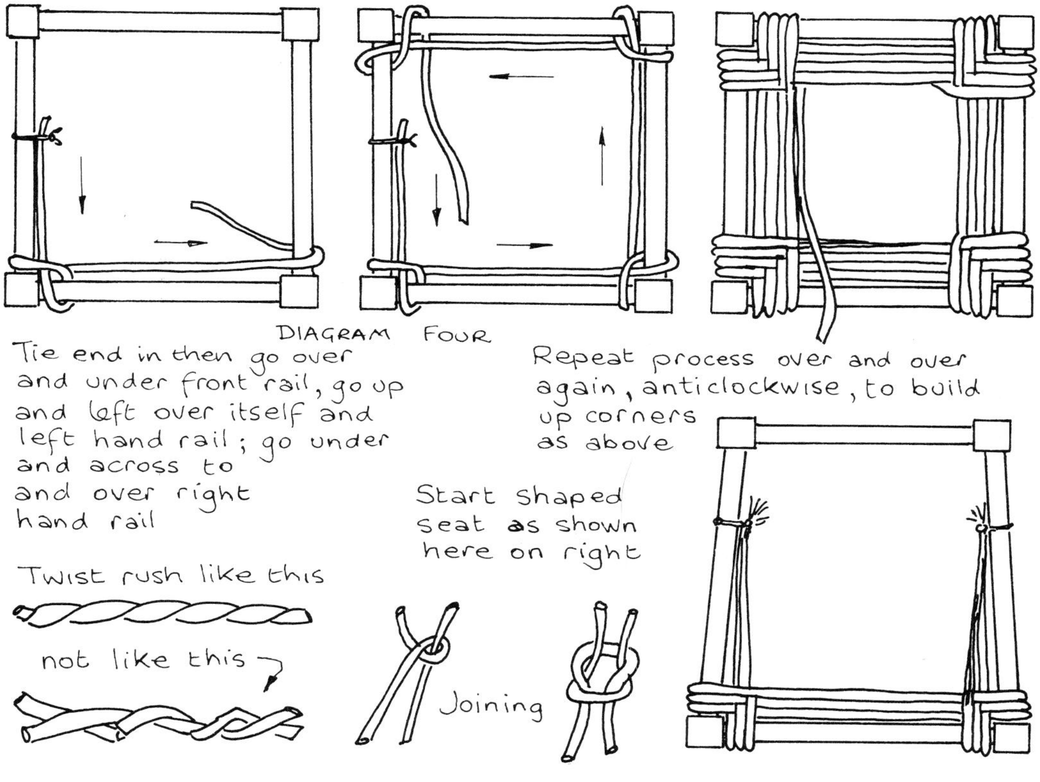
DIAGRAM FOUR
Tie end in then go over and under front rail, go up and left over itself and left hand rail; go under and across to and over right hand rail
Repeat process over and over again, anticlockwise, to build up corners as above
Start shaped seat as shown here on right
Twist rush like this
not like this
Joining

new length of rush as necessary. Coils must be well-made for this; and knotting, although it takes a little longer, is recommended to begin with.

Rush seats are padded in order to firm the centre and raise it slightly above the edges of the chair frame. Padding also tightens up the weaving and makes the seat stronger and therefore more hard-wearing. Short ends and broken pieces of rush can be used for this, but they must be thoroughly dry. Clean straw is also suitable for use as a padding material. The padding is built up gradually, usually working from the underside of the seat, by using the fingers to push handfuls of material into the pockets of rush which form at the corners. This is done after every ten or eleven rounds of weaving. A packing stick is used to push the padding firmly in as the pockets get deeper and the space between them smaller.

The coiled rushes shrink a little as they dry out. For this reason a seat is best made in two or three stages, leaving it at least overnight between each stage. After this the coils can be pushed closer together, resulting ultimately in a much firmer finish. The final coils should be worked as close together as possible.

The various types of turned, stick or peg-leg stools have been used for thousands of years; they were, perhaps, the next logical development from sitting on a log. Early examples were crudely constructed and some, in the form of the traditional three-legged milking stool, were still to be seen in use in country areas up to recent times. The tripod legs were advantageous as an aid to stability when used on an uneven surface and this carried over into the use of splayed three- and four-leg stools and, later, similar chairs on the often uneven stone-flagged floors of early dwelling houses.

Stool tops were often cut from thick planks of elm or oak, while legs were generally of ash or beech, coppiced material used either in the round or cleft and shaped by hand. Each leg, round at the top, was socketed directly into an angled hole bored right through the solid seat. This was secured by means of a hardwood wedge which, when driven down into a saw cut made in the top of the leg prior to fitting, effectively spread and thus tightened the socketed end.

This simple, round, wedged joint was widely used by those who found it easier to obtain or make wood roughly round than accurately square. The wedge took care of any problems and, furthermore, the joint did not require glue. Later, when the round joint

Plate 6 Ash plank marked out for a stool

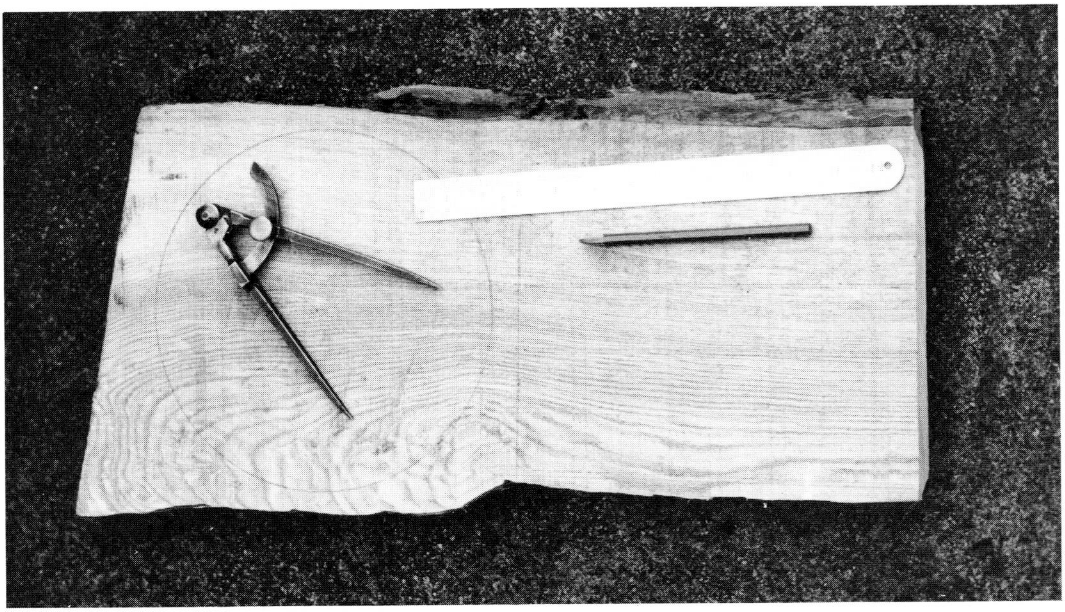

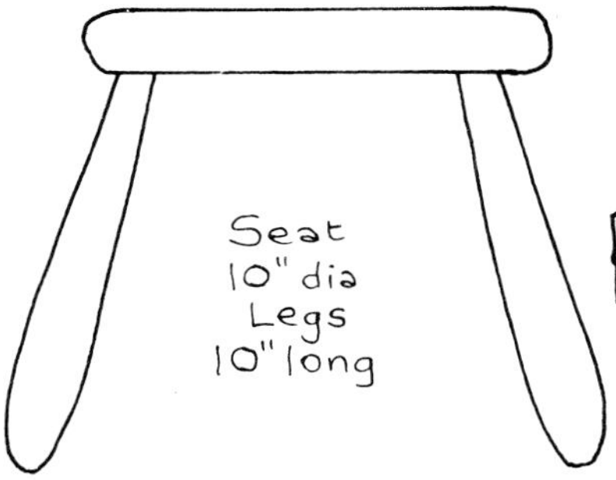

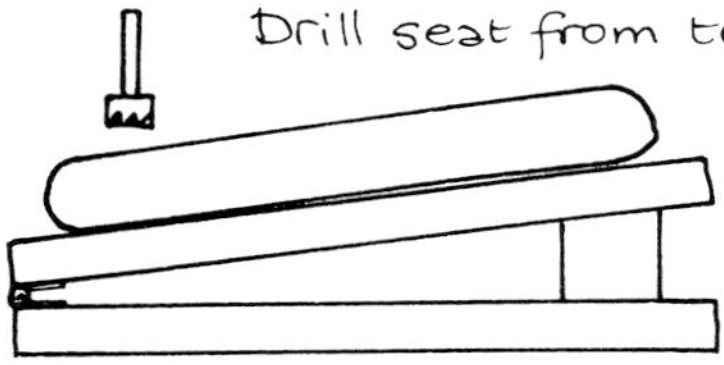

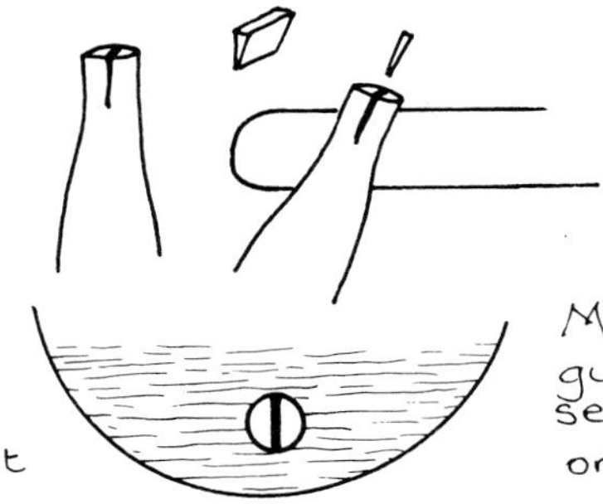

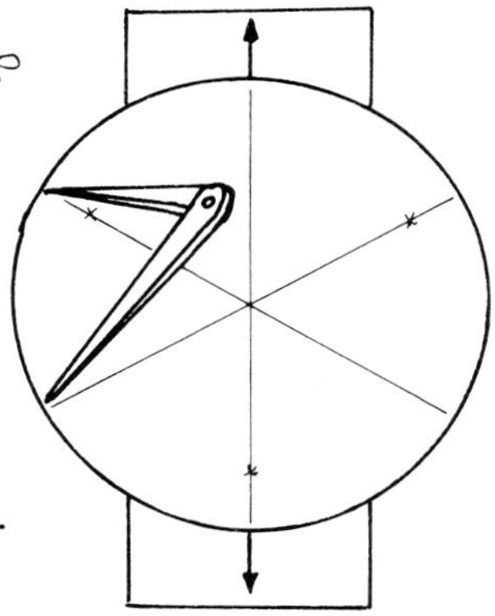

DIAGRAM FIVE

Round stool. The three legs are secured by the wedges as shown on right.

Keep wedges at right angles to grain of seat

Mark out and align guide lines on top of seat with centre line on drilling jig, as above

Square stool, fitted with four legs

Legs, 10" long

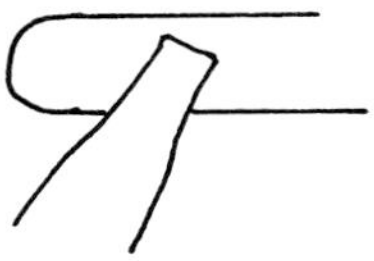

Here the leg joint is 'blind' and the seat is drilled from underneath

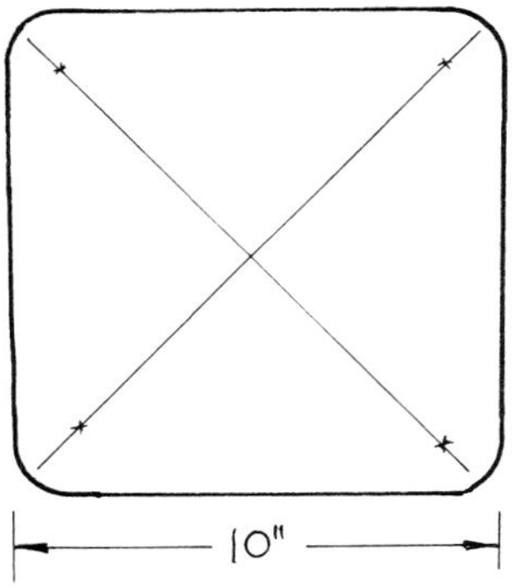

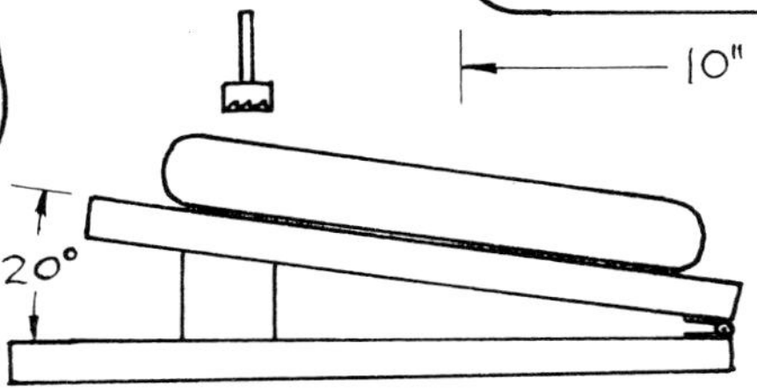

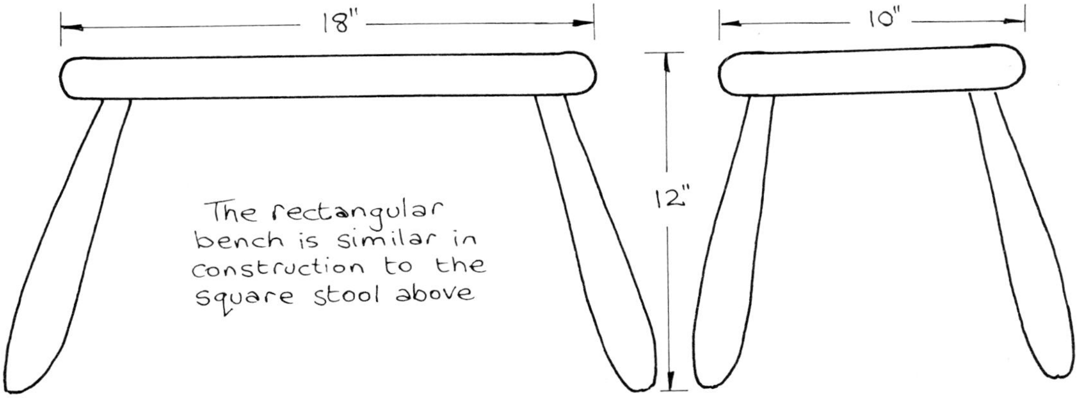

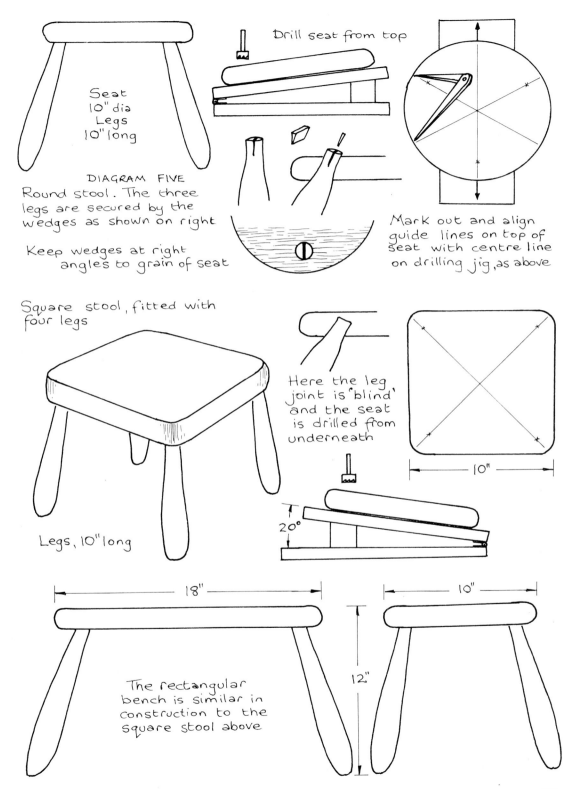

The rectangular bench is similar in construction to the square stool above

could be made more precisely and suitable glues were more readily available, it could be made without the wedge and socketed and glued into blind or closed holes in the seat. Modern turned furniture parts continue to be fitted together in this same manner.

The round-top, three-legged stool shown in Diagram Five has 10in legs and a 10in diameter top, all made from 1½in-thick, well-seasoned ash. First, the top is cut to size and the position of the three leg socket holes marked out using the compasses set at the radius of the top. This gives the 'guide lines' used to align with the centre line of the drilling jig to ensure correct splay or angle of legs. Mark out on the top of the seat. Drill 1in-diameter socket holes right through the seat using the sloping platform jig as described on p44. Clean up the top and bevel or round over its edges.

Plate 7 'Turning' stool legs by hand with a rotary plane

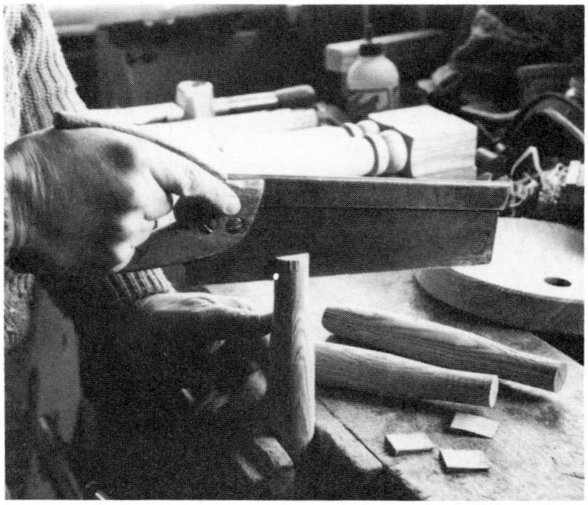

Plate 8 Preparing a stool leg for wedging

Next, the legs are turned to size, either on the lathe or using the rotary planes. Obviously, the top joint is taken down to 1in diameter to match up with its hole in the top. Don't forget to make the saw cuts for the wedges – about 1in deep – into the top of each leg joint and cut three wedges to fit. When assembling the legs into the seat top it is important that these saw cuts lie at right angles to the grain of the seat (see Diagram Five). A wedge put in along the grain would cause the seat to split.

Assemble the legs correctly into their holes and drive in the wedges. To be safe, with stools to be used in centrally heated homes, it is advisable to put glue into the socket holes. Then cut the stub ends flush and clean off the surface. A tenon saw followed by a sharp plane or wide chisel does this job efficiently; hold each leg in turn in the vice and work on that leg.

The square stool and the rectangular short bench are made similarly, their leg joints in each case being of the blind or closed-socket type instead of the through-wedged joint. This is done here only to demonstrate the different jointing methods and may be changed as required. The marking out for the leg sockets is done in the underside of the seat top using the diagonals as guide lines. The socket holes are drilled from the underside also, the stop on the drill being adjusted to go in no more than 1in at its lowest point into the seat. To be successful these leg joints must be a good tight fit; do not rely entirely on the glue. Before final assembly, have a dry run to check that, unintentionally, you do not have a rocking stool. If you have, ascertain which leg is causing the trouble and shorten it. It is a good idea to number legs and matching sockets in case there are some slight discrepancies.

For a finish on these stools, like that on most furniture, I prefer a clear wax. Scrape and sand the surfaces first, apply a sanding sealer and in turn rub this down, too. Then apply beeswax with turpentine and plenty of the traditional elbow grease to bring a gentle glow to the wood.

Plates 9–12 (*above*) Drilling leg socket holes; (*below*) Parts for an elm bench; (*above right*) Rounding over the edge of a burr elm seat; (*below right*) Fitting the stool legs

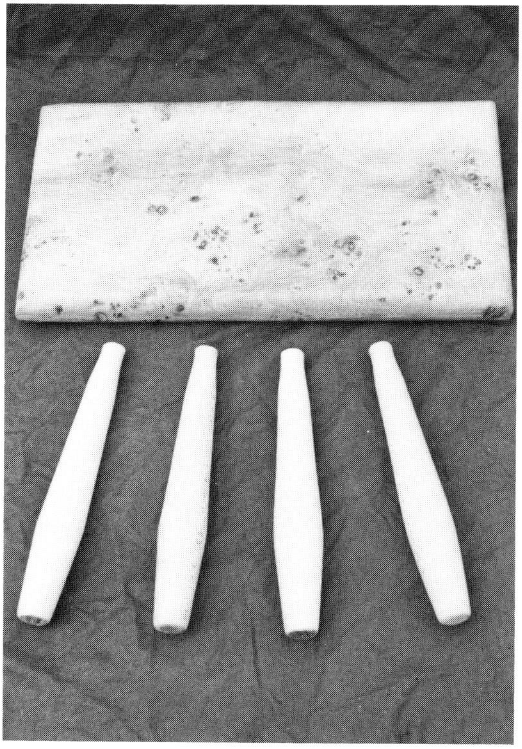

MATERIALS REQUIREMENT LIST. (CUTTING LIST IN INCHES)

No.	PURPOSE	MATERIAL	INITIAL SIZES		
	TRESTLE STOOL				
	All cut from a single board, 5ft long ~				
1	TOP	PINE	18 × 11 × 3/4		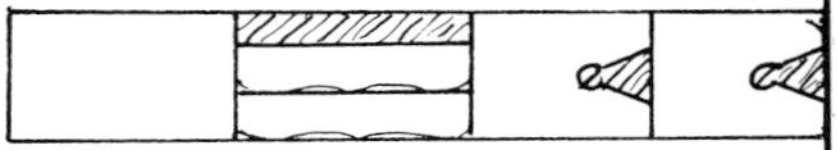
2	LEGS		12 × 11 × 3/4		
2	SIDE PIECES		17½ × 3½ × 3/4		
	JOYNED STOOL				
4	LEGS	OAK	14 × 2 × 2	TURNED	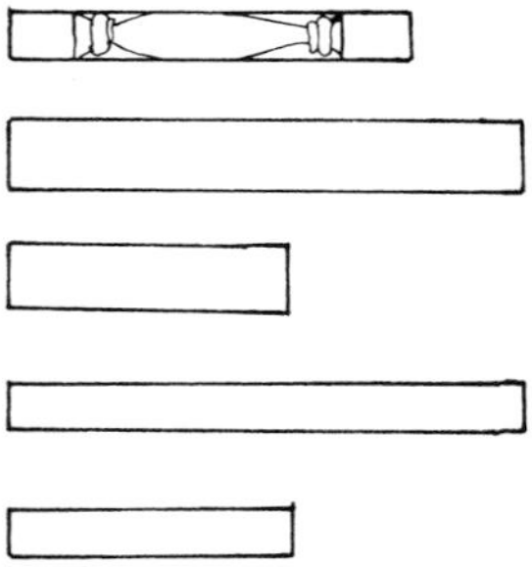
2	LONG TOP RAILS		18 × 3 × 1	PLANED	
2	SHORT TOP RAILS		10 × 3 × 1	&	
2	LONG BOTTOM RAILS		18 × 2 × 1	JOINTED	
2	SHORT BOTTOM RAILS		10 × 2 × 1		
	WOVEN SEAT STOOL				
4	LEGS	BEECH	12 × 1½ × 1½	TURNED OR LEFT SQUARE	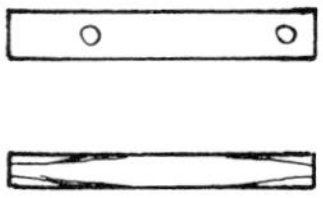
8	STRETCHERS		12 × 1 × 1	TURNED	
	Material for weaving seat				
	ROUND STOOL				
1	TOP	ASH	10 × 10 × 1½	PLANED	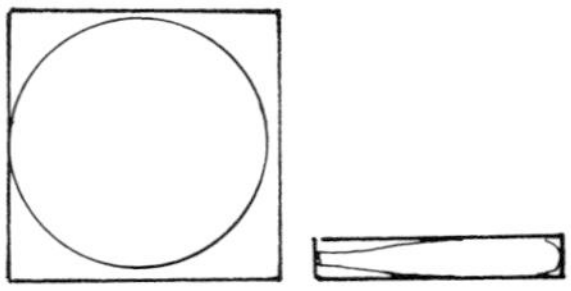
3	LEGS		10 × 1½ × 1½	TURNED	
	SQUARE STOOL				
1	TOP	ELM	10 × 10 × 1½	PLANED	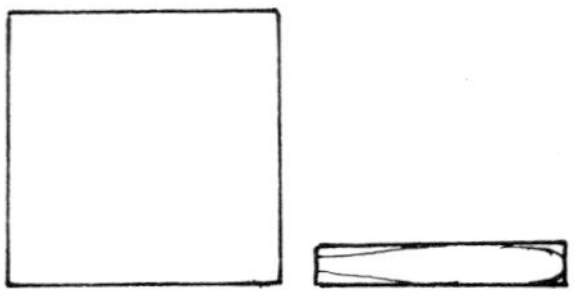
4	LEGS	ASH	10 × 1½ × 1½	TURNED	
	ELM BENCH				
1	TOP	BURR ELM	18 × 10 × 2	PLANED	
4	LEGS	ASH	12 × 2 × 2	TURNED	

3

Spinning Chair

Illustrated on page 83

The item of furniture described here as a spinning chair is also known, more generally, as a back or backed stool. Before Elizabethan times the more usual seating in most houses would have been long communal benches or individual stools, the latter often three-legged so that they stood firm on the uneven stone floors commonplace in dwelling houses of the period. In the larger houses there might be, in addition, a single large chair for the exclusive use of the head of the family or the lord of the manor, or whoever. Occupancy of this chair at meals and other gatherings, while everyone else sat on benches or stools, carried with it an important social status, one handed down to the present day in the title of chairman.

With the eventual idea of extending or adding a back to stools in an effort to give a greater degree of comfort to everyone came the problem of what to call these new pieces of furniture. To call them chairs would offend the dignity of the chair-man and they clearly could not continue to call them stools. So, stools with backs or back stools became the accepted name.

They were made in a variety of styles; some had a row of spindles carrying a cresting rail or comb and, it appears, that these in due course gave rise to the various types of Windsor chair, while others, in which two legs were extended to form two back posts, held solid panels or later, open bars. Regional styles developed and one, usually attributed to Wales, had a solid back socketed into or often through the seat where it was held in place by wooden pegs. It is this latter type which may have been favoured by Welsh wool spinners, hence its present-day name. However, you need not be a wool spinner or any other kind of spinner to sit on a spinning chair. Their low seat makes them extremely functional and ideal for children's use, and one is worth having for its decorative quality alone. All the various types had carving of one type or another and this is no exception. That on this chair is a six-part design based on radius arcs, but the choice is open to the individual.

Beech or ash are both suitable for the construction of the spinning chair described here which was cut from a single piece of board which measured 28 × 16 × 2in (see Diagram One). With the separate pieces cut out, the seat is first planed smooth both sides – the seat remains flat and is not hollowed. Next, it is sawn to shape using the pattern given in Diagram Two as a guide and the cut edges cleaned up with a spokeshave. Chamfer both top and bottom edges and sand smooth. The three legs, cut to 2 × 2in from the board, are

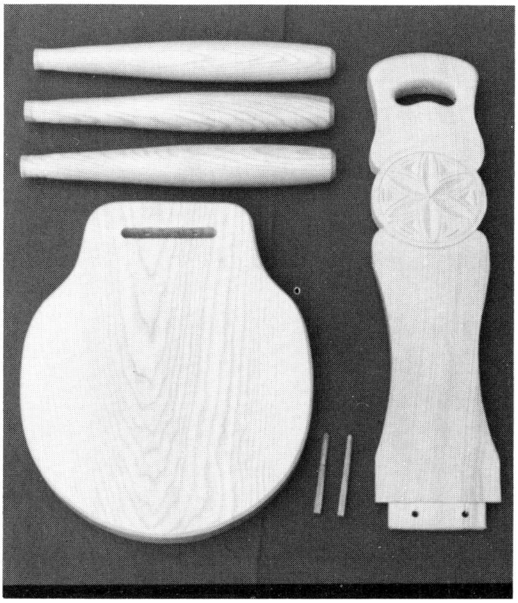

Plate 1 Components for a spinning chair

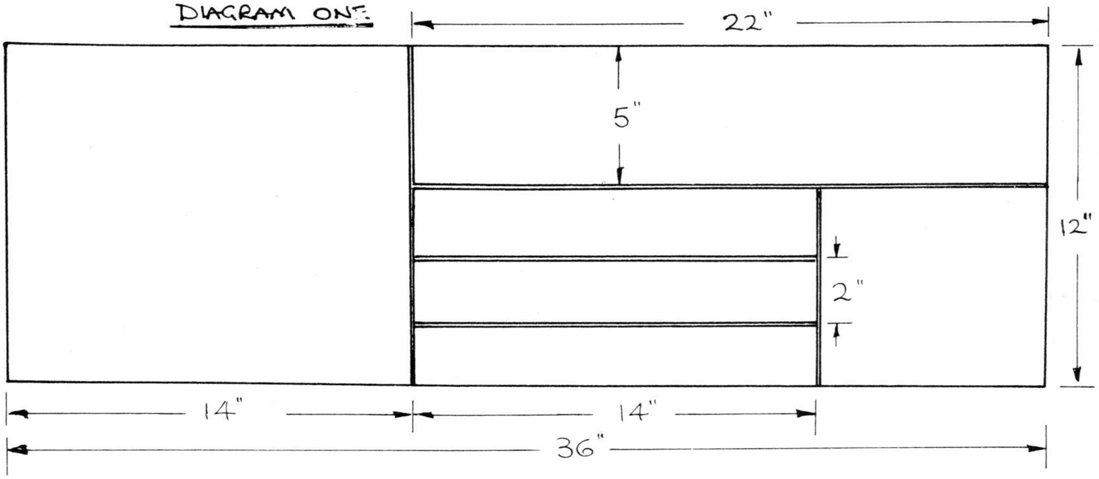

The spinning chair is cut out from a single board as shown above to the dimensions as given. The small off-cut is not wasted but can be used to make a top for a small stool. The board is 2" thick

Board being sawn on a bandsaw, right

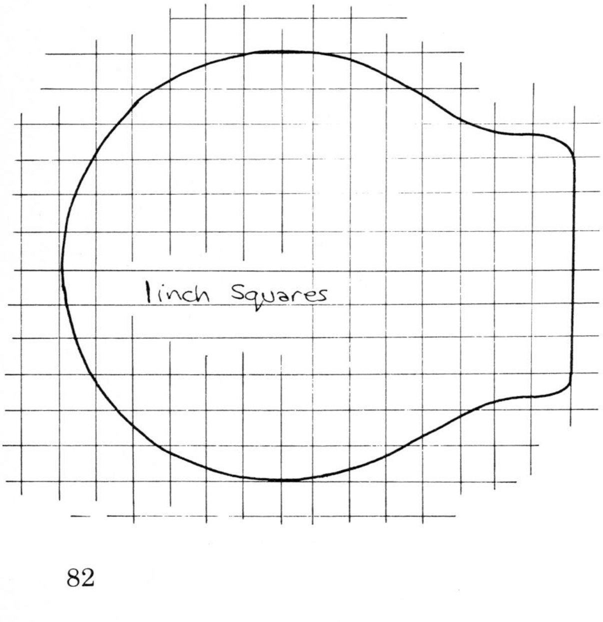

DIAGRAM TWO

Seat is sawn to shape as shown. This is based on a circle, 6 in. in diameter. The extension towards this side accommodates the mortice slot which is cut into it to support the back which is fitted into it later

(*opposite*) Spinning chair (*see pp81–9*) and spinning wheel (*see pp207–18*)

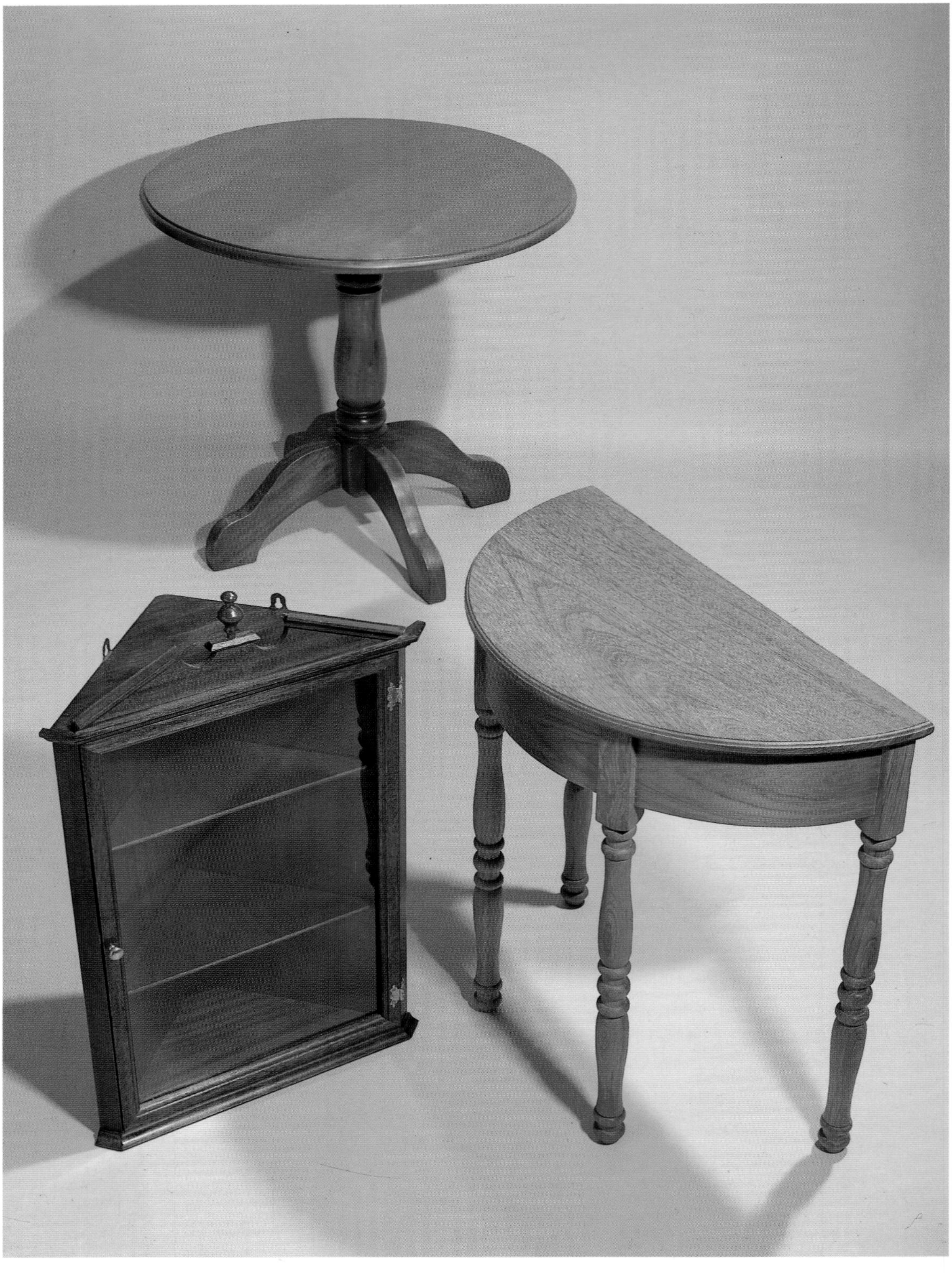

turned on the lathe, first cylindrical and then to the plain, tapered shape shown. They can be more elaborate than this, if you wish, turned with beads and coves, etc, but the simple shape of the chair is complemented, I believe, by the simple plain legs. The top of each leg is finished to be a tight fit in a 1in-diameter hole.

The back of the chair functions not only as a back rest but also in providing a means of carrying the chair from place to place with only one hand. It is shaped in two planes, ie both in its thickness and across its width and is provided with an elongated hand-hole close to its top edge. This produces an interesting back shape which is traditional in its frontal appearance while having something of the feel of a contemporary shooting stick when grasped by the hand for carrying purposes. The shaping process is best carried out in the described manner; plane one face to become the front and mark out the shapes on the front and one edge, according to the patterns given in Diagram Three. Cut the shape in the thickness of the piece first and follow this by cutting out the frontal shape.

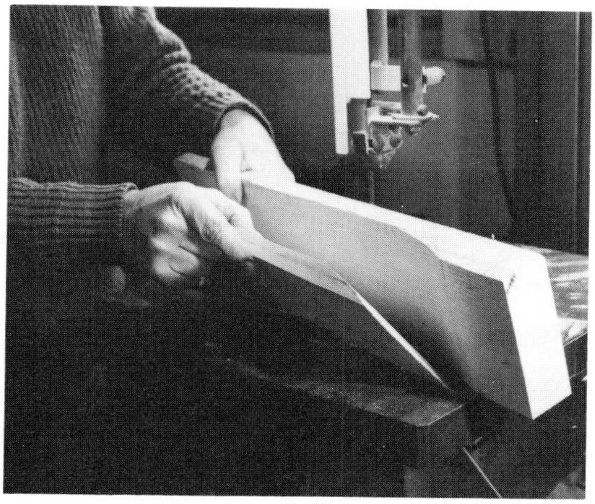

Plate 2 Cutting the back on a band saw

A band saw was used for cutting both shapes, but alternative methods include sawing along the straight portion of the line marked on the edge with a rip saw, making a

(*opposite*) Back: pedestal table (*see pp96–100*); front left: corner cabinet (*see pp90–5*); front right: half-round hall table (*see pp161–7*)

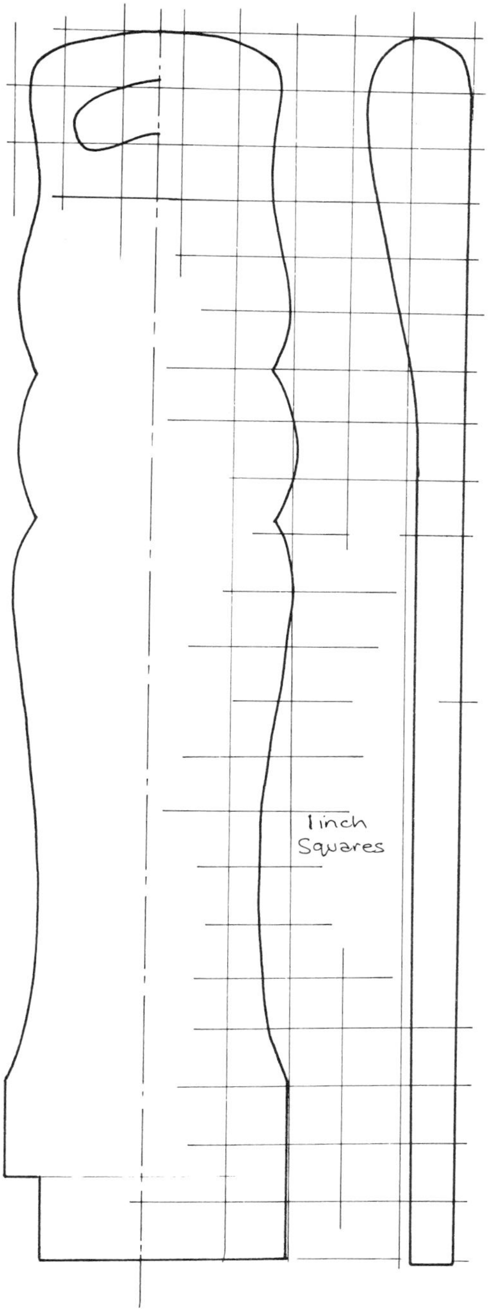

DIAGRAM THREE

Back of chair is cut in two planes to patterns shown here. Further details of shaping are given in other illustrations

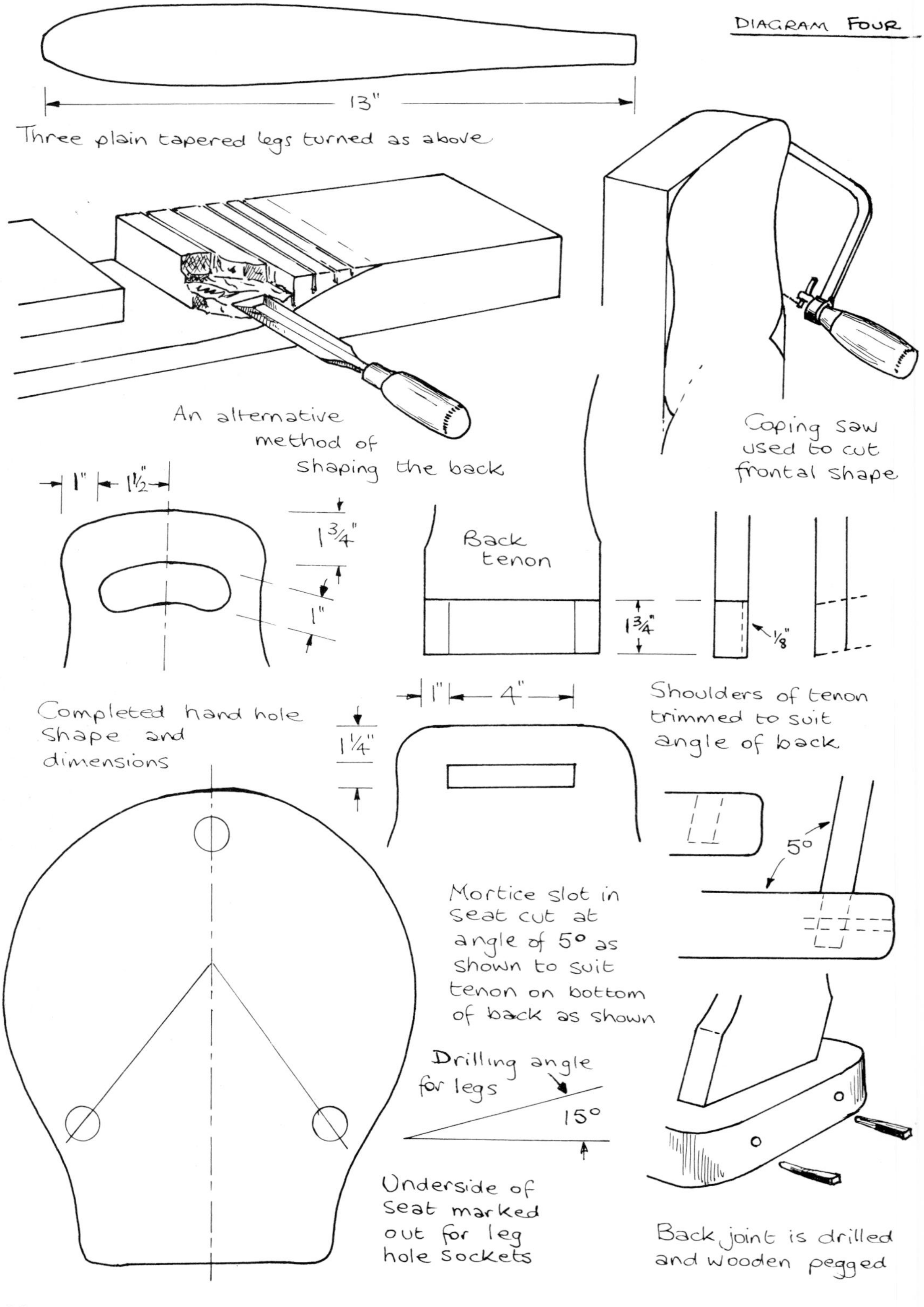
DIAGRAM FOUR
13"
Three plain tapered legs turned as above
An alternative method of shaping the back
Coping saw used to cut frontal shape
1" 1½"
1¾"
1"
Completed hand hole shape and dimensions
Back tenon
1¾"
1/8"
1" 4"
1¼"
Shoulders of tenon trimmed to suit angle of back
5°
Mortice slot in seat cut at angle of 5° as shown to suit tenon on bottom of back as shown
Drilling angle for legs
15°
Underside of seat marked out for leg hole sockets
Back joint is drilled and wooden pegged

series of cuts down to the curved section of the line with a tenon saw and chiselling out the waste, and using a coping saw to cut out the frontal shape (see Diagram Four).

Whatever the method used to cut out the back, it will require cleaning up with a spokeshave. Small files are helpful in getting into those parts of the shaped edges which the spokeshave cannot reach. Keep the edges crisp but aim to produce a nicely contoured shape. The carving on the back may now be carried out. Transfer the drawn design on to the wood and with the piece clamped firmly to the bench proceed with the carving as described earlier. The chip-carved design shown in Plate 4 is given in the chapter on Carved Decoration (p47). Next, mark out and cut the tenon on the bottom edge of the back as shown in Diagram Four. Initially, the tenon is best kept a little oversize so that it may be trimmed later to fit the mortice cut into the seat. The hand-hole located at the top of the back is formed by drilling five overlapping holes 1in in diameter, preferably with a Forstner bit, inside the marked lines as shown in Diagram Three. Clean up with a chisel and half-round file. Then smooth away any roughness with glass-paper [sandpaper] to achieve a nice feel to the whole of the back, paying particular attention to the area around the hand-hole.

Attention may now be focused on finishing the seat. The three 1in-diameter leg-

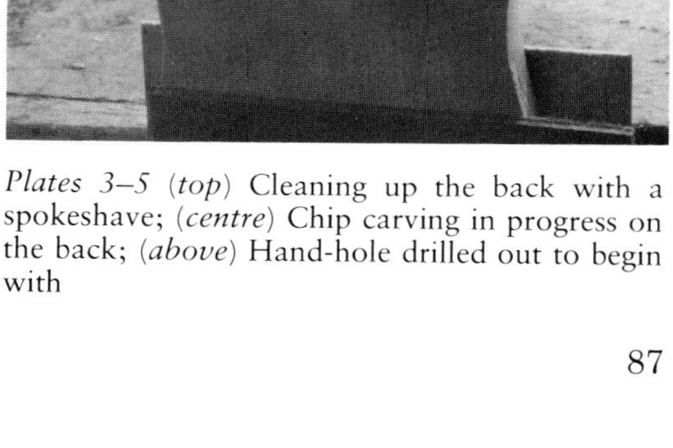

Plates 3–5 (*top*) Cleaning up the back with a spokeshave; (*centre*) Chip carving in progress on the back; (*above*) Hand-hole drilled out to begin with

Plate 6 The hand-hole is cleaned up with a half-round file

Plate 7 Waste in the seat mortice is removed by drilling

socket holes are marked out on the underside as in Diagram Three and drilled at the appropriate angle by any of the methods described elsewhere. On the top surface of the seat mark out the position of the mortice which is to accommodate the back according to Diagram Four. The bulk of the waste in the mortice may be removed by drilling and the slot squared off and cleaned up with a sharp chisel. Note that the back is raked, ie it leans back at an angle of approximately 5°, so carry out the drilling at this angle and keep it in mind when chiselling to size. The shoulders on the tenon should be cut to match this same angle when the tenon is being trimmed to fit the mortice. Test fit the back into the seat to ensure a good fit.

When the tenon is a good fit in the mortice it should be drilled ready for pegging, as shown in the bottom corner of Diagram Four. Mark the position of the pegs on the back edge of the seat, put the back into place and drill a small hole through the seat, just marking the tenon with the point of the drill but not going through it. Remove the back and make new centre marks on the tenon

Plate 8 Test-fitting the back into the seat

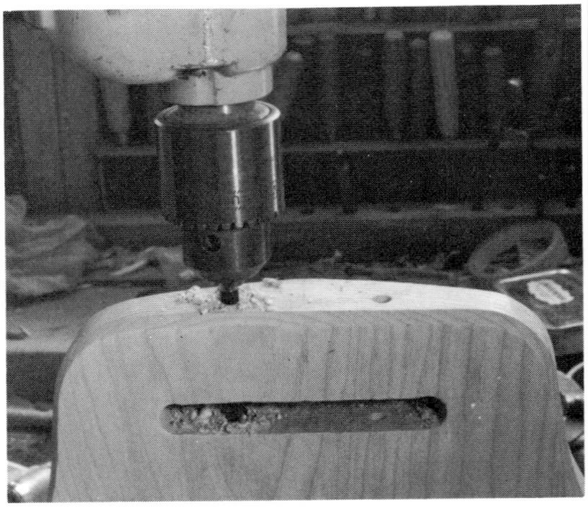

Plate 9 Drilling across the mortice for pegging

just above those made by the drill. At these new marks bore through the tenon with a ⅜in drill and with the same drill enlarge the small holes in the edge of the seat and go through across the mortice slot and into the seat again. This makes the holes in the tenon slightly out of line with those in the seat, ensuring a downward pull on the tenon as the pegs are driven in and bringing the joint shoulders in firm contact with the seat top, thus tightening and neatening the joint when the chair is assembled. Pegs cut ⅜in square and 2in long are whittled round and very slightly tapered over half of their length to leave the head square. Put glue in the mortice, fit the back tenon into place and carefully tap in the pegs to complete the joint. The legs may also be glued into place at this time; put glue into the socket holes and tap the legs in with a soft mallet. Remove all traces of surplus glue, especially from around the joint between the seat and back.

When the glue is set the chair should be given a light sanding to clean it up, followed by an application of sanding sealer and a further light sanding. A wax finish was applied to the chair shown.

	MATERIALS REQUIREMENT LIST.			(CUTTING LIST IN INCHES)	
Nº	PURPOSE	MATERIAL	INITIAL SIZES		
1	SEAT	ASH OR BEECH	14 × 12 × 2	PLANED & SHAPED	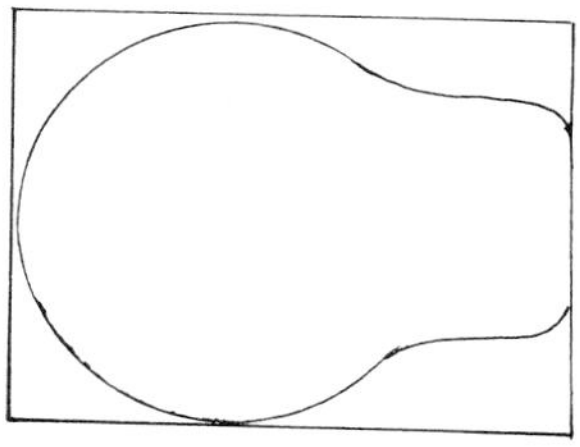
1	BACK	"	22 × 5 × 2	CARVED & SHAPED 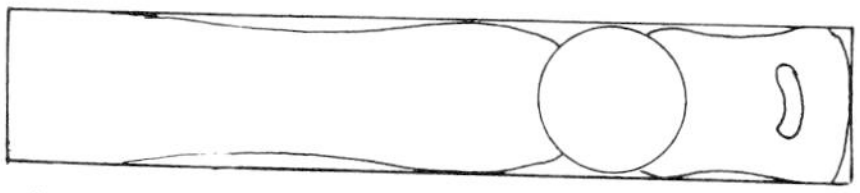	
3	LEGS	"	14 × 2 × 2	TURNED	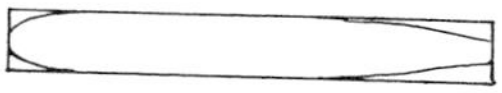

4

Corner Cabinet

Illustrated on page 84

Corner cabinets, like corner shelves and cupboards, were developed so that use might be made of an 'awkward' part of a room. Known from the seventeenth century, early examples were actually built in and panelled along with the rest of the room. Some were used as food cupboards and many simply for the storage of household goods, but by about 1750 they had become separate pieces of furniture, often with glazed doors. They became lighter in construction and more elegant in their design, being used extensively for the display of fine china and silverware.

Some cabinets were of the floor-standing, two-tier type and quite large, while others were made as a single unit to fit to a wall and known as hanging corner cupboards. The one described here is of the latter type, small in size to fit unobtrusively into a corner of a modern room. Made by Bernard Yaffe of Manchester, a photographer by profession but with a keen interest in cabinet making, it is constructed in mahogany, making use of both solid wood and veneered sheet material.

The exploded view given in Diagram One shows the general method of construction and it will be seen that the method of joining the side panels to the two front stiles and back post is to use loose tongues. These are made from thin strips of ply glued into grooves cut into the mating edges of panels, stiles and back post. This method may be employed with either solid panels or veneered blockboard or ply panels.

After obtaining all the necessary materials a good point to begin with is the shaping of the two front stiles. These are made from 1½ × 1in solid mahogany. Start by cutting in the groove for the loose tongue joint. A circular saw does a quick job or a suitable cutter in a power router is equally effective. Grooves can be cut by hand using a plough plane fitted with an appropriate blade. Match the width of the cut to the thickness of the plywood strip to be used and make the groove at least ⅜in deep. After this make the angled cut at 45° to complete the stiles. Top and bottom rails may then be cut to length and both stiles and rails drilled for the dowel joints which join these parts together.

The back post is also made from 1½ × 1in material, its edges shaped to the correct angle and grooved. The two side panels may be made from solid mahogany, each panel consisting of two pieces approximately ½in in thickness, edge glued to make up the required width or suitable sheet material with a mahogany veneer. Either blockboard or plywood may be used. The two edges of both panels will require slotting. With this completed and the four ply strips cut to size, it is a good idea to try out the assembly of the parts prepared so far. Carry out this carcase assembly without gluing – a dry run as it is

Plate 1 Inserting a plywood strip into the slotted edge

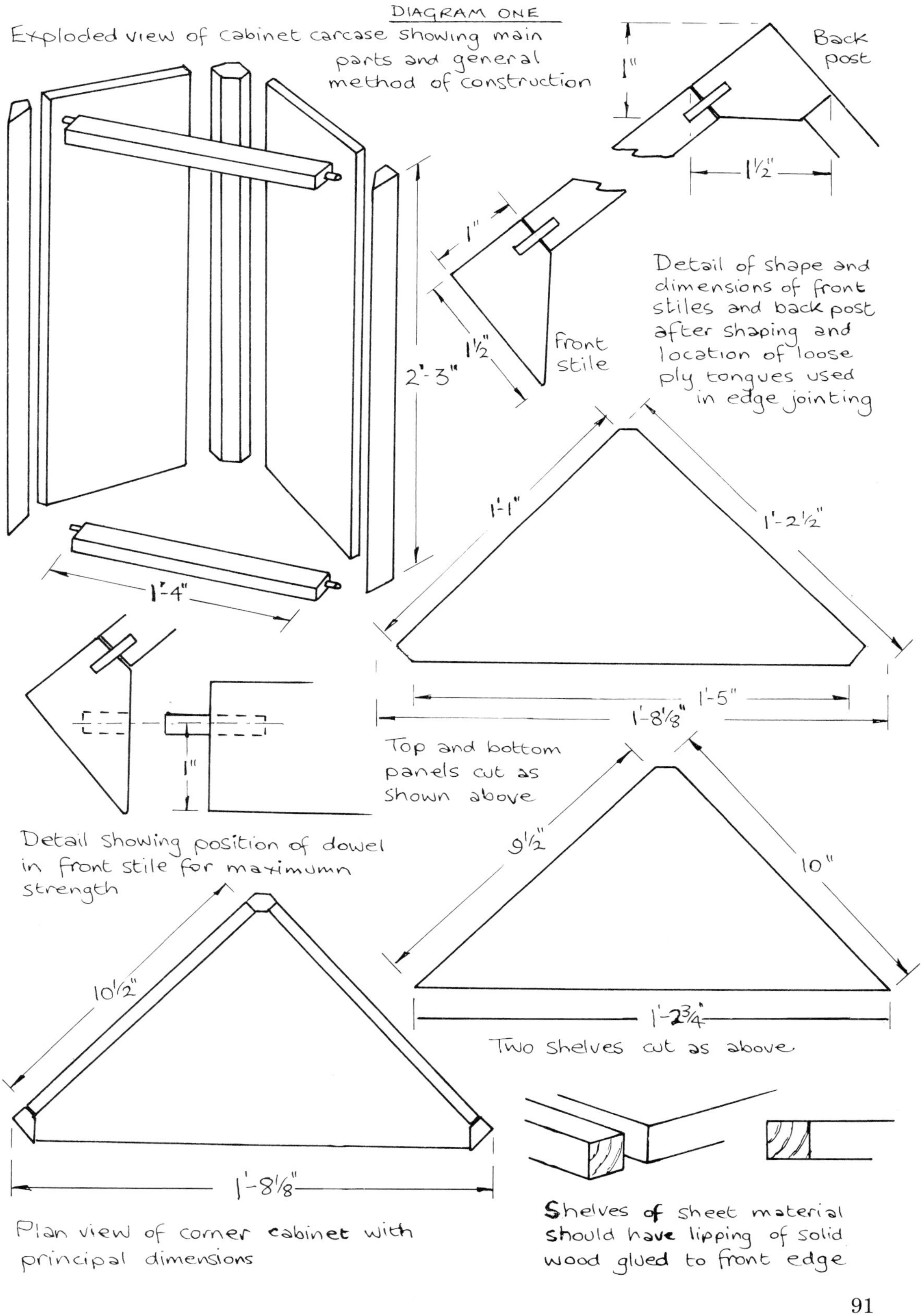
DIAGRAM ONE
Exploded view of cabinet carcase showing main parts and general method of construction
2'-3"
1'-4"
1"
Back post
1½"
1"
1½"
front stile
Detail of shape and dimensions of front stiles and back post after shaping and location of loose ply tongues used in edge jointing
1'-1"
1'-2½"
1'-5"
1'-8⅛"
Top and bottom panels cut as shown above
1"
Detail showing position of dowel in front stile for maximumn strength
9½"
10"
1'-2¾"
Two shelves cut as above
10½"
1'-8⅛"
Plan view of corner cabinet with principal dimensions
Shelves of sheet material should have lipping of solid wood glued to front edge

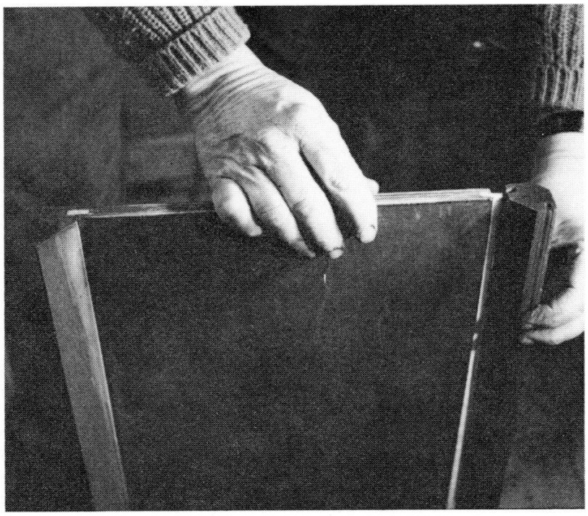

Plate 2 Assembling the back post on to the side panel

known – to ensure that everything fits together in a satisfactory way. While these parts are together measurements should be taken for the top and bottom and also for the shelves inside the cabinet and checked against the dimensions given; there may be slight differences, although there should not be.

Top and bottom can be of ¼in veneered ply, cut to fit flush to the outside dimensions of the cabinet. Top and bottom mouldings will conceal the front edges. The two internal shelves are best made in solid mahogany, but veneered ply or blockboard can be used if a solid lipping is put along the front edge (see Diagram One). Do this by gluing and cramping [clamping] the lipping in place before cutting the shelves in a triangular shape. Note how the front edge of each shelf is kept back from the space which will be occupied by the door. Shelf supports consist simply of mahogany strips screwed and glued to the side panels.

The carcase can now be glued up. Start by gluing the ply strips into both edges of each side panel, then assemble panels and front stiles and back post together. Glue up and dowel into place the top and bottom rails across the front. Place sash cramps [clamps] across all three surfaces and, using softwood blocks on the corners, cramp [clamp] up until the glue is set. Ensure that everything stays square or, to be more precise, at 45°, during this process, especially the front as

Plate 3 The main cabinet components glued together

Plate 4 Close up of the cabinet top before fitting the top panel

Plate 5 The top panel in position

DIAGRAM TWO

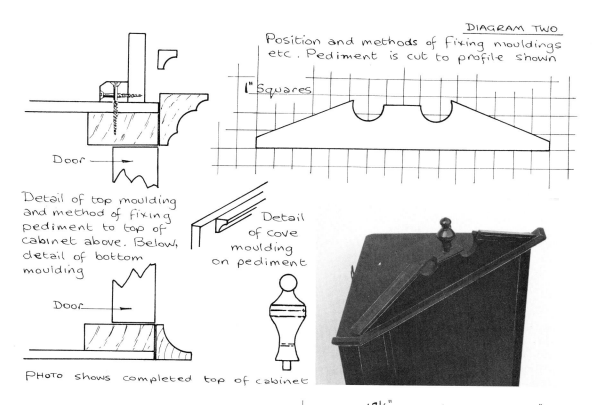

Position and methods of fixing mouldings etc. Pediment is cut to profile shown

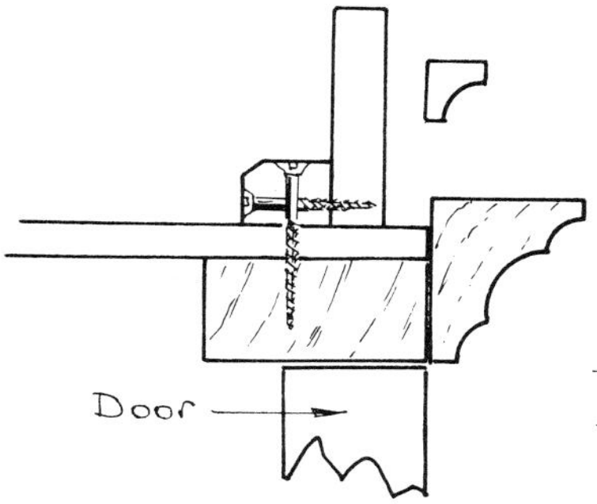

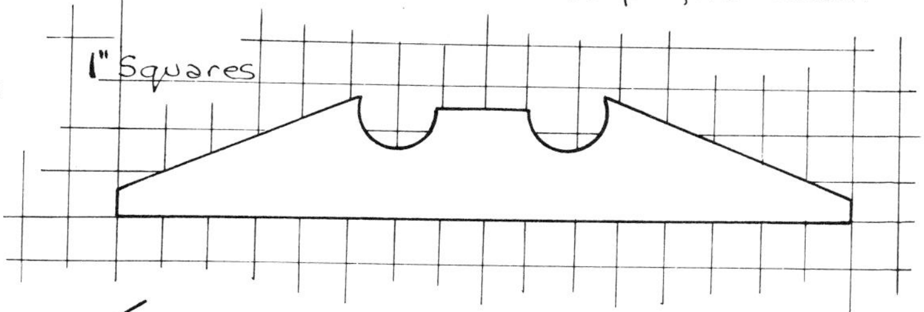

Detail of top moulding and method of fixing pediment to top of cabinet above. Below, detail of bottom moulding

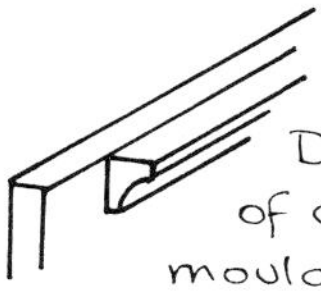

Detail of cove moulding on pediment

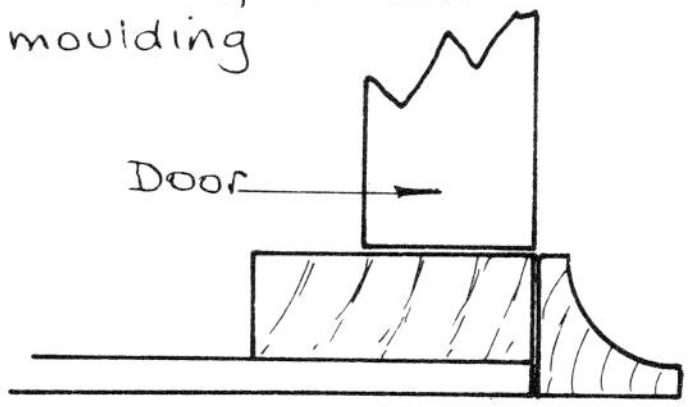

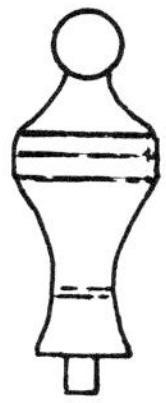

PHOTO shows completed top of cabinet

this forms the frame around the door and if this is out of true it will not only give problems when fitting the door but be very noticeably wrong on completion.

Top and bottom panels can be fitted while the main carcase is held in cramps [clamps]. These are glued and held in position either by panel pinning or screwing.

The bottom moulding, a 1¼in square cove moulding, and the top moulding, which forms the cabinet cornice, are both mitred at 22½° to turn the corners formed by the front stiles. The top moulding needs to be at least 1½in deep to cover both the top rail and the ply top. Both mouldings are glued and panel pinned into place, the pins punched beneath the surface and filled.

The pediment which surmounts the cabinet is cut to the pattern shown in Diagram Two. It can be of solid mahogany or veneered ply. It is fixed in place by means of a fillet of wood glued and screwed behind it and to the top of the cabinet. A narrow cove moulding is glued and panel pinned along its top edge and a turned finial in the centre completes this feature.

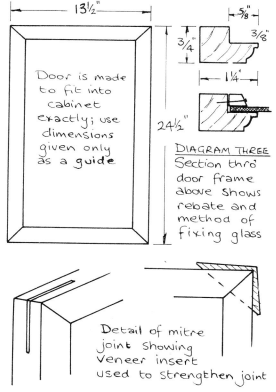

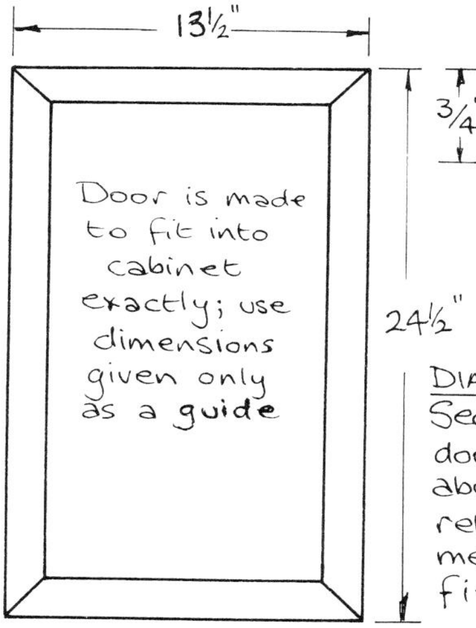

13½"
24½"
Door is made to fit into cabinet exactly; use dimensions given only as a guide

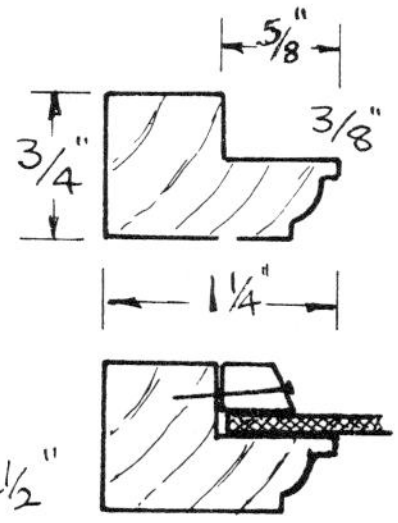

DIAGRAM THREE
Section thro' door frame above shows rebate and method of fixing glass

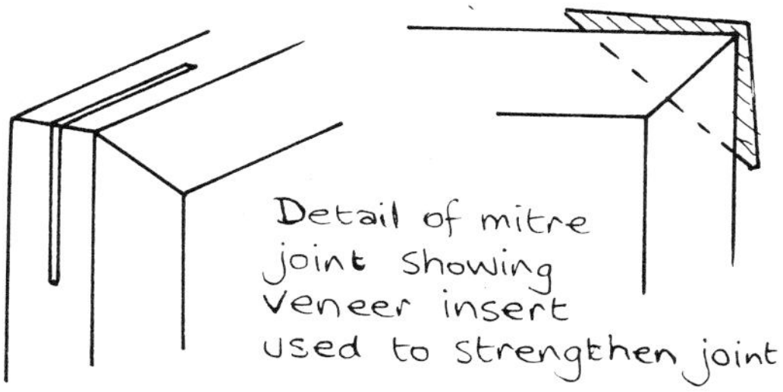

Detail of mitre joint showing veneer insert used to strengthen joint

MATERIALS CUTTING LIST. (CUTTING LIST IN INCHES & FEET.)

No	PURPOSE	MATERIAL	INITIAL SIZES	
2	FRONT STILES	MAHOGANY	2'-3" x 1½" x 1"	
1	BACK POST	"	2'-3" x 1½" x 1"	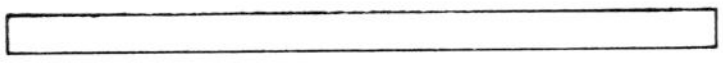
1	TOP RAIL	"	1'-4" x 1½" x 1"	
1	BOTTOM RAIL	"	1'-4" x 1½" x 1"	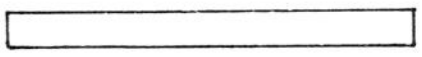
2	SIDE PANELS	VENEERED PLY	2'-3" x 10½" x ½"	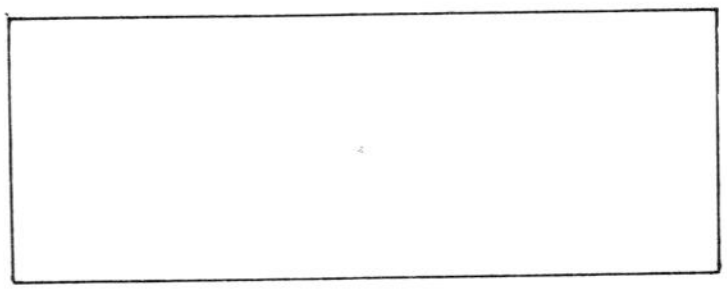
1 1	TOP PANEL BASE PANEL	" "	} 1'-2½" x 1-2½" x ¼"	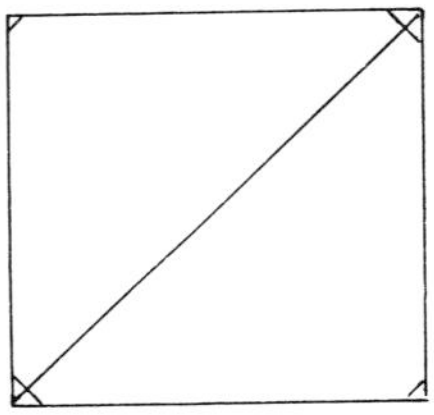
2	SHELVES	"	10½" x 10½" x ¼"	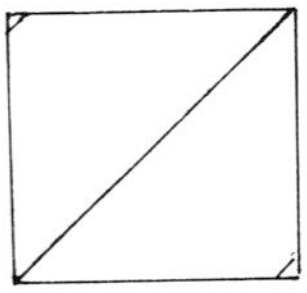
2	DOOR UPRIGHTS	MAHOGANY	2'-1" x 1¼" x ¾"	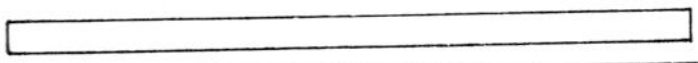
2	DOOR RAILS	"	1'-2" x 1¼" x ¾"	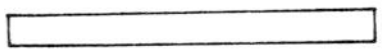
1	PEDIMENT	"	1'-4" x 3" x ½"	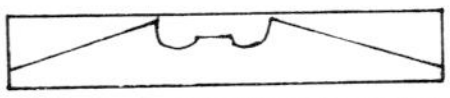

SUITABLE MOULDINGS. LIPPING FOR SHELVES. FINIAL. GLASS FOR DOOR. PAIR BRASS HINGES. HANDLE and BALL CATCH. DOWELS. PLY STRIPS.

A start can now be made on making the door. First measure the actual size of the door aperture of your cabinet and work to those measurements. (Those given in the diagrams, etc, may differ slightly from those of your own cabinet.) The door frame is $1\frac{1}{4} \times \frac{3}{4}$in in section and this is first rebated to accept the glass panel. The corners are then mitred and prepared for jointing by means of veneer inserts. Cuts are made with a tenon saw across the corners and pieces of veneer inserted when gluing up. Clean off any protruding veneer when the glue has set. A light moulding may be cut around the inner edge of the door frame. Glue up and cramp [clamp] the frame ensuring that it is kept properly square while doing so. When set, the glass may be fitted, held secure by strips of wood panel pinned into place (Diagram Three).

The door is hung by means of decorative brass hinges and the door held in the closed position with a ball catch fitted inside the door frame. A small brass knob completes the cabinet.

The wood is finished by staining down with spirit stain to ensure a uniform colour both inside and out and then sealed and polished as described elsewhere.

Plate 6 The completed parts of the cabinet ready for final assembly

5

Pedestal Table

Illustrated on page 84

DIAGRAM ONE

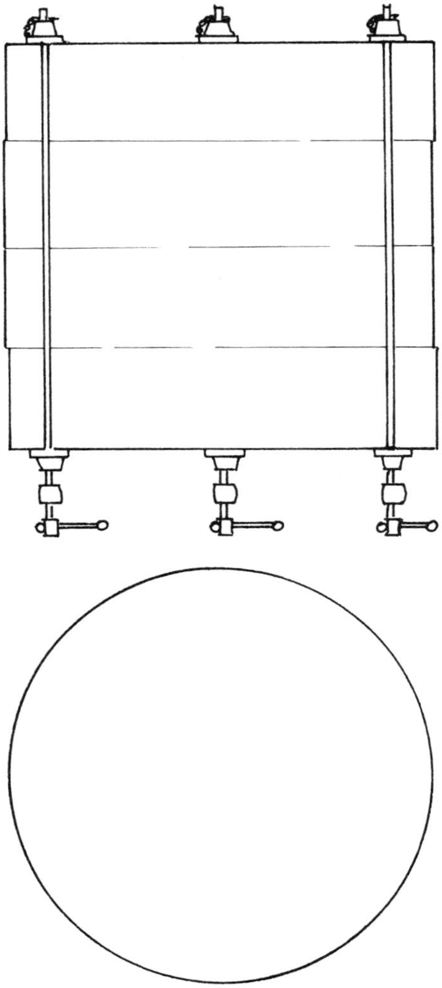

Method of constructing table top

This style of table came into vogue during the second half of the eighteenth century owing largely, it seems, to the increasing popularity of afternoon tea as a socially acceptable pastime for the ladies of the day. Sometimes called a pillar table, many had a much smaller top than the one described here and most early ones, while still having the single central leg, had three 'feet' only and were known as tripod tables. Pie-crust edgings were often used around the top edges of these smaller tables and sometimes the top was hinged so that it could be tilted to a vertical position, thus allowing the table to stand close to a wall when not in use. Mahogany was the most popular wood to be used in their construction.

The table described here, while lacking the refinements of tilting top and pie-crust edging, is otherwise made true to the late-eighteenth-century style. It was made in mahogany by Ian Massey of the Broadmere Loft Workshop. The top is constructed by first edge gluing together a number of selected mahogany boards (see Diagram One). These were chosen from dry stock for uniformity and flatness. This was then marked out with a 34in circle and band sawn to this size and shape. Both surfaces were scraped flat and clean and a light moulding was cut around the edge with a power router.

Turning the centre column is the next main job. This was turned from a piece initially measuring 4 × 4in and 25in long. As will be seen from Plate 2, this is left square at top and bottom, the top to carry the cross-pieces which make up the supports for the top, the bottom to accommodate the jointing in of the four legs. First, centres are marked on both ends and the two parts to be left square are clearly marked (see Diagram Two). The procedure for turning follows

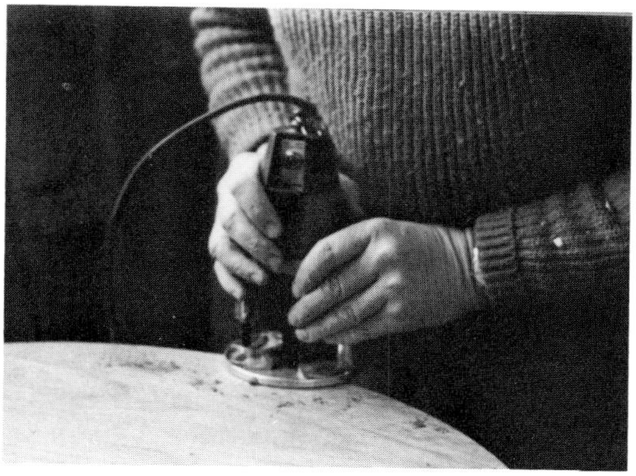

Plate 1 Router in use to put light moulding on the edge of the table top

Plate 2 (*right*) The top being scraped clean

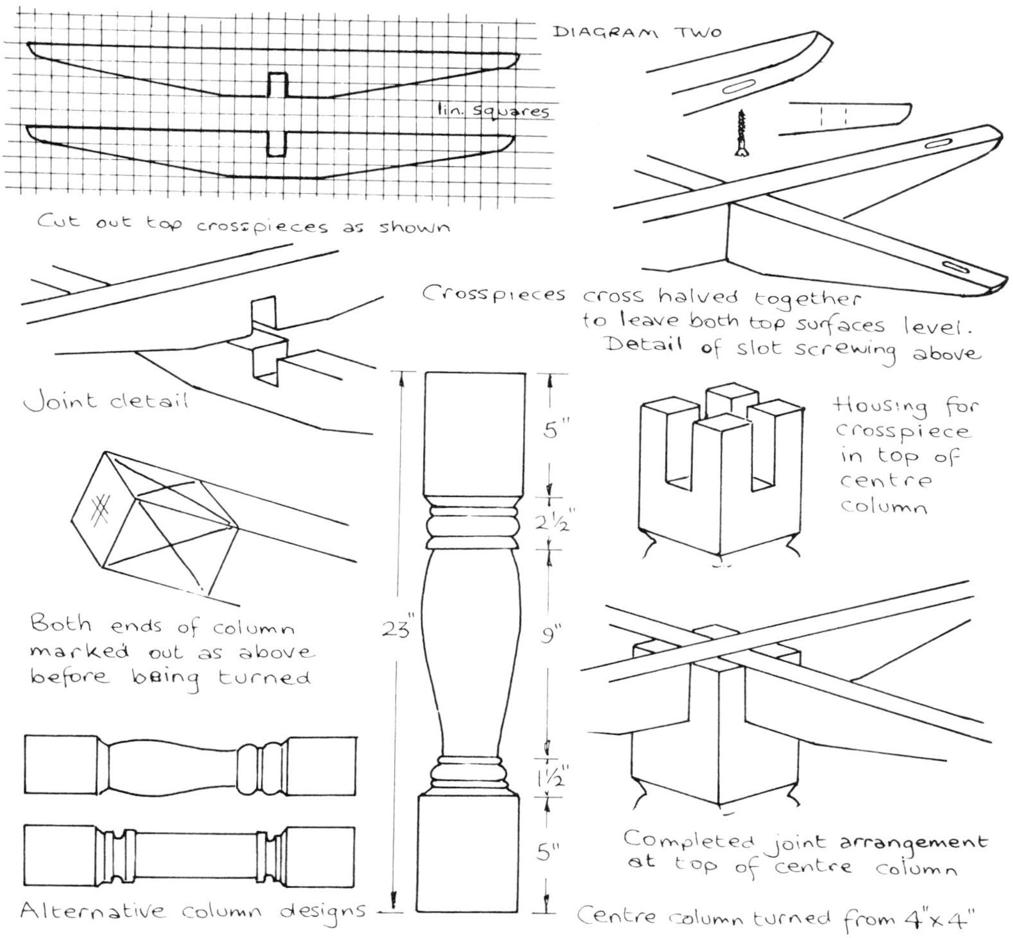

Plate 3 The pedestal leg being turned on the lathe

that described later for the legs of the dining table. Here there are two areas left square and the waste between the two is removed with a gouge; this section is turned to a cylinder before marking out and turning to the suggested profile or any other of your choice. One consolation here is that there is only one member to turn – you don't then have to go on to make three more, and to match! Again, finish by sanding but do not wax on the lathe as the completed table is to be stained before being polished.

The four legs or feet may be attached to the turned column in a number of ways. Dowelled joints, provided the mating surfaces of the leg and the square face of the pillar are flat and true and the dowels enter the respective parts by at least 1¼in, are satisfactory, as are simple shouldered mortice-and-tenon joints. The joint most often recommended for this particular application is a slot dovetail, correctly made with both the dovetail and the socket slightly tapered along their length so that entry is eased and the risk of splitting eliminated. But this is not an easy joint to make well and, with modern adhesives, either of the other two methods may be used, although there is some personal preference for the tenon method rather than the dowel method, which was used here.

Plate 4 Marking out the legs

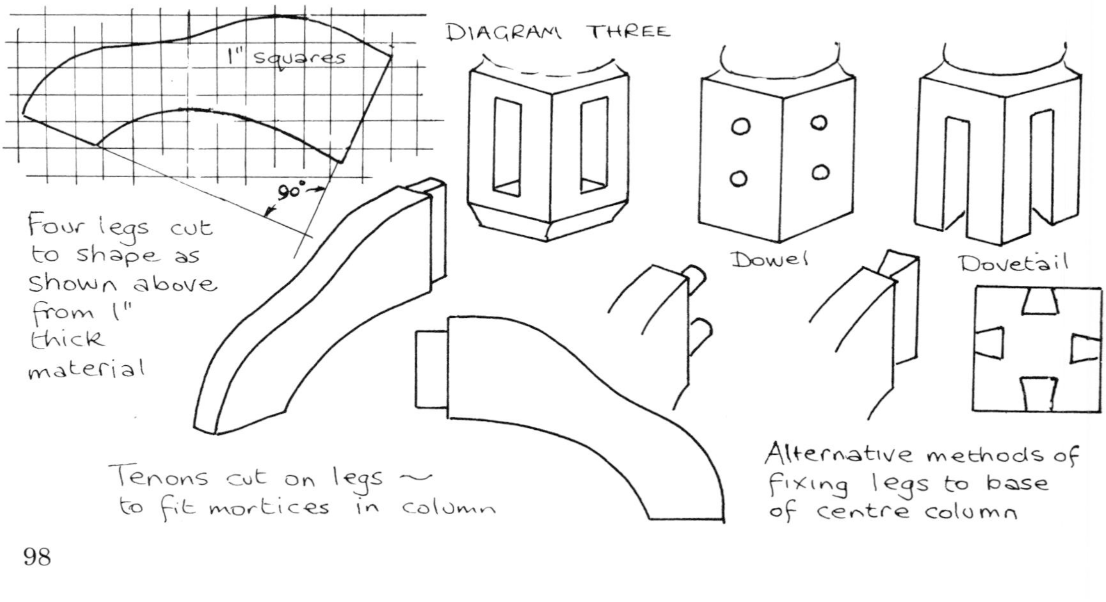

Plate 5 Cutting out the legs on a band saw

Plate 6 Ian Massey completing the underframing

Cut the legs to shape to the profile shown in Diagram Three. Ideally, make a full-size template from the diagram and use this to mark out and cut the first leg and use this as a pattern to mark out the other three. Note that the mating face to the pillar and the face of the foot to be in contact with the ground are at right angles to each other, ie at 90°. It is important to have regard to the grain direction of the wood when marking out so as to avoid having too much short grain across a leg at any point. Hand sawn or band sawn to shape, these can be cleaned up on a rotary sander or with a spokeshave. Tenons on each are cut in the normal way (see Joints, p29). The corresponding mortices are now cut in the lower square area of the turned column and the legs tested for fit. Good tight joints are obviously very important. Details of the slot dovetail are given in Diagram Three should you wish to try it.

The round top is supported on shaped crosspieces which are joined together by means of a cross-halving or housing joint and which are themselves housed in the square top of the turned column to lie flush with the top of the square section. The top is fixed to the supportive crosspieces by the method known as slot screwing. Screws are used to fasten the top to the supports, but these pass through slots rather than through holes, the slots allowing for any possible lateral movement of the top due to shrinkage or expansion (see Diagram Two for details).

As mentioned earlier, the completed table was stained before being polished. This was partly because Brazilian mahogany was used and this is paler in colour than the now difficult to obtain Cuban variety, and partly to compensate for some slight variation in shade in the mahogany available. To darken the wood uniformly, a dark mahogany spirit stain was used and, when dry, this was sealed and finally wax polished to give a rich warm tone.

MATERIAL REQUIREMENTS LIST. (CUTTING LIST IN INCHES)

Nº	PURPOSE	MATERIAL	INITIAL SIZES		
4	BOARDS FOR TOP	MAHOGANY	34 x 8½ x 1	GLUED EDGE TO EDGE	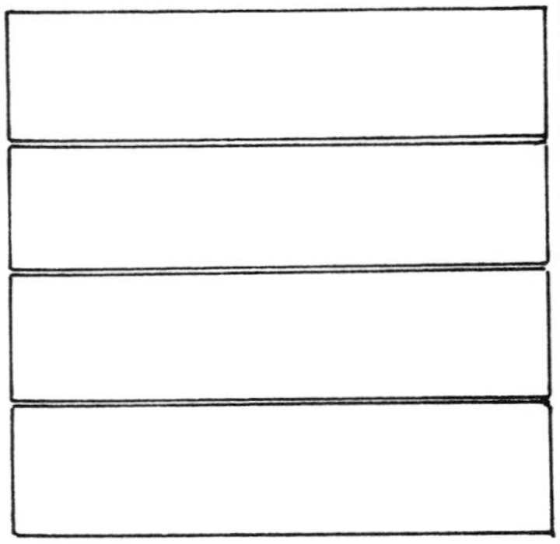
1	PEDESTAL		24 x 4 x 4	TURNED	
2	CROSSPIECES		30 x 3 x 1	SHAPED	
4	LEGS		14 x 6 . x 1	SHAPED	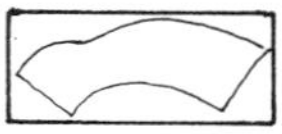

6

Chest

Illustrated on page 117

The chest, one of the earliest examples of early furniture, fulfilled a multi-purpose role in the otherwise sparsely furnished homes of the Medieval and Tudor period. It was used for storage purposes, for simple things like clothing and books as well as treasure; it served as a table, seat and sometimes bed, and it was always ready to travel when the household moved, as they often did in those unsettled times.

The earliest chests were crudely dug out from solid sections of tree trunks – hence, presumably, the still current usage of the name trunk for boxes used similarly today. These were bound with iron straps against the effects of deformation and splitting through shrinkage of the wood. So, too, were the later planked or boarded chests which consisted of six or more wide boards nailed or wooden pegged together.

During the fourteenth and fifteenth centuries the 'joyned' chest was developed; the boards of these, instead of all being wide and horizontal as before, had two end pieces placed at right angles at each corner. Known as stiles, these vertical timbers had long grooves cut into them which housed the ends of the now thinner horizontal boards. This made a stronger construction, less vulnerable to shrinkage.

Later, these stiles became narrower and extended below the chest to form feet. The solid boards were changed to separate top and bottom rails with intermediate uprights known as muntins. These were all connected by pegged mortice-and-tenon joints and the space within filled by panels loosely held in grooves so that movement of individual pieces was not detrimental to the structure as a whole. This type of construction, known as framed or panelled, has formed a basis for most furniture making in solid timber since that time.

Many early chests were decorated, either painted or carved, or both. The earliest carved designs were geometric chip carvings and later the familiar linen fold became popular while the Renaissance saw the introduction of Italian-style motifs and portrait panels.

Oak was the timber most commonly used, but chests were also made in pine, chestnut, walnut and elm; cypress wood was also used, so it is said, as a deterrent against moths.

I made the chest described here in English oak using material saved from a number of old school desks, probably made late last century. The wood was mostly quarter sawn and I had been saving it for a worthwhile project such as this. There were a number of rails, 1¼in thick and between 3in and 5in wide and some 12in wide, joined pieces which had been part of the desk tops. The latter varied in thickness but averaged about ¾in and bore the evidence of pupil misuse – carved initials, compass arc patterns and, of course, ink stains from pre-ball-point pen days.

After checking that the wood was metal-free – no broken-in screws, etc – everything was machine planed, the rails to a full 1in thickness, the wide joined boards progressively until all carving and staining had gone, then to a uniform thickness of ⅜in. These would be used, unaltered, for the chest's panels. Almost every rail had a screw hole in it somewhere but all pieces had one good face; screw holes were wooden plugged and kept mainly to the inside of the chest.

To some extent the dimensions of the chest were governed by the dimensions of the original desks and the sizes of the material which they provided. The 12in-wide desk tops – reduced to 11¾in to pass through a 12in planer – were 31in long. Cut

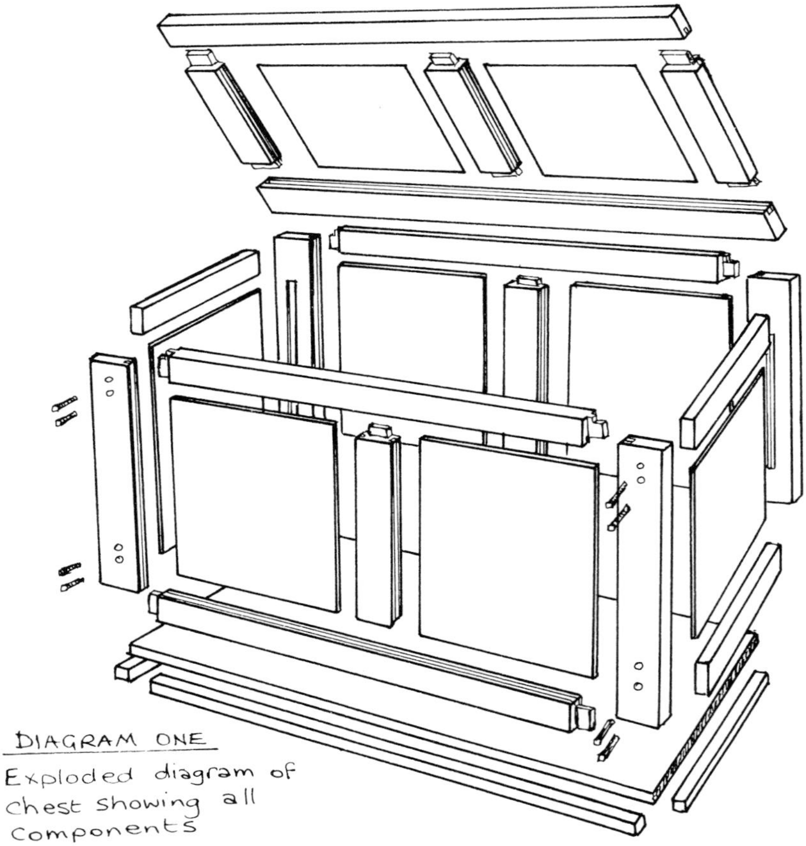

in half and squared up, these produced eight usable panels measuring 15¼ × 11¾in and these formed the basis for the chest's finished size.

The design is largely traditional: framed panels, the frames morticed and tenoned, the panels, loose, in slots in the frames (see Diagram One). The four main corner joints have their tenons secured with oak pegs as was the practice in years gone by. What is not strictly traditional is that these pegs continue through the end rails and out the other side to form substantial dowels which are used to joint the side panels to front and back panels.

First, the wood to be used was selected for its particular function, cut to size and marked accordingly. For front and back panels top and bottom rails are 2in wide, the two end rails and the central muntins, 3in wide. All these rails were slotted ⅜ × ⅜in to take the panels and then marked out for

Plate 1 Cleaning up the slots in the rails

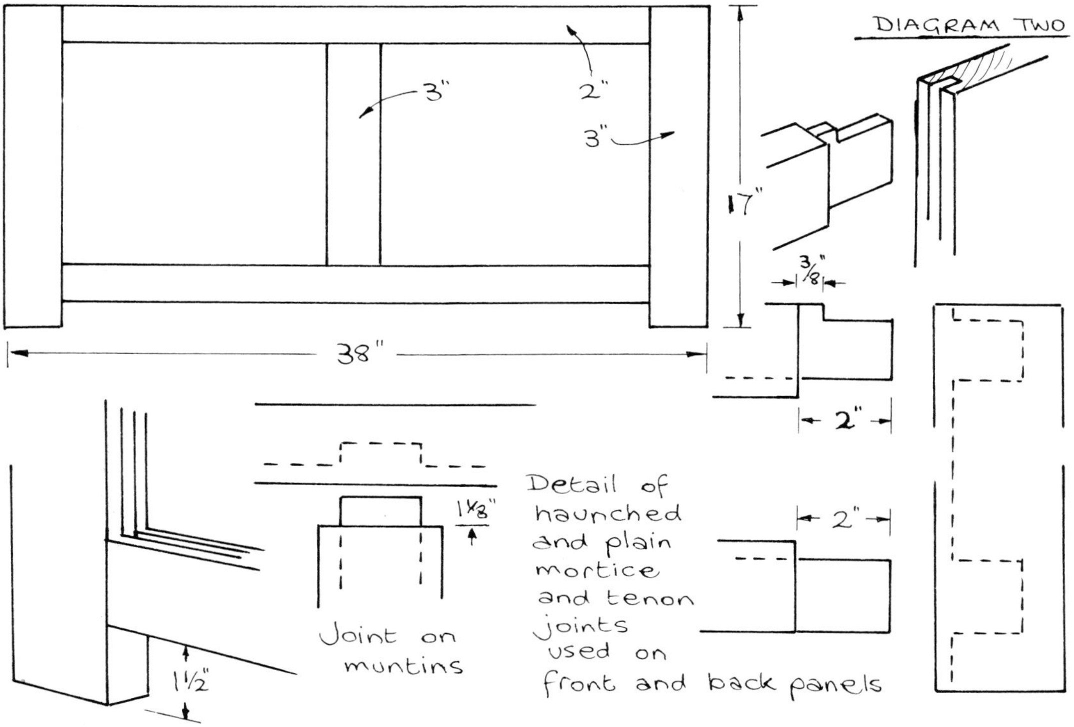

jointing. Note that haunched tenons are used at the top of the end rails – the haunch conveniently filling the panel slot where it comes through on the end of the rail – with plain tenons on the bottom. Centre rails or muntins have short stub tenons. Mark and cut the tenons first, then mark and cut the mortices to suit. When marking out note that the bottom rail is positioned 1½in up from the lower end of the end rail (Diagram Two).

Before assembly, these rails require slotting to accommodate the side panels which abut to them. See Diagram Three for details of this and note that the slots, ⅜in wide to take the panels, are only made ¼in deep so as not to break through into the mortices and thus perhaps weaken the end rail. These slots can be cut with a router.

With this work completed, rails and panels should be lightly hand planed and/or scraped to bring all to an acceptable finish. It is easier to do the bulk of this now before the assembly stage begins. Now a dry assembly may be undertaken to check that everything goes together nicely. Remember that panels should be just undersize so they do not 'bottom' in the slots before the joints close,

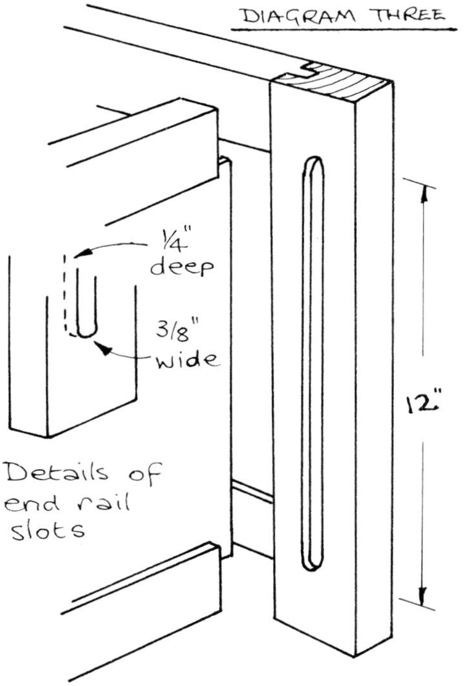

thus preventing the joint shoulders from making close contact. Select the panels for continuity of grain and pencil mark everything so it goes back in the same way when gluing up. If all is well, prepare for gluing – have a clear space to work in, cramps [clamps], etc, ready to hand – and glue up the joints – put glue in the mortices and on the shoulders – but no glue in the slots, not even in the corners; wipe it off if it oozes from the joint and into the slot at this point. The panels are put in loose so that if shrinkage or expansion of the wood takes place the panels are free to move, thus reducing the risk of distortion and splitting. Cramp [clamp] up, check with the try square and across the diagonals that the panel is square and not twisted and leave for the glue to set.

Meanwhile, the two ends or sides can be prepared. These consist simply of the side panels and a top and bottom rail; there are no end rails as the ends of the panels fit into the slots previously cut in the end rails of the front and back panels respectively. Top and bottom rails, 2in wide, are slotted to fit the panels. Using sash cramps [clamps] – and an

Plate 2 Putting the centre muntin in place

Plate 4 Adding the slotted end piece

Plate 3 Fitting the top rail

Plate 5 The completed panel in cramps [clamps]

Plate 6 The front and one end in position

extra pair of hands is also useful here if you can find a volunteer – the ends are put into place and held between front and back panels; the ends of the side panels are entered into the slots cut for them and top and bottom rails placed in their correct positions. Make sure everything is square and true, then mark and drill the peg holes as shown in Diagram Four. Use a ⅜in drill and bore right through the end rail and into the ends of the top and bottom rails of the end panels. The depth into the end of the end rails should be 1½in. Mark the mating pieces – this is very important, otherwise the drilled holes will almost certainly not line up if rearranged – and remove the cramps [clamps].

A total of sixteen oak pegs are needed. These treenails, as they used to be called, are made to the detail shown in Diagram Four, being ⅜in cylindrical over the majority of their length but with the head portion left square. They can be whittled with a hand knife or cut with a chisel – some might like to try turning them on the lathe. They do not have to have square heads – it is easier to make them round all the way along – and they do not have to protrude as the ones illustrated; they can be cut flush with the

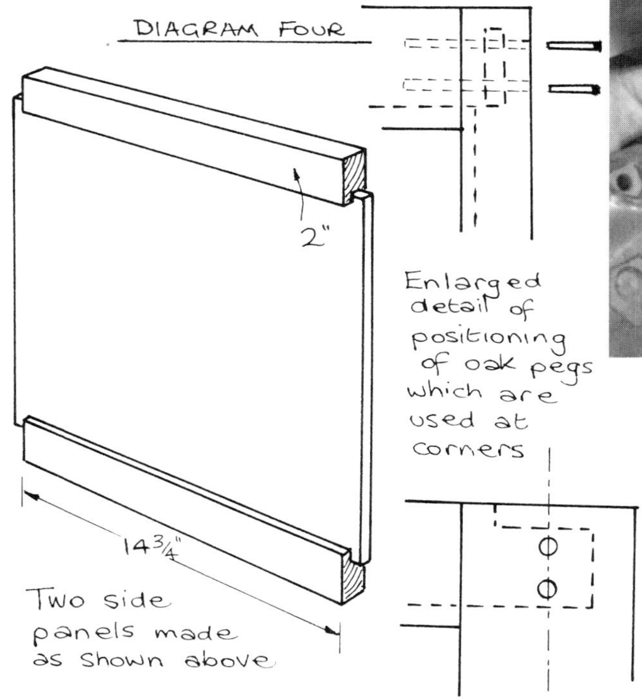

Above – Drilling holes for pegs

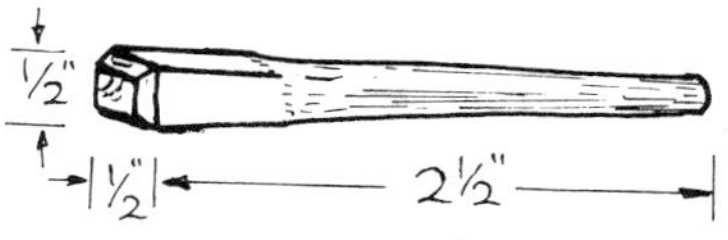

Make 16 oak pegs as here

surface if required. But the slightly protruding square heads do make quite a distinctive and authentic feature on what is otherwise a rather plain chest.

Test the pegs for fit, initially in a 3/8in hole drilled through a piece of scrap oak to avoid over-enlarging the holes in the chest. They should be a push fit to within about 1/2in of their square end at this stage.

After hand planing or scraping the end panels and rails, enlist the services of your volunteer assistant again and, with the help of the sash cramps [clamps] assemble ends to front and back sections; put glue in the dowel holes in both pieces and on the ends of top and bottom rails, but the panel slots should again be left dry. Tap in the pegs, part way, and check that everything is square and true. Tighten the sash cramps [clamps] and check again. Then, using a hammer and a block of wood to protect the head of the peg, knock each one in until approximately 1/4in is left protruding. Leave the cramps [clamps] in place until the glue has set.

The top or lid is made with all its rails 3in wide. This provides the extra width for an overlap to its front edge. The long rails run through from end to end with the end rails and centre muntin set between. This is done so that the corner joints appear on the ends and are not visible from the front or back. Haunched tenons are again used, this time on both ends, with stub tenons for the centre muntin (see Diagram Five). Mark and cut these out as shown and have a dry run with the panels in place. Then, plane or scrape the rails and panels and glue up the joints – but no glue in the slots – fit the panels and assemble. Again check that everything is square and out of twist and leave in cramps [clamps] until the glue is set.

A base is fitted inside the chest, resting on fixing rails screwed and glued to the inside of the bottom rails as shown in Diagram Five. This fixing rail should measure approximately 1 × 1in or a little less. The base itself can be of solid material or a piece of sheet material may be used. A piece of 3/4in blockboard, veneered with oak on one face, was used in this chest, but it will eventually be replaced with solid oak. I have no particular objection to the veneered blockboard as regards its suitability to make a substantial base, but I would prefer 'proper oak'.

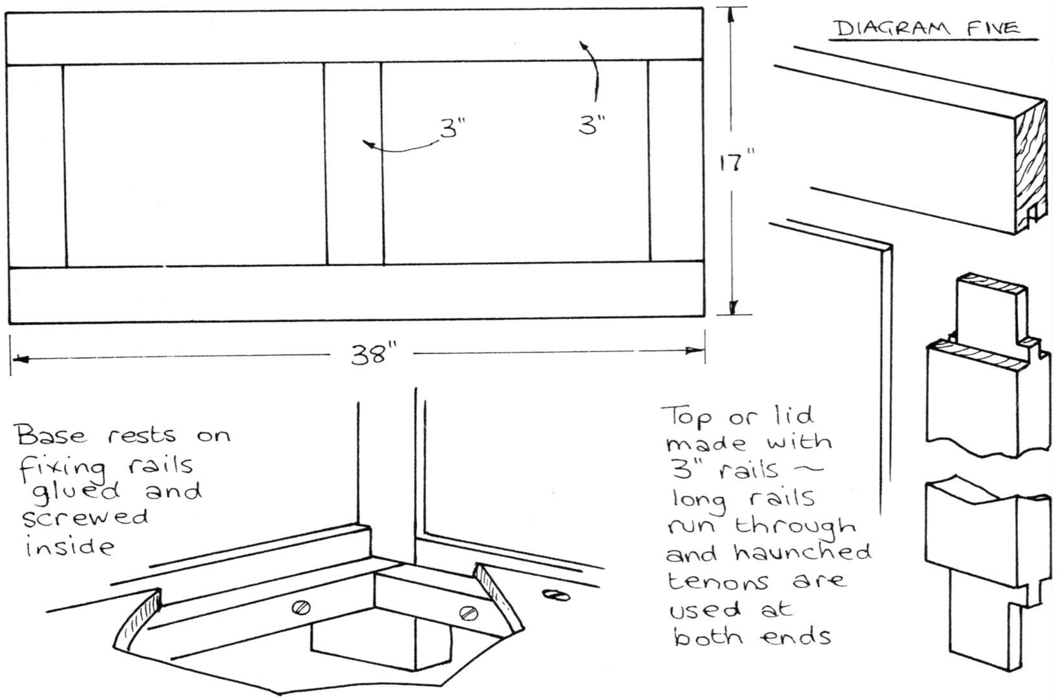

DIAGRAM FIVE
3"
3"
17"
38"
Base rests on fixing rails glued and screwed inside
Top or lid made with 3" rails ~ long rails run through and haunched tenons are used at both ends

The chest and the still separate lid were lightly sanded all over to remove pencilled identification marks, etc, after which a clear sealer was applied inside and out and sanded smooth. The lid was then fitted using three 3in solid drawn, brass butt hinges. A substantial lock could also be fitted centrally above the front centre muntin for maximum strength. Finally, the exterior of the chest was wax polished until the ancient oak glowed, honey coloured and warm looking, a fitting new lease of life for those old desks now destined to go on in use, albeit in a different form, well into the next century and perhaps beyond.

Plate 7 (*left*) The chest in cramps [clamps] while the glue sets

Plate 8 (*below*) Checking the lid after fitting

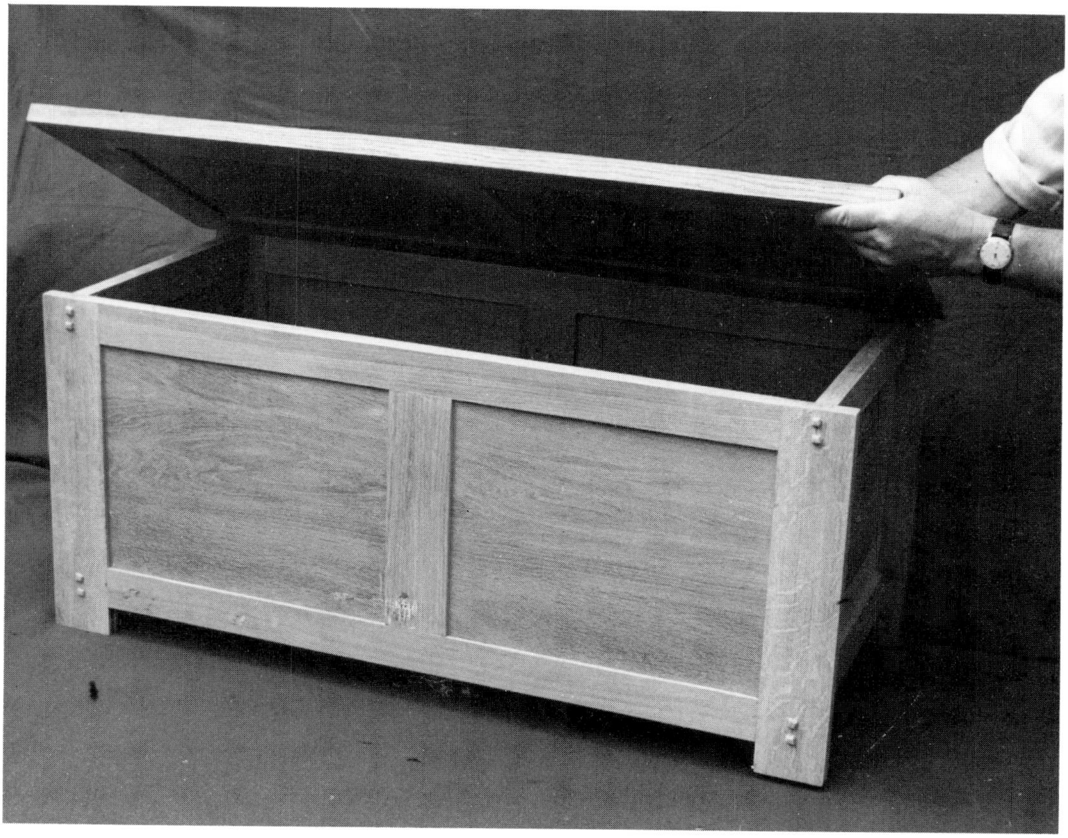

MATERIALS REQUIREMENTS LIST. (CUTTING LIST IN INCHES)

Nº	PURPOSE	MATERIAL	SIZES		
	FRONT and BACK PANELS. (TWO IDENTICAL)				
4	UPRIGHTS	OAK	17 × 3 × 1		
2	MUNTINS	"	13½ × 3 × 1		
2	TOP RAILS	"	32 × 2 × 1		
2	BOTTOM RAILS	"	32 × 2 × 1		
4	PANELS	"	15¼ × 11¾ × ⅜		
	ENDS (TWO IDENTICAL)				
2	TOP RAILS	"	14¾ × 2 × 1		
2	BOTTOM RAILS	"	14¾ × 2 × 1		
2	PANELS	"	15¼ × 11¾ × ⅜		
	LID				
1	FRONT RAIL	"	38 × 3 × 1		
1	BACK RAIL	"	38 × 3 × 1		
2	END RAILS	"	13½ × 3 × 1		

MATERIALS REQUIREMENTS LIST (CONTINUED)

Nº	PURPOSE	MATERIAL	SIZES		
	LID (CONTINUED)				
1	MUNTIN	OAK	13½ x 3 x 1		
2	PANELS	"	15¼ x 11¾ x ⅜		
	BASE				
2	FIXING RAILS	"	32 x 1 x 1		
2	FIXING RAILS	"	14¾ x 1 x 1		
1	PANEL	OAK VENEERED BLOCKBOARD	34 x 14¾ x ¾		
	OAK OFFCUTS TO MAKE PEGS (TREENAILS). THREE BRASS HINGES and SCREWS				

7

Cradle

Illustrated on page 117

The name cradle comes from the Old English *cradol* and is related to the Old German *kratto* which meant basket. Early cradles would no doubt have been of rush or osiers (willow) woven like a basket – the biblical basket in which the baby Moses travelled was probably a cradle, after all. Not only would such cradles have been easy and cheap to make, but when one had held a child afflicted by some terrible illness it would be no great loss to burn the cradle as a safeguard against further infection.

The earliest cradles which have survived were made mainly in oak, and had panelled sides and a solid hood at one end, often richly carved. Rockers formed part of the end panels or were inserted into the base of the corner posts. Later cradles, more lightly built and without hoods, had rockers screwed into the base of the framework and are to be found made in a variety of woods, including beech and some fruitwoods. Turned finials on the corner posts have long been popular, providing a convenient place to hold on to when rocking the baby.

Yew was the wood chosen to make the cradle described here, its mellow tones seeming most fitting for this particular subject. Its design incorporates panelled sides and ends with a surrounding open-top rail of short, turned spindles and the top of each corner post has a ball finial turned on it. The contrast in colour between the light sapwood and the darker heart of yew was used to advantage wherever possible.

As yew of satisfactory quality is not always easy to obtain in sufficient quantity, it is as well to begin by getting together all the yew which will be required and to sort it through for colour matching, etc. A timber other than yew could be used, but it should go without saying that whatever material is used it must be properly seasoned and thoroughly dry before the work begins. A total of eighteen pieces measuring $9\frac{1}{2} \times 4\frac{1}{2} \times \frac{1}{4}$in are required for the side and lower end panels and a further four, $15 \times 4\frac{1}{2} \times \frac{1}{4}$in for the longer upper end panels. The materials for these were machine planed before the individual pieces were cut to length, after which they were scraped by hand and sanded smooth.

Plate 1 Panels and rails for both end sections

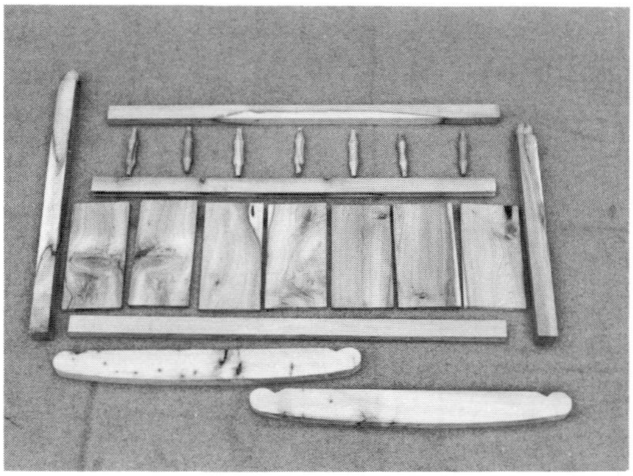

Plate 2 Panels, rails and turned spindles for one side with prototype rockers

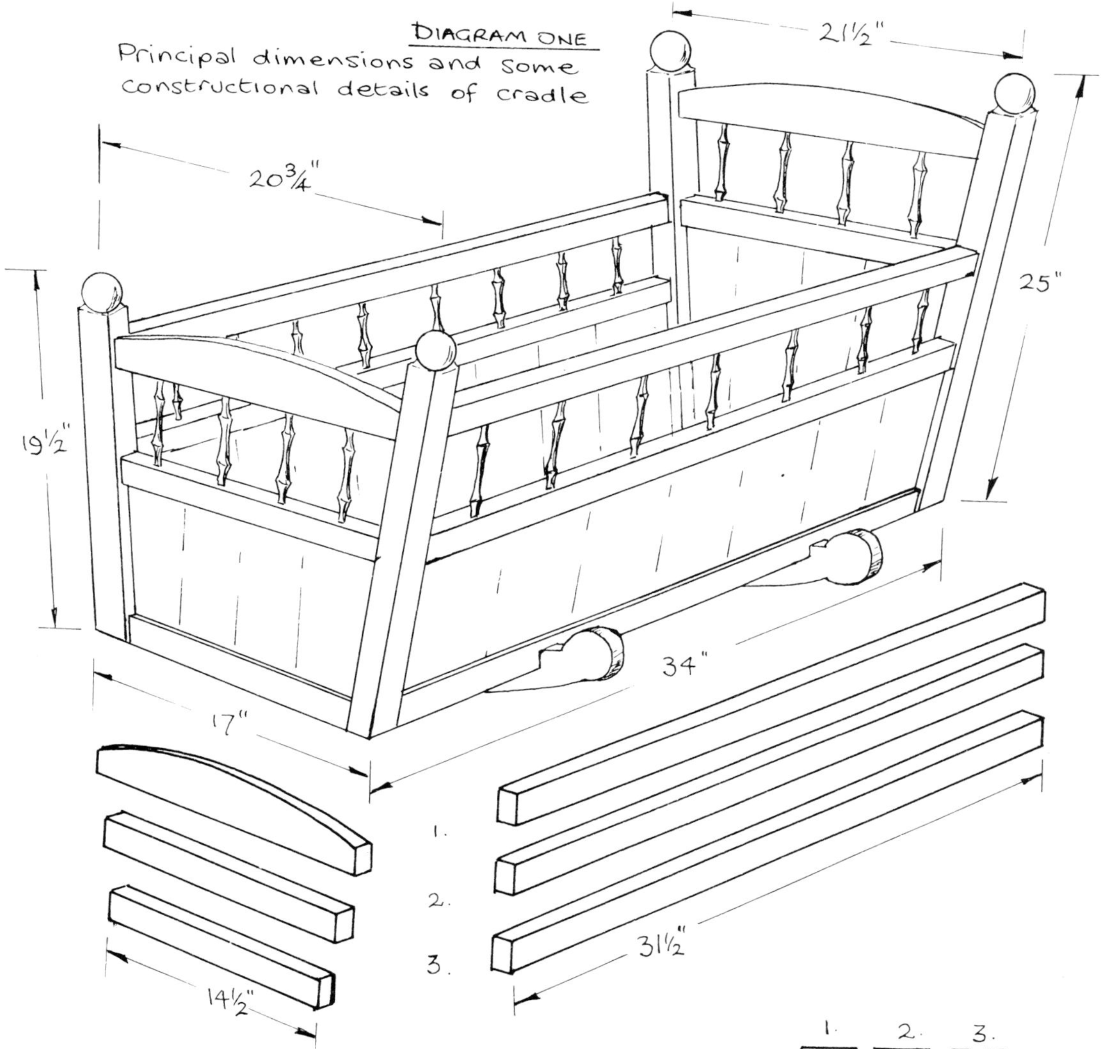

The side rails, three each side, and the end rails, three each end, are next to be prepared. All except the two end top rails are made from 1½ × 1in-section material, planed to 1⅜ × ⅞in. The two end top rails have curved top edges and are cut from 2½ × 1in material. The six side rails are cut to their exact length, but the six end rails are all left overlength to begin with to allow for the later angled cutting at the different lengths determined by the sloping sides of the cradle (see Diagram One). Lower and middle side rails and lower and middle end rails are slotted all along one edge to accommodate the panelling, the slots being ¼in in depth, the width matched to the thickness of the

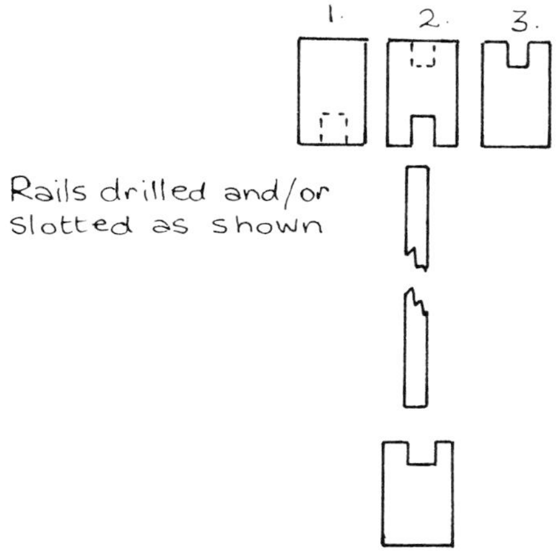

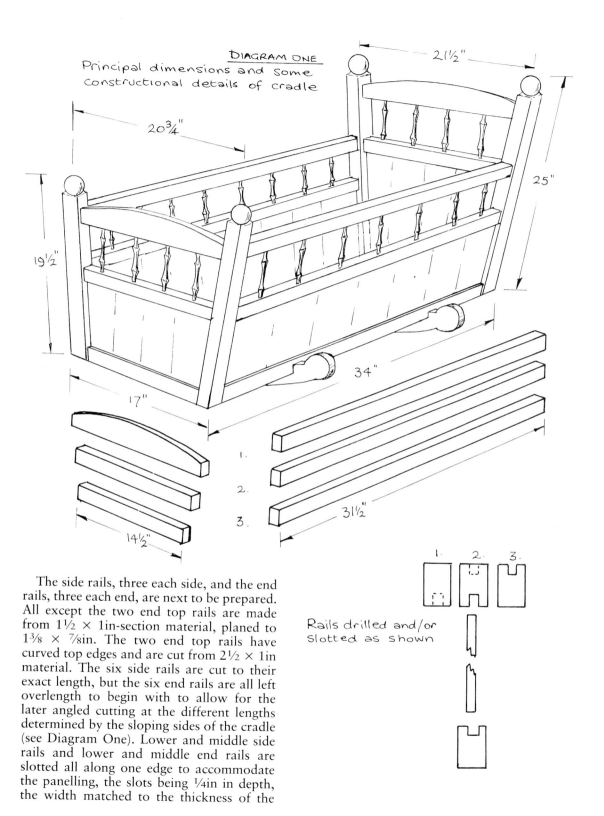

Plate 3 Cleaning up the rails using a cabinet scraper

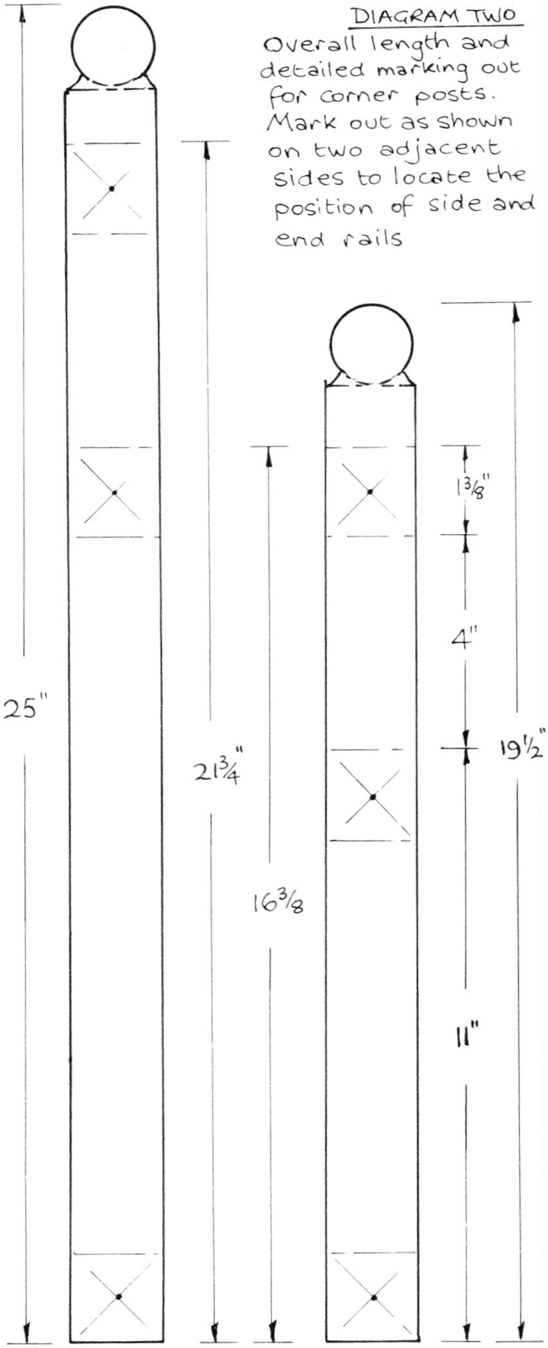
DIAGRAM TWO
Overall length and detailed marking out for corner posts. Mark out as shown on two adjacent sides to locate the position of side and end rails
25"
21¾"
16⅜
1⅜"
4"
19½"
11"

panel pieces (⅜in in the one made).

The four corner posts are then cut to length – don't overlook the extra length of the two top posts – and planed to 1⅜in square. Mounted in the lathe, each post has a ball finial turned on its upper end as shown, after which each post is hand scraped and sanded smooth.

Now the corner posts are marked out to locate the positioning of the side and end rails. Diagram Two shows this marking out in detail. Side and end rails are dowel jointed into the corner posts, a simple but adequate method which can be replaced by some difficult mortice and tenoning by those who wish to do so. The jointing of the corner posts to the side rails is quite straightforward, but a different approach and a little extra care is necessary when drilling for the joints between the corner posts and the end rails due to the angles at which they meet each other.

As a first stage, drill all the dowel holes square into the ends of all the rails irrespective of whether they are side or end rails. Be generous with depth in the case of the six end rails as some wood will be lost in making the angled cuts later. In order to ascertain the true length and the correct angle of each of these end rails it is best to make a full-size drawing of the top end of the cradle from the dimensions given in the diagram. Measurements taken from this will give true lengths. The angle used throughout is 95° and a sliding bevel should be set to this for marking-out purposes. Note that it is necessary to mark out the outer pieces of end panelling to the same angle. End rails and the outer panels can then be cut to the correct length and angle (see Diagram Three).

Now the dowel holes are drilled into the corner posts at the previously marked positions. For the side rails these go in square and will present no problem, but those for the end rails must be drilled at an angle of 95°. Use the sliding bevel at the same setting as before to mark this angle at each drilling position. Refer to the section on chairmaking (p44) for methods of drilling holes at an angle. A dry assembly of end panels into rails and rails to corner posts is a good idea at this stage to check that all will eventually go together correctly.

With one small turned spindle to each piece of panelling a total of twenty-two spindles is required. These, which may be to any design of your choice, were turned mainly from offcuts [cutoffs], mostly single but in some cases, where the piece was long enough, two were turned end to end and separated afterwards. Pieces 5in long and 7/8in square are needed to make a single spindle. The turned tenon at each end of each spindle is 3/8in in diameter and parallel for 1/2in before flaring out to form the spindle shape. Polish the spindles while they are still on the lathe. Part off on the lathe or saw to finished length, which is 4 1/2in overall.

When these are finished drill the holes into which they are to fit into the top edge of the middle rails and the lower edge of the top rails. The drilled holes are 3/8in in diameter and 1/4in in depth. The top edges of all the top rails are rounded over so as to leave no sharp corners.

DIAGRAM THREE
Details of dowel jointing of rails into corner posts and dimensions and spacing-out of turned spindles
Mark out all rails as above and drill central and square. For side rails, corner posts are drilled square as shown here
End rails are cut to angle shown and corner posts are drilled at the same angle
95°
95°
4½"
1"
For spindles, top and middle rails are drilled at centres as shown on right
2¼"
4½"

Final assembly of the cradle body begins with the gluing up of the two end sections. First, dowels are glued into place in the holes drilled in the end rails, then a little glue may be placed in the slots cut to accommodate the pieces of panelling and the panel pieces correctly assembled between the bottom and middle rails. Glue in the spindles between

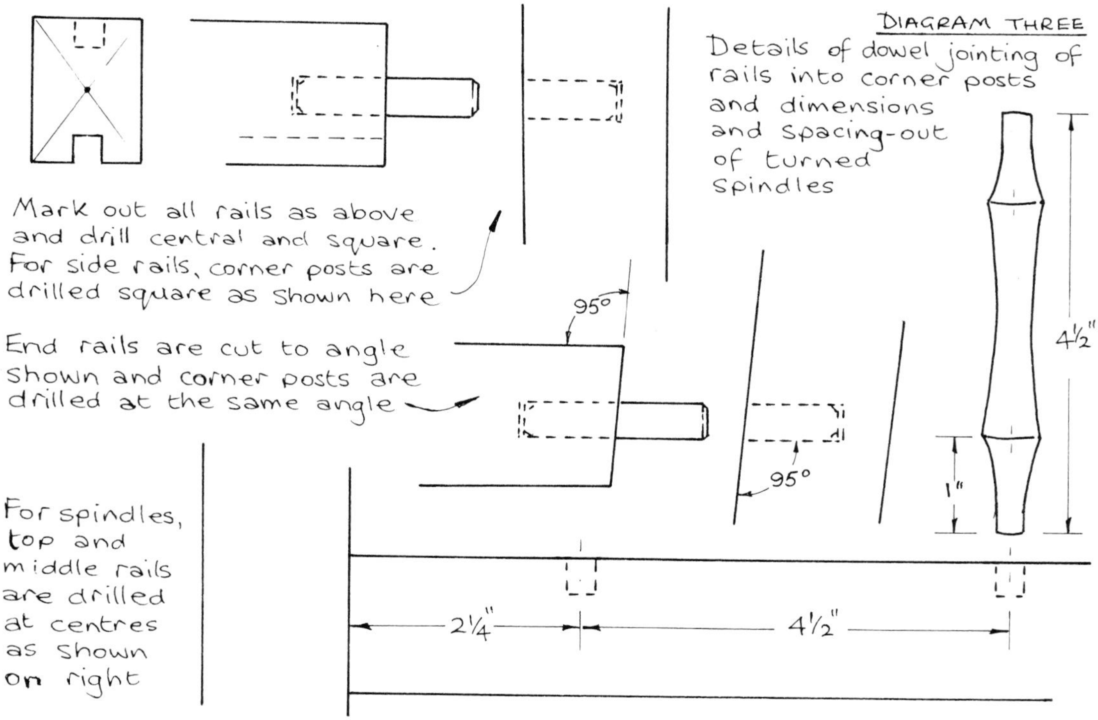

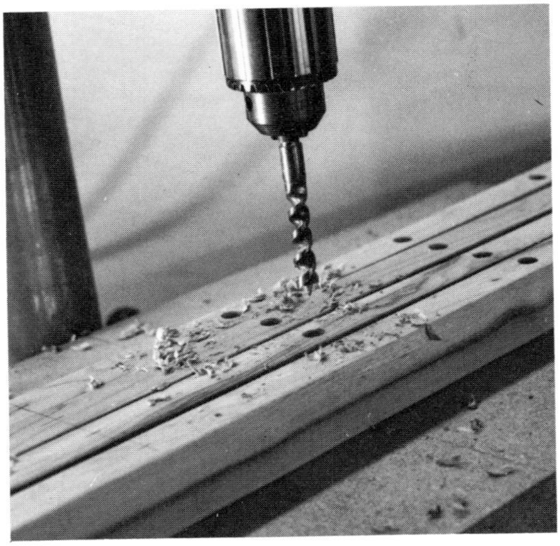

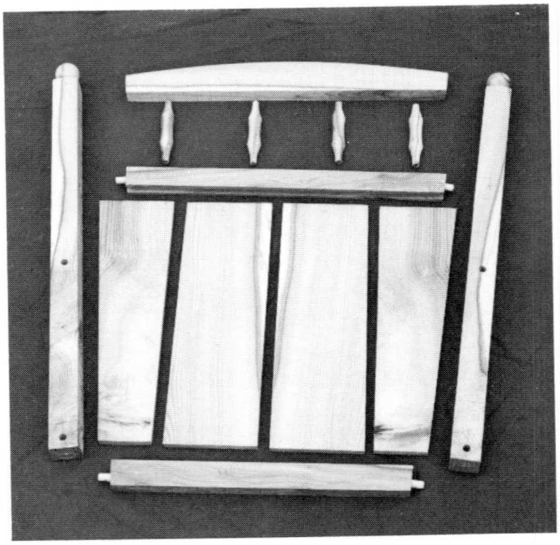

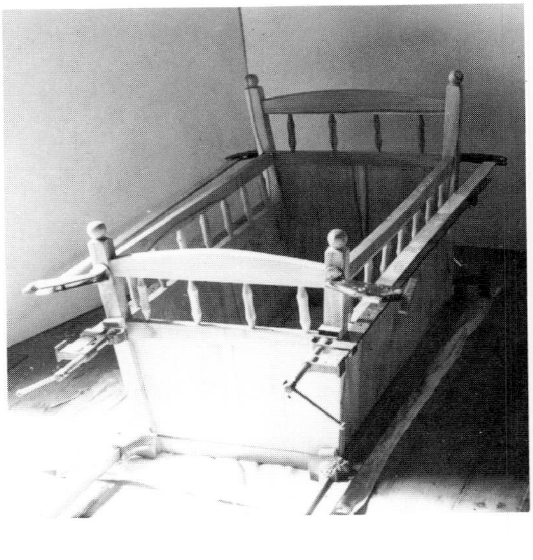

Plates 4–8 (*top*) Drilling spindle holes in the rails; (*above*) Checking that the turned spindles fit into the holes drilled for them; (*opposite top*) The end section ready for gluing up; (*centre*) The end sections glued up and held in cramps [clamps]; (*right*) The assembled cradle glued up and held in cramps [clamps]

middle rails and top rails; then, with glue in the dowel holes in the corner posts and on the ends of the rails the whole end section is brought together. Cramp [clamp] up with sash cramps [clamps], and with the surplus glue cleaned off leave until set, then remove the cramps [clamps].

The assembly is completed by gluing the dowels into the side rails, and the side panels and spindles into their respective slots and holes. Glue is placed in the dowel holes and on the ends of the side rails, the sides then put together with the two end sections and cramped [clamped] up. Check that the cradle body goes together squarely while doing this.

Measurement taken across the inside of the lower part of the cradle will give the precise measurements for the piece of ply which forms the bottom of the cradle. Anyone with an abundance of yew can make the bottom from solid material, but ply is quite suitable. The bottom should be a snug fit down on to the inside edges of the bottom rails. It is held in place by means of the screws which pass through it and into the rockers, as will be seen in Diagram Four.

The final job is to make and fit the rockers. These are marked out with the help of the pattern given in Diagram Four, but check its measurements against your own cradle and adjust for any differences, especially in the shaping of each rocker to accommodate the bottom side rails. Cut to the correct shape and test for fit by having a trial, dry assembly. If all is well, drill and countersink holes through the bottom of the cradle, as shown; glue the rockers into position and screw down into each through the cradle bottom. This has the effect of sandwiching the bottom rails between the cradle bottom and the rockers, thus locking everything securely together.

After a light sanding down, a clear finish is applied to the cradle in order to preserve and enhance the appearance of the yew. A wax finish over a suitable clear sealer makes a nice job, but some, anxious to have a finish less susceptible to finger marking and the effects of moisture, might prefer to use polyurethane varnish or a pre-catalysed lacquer.

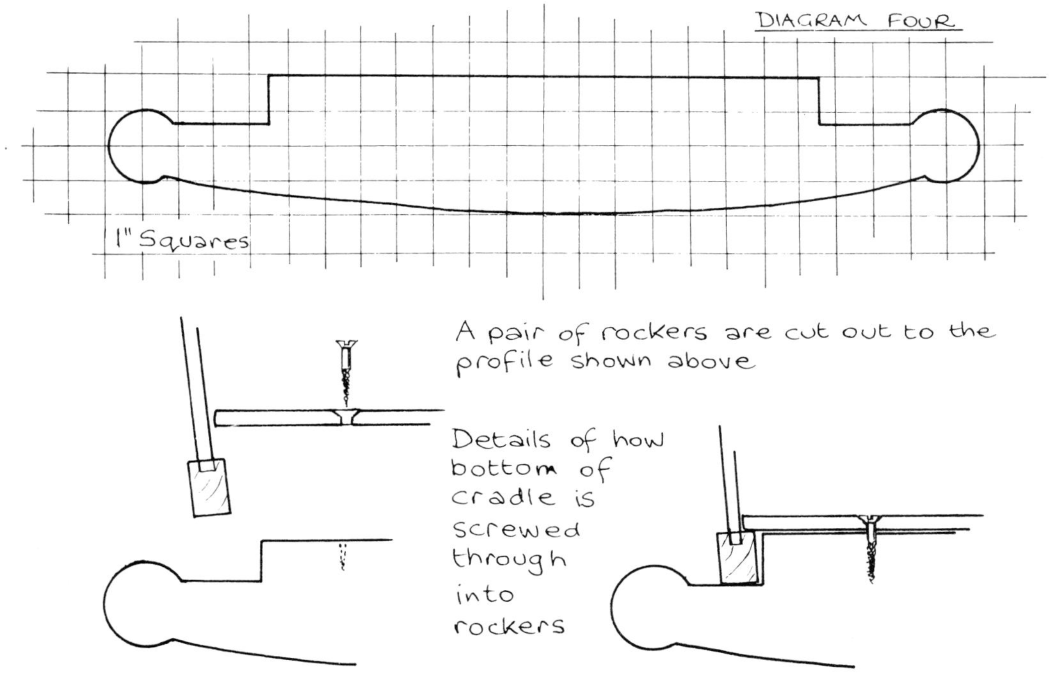

DIAGRAM FOUR
1" Squares
A pair of rockers are cut out to the profile shown above
Details of how bottom of cradle is screwed through into rockers

	MATERIALS REQUIREMENTS LIST. (CUTTING LIST IN INCHES)			
Nº	PURPOSE	MATERIAL	INITIAL SIZES	
2	CORNER POSTS	YEW	25" x 1½" x 1½"	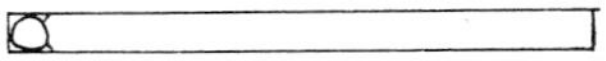
2	CORNER POSTS	"	20" x 1½" x 1½"	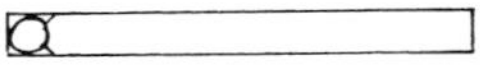
6	SIDE RAILS	"	31½" x 1½" x 1½"	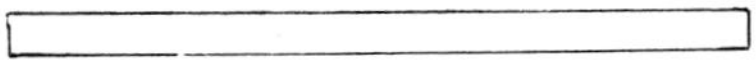
2	END RAILS	"	14½" x 1½" x 1½"	
2	END RAILS	"	16¾" x 1½" x 1½"	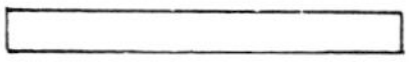
2	END RAILS	"	18" x 2½" x 1½"	
4	PANELS	"	15" x 4½" x ¼"	
18	PANELS	"	9½" x 4½" x ¼"	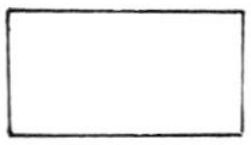
2	ROCKERS	"	24" x 4" x 1"	
1	BOTTOM	PLY	32½" x 18½" x ½"	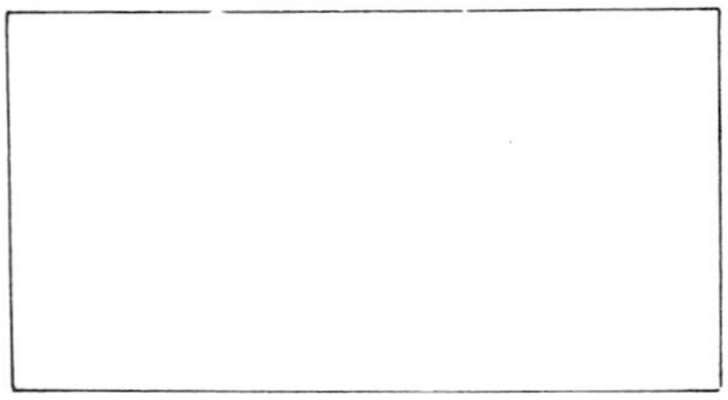
22	TURNED SPINDLES, MAINLY FROM YEW OFFCUTS, EACH, 5" x ⅞" x ⅞"			

(*opposite*) Above: Chest (*see pp101–9*); below: cradle (*pp110–16*)

8

Dining Table

Illustrated on opposite page

Early tables were simply separate boards placed on trestles or, perhaps even earlier, on upturned tree stumps. The boards would have been rough hewn or pit sawn, trimmed with an adze and fixed together with cross-pieces. In due course of time these temporary tables – for they were taken down when not in use – were replaced by more permanent ones. Among these the style popularly known now as the refectory table was prominent, but several other types developed later and some are still in use today. Tables which extend in some way have become extremely popular owing largely to the decreasing size of the dining-room or, to be more precise, the dining area, for many modern, open-plan homes do not now have a separate room. But where space permits, the sturdy four-legged table with its bulbous, turned legs, and plain fixed top is hard to beat. In use from Elizabethan times, they were extremely popular among the large families of the Victorian period.

Many of those from Victorian times were made in pine or deal – some might have tops of sycamore – and it was usual to keep these clean by scouring with sand or by scrubbing. On Sundays they would be covered with a heavy chenille tablecloth. Later, many were painted and now have become prized among those fond of stripped pine furniture.

The table described here was made as a co-operative effort by the occupants of the Broadmere Loft Workshop and myself for a client in Birmingham and, while its method of construction makes it a little heavy, it is not difficult to make and has proved sturdy and practical in use.

Selected waney-edge boards of first quality English ash were used and, to ensure stability, these were bought in as kiln dried. A board thickness of 1½in was purchased for the top and under rails and, after being cut to width, this thickness was reduced to a full 1¼in by machine planing. For the turned legs 4 × 4in ash was used. The completed table measured 6ft in length, 34in wide and 29¼in high.

Plate 1 The matched boards which are edge jointed to make the table top

Four matched boards, 8½in wide, were edge jointed to make the top, each inner edge glued and dowelled for extra strength. End pieces were fitted across each end; these were again glued and dowelled, two dowels to each longitudinal board. To overcome the problem of cramping [clamping] when fitting these end pieces, pairs of cramps [clamps] were fastened together to double their effective length. The glued-up top was hand planed and scraped to obtain a good flat surface and finally sides and ends were planed square and their edges given a slight rounding over. An alternative treatment might be to make a moulded edge by means of a hand or power router (see Diagram One).

The underframing, consisting of two side rails, two end rails and a centre cross-rail

Plate 2 The table top is hand planed and scraped to obtain a good flat surface

were cut at 4in wide from the 1¼in planed material. The side and end rails fit into the legs by means of mortice-and-tenon joints while the cross rail is dowelled into the inner face of each side rail. The mortice and tenons are worked out and cut as in Diagram Three (see section on Joints, p29, for further details).

Obtaining 4 × 4in ash for the legs was not easy and we had to consider at one stage building up this section by gluing together two pieces of 4 × 2in. In case of real difficulty this is a way out of the problem and if the wood used is chosen and matched with care it can be reasonably satisfactory when turned to shape. However, it is obviously better to use the full-size timber if it is available. The legs, it will be seen, are left square at the top for the mortice-and-tenon joints, the turned part then extending down to ground level. Any turned design of your choice can be used. The shape used here was based upon a traditional Victorian design (see Diagram Two).

Avoid the temptation of making the turning too elaborate. This is a large piece of material to have revolving in a lathe, and remember, there are four to make. First, mark centres at both ends of the piece, then mark out the part to be left square. Do this on all four sides; it is customary to mark this area with crosses, as shown, to remind you to keep it square. Although it is easy enough to turn the leg, the problem for some lies in obtaining a clean transition from the square to round and finishing up to the square. Part of the answer is to begin the work at this very spot and to use the long point of a sharp skew chisel to do the work. With the wood revolving at about 800rpm, present the chisel on its edge and angled slightly away from the square (see Diagram Two). Lift the chisel handle and the point will go down to

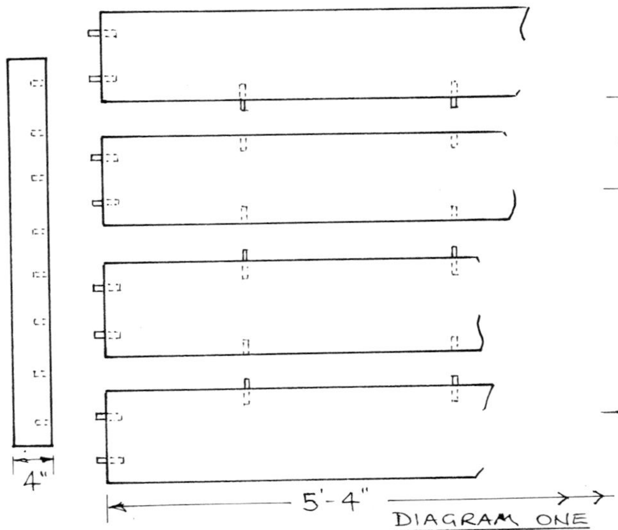

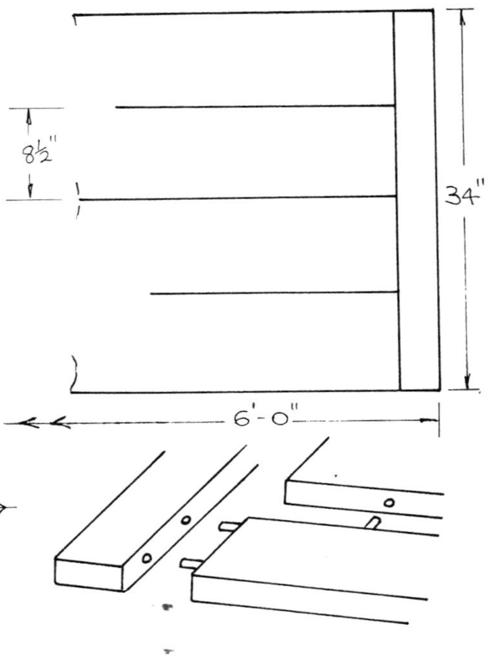

DIAGRAM ONE

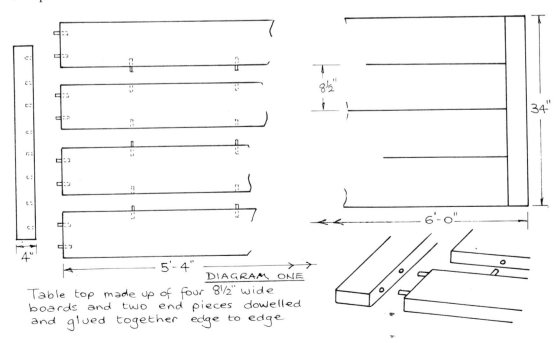

Table top made up of four 8½" wide boards and two end pieces dowelled and glued together edge to edge

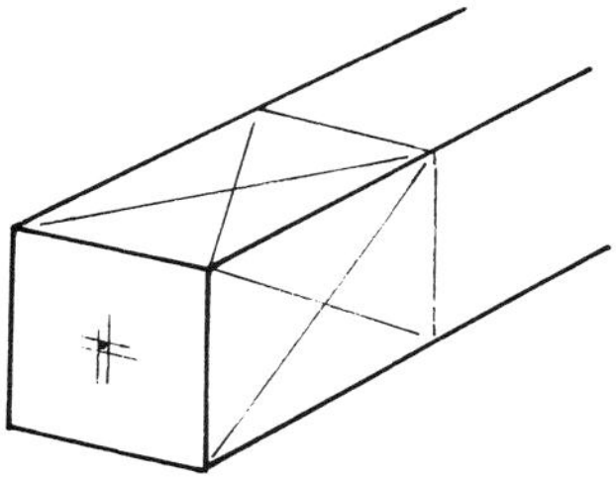

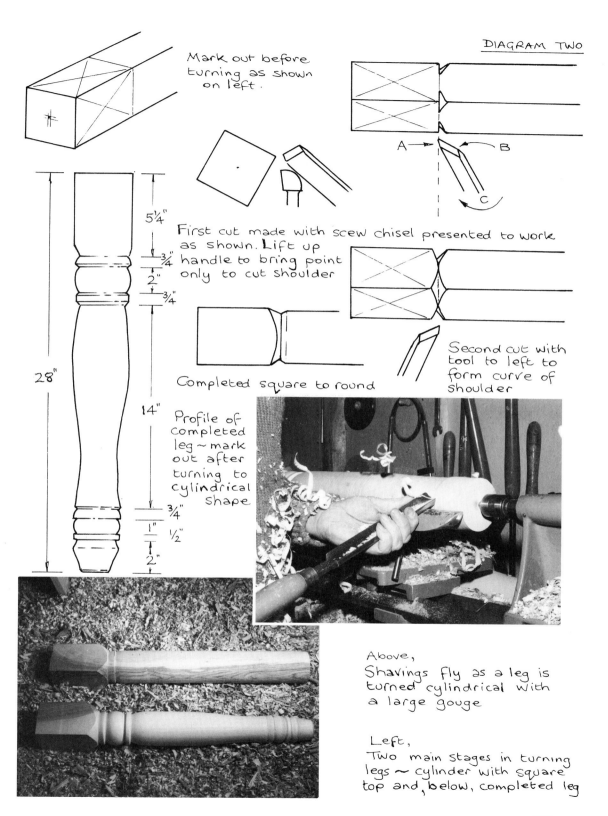

Mark out before turning as shown on left.

DIAGRAM TWO

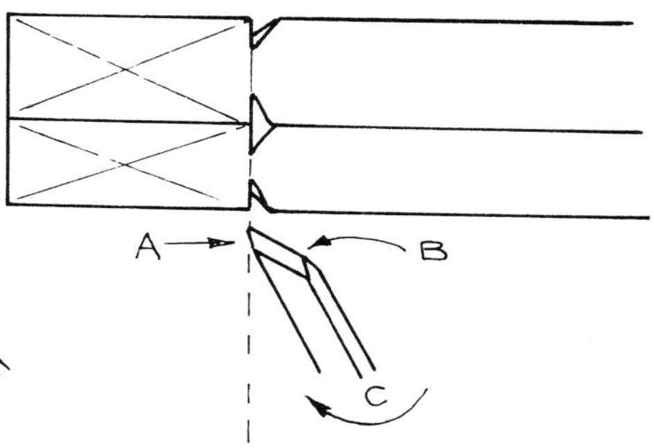

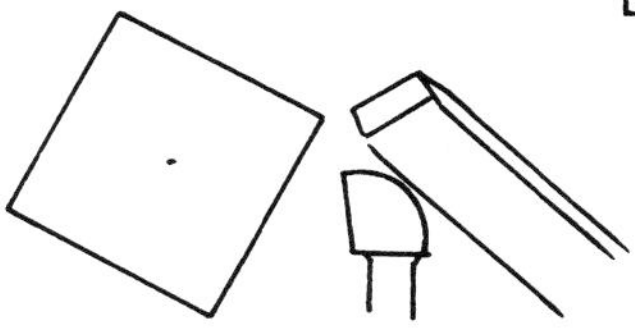

First cut made with scew chisel presented to work as shown. Lift up handle to bring point only to cut shoulder

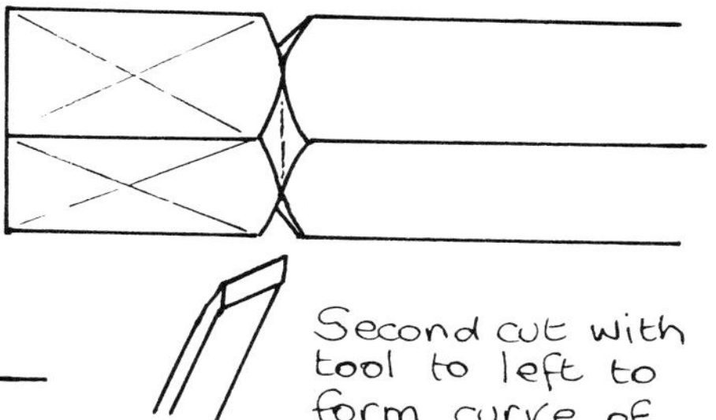

Second cut with tool to left to form curve of shoulder

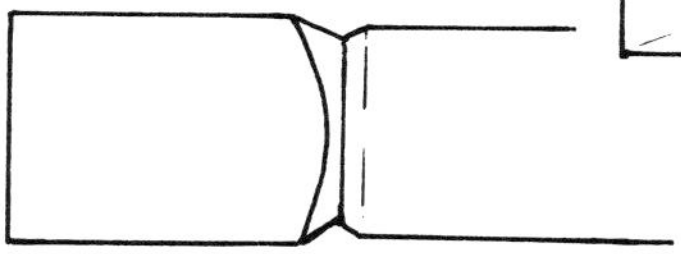

Completed square to round

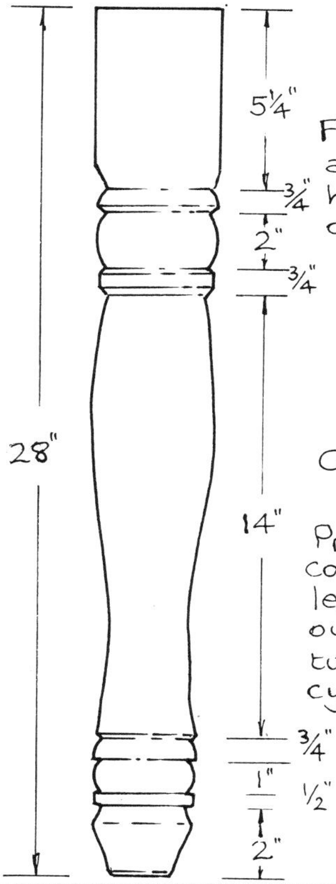

Profile of completed leg ~ mark out after turning to cylindrical shape

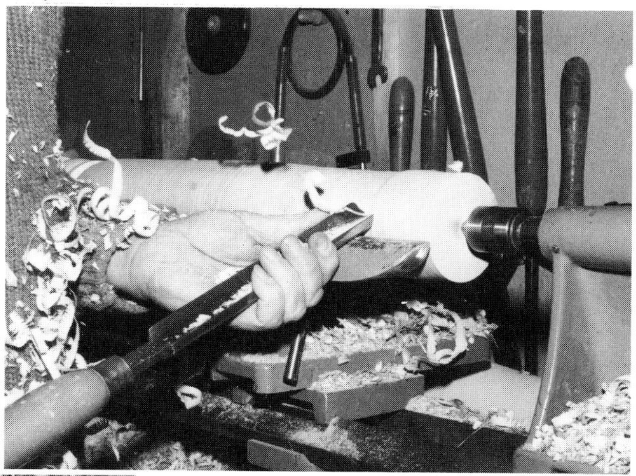

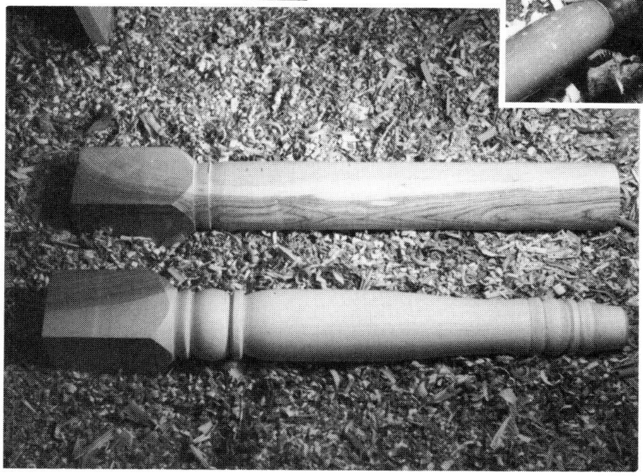

Above,
Shavings fly as a leg is turned cylindrical with a large gouge

Left,
Two main stages in turning legs ~ cylinder with square top and, below, completed leg

cut triangular shavings as shown. Hold the chisel so that bevel A is in line with the cut, while bevel B, underneath, rubs the work and reduces the chance of digging in. Gradually, bring the tool to an upright position and square to the work; do not let the chisel go in too far or it will begin to take too big a cut. For the second cut, angle the tool to the opposite side, lift the handle as before and again bring the tool upright and square to the work. This second cut forms the curved shoulders of the square section. Note that only the point of the chisel cuts. Repeat until there is a continuous line around the work. The rest of the leg is then first turned to a cylinder using a large gouge before being marked out and turned to the profile given, or to any other of your choice. Finish by sanding and, if the finished table is to be wax polished, the legs can be waxed while revolving on the lathe. Observe the usual precautions when sanding and polishing work on the lathe.

Mark out and cut the mortices in the squares left on each of the legs and follow this by marking out and cutting the tenons of the side and end rails (see Diagram Three). Test fit these joints, 'marrying' each leg mortice to its respective tenons and pencil in identification marks. Mark out and drill the

Plate 3 The leg mortice is 'married' to its respective tenon

DIAGRAM THREE

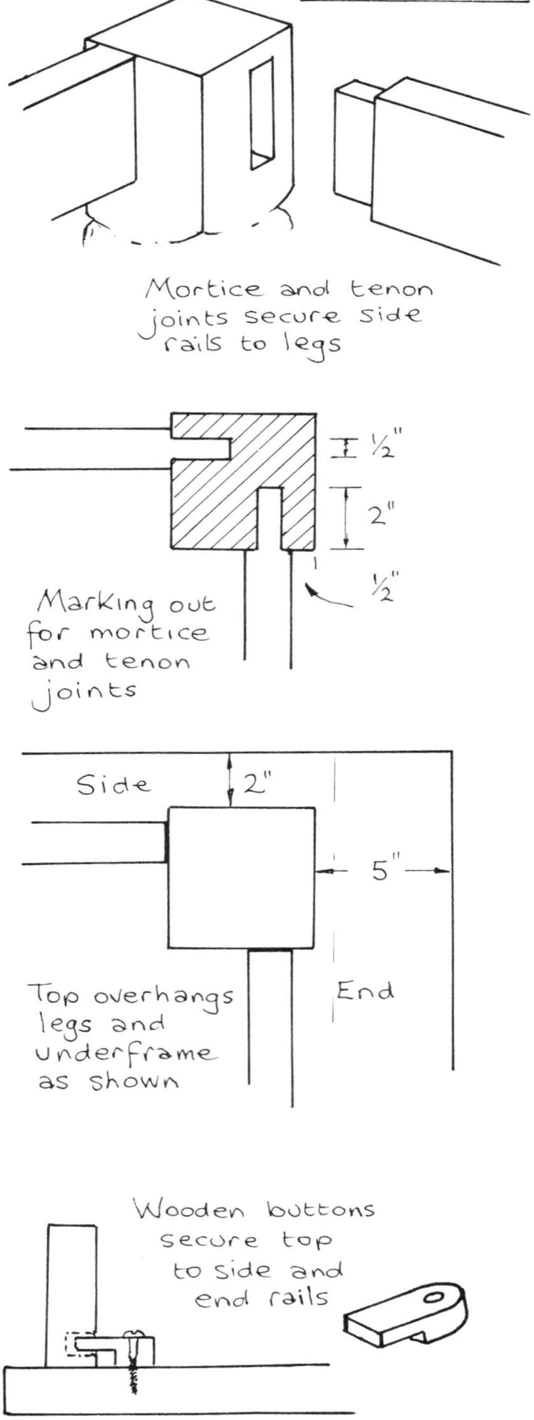
Mortice and tenon joints secure side rails to legs
½"
2"
½"
Marking out for mortice and tenon joints
Side
2"
5"
End
Top overhangs legs and underframe as shown
Wooden buttons secure top to side and end rails

dowel holes for the centre rail and assemble and check the whole underframe for squareness. When satisfied, glue up the joints and assemble the underframe, check again that it is true and square and place under pressure by means of sash cramps [clamps].

The top is held to the underframe by means of hardwood buttons. Use the same method as described on p166. Remember that the thickness of the buttons should be slightly less than the distance between the groove and the table top so that the top is pulled down tight as the buttons are screwed up. Note that here the buttons are a little larger as is the groove into which they fit.

When the table is assembled it should be cleaned up and given a light sanding over if necessary before a suitable finish is applied. Mention has already been made of a wax finish in connection with the turned legs and this was indeed the finish applied to the legs and the underframing of this particular table. However, a different finish was applied to the top. A heat- and damp-resistant finish seemed a more practical proposition in the circumstances and to this end a pre-catalysed lacquer was used. This was buffed to give a semi-matt finish which matched well with the waxed finish elsewhere.

Plate 4 Joints are glued up and the underframe assembled. When it is true and square, place under sash cramps [clamps]

Plate 5 The table top is held to the underframe by hardwood buttons

MATERIALS REQUIREMENT LIST. (CUTTING LIST IN INCHES)

Nº	PURPOSE	MATERIAL	INITIAL SIZE		
4	TOP BOARDS	ASH	5'-4" x 8½" x 1½"		
2	END PIECES	"	2'-10" x 4" x 1½"	PLANED & JOINTED	
2	SIDE RAILS	"	4'-10" x 4" x 1½"	"	
2	END RAILS	"	2'-4" x 4" x 1½"	"	
1	MID RAIL	"	2'-3½" x 4" x 1½"	"	
4.	LEGS	"	2'-5" x 4" x 4"	TURNED	
	DOWELS, PIECES TO MAKE 8 BUTTONS				

9

Ladderback Chair

Illustrated on page 135

One of the finest examples of traditional country furniture, the ladderback chair, has been popular in Britain since the early seventeenth century. Over the years its design has undergone considerable change, from the simple rush-seated example discussed here to the more elaborate designs of the Chippendale period with their ornate and sometimes pierced back splats, cabriole legs, and so on. Some of these have solid wooden seats, others are upholstered and many bear little resemblance to their ancestors.

The original ladderback was a woodturner's rather than a joiner's or cabinetmaker's chair; all its main components, round in section, joined by means of round tenons turned on the ends of components which are glued and sometimes pegged into holes drilled and angled to receive them. Horizontal back slats, any number from three to seven, are of thin section material, steam bent to a shallow curve and housed in mortices cut in the back uprights. The seat was always of woven rush, although in the United States of America fabric tape was a popular alternative.

Almost any kind of hardwood is suitable for the frame; softwood is frequently used commercially today, but it is not pretty nor is it recommended. The chair described, one of a set of four, was made in ash; beech would also be very suitable. For sound construction ensure that the timber is straight grained and knot-free. Many of the components are quite slender and straight grain is necessary for flexibility and strength. For the same reasons, tight joints are essential.

Begin by cutting to length all the turned members, leaving a little over for waste in each case. The two long back uprights may present some problems associated with 'whipping' when being turned or, if your lathe bed is too short, it may be necessary to resort to having them made. I overcame the problems by using the rotary planes described elsewhere. In cases of real difficulty these two long members could be shaped by hand using plane and spokeshave; some early chairs were in fact entirely made by this means.

All stretchers of the underframing are turned full from 1in material, gradually tapered to form tight ¾in tenons at each end. The four rails which make up the seat frame can be turned in the same way but need not be given a smooth finish as they will be covered by the seat weaving.

Now to make a start on drilling all those rail and stretcher holes, and here you have a choice of making the job easy or difficult. Ideally, the seat of a ladderback is not square but is wider at the front than at the back (see Diagram One). In a square seat all the holes are drilled at right angles – in the shaped seat the angles vary. For simplicity I made these chairs with square seats, but I have made both types and will describe both methods.

A simple jig is a useful aid in alignment when drilling these holes, both in keeping them in line with each other and in ascertaining the correct drilling angle (see Diagram Two). The saw-tooth Forstner-type bit is the ideal drill to use as it produces the necessary flat-bottomed hole and, as in other descriptions of the use of these drills, for accuracy in drilling vertical and angled holes, a pillar or bench drilling machine [drill press] is advocated.

The first stage involves making up the front section and the back section of the chair. In fact, throughout its construction, these two sections form the basis of the chair, the side rails and stretchers being added to join these two sections together to form the completed chair. Whether the seat be square or shaped the drilling of these two

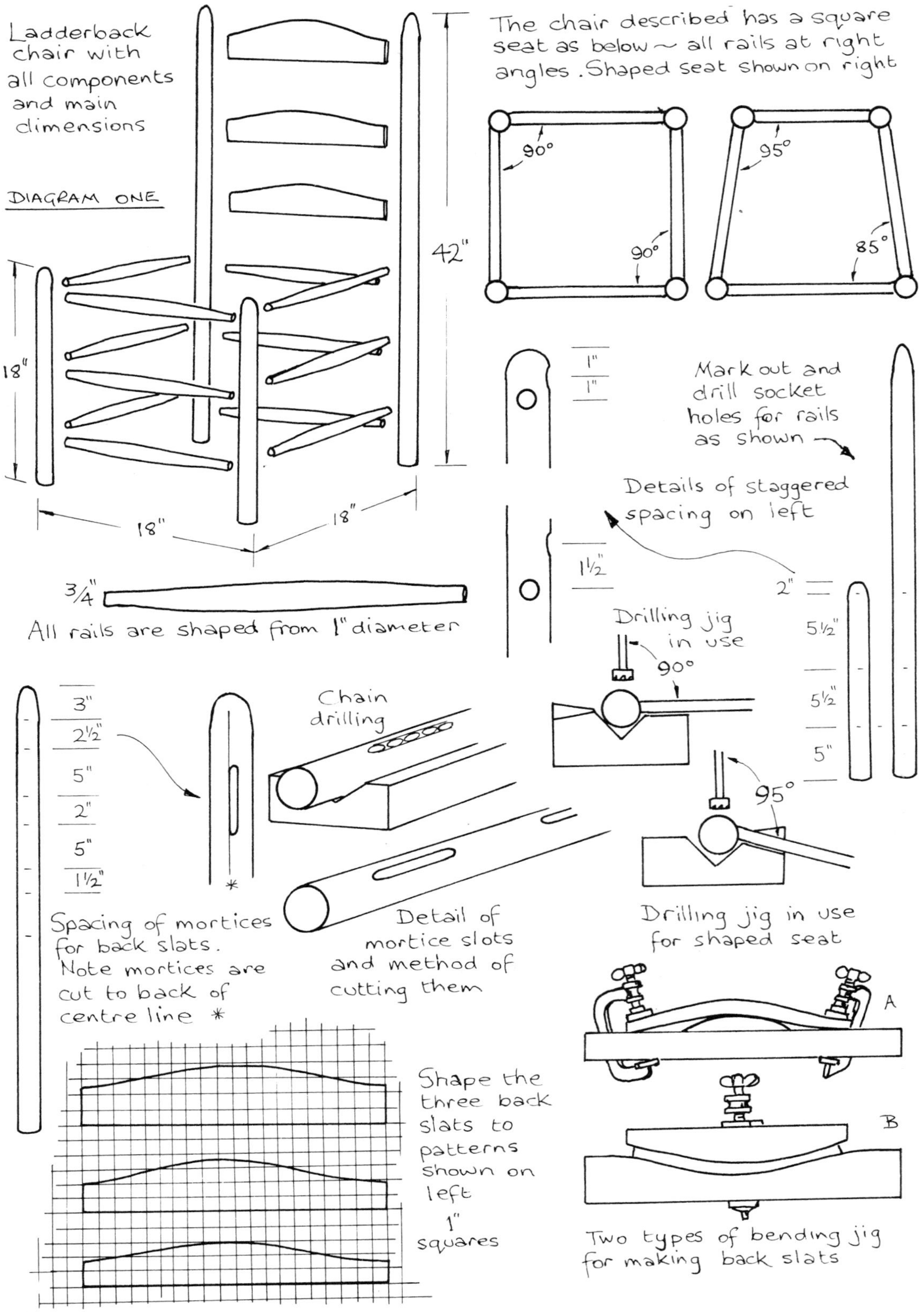

Ladderback chair with all components and main dimensions
DIAGRAM ONE
42"
18"
18"
18"
3/4"
All rails are shaped from 1" diameter
The chair described has a square seat as below ~ all rails at right angles. Shaped seat shown on right
90°
90°
95°
85°
1"
1"
1½"
2"
Mark out and drill socket holes for rails as shown
Details of staggered spacing on left
5½"
5½"
5"
Drilling jig in use
90°
95°
Drilling jig in use for shaped seat
3"
2½"
5"
2"
5"
1½"
*
Spacing of mortices for back slats. Note mortices are cut to back of centre line *
Chain drilling
Detail of mortice slots and method of cutting them
A
B
Two types of bending jig for making back slats
Shape the three back slats to patterns shown on left
1" squares

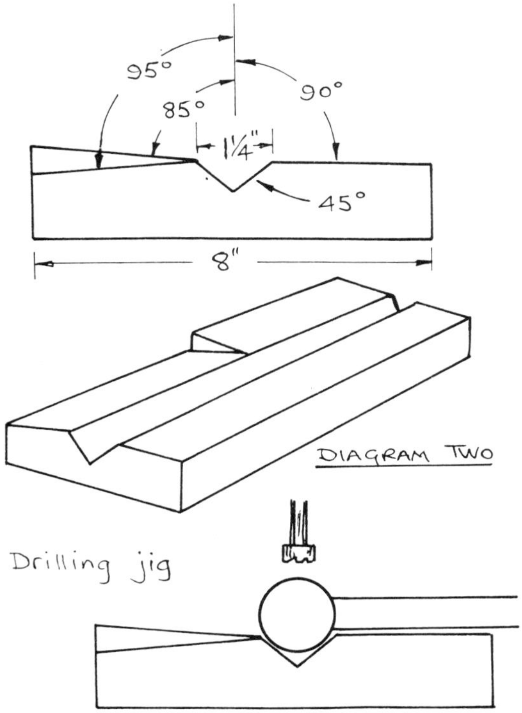

Plate 1 Drilling socket holes using a V-cradle and pillar drill

sections is the same as both are parallel to each other in each case. First mark out the position of the holes as in Diagram One along a line drawn the length of the leg or leg section of the back uprights. Use the jig to hold components while drilling at the marked positions, setting the depth stop of the drill to a touch over ¾in. This is in keeping with the adage of tenon depth equal to tenon diameter plus at least ⅛in. In this case there is not much wood to spare in the leg section, so do not go deeper than this otherwise the leg will be weakened. This applies especially to the seat rail holes in the two back uprights.

With these front and back holes drilled the problem of drilling holes for the side rails can be tackled. Mark out the hole positions as in Diagram One, noting that all side rail holes are higher than their corresponding front and back holes. This staggering arrangement causes less weakening of the leg members at these points. With a short length of ¾in dowel in one of the previously drilled holes, place the leg in the jig on the drilling machine [drill press] so that the dowel lies on top of the square face of the jig, bring the drill down and a hole at right angles (90°) to the previous one will appear. Repeat this procedure until all the holes are drilled.

In the case of the shaped seat the use of the jig described makes the actual drilling almost as easy, but you do have to drill the correct angles for left and right sides. It helps to remember that side holes in the back section are angled outwards while those in the front section are angled inward. Again, with a short length of ¾in dowel in one of the previously drilled holes, the leg is placed in the jig with the dowel lying on the appropriate sloping part of the jig. This will give the correct angle for drilling.

The mortice slots which accommodate the back slats should now be made to complete this stage of the work. To allow for the curvature of each slat do not cut their mortice slots directly on the centre line of the uprights but slightly towards the back of the chair (see Diagram One). Mark the position of each as shown and then, using the V-cradle jig as before, drill a line of holes – chain drilling as it is sometimes called – inside the pencilled marks. Clean up with a bevelled chisel, leaving the ends of the slots

Plate 2 Cleaning up the top curve on back slats

Plate 3 (*below*) Back slats in a bending jig

as left by the drill to give a rounded shape. The completed mortices should be about ½in deep. The slats, when made, are shaped and trimmed to form full-width tenons, ie not shouldered, to fit into the mortice slots.

When this drilling and morticing is completed, it is a good idea to have a dry assembly of all the components made so far. Assemble the back and front sections first to form separate 'units', then insert the side rails and stretchers to complete. Check that all side rail and stretcher tenons enter their respective holes to the required depth. When satisfied that all is well, check that the two back uprights are parallel and take note of the measurement between the two. (There may sometimes be a slight discrepancy between what it should be and what it actually is.) Then separate the components and turn your attention to making and fitting the back slats.

As has been said, the slats may vary in number and, as a consequence, in width. Some are left quite plain, others ornately

shaped, even carved. The final choice is up to the maker (or his client), but the number, size, etc, must be decided upon at the offset. Instructions are given here for the simple three-slat back as illustrated. Each slat is cut from straight-grained material, $1/4$–$3/16$in in thickness and is made a full 2in longer than the measurement as taken between the two back uprights. This allows for the reduction in overall length owing to the curvature of the bend and provides sufficient material for jointing into the slot mortices cut in the back uprights. The top curve to each slat is also cut at this stage.

The bending of these slats should present no difficulties; they are quite thin in section and their curvature comparatively shallow. Two types of bending jig are illustrated in Diagram One; both work well but the more sophisticated type B is marginally better. Steam-bending procedures are fully described on p42. Allow time for the slats to dry out properly and set to shape. When dry, they will need scraping and sanding smooth. Then trim each one individually to fit its mortice slot and mark accordingly.

Another dry run is now necessary, this time just of the entire back section, ie two back uprights together with seat rails, stretchers and the slats or ladder bars. Check that all components go together correctly, tenons to their correct depth with the two uprights remaining parallel. Carry out any trimming to size and fit at this stage. When satisfied that all is well, separate the back parts ready for final finishing and assembly.

It will be found to be advantageous to sand everything smooth while all the components are separate. Avoid sanding the ends of stretchers, etc. as this may result in loose joints. After this initial smoothing I like to apply a coat of sanding sealer and this operation is also simplified if done while the chair components are still separate. Extreme care must be taken not to get sealer on or in any of the joint areas as this will inhibit glue adhesion. When the sealer is dry, give a final light sanding, wipe off the dust and the chair is ready for gluing up. Use a synthetic resin glue such as Cascamite or Aerolite. The correct sequence of assembly is important and follows the earlier mentioned procedure of making up the front section and back section as separate 'units' and then joining these

Plate 4 Back parts ready for gluing up

Plate 5 The back cramped [clamped] up after gluing

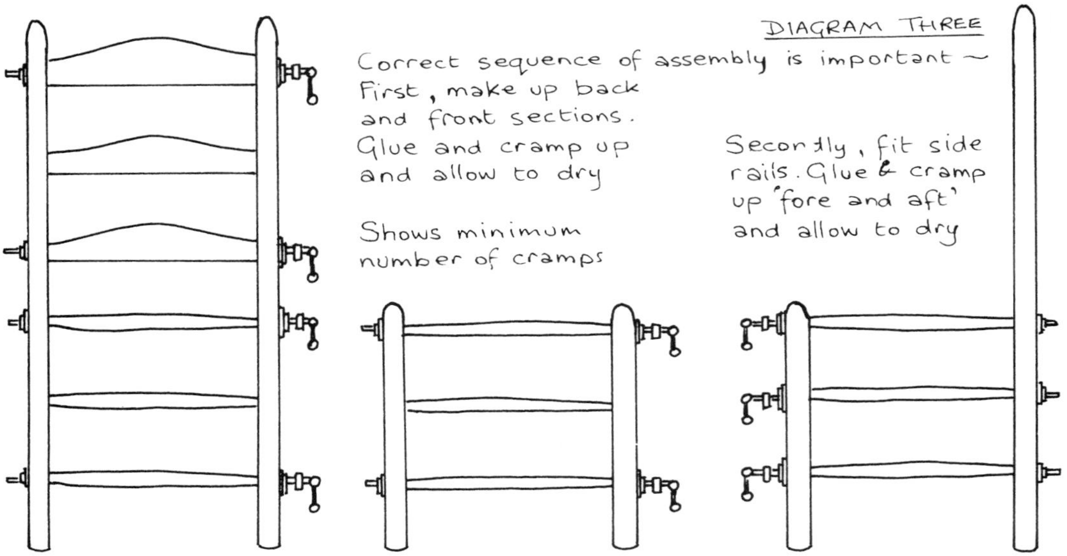

with side rails and stretchers to form the complete chair (see Diagram Three). Put glue into tenon holes and mortice slots, assemble front and back sections and cramp [clamp] up. When cramping [clamping] ensure the cramps [clamps] are placed opposite and in line with stretchers and other horizontal cross-members and that the parts pull together squarely. Protect cramping [clamping] points with softwood blocks.

DIAGRAM THREE
Correct sequence of assembly is important ~
First, make up back
and front sections.
Glue and cramp up
and allow to dry
Shows minimum
number of cramps
Secondly, fit side
rails. Glue & cramp
up 'fore and aft'
and allow to dry

When the glue is dry, the cramps [clamps] are removed and the separate back and front sections have glue placed in their tenon holes and are joined together by means of their respective side seat rails and stretchers. Cramp [clamp] up again, 'fore and aft', and, checking that the chair stands square on its four legs, leave under pressure until the glue is set.

The chair is now ready to have its seat woven. Basic instructions for seat weaving were given for the rush-bottomed stool (p74), and these should be referred to here. Alternatively, other materials and methods such as the fabric tape or woven cord weaving mentioned on p74 may be used. If the chair has a square seat, then the instructions given for the square stool may be strictly adhered to. If, however, the chair seat is wider at the front than at the back, then a slightly different technique is required to begin with for square corners are essential when seat weaving and the extra space on the front rail must first be filled and squared off. After this the sequence for square seats is followed. There are several ways of filling this space but only one is described, as in the diagram on p75.

First, the length of the back rail is measured and this distance is marked in pencil on the front rail leaving an equal space at each end. These are the spaces which have to be filled to square off the seat. The weaving rushes or cord are tied into the left-hand rail as in a normal start, passed over the front rail and worked around the front corner as before, then taken across to the opposite front corner and again worked over in the normal way. Instead of continuing to the back corner, however, the rushes are cut and tied off to the right-hand rail as in the diagram. New weavers are tied in each time and worked over the two front corners only until the pencil marks on the rail are reached. After this the weaving is continued and completed in the usual way.

Finally, the chair is wax polished and a start can now be made on the others to make up the set of four – or eight. Seriously, if a set of chairs is to be made, there are advantages in making all the components at one time, doing all the drilling together, and so on. But, if you are not too sure, then do the sensible thing and just make one to begin with.

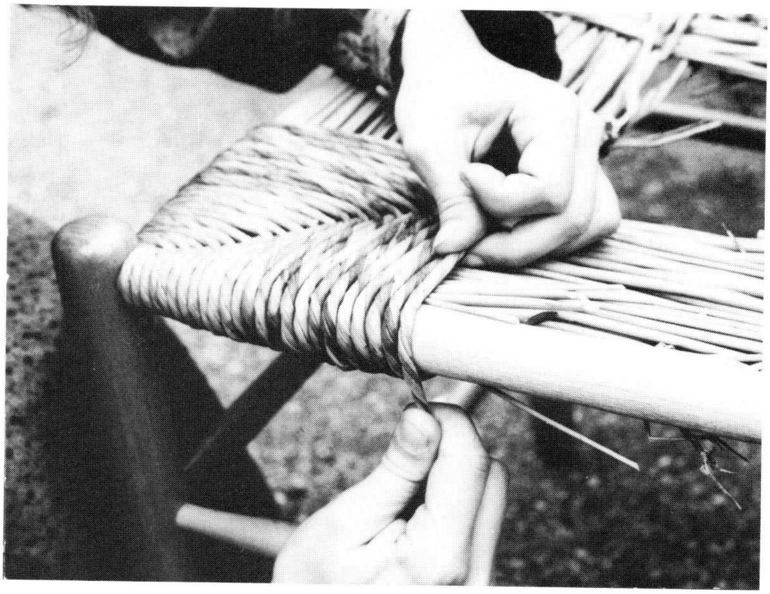

Plate 6 The seat being woven with rush

MATERIAL REQUIREMENTS LIST. (CUTTING LIST IN INCHES)

2	BACK UPRIGHTS	ASH	42 × 1½ × 1½	TURNED	
2	FRONT LEGS		18 × 1½ × 1½		
12	STRETCHERS		18 × 1 × 1		
	SUFFICIENT RUSH (1 BOLT) or SEA GRASS CORD (1½ - 2 HANKS) TO WEAVE SEAT OF CHAIR				

10
Doll's House

Illustrated on page 239

Doll's houses have delighted little girls for generations, holding, it seems, a special place in the make-believe world of childhood. As the style of 'real' houses has changed over the years so, too, has the type of doll's house, from the miniature mansion to the traditional town house, from the suburban bungalow to the seaside villa. Some have been simply and quite cheaply made, destined, like too many playthings, to be discarded in due course, while others, better made and perhaps more elaborate, have continued in use throughout the childhood and into the adulthood of several members of the same family. Some of the most elaborate have become quite famous – for example, that which once belonged to Queen Victoria and is now on public view at Osborne House – while others are now much sought after as collectors' pieces, especially those of traditional design.

Sid Cooke of Redditch in Worcestershire makes traditional doll's houses which are truly collectors' pieces and the one described here is one of a range which he constructs, all to one-twelfth scale. This particular house is in the Georgian style, its well-proportioned fascia opening fully for access to its interior. The overall outside dimensions are 24in wide, 22½in high and 11in deep, ie front to back. On completion, the house is intended to be decorated, ie, painted inside and out or covered in patterned paper made true to scale especially for this purpose.

A good quality birch plywood is recommended for the construction of its main components, ie walls, floors, roof, etc. The two sides, interior floors and ceiling, the two interior walls and the front fascia are cut from ⅜in-thick material; the back and roof panels from $^3/_{16}$in-thick material. (The nearest metric equivalents are 9mm and

Plate 1 Parts of the doll's house ready for assembly

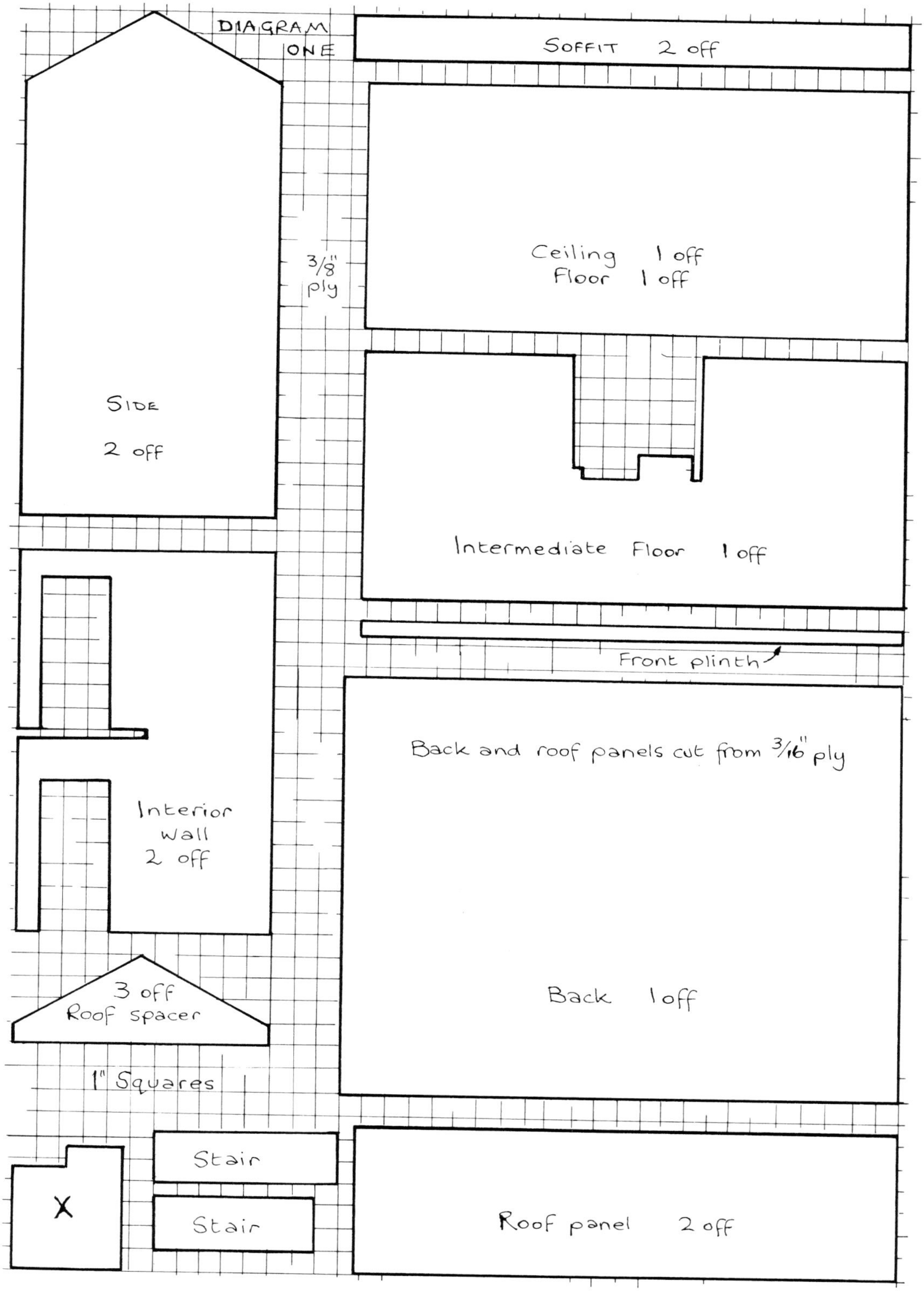
DIAGRAM ONE
SOFFIT 2 off
Side
2 off
3/8" ply
Ceiling 1 off
Floor 1 off
Intermediate Floor 1 off
Front plinth
Back and roof panels cut from 3/16" ply
Interior wall
2 off
3 off
Roof spacer
Back 1 off
1" Squares
Stair
Stair
X
Roof panel 2 off

4mm respectively – see Materials Requirement List, p141.) The window frames, door, interior, stairs, etc, are made from either hardwood or softwood and as these are all quite small suitable offcuts [cutoffs] may be utilised.

Begin by measuring up and marking out the carcase components on the birch ply sheets according to Diagram One. Cut all pieces to size using a fine tooth saw to eliminate the possibility of splintering out along the cut edges. Note that the roof angle on each of the gable ends is 30°. After sawing, smooth all edges with glass-paper [sandpaper], but work carefully so as not to round over the corners.

Glue and panel pin the upper ceiling and lower floor inside the two gable ends to form the main box assembly of the house. Note the positioning of the ceiling and that the floor is set up 1in from the bottom. Fit the back with glue and panel pins, ensuring as you do that the box assembly remains square. Fit the plinth which occupies the front space below the floor and put aside to dry while continuing work on the other components (see Diagram Two).

The two interior walls and the intermediate floor are cut out and slotted as shown in the diagram, the cut-outs forming the interior door openings and stair well, while the slots enable the three pieces to be assembled together quickly and simply. These three pieces can be easily slid into the house as a single unit and do not require gluing or pinning in place. They are made purposely this way so that they can just as easily be slid out to enable the interior decoration of the house to be carried out.

Plate 2 The intermediate floor slides out easily

The stairs, too, are made to slot into place and are removable for the same purpose. Both stair sections are similar in their basic construction but one, the lower section, has eight steps and has its newel post at the bottom, while the other, the upper section, has one step less and has its newel post, naturally, at the top. The angle of the stairs is 45° so all sloping cuts are made to this angle. For the lower section a piece of ply, 8 × 2¼ × 3⁄16in is used for the base and to this are glued the steps which are cut from either ¾in-section hardwood or ¾in softwood of your choice. Each step has a ⅛in hole drilled into it to accept the side rails. The hand rail is similarly drilled and the newel post is morticed to take the hand rail. The dowel, ⅛in in diameter, is cut to length for the side rails. For the upper section the ply base measures 7 × 2¼ × 3⁄16in and all other parts are made as for the lower section. Assemble and glue up as shown in Diagram Three. Make also the short piece of rail as shown which fits at the head of the stairs.

The item marked X in Diagram One is cut from ply and, when glued in position to the inside surface of the back of the house, acts as a spacer for the interior walls and as a support for the stairs. Two strips glued to the inside of the sides support the ends of the intermediate floor.

The house must have a roof and this is made separately and added to the main box assembly. It consists of the two roof panels supported on three roof spacers cut as in Diagram One. The roof panels are glued and panel pinned into place on the spacers which in turn rest on the ceiling, the two end spacers being glued and pinned to the gable ends. Fascia boards or soffits, 1¾in deep and 24in long, are fitted to both the back and the front of the house to cover the space between the ceiling and the roof. Note that the roof section, when in place, lies ½in below the top edge of the gable ends. The two chimney stacks, consisting of wood blocks cut to fit

(*opposite*) Ladderback chair (*see pp125–31*)
(*overleaf*) Welsh dresser (*see pp151–60*)

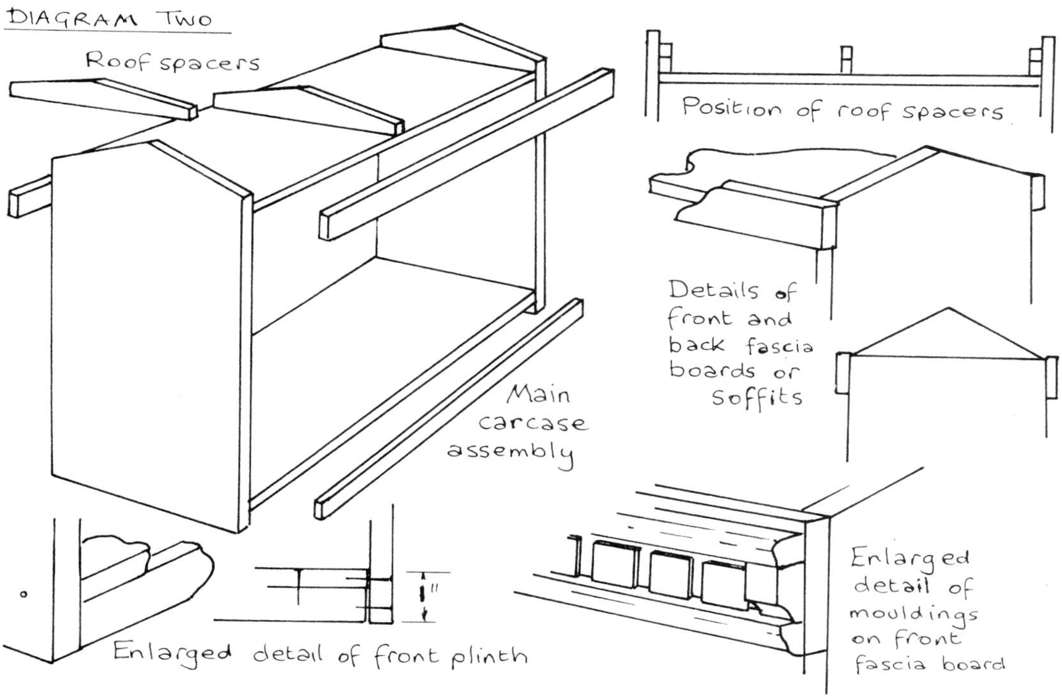
DIAGRAM TWO
Roof spacers
Position of roof spacers
Details of front and back fascia boards or soffits
Main carcase assembly
1"
Enlarged detail of front plinth
Enlarged detail of mouldings on front fascia board

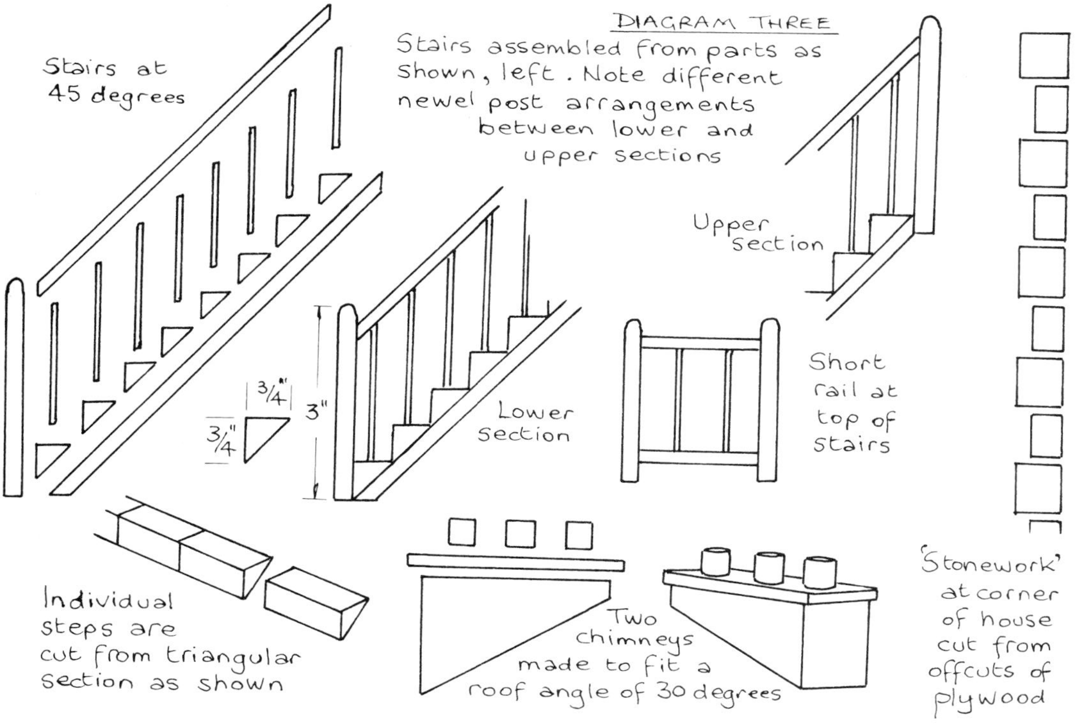
DIAGRAM THREE
Stairs assembled from parts as shown, left. Note different newel post arrangements between lower and upper sections
Stairs at 45 degrees
Upper section
3/4"
3/4"
3"
Lower section
Short rail at top of stairs
Individual steps are cut from triangular section as shown
Two chimneys made to fit a roof angle of 30 degrees
'Stonework' at corner of house cut from offcuts of plywood

DIAGRAM FOUR

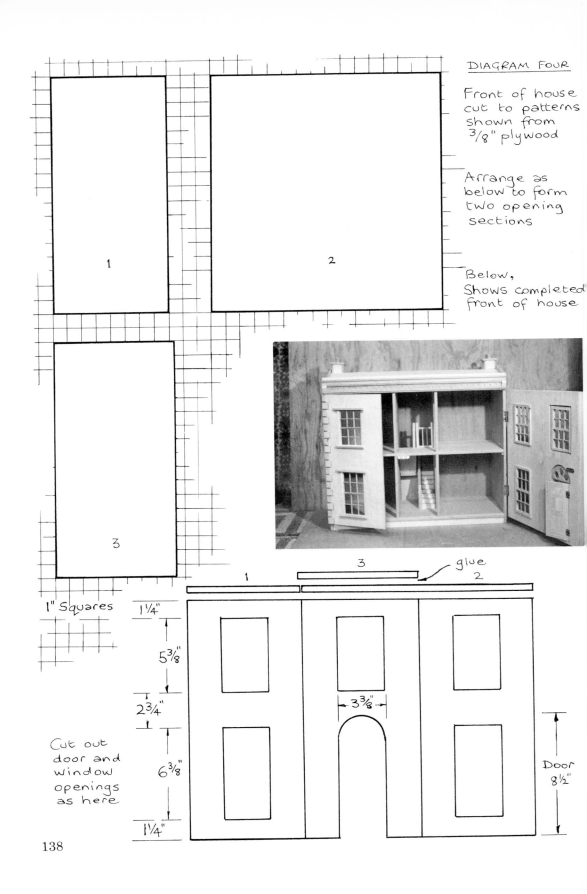

Front of house cut to patterns shown from 3/8" plywood

Arrange as below to form two opening sections

Below, Shows completed front of house

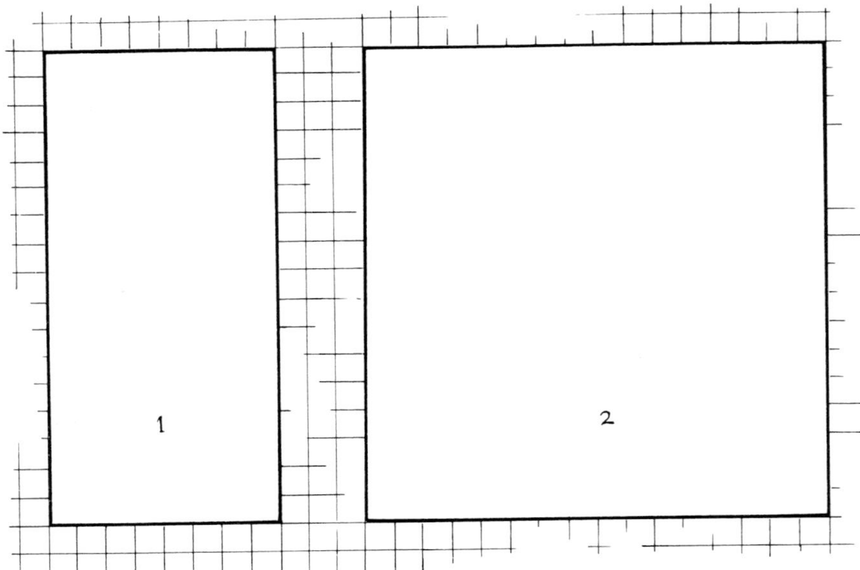

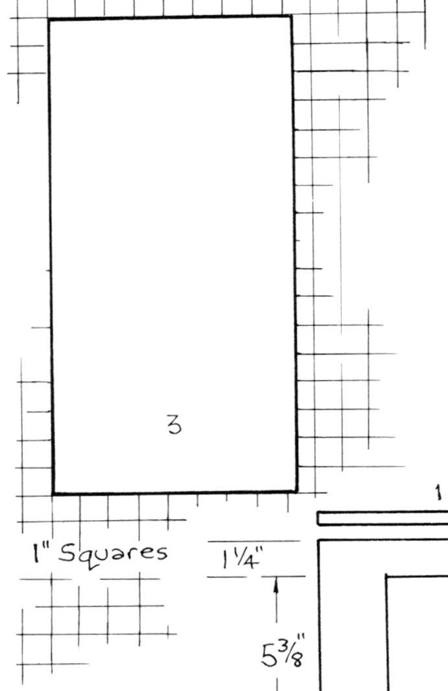

Cut out door and window openings as here

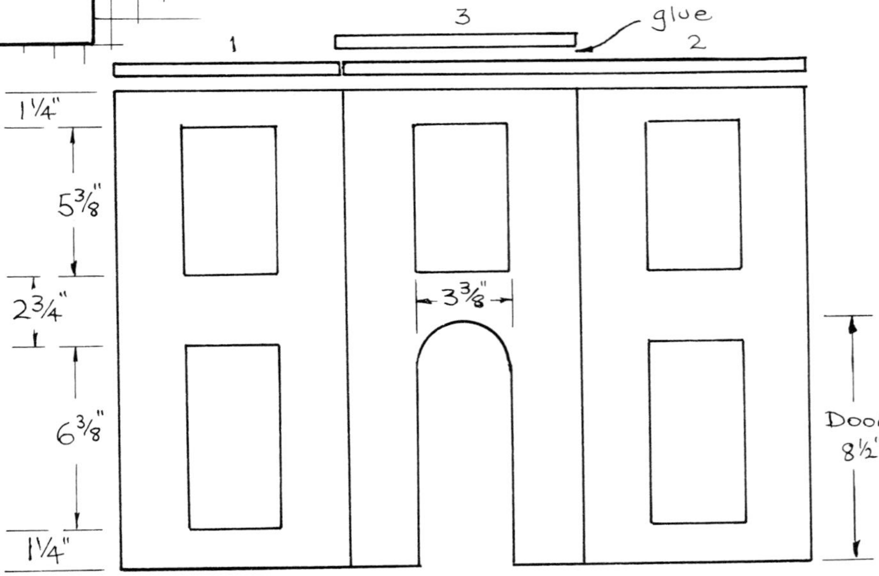

the 30° angle of the roof and with three short pieces of 3/4in dowel glued on as chimney pots, are made to be put into place after the roof is decorated.

Attention may now be concentrated on the hinged front which is where most of the intricate but perhaps the most interesting work takes place. It is made up of three pieces, two of them overlaid and fixed together by gluing as shown in Diagram Four to form two parts. In the closed position the slight overlap conceals the joint between the two parts. Openings for windows and the door are marked out and cut out using a coping saw or fret saw. Saw carefully and glass-paper [sandpaper] the edges smooth without rounding them over. Note that the two lower windows are larger than the three windows upstairs.

Make the window frames in either softwood or hardwood. All dimensions are given in Diagram Five and these should be strictly adhered to for it is the proportions of the windows of the Georgian period which gave the architecture of the era its timeless elegance. The outer frames are made slightly larger than the window openings and are

Plate 3 Window frames can be made in hardwood or softwood

rebated to fit. The inner framework is made up of thin strips which are half lapped where they cross; it is not difficult to do if you have the patience, or a circular saw. Glue holds the whole window frame together when it is assembled and the simple cramping [clamping] jig shown in Diagram Six will hold them firm and square while the glue sets. Varnish

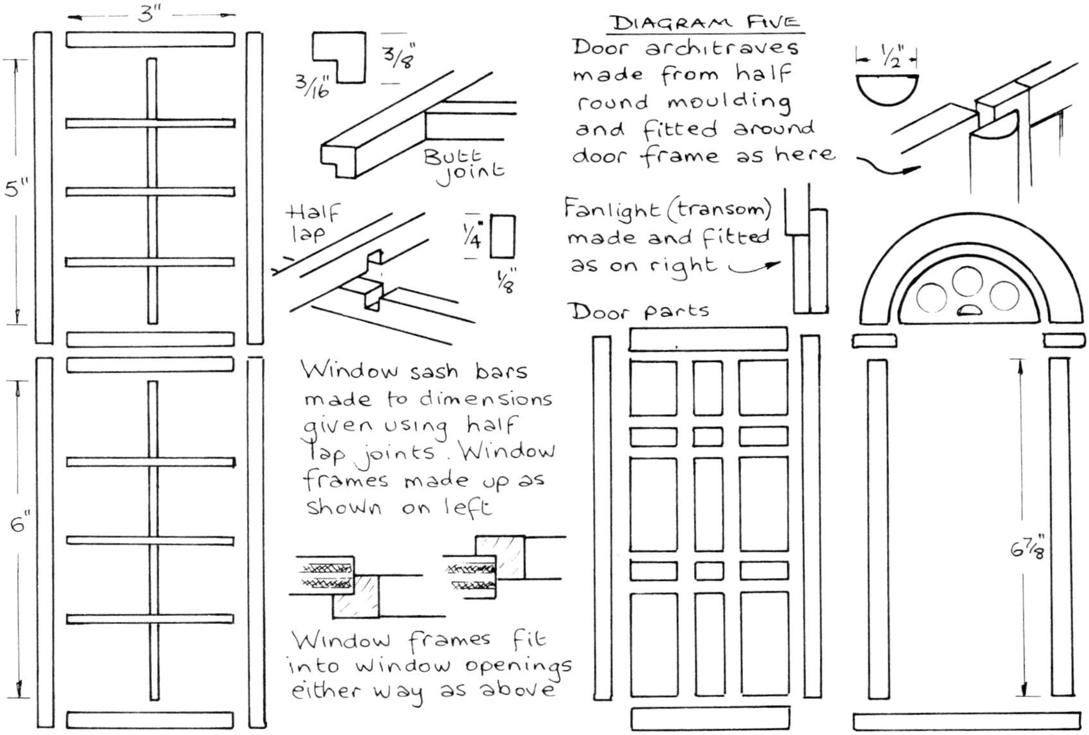

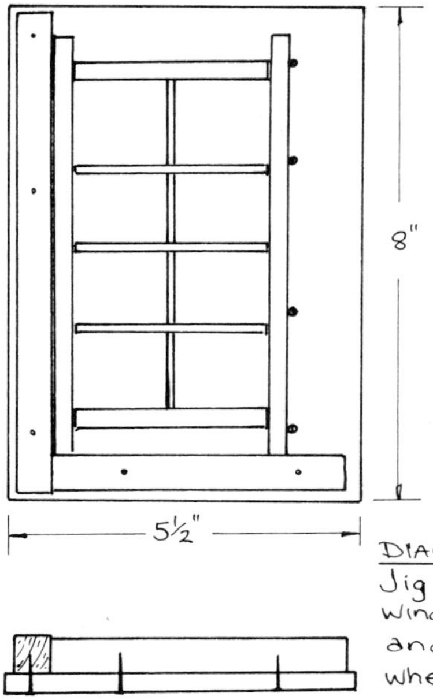

DIAGRAM SIX
Jig to hold window frames and doors when gluing

or wax the jig if you want to avoid gluing your window frame permanently to it.

The 'panelled' door is not panelled at all but is made up of the separate parts shown in Diagram Five and simply glued together. The centre pieces are lightly bevelled before gluing up to give the fielded panel effect. Again, the cramping [clamping] jig may be used to hold the door square and firm after gluing.

The fanlight or transom – the window above the door – is cut from thin ply as is the semi-circular moulding which goes round it. Both are glued together and then glued into place above the door. Each side of the door opening has a rebated [rabbeted] strip of wood glued to it to form the door architrave. This is shaped to give the appearance of a slender pillar on each side of the door. The top of each pillar has a small finial glued on and at the bottom a strip of wood forms the door step. Window sills are similar but have smaller strips glued on beneath each window, while the moulding above them is cut from short lengths of picture-frame moulding. Pieces of deeper moulding are used along the top edge of the roof fascia. Window mouldings and the fascia moulding have small shaped supporting blocks or corbels glued below them at each end. The 'stonework' on both front corners, which forms such a decorative feature of the house, consists of separate pieces of thin ply cut to size from scrap material and glued into place – a time-consuming procedure but one which gives a visual effect well worth the effort.

All the windows should be ready for gluing into position by now and the door hung by means of tiny brass hinges (see Diagram Six). The accuracy with which these fit will depend upon the skill of the maker, especially as regards marking out and the ability to cut up to a marked line. Small adjustments may be necessary to ensure a snug fit, but remember, these can only be made if there is a surplus of wood to be removed. If a window frame or the door has been made too small there is only one proper way out of that problem and that is to make another frame or another door. The door should ideally be a push-tight fit to avoid the need to fit a catch.

When all windows and the door are satisfactorily fitted, the two panels which make up the front of the house may be fitted. These are hinged to the sides or gable ends of the house and so positioned that they are close up under the roof fascia leaving approximately 1in at the bottom to give clearance when the front is swung open while standing on a table. In the closed position the overlap of the two panels conceals the joint between them and they are held shut by means of a magnetic catch.

Plate 4 The two panels which make up the front of the house are hinged to swing open

After a final light sanding the house is completed and ready to be decorated. As this entails the use of methods and materials somewhat outside the scope of this book and is, anyway, very much a matter of personal choice from a wide range of treatments, decoration in detail is not discussed here. Suffice to say that the house, as mentioned earlier, may simply be painted both inside and out, or it may be covered inside with twelfth-scale wallpaper and outside with brick- or stone-patterned paper specially made to scale for this purpose. An address where these materials may be obtained is given in the Appendix.

MATERIALS REQUIREMENT LIST.			
Nº	MATERIAL	INITIAL SIZES	
1 PIECE	BIRCH PLY	NOTE:- In Britain plywood is only available in metric thicknesses; other dimensions are still in feet/inches. 5'-0" x 4'-0" x 3/8" (9mm)	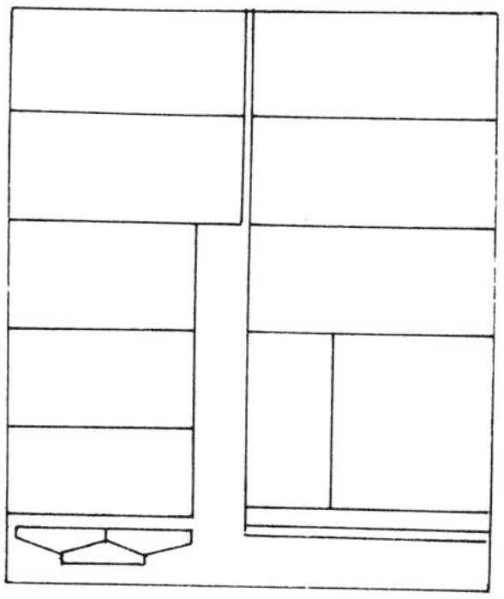
1 PIECE	"	3'-0" x 2'-0" x 3/16" (4mm)	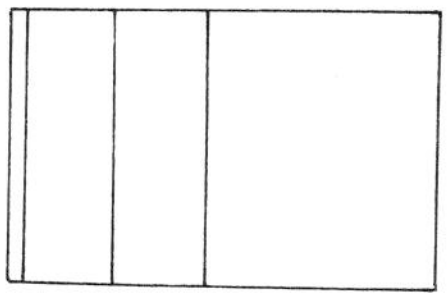
OFFCUTS TO MAKE STAIRS, WINDOW FRAMES, ETC. MOULDING. TWO PAIRS HINGES. ONE MAGNETIC CATCH.			

11

Long Case Clock

Illustrated on page 169

A growing interest in the science of horology towards the end of the seventeenth century, and developments which took place within that science, gave cabinet makers of the period a rather different piece of furniture upon which to demonstrate their skills. Clocks of various types had been around for some time, many of them of the wall-hanging variety, driven by weights hanging below and wound by pulling on a length of chain. In the late 1650s the chains were replaced by catgut wound on a drum and the pendulum came into use as a regulator.

At first the pendulum required a very wide arc of swing, but replacement of the verge escarpment with the anchor escarpment about 1670 overcame this. The pendulum and weights could now be housed in the box-like cases which had originally been devised to protect the weights and chains of earlier hanging clocks. Longer pendulums in turn meant longer cases and it was not long before someone added a base to the long case and stood it on the floor.

Many early long case clocks had strong architectural features with turned columns and pediments, while carved and gilded capitals and moulded panels predominated. Some were richly decorated with inlay and marquetry and many were made in choice woods such as walnut, burr chestnut and mahogany.

Appropriately, mahogany was the wood chosen for the clock case described here. Its design, although still somewhat architectural, has sufficient restraint to give it a look of elegance. It was made by a young lady furniture maker of my acquaintance, Judith K. Wrightson. Its construction is traditionally based upon three separate box sections – base, trunk and hood – which join together to make the complete clock case. Base and trunk are permanently joined but the hood remains removable for access to the clock movement. The overall height, including the pediment and top finial, is 82in or 6ft 10in, and at its base the plinth area measures 17 × 10in. Most of its components can be cut

Plate 1 Some of the main components of the long case clock

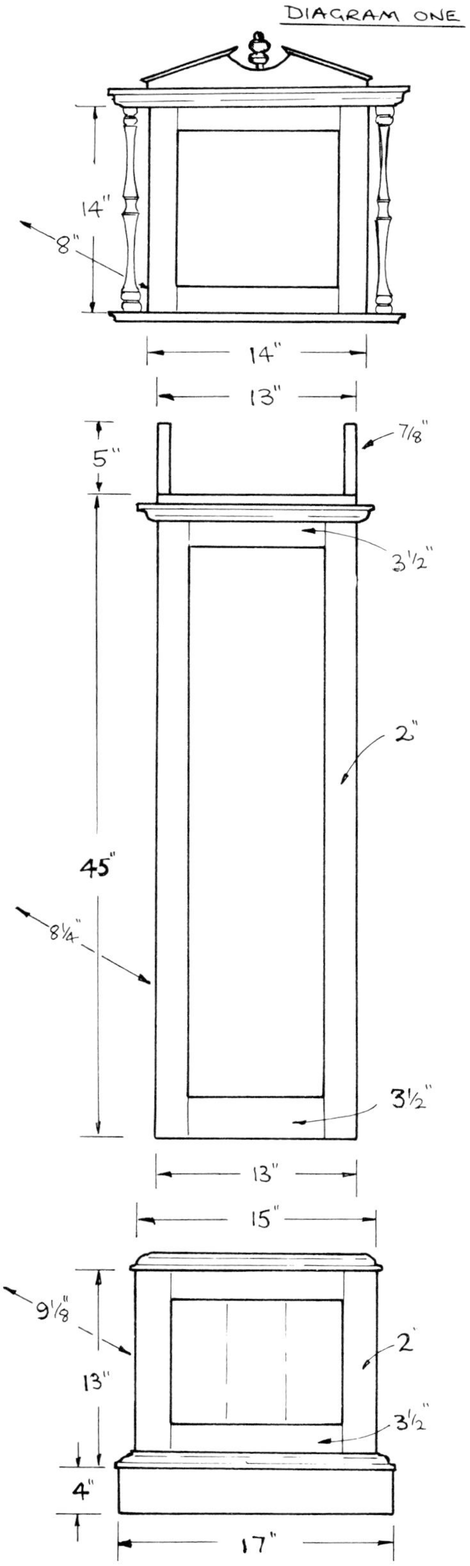

from 1in thick boards, sawn and planed to finish at the required sizes. With the exception of the back, which is of veneered ply, solid mahogany was used throughout. Veneered sheet material could be substituted for the side pieces and for the door if absolutely necessary (see Diagram One).

The required number of boards are first planed to 7/8in, then sufficient of this is sawn and edge planed to make the rails and side pieces in the construction of the base and plinth.

Plate 2 Base section – the panel for the front in cramps [clamps] in the foreground

To begin with the base: two 2in-wide side rails, 15in long, and one 11in-long top rail, together with a bottom rail also 11in long but 3½in wide, are slotted to accept the front panel as shown in Diagram Two. The panel is made up from three 3/8in pieces edge jointed together. The two side rails are rebated [rabbeted] for jointing to the side pieces which are in turn rebated [rabbeted] on their back inside edge to accommodate the back panel. The extra width of the bottom rail is required because in the assembly 1½in of it will be concealed when the plinth and plinth moulding are fitted, leaving a 2in rail visible to match in with the other rails.

The front frame is dowel jointed together – the front panel left loose in its slot, and the side pieces are added, glued and cramped [clamped] into the rebated [rabbeted] side rails. Corners are strengthened by means of glued blocks (see Diagram Three).

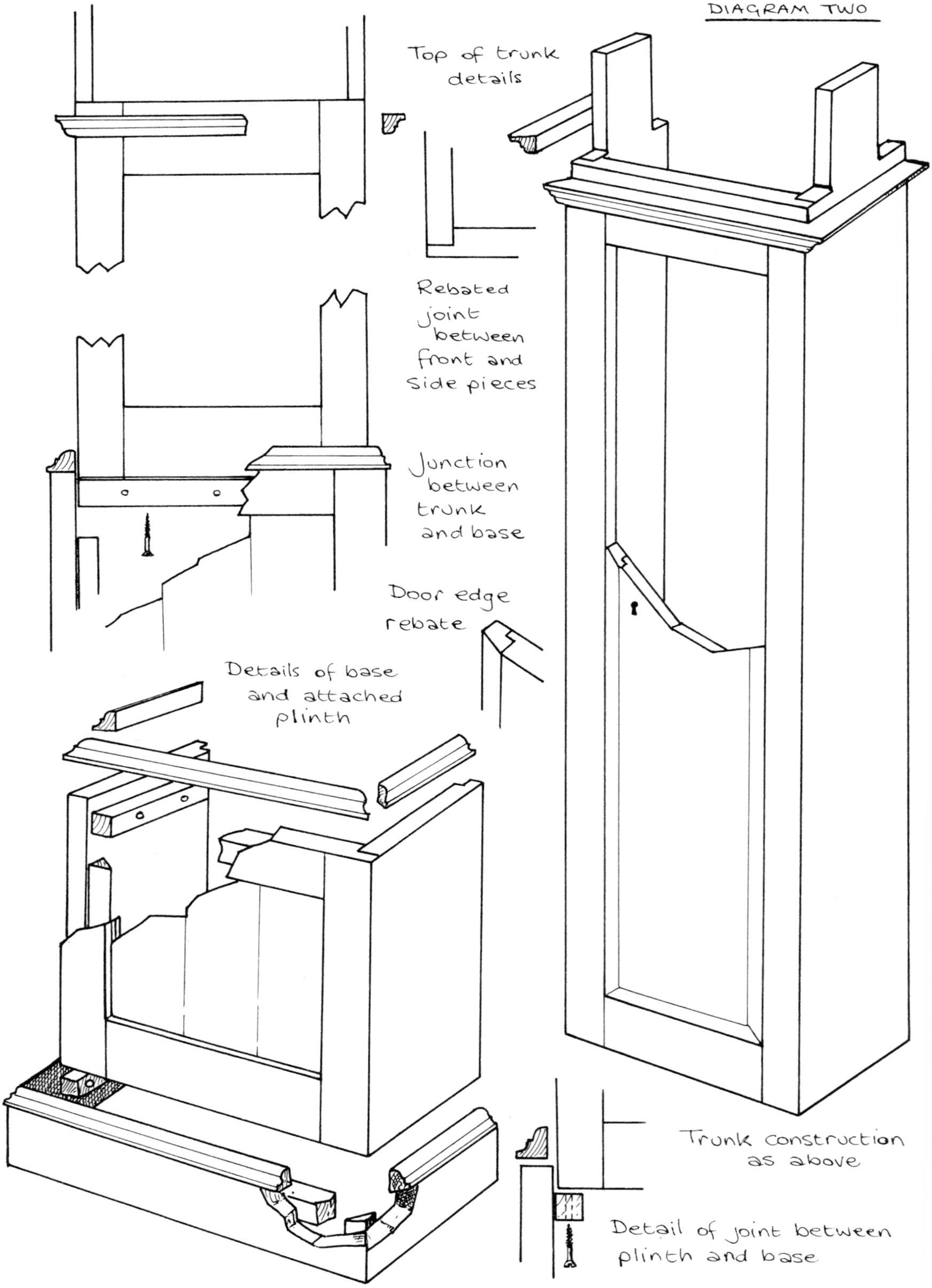
DIAGRAM TWO
Top of trunk details
Rebated joint between front and side pieces
Junction between trunk and base
Door edge rebate
Details of base and attached plinth
Trunk construction as above
Detail of joint between plinth and base

Plate 3 Fitting the moulding to the base

The plinth portion of the base is made separately, using the ⅞in material again, three pieces 4in wide. Corners are mitred and strengthened with triangular glued blocks and, for jointing to the base, blocks are glued and screwed inside. The base rests on these blocks and is held by screws which pass up through them (see detail in Diagram Two). Moulding is attached at the junction of the plinth and base, glued to both sections as this is a permanent joint.

Incidentally, where mouldings are bought in, and as these may vary in size from one source of supply to another, it is perhaps wise in some cases to have the moulding to hand and work directly to its dimensions in those areas where its fitting is critical. If the moulding obtained is too large in section it can be modified, but if it is too small there will be unsightly gaps in the finished work.

The trunk, which is basically a narrower, elongated version of the base, is constructed in a similar way with one or two important differences. In order to keep weight low down for reasons of stability the materials used in the trunk are reduced in thickness to ¾in. The two long side rails are 2in wide again, but both top and bottom rails are wider, both 3½in. As with the joining of plinth and base, 1½in of the bottom rail is concealed in the joint between base and trunk, while at the top of the trunk the same thing happens in the joint between it and the hood.

For the trunk the two long side rails are 45in long, top and bottom rails 9in long. Their inside edges are left plain for the inset door, but the two long rails are rebated [rabbeted] as before for the solid side pieces. These are ¾in thick and 8in wide and have the rebate [rabbet] along their back inside edges to accommodate the back panel. Note that the side pieces extend above the top moulding for several inches to provide location for the hood and, where required, to act as supports for the seat board used to carry some types of clock movement. The front frame is dowel jointed, then all is glued up and cramped [clamped] as described previously.

The trunk rests on and is joined to the base by means of screws which pass up through blocks glued and screwed in the base (see detail in Diagram Two). Carry out this work with base and trunk lying horizontal – it's easier that way – but if you are of average height or less it's easier still to leave the joining together until later. Further work on the trunk and fitting the hood are both best done with the trunk separate from the base and

Plate 4 Base and trunk nearing completion

Plate 5 Base and trunk joined together. Door not yet fitted.

In many clock-case designs the making of the hood is often the most difficult part, partly because of its function but also partly due to an obsession, it seems, to make them as complex as possible with elaborate over-ornamentation of the area surrounding the clock face. The hood's function is simply to house and protect the clock movement and to display adequately the clock's face so that one may ascertain with ease the time of day or night. Access to the clock movement is necessary and this is usually provided for by making the hood so that it slides forward and lifts off the case. Separate and easier access to the clock face is also required and for this the glass front is usually hinged.

The hood of this clock meets these criteria without being too complex or over-elaborate. For added security it is made to lift up and off rather than slide forward for access to the movement. Access through a hinged door at the back as at the front would probably have been even more simple. The hood holds an 11in-square face or dial and will accommodate a variety of clock movements. Suppliers of movements and faces give dimensions in their catalogues and it is

Plate 6 Door under cramping [clamping] pressure after gluing on rebated [rabbeted] lipping

left standing upright on the floor for the time being.

The door to this clock case is of solid construction, but it could be framed up and panelled; or, if a weighted or pendulum movement were to be fitted the door could be framed and glazed. A nicely figured piece of mahogany was chosen and planed to $^5/_8$in in thickness and this then had a lipping, mitred at the corners, rebated [rabbeted] on all around. A slight chamfer was given to the front face of the lipping and, when hung, the door is slightly proud of the surrounding frame. Because the door is inset it should initially be made a little oversize and trimmed carefully to be a nice fit in the door frame.

Final work on the trunk is to fit 1in mouldings to top and bottom. Both are positioned $^1/_2$in in from the end of the trunk as shown in Diagram Three. This $^1/_2$in projection beyond the moulding facilitates joining to base and hood.

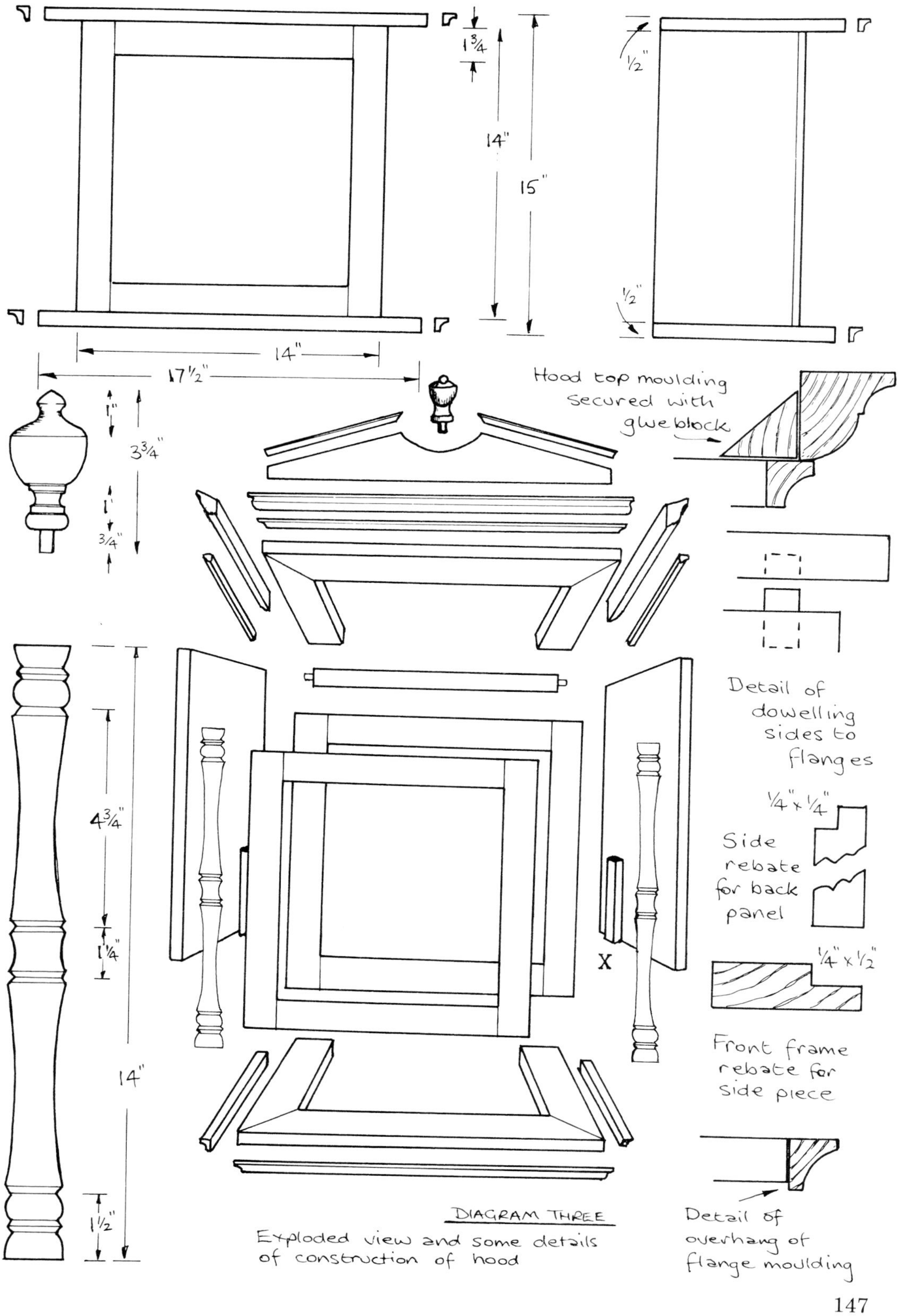

DIAGRAM THREE

Exploded view and some details of construction of hood

as well to check these against the dimensions given here.

Based on the front frame measurements of a 14in square, the hood is again purposely made lighter in weight than the rest of the case for added stability. The front frame and the identical frame for the hinged door both have $1^3/_4 \times {}^5/_8$in rails and the side pieces are of only $^1/_2$in thickness. The door frame is rebated all around its inside edges to accommodate a pane of glass. Top and bottom of the hood consist of two partial frames or flanges made up as shown in Diagram Three. These are dowelled to the front frame and side pieces to make a solid-sided but otherwise open box. A back rail dowelled across the top at the rear of the hood helps stiffen the construction.

The internal measurement across the hood should be such as to allow it to slide down easily each side of the extensions to the side pieces of the trunk above the top moulding. This measurement should be 13in, but it is as well to check it. A strip of wood glued inside each side of the hood retains the hood when it is in position. This is the item marked X in Diagram Three. Furthermore, the hood's external dimensions should enable it to sit correctly on the top edge of the trunk and to match in with the top moulding thereon, so some careful measurements should be taken.

To enclose the hood, a top is fitted and this may simply be a rectangle of wood or of plywood, glued and screwed to the top of the top flange. It is concealed by the hood top moulding. The ply back, which encloses the back of the base and trunk and extends up behind the hood, is cut to size and fitted into the prepared rebate in all three sections but fixed only to the base and trunk by small screws.

The illustrations in Diagram Three show that the two hood flanges have a narrow moulding applied to their outward edges. This helps the lower flange to blend with the top trunk moulding and, if the flange moulding is fitted with a slight downward overhang, as shown in the detail in the diagram, this helps conceal the joint between the two. To the top flange is added a further piece of 1in moulding to balance the lower arrangement and above this is fitted a shaped pediment and turned finial. Two turned pillars are added, one to each side of the hood, these being simply cut to a nice fit between the two flanges to which they are glued and held by a panel pin, top and bottom.

An 11in-square brass face was purchased from an horological supplier and, in this instance, was fitted behind the front frame by means of small screws in its corners. An electronic quartz clock movement was fitted

Plate 7 The hood nearing completion

Plate 8 Face and fingers fitted into the hood

– these are very light in weight and are held by means of a threaded spigot which simply passes through the central hole in the face where it is secured with a small knurled nut. A clock case of such stature demands a genuine mechanical movement and, perhaps, one day such a movement will be fitted. Meanwhile, the quartz keeps time with quiet accuracy and does not need winding up.

Ideally, the case should have been French polished, but instead it was lightly stained to bring the mahogany to a uniform colour after which it was sealed with two applications of clear matt polyurethane well rubbed down between each coat. Finally, it was polished with a proprietary [commercial] wax polish. Subsequent polishing will enhance the warm tones of the mahogany.

MATERIAL REQUIREMENTS LIST. (CUTTING LIST IN INCHES)

No	PURPOSE	MATERIAL	INITIAL SIZES	
	PLINTH			
1	FRONT	MAHOGANY	17 × 4 × 7/8	PLANED
2	SIDES	"	10 × 4 × 7/8	–
	BASE			
2	SIDEPIECES	"	13 × 9 × 7/8	PLANED & REBATED
2	VERTICAL RAILS	"	13 × 2 × 7/8	"
1	TOP RAIL	"	11 × 2 × 7/8	–
1	BOTTOM RAIL	"	11 × 3½ × 7/8	–
1	FRONT PANEL	"	15¾ × 10¼ × 3/8	EDGEGLUED
	TRUNK			
2	SIDEPIECES	"	50 × 8 × 3/4	PLANED & REBATED
2	VERTICAL RAILS	"	45 × 2 × 3/4	PLANED
1	TOP RAIL	"	9 × 3½ × 3/4	–
1	BOTTOM RAIL	"	9 × 3½ × 3/4	–
1	DOOR	"	37 × 8 × 5/8	–
	DOOR EDGING	"	3/4 × 5/8 ABOUT 8 ft.	REBATED

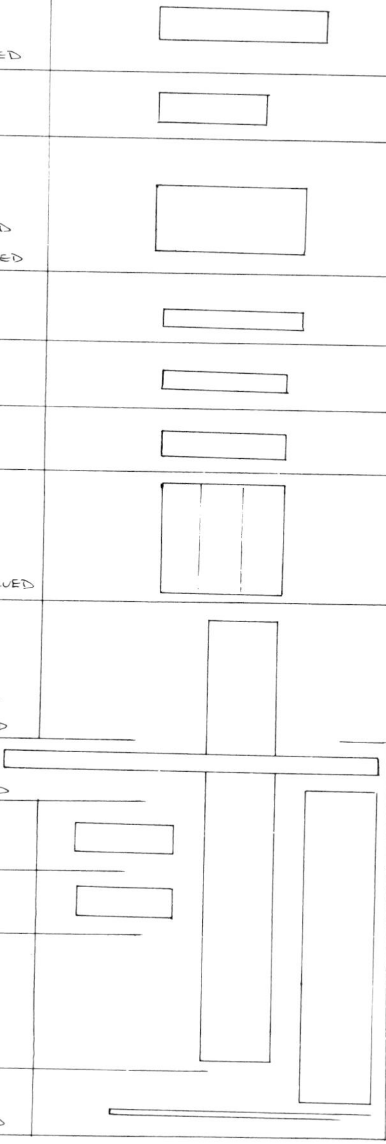

MATERIAL REQUIREMENTS LIST. continued

No.	PURPOSE	MATERIAL	INITIAL SIZES	
	HOOD			
2	SIDEPIECES	MAHOGANY	14 × 1 3/4 × 5/8	PLANED & REBATED
4	VERTICAL RAILS	"	14 × 8 × 1/2	"
2	TOP RAILS	"	14 × 1 3/4 × 5/8	PLANED
2	BOTTOM RAILS	"	14 × 1 3/4 × 5/8	"
2	FLANGE FRONTS	"	16 × 1 1/2 × 1/2	"
4	FLANGE SIDES	"	10 × 1 1/2 × 1/2	"
1	BACK RAIL	"	13 × 1 1/2 × 1	"
1	PEDIMENT	"	16 × 3 × 1/2	PLANED & SHAPED
2	PILLARS	"	15 × 1 1/4 × 1 1/4	TURNED
1	FINIAL	"	4 × 2 × 2	"
1	BACK	VENEERED PLYWOOD	80 × 14 × 3/16	CUT TO SHAPE

1 INCH. MAHOGANY MOULDING, 12 FT. 1/2 INCH MAHOGANY MOULDING. 8 FT.
SCRAP PIECES FOR GLUE BLOCKS. WOOD SCREWS FOR BASE. GLASS, 11" × 11"

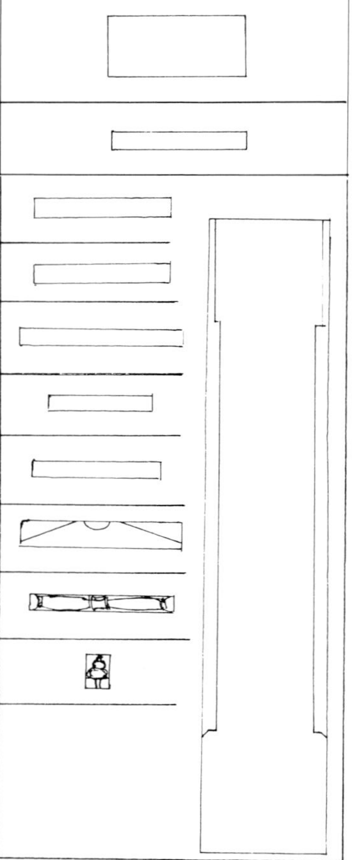

12

Welsh Dresser

Illustrated on page 136

The so-called Welsh dresser was and still is made in many different areas and there are a number of regional variations ranging from Devon to the North of England. The cupboard bottom, originally used without the tall dresser back and in general use mainly in farm and cottage kitchens from the early part of the eighteenth century, appears to have developed from the medieval raised board on which to stand cups – hence cupboard. While in wealthy households this simple board developed in tiers to become the more elaborate court cupboard or buffet, in the cottagers' homes drawers and cupboard doors were added. Some were used with an open plate rack fixed to the wall behind and this in turn gave rise to the tall dresser back with which we are familiar today.

J. C. Louden, in his *Encyclopaedia of Cottage, Farm and Villa Architecture*, published in 1833, tells us that:

> dressers are fixtures essential to every kitchen, but more especially to that of the cottager, to whom they serve both as dressers and sideboards. They are generally made of deal (pine) by local joiners, and seldom painted, it being the pride of good housewives, in most parts of England, to keep the boards of which they are composed as white as snow by frequently scouring them with fine sand.

In its familiar form, comprising of a lower part containing cupboards and drawers and an attached tall back with shelves, shaped side uprights and moulded top, it is a well-known and much-loved example of traditional country furniture.

The example shown and described here was designed and made throughout in pine by furniture-making colleague and friend of mine, Ian Massey. It goes without saying that good-quality pine should be chosen; there is a lot of second-grade wood on the market intended primarily for the building trade and this should not be used for furniture making. The pine should be well seasoned and free from loose knots and shakes (splits); furthermore, as the boarded back and panels are an important feature of this design, the boards used should be well matched.

Begin by making the lower, cupboard section and start this by making up its carcase as shown in Diagram One. For clarity, this exploded view has been purposely kept simple, its main objective being to show the basic method of construction; details and dimensions can be found in the Materials Requirement List (p159) and elsewhere. Again, for simplicity – why make life complicated when there is no need? – it will be noted that most of the carcase timber sizes have been standardised as far as possible. The four legs or corner posts are $2\frac{1}{4} \times 2\frac{1}{4}$in, while most of the various rails are $2\frac{1}{4} \times 1$in.

All the timber is prepared to size and marked out as required. Mortices are cut in the corner posts (A) and top and bottom end rails (B) are tenoned into them to form a pair of end frames. Where panels are to be fitted directly into these end frames they will need to be slotted to accept their panels. Details of this method are given on p36 and again on p103 in the chapter on the oak chest. However, because the piece of furniture being described was made as part of a complete kitchen a somewhat different method was adopted. The entire carcase was put together without slotting and separate framed panels were made and inserted at each end. Whatever method is chosen, these frame ends are joined together by means of the top front and back rails and bottom front and back rails to form the main carcase framing. Top rails (Diagram One, C) are

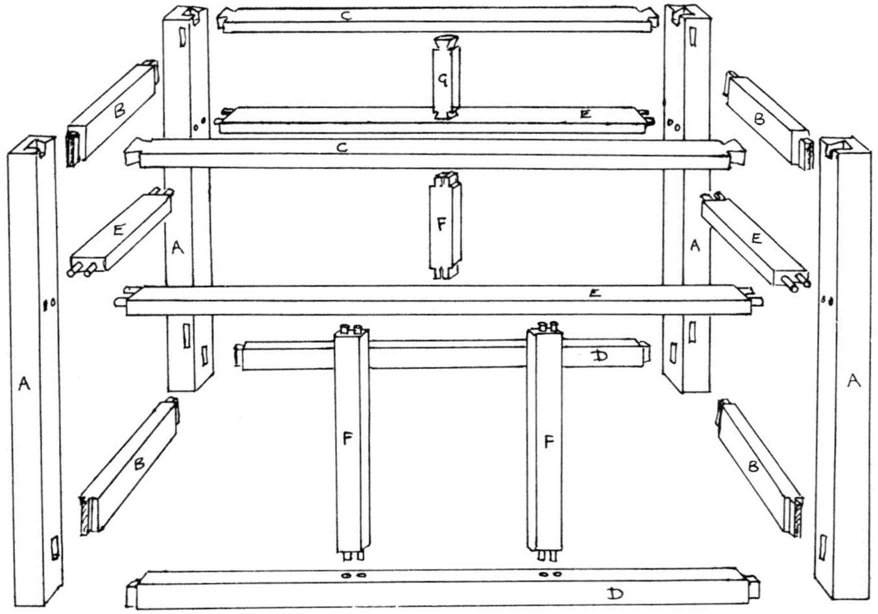

DIAGRAM ONE

Main components of lower section shown in exploded view

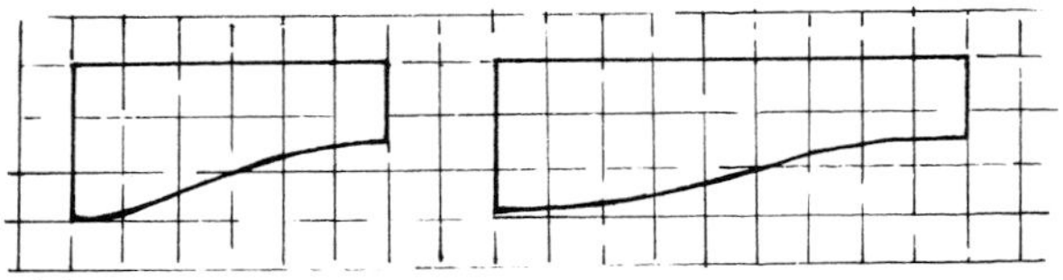

1ins squares

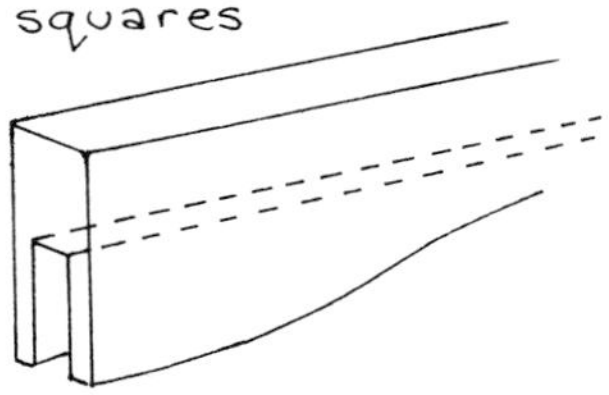

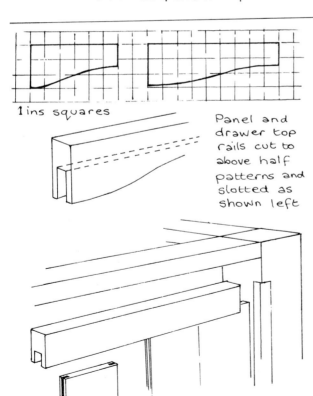

Panel and drawer top rails cut to above half patterns and slotted as shown left

Above, Cupboard end panel

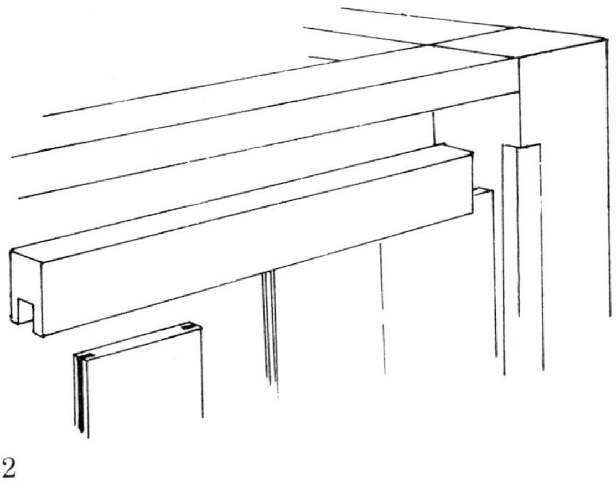

DIAGRAM TWO

Detail to show how the back panel of cupboard is made up and fitted into rebate

Plate 1 The lower section partially completed

dovetailed into sockets cut into the top of the corner posts and may be further strengthened by dowelled fillets dovetailed into the side rails; bottom rails (Diagram One, D) are joined to corner posts by means of mortice-and-tenon joints.

It is a good idea to assemble this basic carcase frame dry in order to check all joints for fit and squareness. It is at this stage also when final decisions about the arrangement of drawers and cupboards can be made. The arrangement used here can be altered to suit individual requirements, but as this affects the placement of intermediary carcase components such as drawer rails, uprights and shelf bearers, any changes must be made now before the next stage begins.

In this design the client required two drawers and one continuous cupboard with two opening doors, the centre 'door' being a fixed panel. Bearing firmly in mind the drawer sizes and the dimensions of the cupboard doors (together with the fact that these overlie the front drawer rails and front uprights), mark out the carcase members and the intermediary rails, etc, jointed into them. Most of these joints are shown dowelled and this is quite adequate. Alternatively, mortice and tenons could be used, as in other parts of the carcase, for fixing drawer rails (E) to corner posts while front uprights (F) could be through-tenoned and wedged into rails. The short back intermediary rail, known as the muntin, (G) can be similarly jointed but is shown in the diagram with the more desirable single dovetails top and bottom.

These intermediary members serve a number of purposes: they delineate the position of drawer and cupboard-door spaces; drawer rails take some of the weight and sliding action of drawers while uprights may provide firm fixing for cupboard doors and, last but by no means least, they add considerable strength to the complete carcase.

The end panels, mentioned earlier, are made as described before on p36, with two minor changes. The usual practice of the frame slot being made one-third the thickness of the frame was not followed. The panels are made up from the same loose-tongued boards as used in the dresser back and, as a consequence of their being $\frac{7}{16}$in thick, this leaves a full $\frac{1}{4}$in each side of the slot in the 1in frame; in this case, an adequate amount. The shaped top rail is cut from a piece 3 × 1in. Cupboard doors are similarly constructed. The framed panels are made a close fit in each of the carcase ends and are secured by screws through from the inside of the top and bottom end rails.

The back of the cupboard is also made from the tongued boards fixed vertically in a simple panel arrangement. This is made up of slotted top and bottom rails into which are fitted the tongued boards, as shown. Only the two end boards are glued into place; the others are left free to take account of any subsequent movement in the wood. This back panel is secured by screws into a rebate [rabbet] cut into the back inner edge of each of the back corner posts. It fits under the back top rail and is there further held by woodscrews (Diagram Two).

Drawer and kickers can now be fitted as described on p37. Then it is time to make the drawers – the part everyone has been looking forward to (or dreading!) Follow the directions and diagrams on pp37–9, work carefully, and success will be yours.

Two important changes to note with the drawers for this project are, first, that they have panelled fronts to match with the cupboard doors and end panels and secondly that they overlie the front top and drawer rails and the centre muntin. Simply make up plain-fronted drawers to fit the drawer openings and ensure they run easily against runners and guides and then make suitable front panels to fit, securing them to the drawers by means of screws through from the inside. In this case there is no need to make lap dovetails on the drawer fronts as they are covered by the front panels (Diagram Three).

Three identical cupboard doors are made, the two outer ones hinged from the corner posts to close half over the two front uprights. The centre 'door', as has already been mentioned, is fixed in by being screwed into place half over the two uprights and through the drawer rail and bottom rail. The cupboard bottom consists of tongued boards running front to back and supported on the front and back bottom rails.

Because the top of the cupboard was required for use as a kitchen working surface, a substantial top was made from $1\frac{1}{2}$in pine boards, edge joined and dowelled. Its front corners were rounded and a $\frac{1}{2}$in ogee moulding worked round its upper edge. The top is made to overlap front and sides and is secured into place by pocket screwing.

With the lower section completed, work can now begin on the dresser back. The simplified exploded view in Diagram Four shows the principle of construction. Once

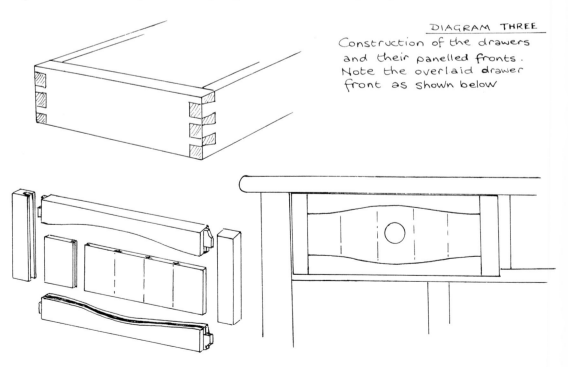

DIAGRAM THREE
Construction of the drawers and their panelled fronts. Note the overlaid drawer front as shown below

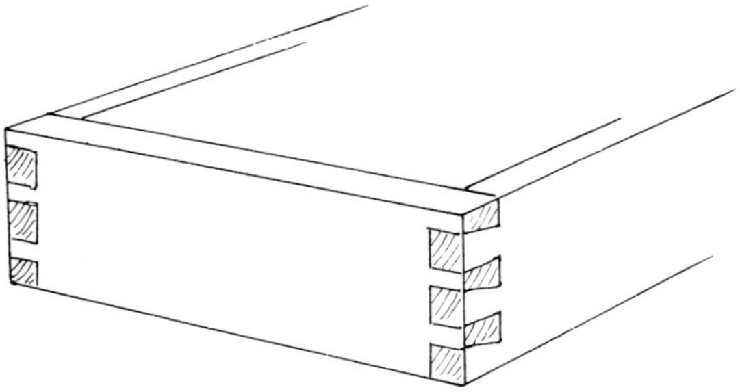

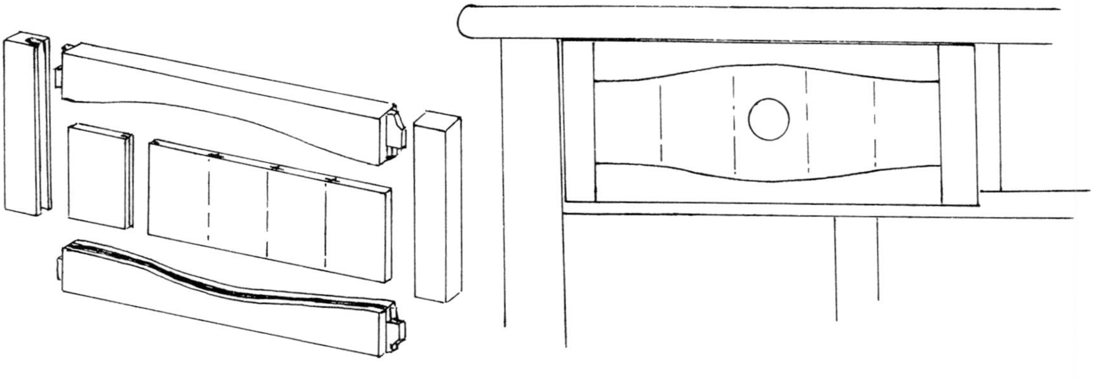

Plate 2 Fitting the top to the lower section

Plate 3 (*below*) Completed lower section

the overall height and the number and arrangement of shelves is decided upon, prepare the two end uprights (1). Single boards of this width, 10in, are available, but they must be sound and well seasoned for they must not 'cup' in use. If there is any doubt, edge joint two narrower boards to make up the width as was done in this case. These uprights are band sawn to a wavy edge according to the shelf arrangement. The top frieze (2) may also be shaped at the same time. Uprights and frieze are finished with spokeshave and, finally, glass-paper [sand-paper].

As the shelves are held in stopped housings in the uprights these are next cut in. The stop gives a neater appearance from the front but don't forget to cut the shelves long enough to reach into both housings and to notch the front of each shelf to take care of the stopped end. The back inner edge of the two uprights has to be rebated [rabbeted] to accommodate the back boards. Now the top and bottom rails (Diagram Four, 3) can be dovetailed into the uprights which in effect makes up the frame into which the back boards will eventually be fitted. The dovetails are glued in and work begun on the top.

The top (4), which can be of edge-joined

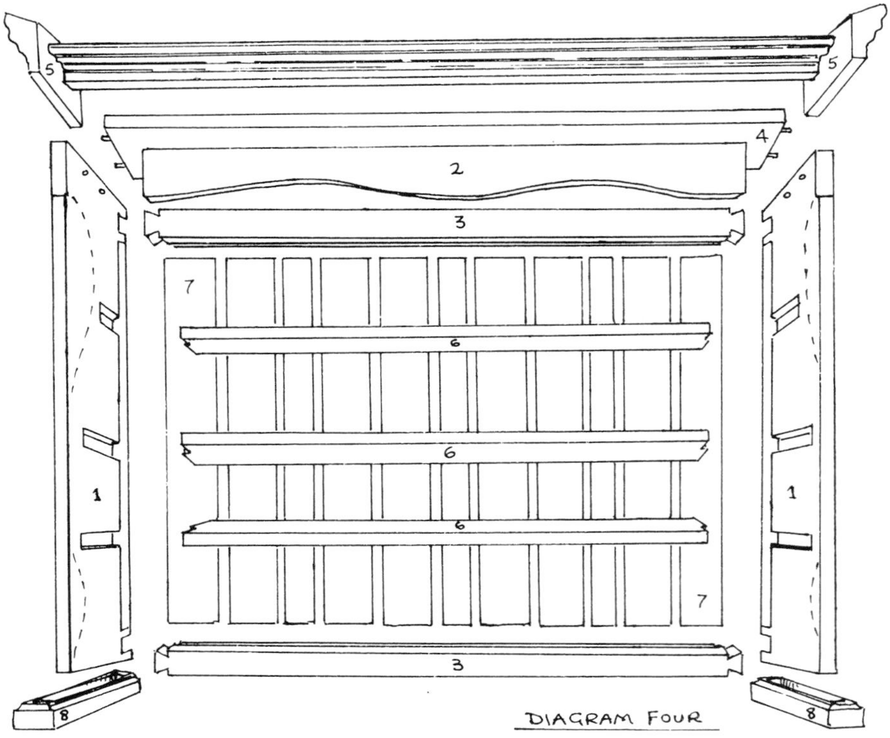

Exploded view of upper section

Plate 4 Completed upper section

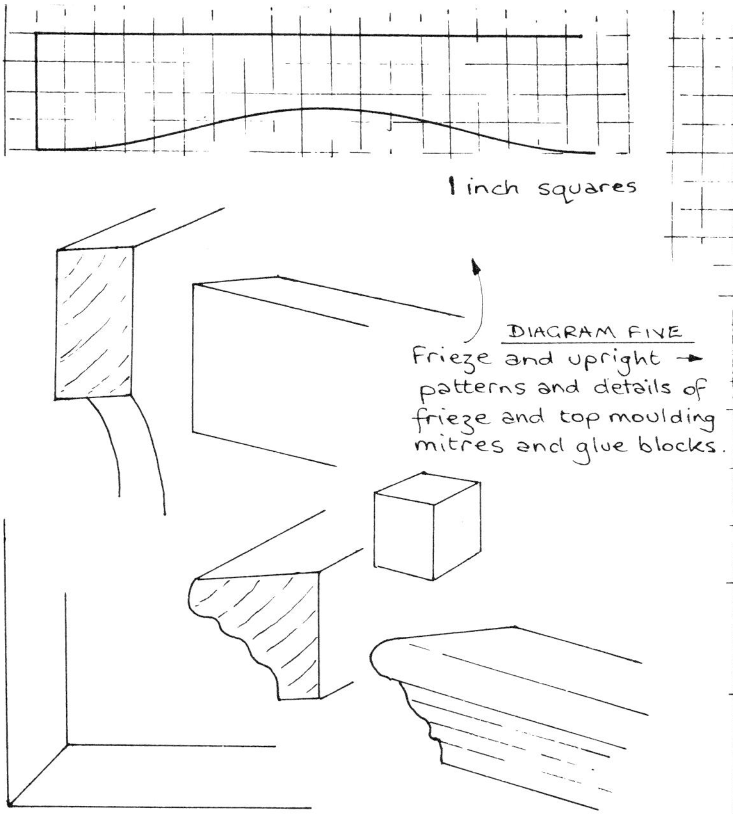

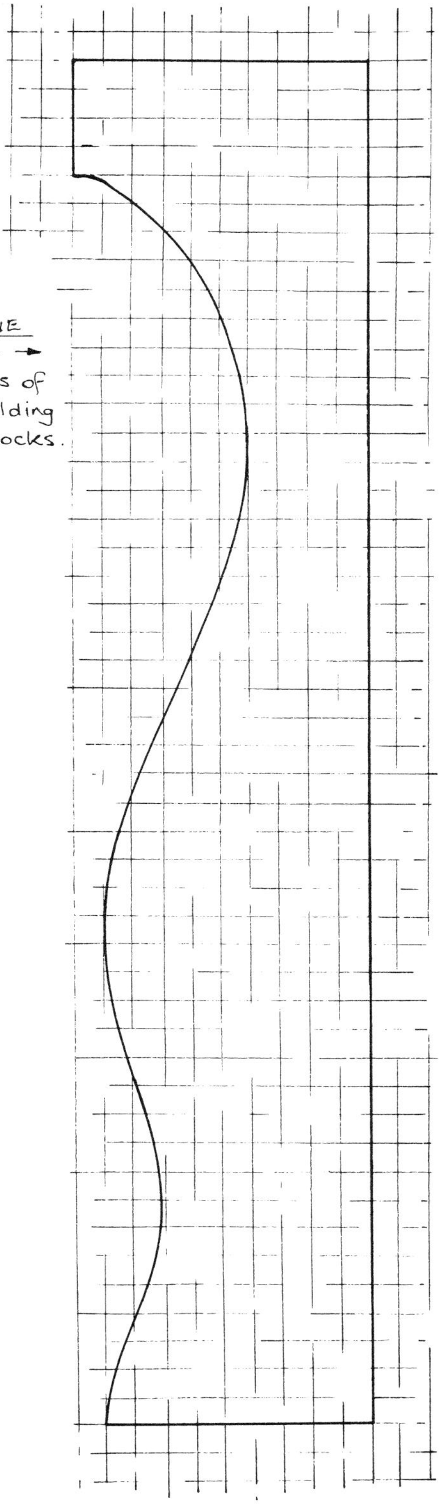

narrow boards to make up the width, is secured to the uprights by means of dowels. The shaped frieze is now attached and the top completed by a deep attached moulding (Diagram Four, 5) fixed to the front and two side edges of the top board. The corners of the moulding are mitred and glued blocks help to support it. Details are given in Diagram Five.

Shelves (Diagram Four, 6) are cut to length and notched for the stopped housing in the uprights. Their front edges can be gently rounded and you may like to run a round-bottomed groove along the length of one or two of the shelves, about 1¼in from their back edge to act as a plate groove. This prevents plates displayed on their edge from sliding forward and the groove is much nicer than the quadrant beading sometimes placed on shelves for the same purpose.

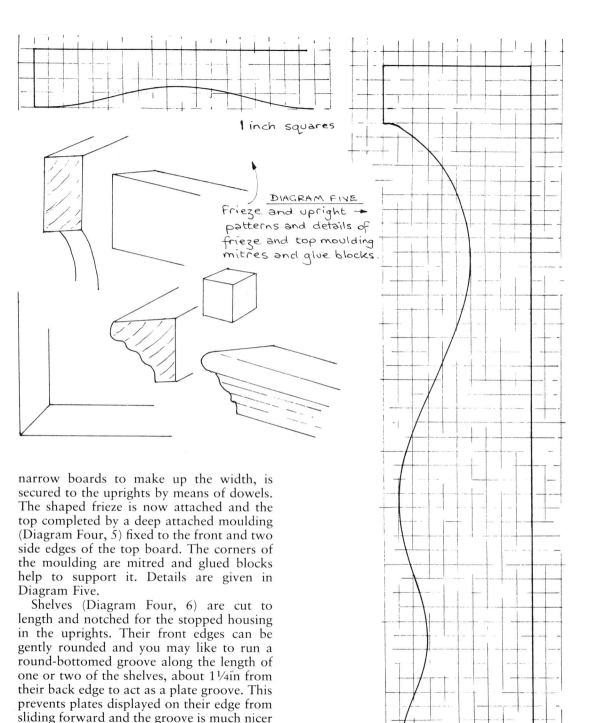

With the shelves slid into place the back can now be fitted. The tongued boards used in the back are accommodated in the rebate in the two uprights and are screwed or panel pinned to the top and bottom back rails. For aesthetic reasons the boards were made in two widths and arranged, as may be noted, with two wide boards interspaced with a narrower one.

One final job: for stability each upright is fitted with a foot (Diagram Four, 8), basically a thicker and wider piece of wood with the end of the upright going into a housing in its upper surface. There are numerous ideas about fixing top sections to bottom sections – and some about not fixing them at all. Some advocate pocket-screwing through the bottom rail of the dresser back down into the cupboard top or screws up through the top and into the bottom rail, or metal plates (mirror plates) to join the two halves together, and so on. Often a short dowel at each end helps locate the top section in position and the rest is left to gravity, the weight of the top being enough to keep it there. If a fixing must be used, I personally favour the mirror plates; they are totally adequate and don't mar the surface of the cupboard section should it be used without the shelves.

Ideas about finishing pine have ranged widely, from no finish at all – just scrubbing with sand – through painting, staining and most recently, polyurethane, usually the high-gloss variety. My preference is to use a satin-finish polyurethane, well thinned and applied initially with a brush as a sealer. When thoroughly dry, rub down the first coat with fine glass-paper [sandpaper] or wire wool and apply one or two further coats in a dust-free place, carefully rubbing down each coat when dry.

MATERIALS REQUIREMENT LIST. (CUTTING LIST IN INCHES)

Nº	PURPOSE	INITIAL SIZES		
	FOR CUPBOARD SECTION			
4	CORNER POSTS	36 × 2¼ × 2¼	Planed	
4	END RAILS	18 × 2¼ × 1	"	
2	TOP RAILS	48 × 2¼ × 1	"	
2	BOTTOM RAILS	48 × 2¼ × 1	"	
2	DRAWER RAILS	48 × 2¼ × 1	"	
2	DRAWER RUNNERS	18 × 2¼ × 1	Shaped	
1	CENTRE RAIL	18 × 3 × 1	Planed	
2	DRAWER MUNTINS	11 × 2 × 1	"	
2	CUPBOARD MUNTINS	24 × 2 × 1	"	
12	BACKBOARDS	32 × 4 × 5/16	Tongued	
2	B/board RAILS		Planed	
1	CUPBOARD TOP	52 × 21 × 1½ (3 @ 52 × 7 × 1½)	Edge joined	
	FOR END PANELS & CUPBOARD DOORS			
4	END UPRIGHTS	32 × 1½ × 1	Planed	
2	END RAILS	14 × 3 × 1	"	
2	END RAILS	14 × 1½ × 1	"	
2	PANELS	30 × 13 × 5/16 (4 @ 30 × 3¼ × 5/16)	Tongued	
6	DOOR UPRIGHTS	24 × 1½ × 1	Planed	
3	DOOR RAILS	14 × 3 × 1	Shaped	
3	DOOR RAILS	14 × 1½ × 1	Planed	
3	DOOR PANELS	24 × 13 × 5/16 (4 @ 24 × 3¼ × 5/16)	Tongued	

№	PURPOSE	INITIAL SIZES		
	FOR DRAWERS & DRAWER FRONTS			
2	DRAWER FRONTS	22 × 8 × 1	Planed	
4	DRAWER SIDES	19 × 8 × 3/4	"	
2	DRAWER BACKS	22 × 6 × 1/2	"	
2	DRAWER BOTTOMS	20 × 18 × 1/4		
4	FRONT RAILS	21 × 3 × 1	Shaped	
4	END PIECES	9 × 1 1/2 × 1	Planed	
2	PANELS	13 × 7 × 5/16 (5∂7 × 4 × 5/16)	Tongued	
	FOR DRESSER SECTION			
2	UPRIGHTS	48 × 10 × 1	Shaped	
2	BACK RAILS	48 × 2 × 1	Planed	
1	FRIEZE	48 × 4 × 1	Shaped	
1	FRIEZE RAIL	48 × 1 × 1	Planed	
1	TOP	48 × 10 × 1	"	
2	SHELVES	48 × 8 × 1	"	
1	SHELF	48 × 3 × 1	"	
1	FRONT MOULDING	48 × 2 1/2 (approx)	Mitred	
2	SIDE MOULDINGS	12 × 2 1/2 (approx)	"	
8	BACKBOARDS	48 × 4 × 5/16	Tongued	
3	BACKBOARDS	48 × 2 × 5/16	"	
2	FEET	12 × 2 1/4 × 2 1/4		

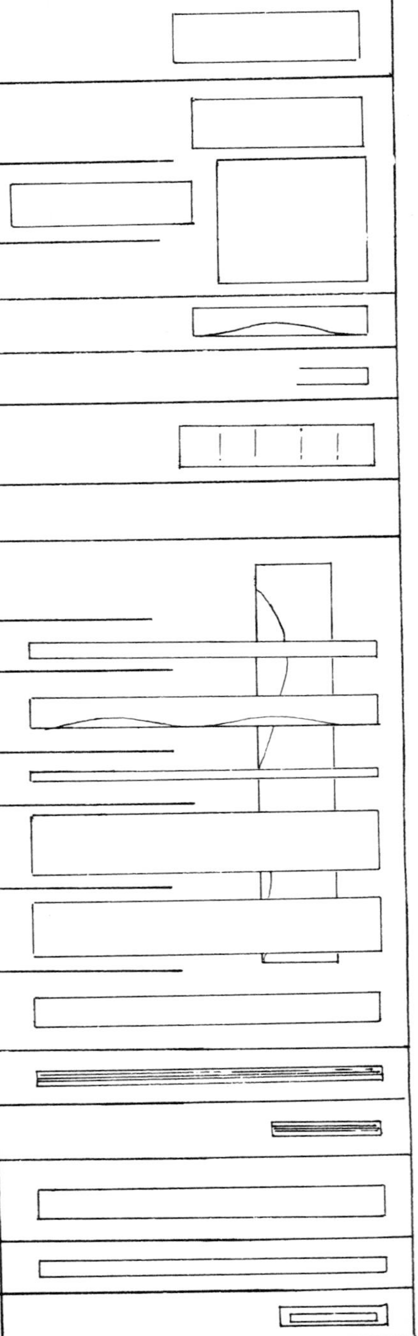

13
Half-round Hall Table

Illustrated on page 84

This type of table comes in various forms and has several uses and numerous names. From the early seventeenth century it was in use in the dining-room and known as a side table, the first examples massively made and three-legged. In Georgian times, four-legged versions with folding tops were popular for use as card tables. Later it became fashionable to use them in pairs, in alcoves or between windows, and these were often carved and extravagantly gilded. Some had marble tops. Sheraton introduced a much simpler form with delicate lines and tapered legs. Smaller side tables came to be used in the hallway and along corridor walls and these became known as hall tables. Some, today, call them semi-circular, bow-fronted or 'D' tables.

The version described here was made to a client's commission to fit into a small hallway. It was made in teak and the turned legs and the teak were chosen to blend in with other furniture in the hall. Iroko is an acceptable substitute for teak or another hardwood and a different treatment of the legs could be effectively used.

It is only fair to begin by saying that the most problematic part of this project is the curved or bow front. There are two or three ways of doing this. First, it can be made as one continuous piece or secondly, it can be made up of three separate parts. For either method solid or laminated wood may be used depending on the sweep of the curve, the wood being used and its thickness. For a table of this small size any of these methods is feasible and the choice is up to the individual. I chose to make it as one continuous piece using laminated material. This helps towards a sound and relatively straightforward method of construction. The alternative methods will be discussed, but first the laminated, continuous piece method will be described.

The first task is to make a bending former [form]. Shown in Diagram One, the male half of the former [form] can be fabricated using shaped wood blocks sandwiched between two sheets of ½in ply. The outside curve is formed of a continuous piece of ⅛in hardboard or ply. Its completed size must correspond to the inside radius of the front

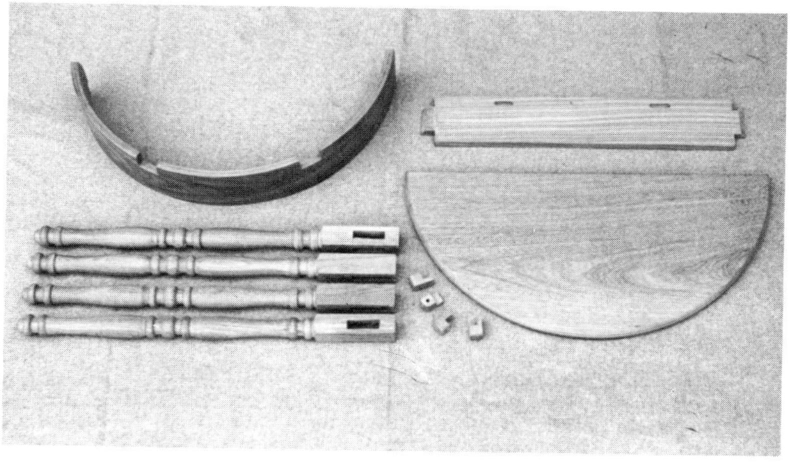

Plate 1 Parts for the half-round hall table

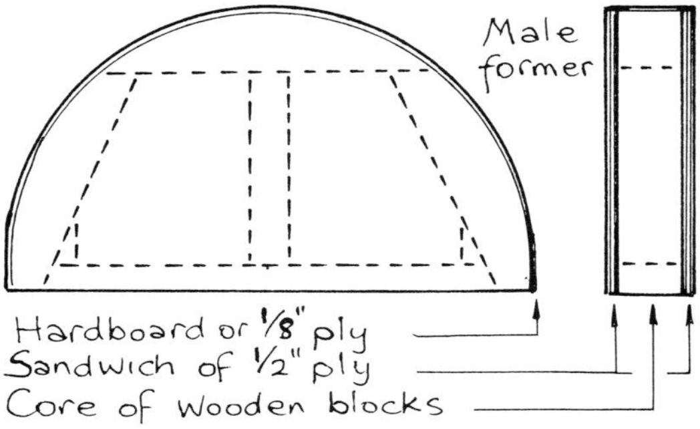

DIAGRAM ONE

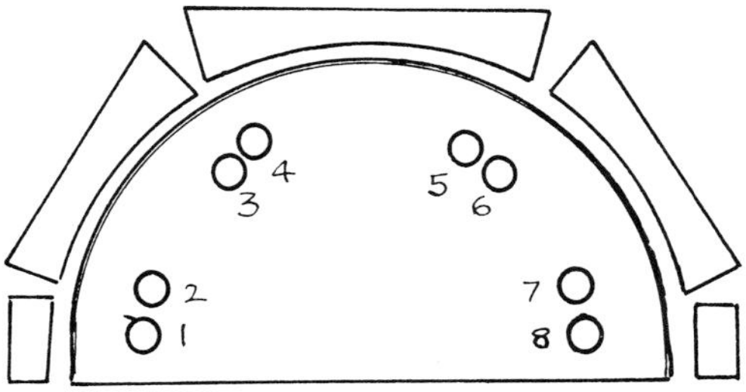

Position of female formers and G cramp location holes

curved rail and to its width; in this case the radius is 11½in and the width 4½in. The shaped blocks which form the female parts of the former [form] have an inside radius not of the male former [form] but of the outside radius of the front rail, in this case, 12¼in. The formers [forms] must be strong enough to withstand the stresses imposed upon them when the glued laminae [laminates] are cramped [clamped] up under pressure. For locating the G-cramps [C-clamps] used to do this, 2in holes are made through the outer layer of ply on the male former [form].

For laminating, furniture veneers may be used, but as these are normally quite thin they will take longer to glue and build up to make the required thickness. Thicker veneers, known as constructional veneers, are made and these at 1/10in in thickness are a better proposition if they can be obtained; or you can do as I did and cut the laminae [laminates] individually from the solid. This is not as difficult as it sounds if machinery is available, ie a circular saw and possibly a planer, but do not try sawing them by hand. Laminae [laminates] a little over the required length and width were cut 3/16in thick and lightly planed to ⅛in. A scraper could do this last stage of the work. Six pieces at ⅛in make up the ¾in thickness required. When making the bend, a continuous outer band of ⅛in ply or hardboard helps to protect the outside surface of the curve and evens out cramping [clamping] pressure.

Bends of laminated wood will retain their shape and will not straighten out because each lamina [laminate] is concentric and of a slightly smaller radius than its neighbour. The adhesive used effectively bonds each piece firmly in position. Tests have shown that well-made laminated sections are actually stronger and stiffer than solid timbers of the same dimensions. The most suitable adhesive would be one of the synthetic resins such as Cascamite or Aerolite.

Success lies in good preparation – a suitable former [form] and adequate means of applying evenly distributed pressure to the work, the use of straight-grained wood and a suitable adhesive and, above all, an organised approach to the work; don't

Plate 2 Laminae [laminates] for the curved front being glued up

Plate 3 Laminae cramped up on a bending jig

fumble about looking for cramps [clamps] halfway through the job, don't run out of adhesive and don't answer the telephone! An extra pair of hands can sometimes be useful.

To assist glue-adhesion work in a warm environment, coat one inside surface of each lamina [laminate] with glue, line up the stack and place centrally on the former [form]. A centre mark is helpful. Place the outer band and the centre segmented female former [form] in position and apply light pressure with G-cramps [C-clamps] 4 and 5 (see Diagram One). Then, working left or right, bend one end down to the former [form], put a second segmented piece in place and hold down with the next G-cramp [C-clamp], either 3 or 6. Add cramps [clamps] 2 or 7 and 1 or 8 and repeat on the opposite side, still applying only light pressure at this stage. After checking that the stack of laminae [laminates], outer band and segmented formers [forms] are all nicely in line, apply full pressure on the cramps [clamps], working from the top centre outwards. Wipe off any surplus glue and leave to set. When dry, the rail is cleaned up and sanded.

Plate 4 The curved front being cleaned up after gluing

Plate 5 The leg being turned on a lathe

Plate 6 Bridle joints fix the front legs to the curved front

The four legs, made from 1¾in square stock, were turned as shown. The legs could, of course, be left square or preferably tapered. Whatever their final shape, the top 5in should be left square to accommodate the jointing in of the top rails. A bridle joint method is used for the two front legs and the front curved rail housed where they join. Where the curved front rail meets the rear legs a mortice-and-tenon joint is used and the back rail is similarly joined into these legs also (see Diagram Two, B for details).

Plate 7 Mortice and tenons join the curved front to the rear legs

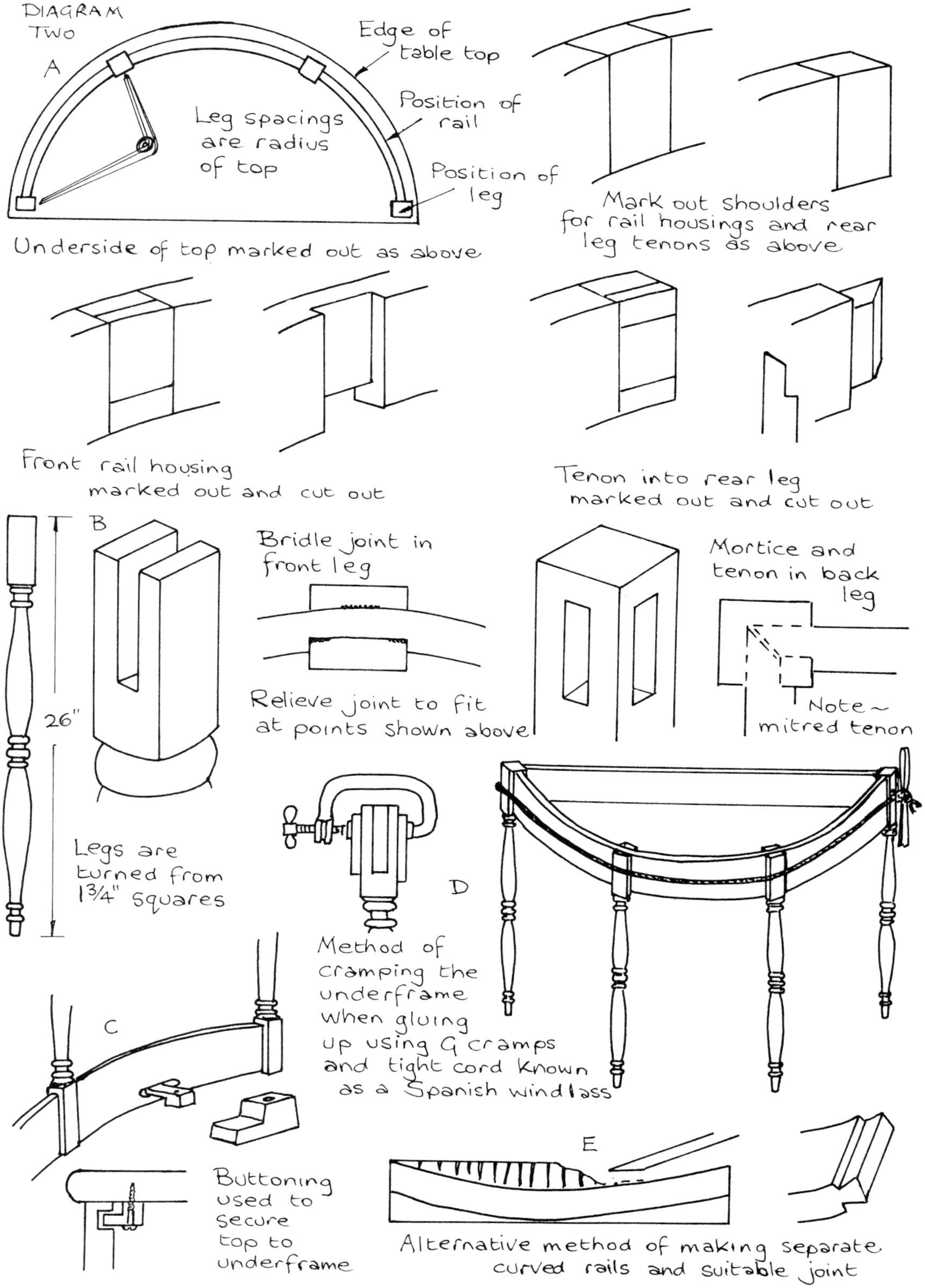
DIAGRAM TWO
A
Edge of table top
Position of rail
Leg spacings are radius of top
Position of leg
Underside of top marked out as above
Mark out shoulders for rail housings and rear leg tenons as above
Front rail housing marked out and cut out
Tenon into rear leg marked out and cut out
B
26"
Bridle joint in front leg
Relieve joint to fit at points shown above
Mortice and tenon in back leg
Note ~ mitred tenon
Legs are turned from 1¾" squares
D
Method of cramping the underframe when gluing up using G cramps and tight cord known as a Spanish windlass
C
Buttoning used to secure top to underframe
E
Alternative method of making separate curved rails and suitable joint

Because a curved rail is to be jointed to a square leg the marking out for the shoulders of these joints is rather different from normal. Working on the underside of the table top, the curve of the front rail is first drawn out and the position of each leg accurately marked on it as in Diagram Two A. Align the top edge of the front rail along the curved line which marks its eventual position and mark, with a marking knife, the points at which the two front leg positions intersect the rail. Each of these is joined across the top edge, squared across the width, front and back and joined again across the bottom edge. This marks the shoulders of the rail housings. Mark out the shoulders for the tenons into the back legs in a similar fashion. The tenons on the back rail are marked out and cut in the normal manner. Ascertain the true length of this back rail by assembling the two back legs to the curved front rail when its tenons are cut and measure the distance across the back between the two legs. By making the back rail a fraction overlong advantage can be taken of the slight springiness of the curved front rail to give a tight, firm fit to the back rail.

Set a marking gauge to one-third the thickness of the curved front rail and at each of the four joint positions scribe a line on top and bottom edges (see Diagram Two, A). Remove the waste as described in the section on Joints (p26). Next, cut out the half-lap housing on the bottom of the front rail for the two front legs and the top and bottom shoulders of the back tenons.

The bridles are now sawn out on the front legs. It will be obvious that when fitting these joints it will be necessary to relieve them slightly to obtain a good fit and this is best done as shown in the diagram. Remember to work carefully and keep checking for size. Finally, cut the mortices through in the back legs. When fitting these joints note that the ends of the tenons are mitred to fit.

A piece of well-seasoned teak, wide enough to make the top in one piece, was available and as it is normally a very stable timber this was used. A top made up of narrower boards edge joined would be equally suitable. The top, planed and cut to shape, had a light moulding cut into its edge using a power router. Remember that the top has an overhang all round. It is fastened to the underframing by the method known as buttoning (see Diagram Two, C). Hardwood buttons are made and screwed to the underside of the table top and located in grooves cut near the top edge of the rails. The grooves should be cut before the underframing is assembled and glued. The thickness of the buttons should be slightly less than the distance between the groove and the table top so that the top is pulled down tight as the buttons are screwed up. This method of fixing allows for any movement of the top.

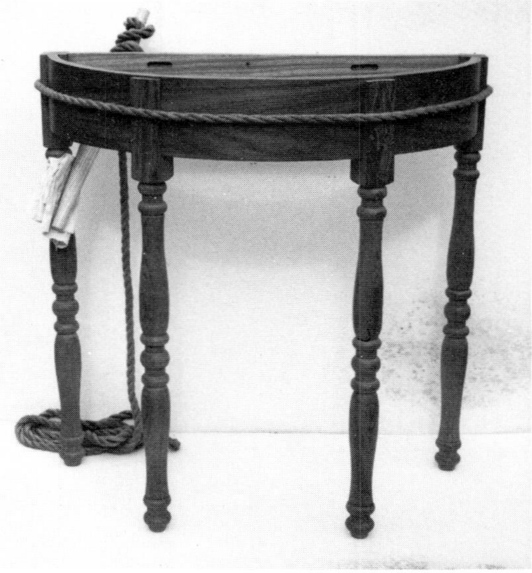

Plate 8 'Spanish windlass' used to secure the table while gluing

Assemble and glue the underframing. A sash cramp [clamp] may be used across the back but, if the advice about making the back rail a little over-length is taken, this is hardly necessary. Cramp [clamp] the curved front by means of cords twisted tight with a stick as shown in Diagram Two D. This is sometimes called a Spanish windlass. Use G-cramps [C-clamps] to apply pressure to the bridle joints of the two front legs; use softwood blocks to protect the leg surfaces. Check that everything is standing square, and clean off any surplus glue. When dry remove all cramps [clamps] and clean up the underframing. When the top has been added, give all a final sanding and apply a finish.

Alternative methods of making a curved

front include steam bending, either a continuous piece or three separate sections, or cutting three separate sections from the solid. For the latter this is easiest done on a band saw, although the method shown in Diagram Two, E is an alternative way. Three separate sections could also be made up by laminating – the former [form] or jig for this would be quite easy to make. Using three separate sections the joints used would need to be different from those used here; short stub tenons or a type of dovetail joint would be necessary. Solid wood sections would have weak cross-grain at the joint areas.

MATERIALS REQUIREMENT LIST. (CUTTING LIST IN INCHES)

NO	PURPOSE	MATERIAL	INITIAL SIZE	
1	TOP	TEAK	26 × 13 × 3/4	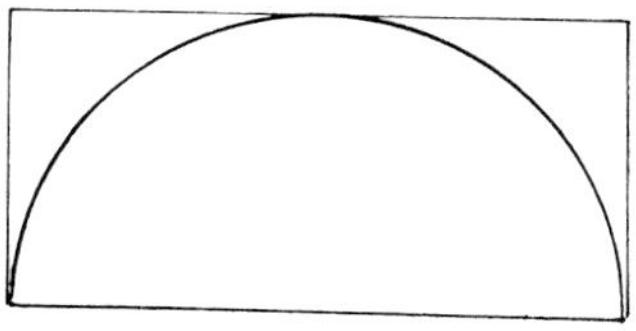
1	CURVED FRONT RAIL		40 × 4 × 1½	 SAWN INTO LAMINAE
	OR SUFFICIENT TEAK VENEER TO MAKE UP 3/4" THICKNESS			
1	BACK RAIL		28 × 4 × 3/4	
4	LEGS		26 × 1¾ × 1¾	TURNED 

14
Tall Display Cabinet

It was the interest in collecting products and artefacts from abroad, notably the East, during the second half of the seventeenth century, which gave rise to the design and manufacture of cabinets fitted with glass doors in which to display these collectables. Nothing was quite so highly prized as the exquisite Chinese porcelain and many of these display cabinets were given the name china cabinets and used exclusively for this purpose.

The diarist Samuel Pepys popularised their use as movable bookcases – hitherto books were mostly kept on shelves fixed to the wall – and when in the eighteenth century porcelain was produced in English potteries the demand for 'china' cabinets increased. Many different designs appeared, the bureau-bookcase is one of them, while another, the chiffonier, had a glazed cabinet placed on top of a sideboard-type cupboard.

During the nineteenth century such cabinets and cupboards were used to display the treasures of the Victorian collector: rocks and minerals, birds' eggs, sea shells and seaside souvenirs. They remained a favourite piece of furniture in many a sitting-room into the twentieth century. After the heavy Victorian designs some became plain, well made and elegant, but a large number, fitted with coloured mirror backs and electric lights, became ugly. As a consequence, the display cabinet tended to go out of fashion in many contemporary homes. Fortunately, however, sufficient interest has remained in keeping treasured possessions on view and for the majority a well-made cabinet is a prerequisite.

Originally conceived as a gun cabinet and therefore purposely made tall and slim, this piece of furniture goes well in a modern setting, ideal for one of those awkward, narrow alcoves which almost everyone seems to have. It may be made, as this was, for its intended purpose, or, by fitting shelves in the upper, glazed section, it can be used to store and display pottery, silverware, etc, or as a bookcase. The lower section consists of a single wide drawer and a cupboard with shelves. Ian Massey made the cabinet illustrated in English elm but any other suitable

Plate 1 The completed tall display cabinet

(*opposite*) Left: long-case clock (*see pp142–50*); right: tall display cabinet
(*overleaf*) High chair (*see pp180–6*)

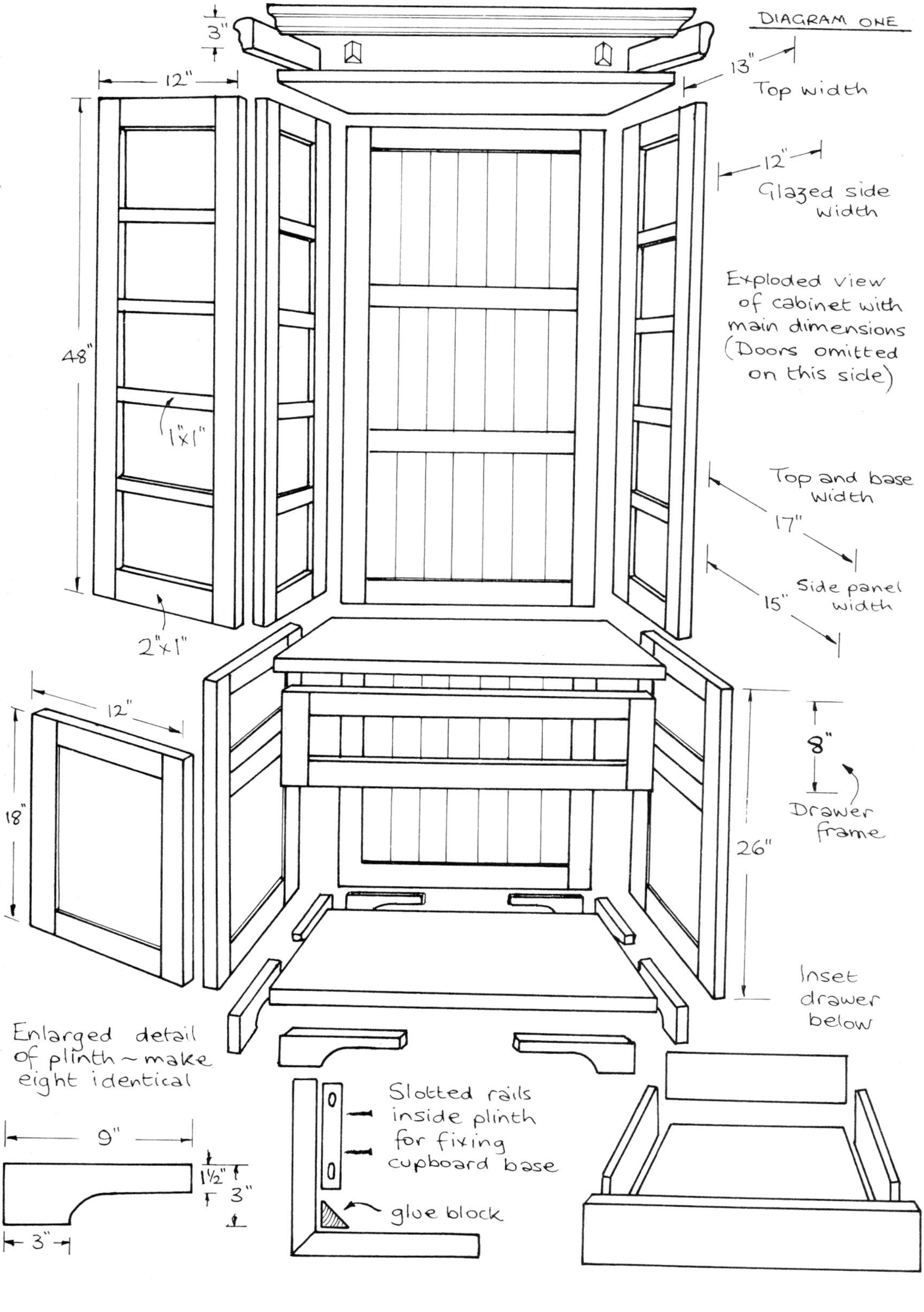
DIAGRAM ONE
3"
12"
13"
Top width
12"
Glazed side width
Exploded view of cabinet with main dimensions (Doors omitted on this side)
48"
1"x1"
2"x1"
Top and base width
17"
Side panel width
15"
12"
18"
8"
Drawer frame
26"
Inset drawer below
Enlarged detail of plinth ~ make eight identical
9"
1½"
3"
3"
Slotted rails inside plinth for fixing cupboard base
glue block

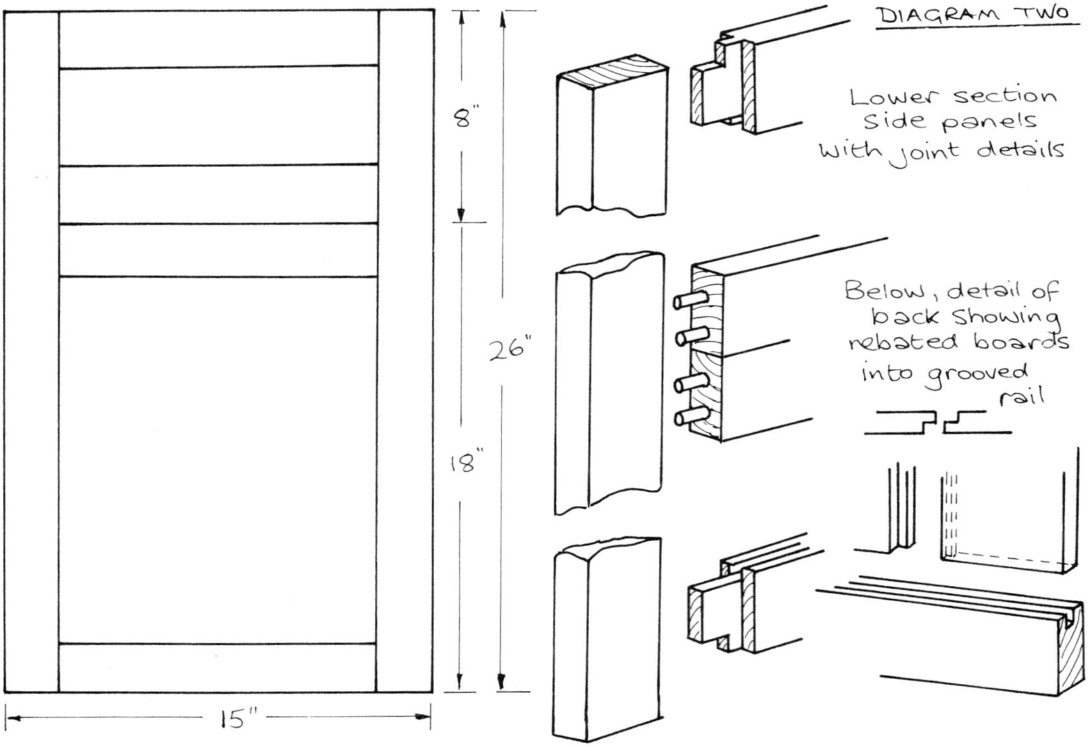
DIAGRAM TWO
Lower section side panels with joint details
Below, detail of back showing rebated boards into grooved rail
8"
26"
18"
15"

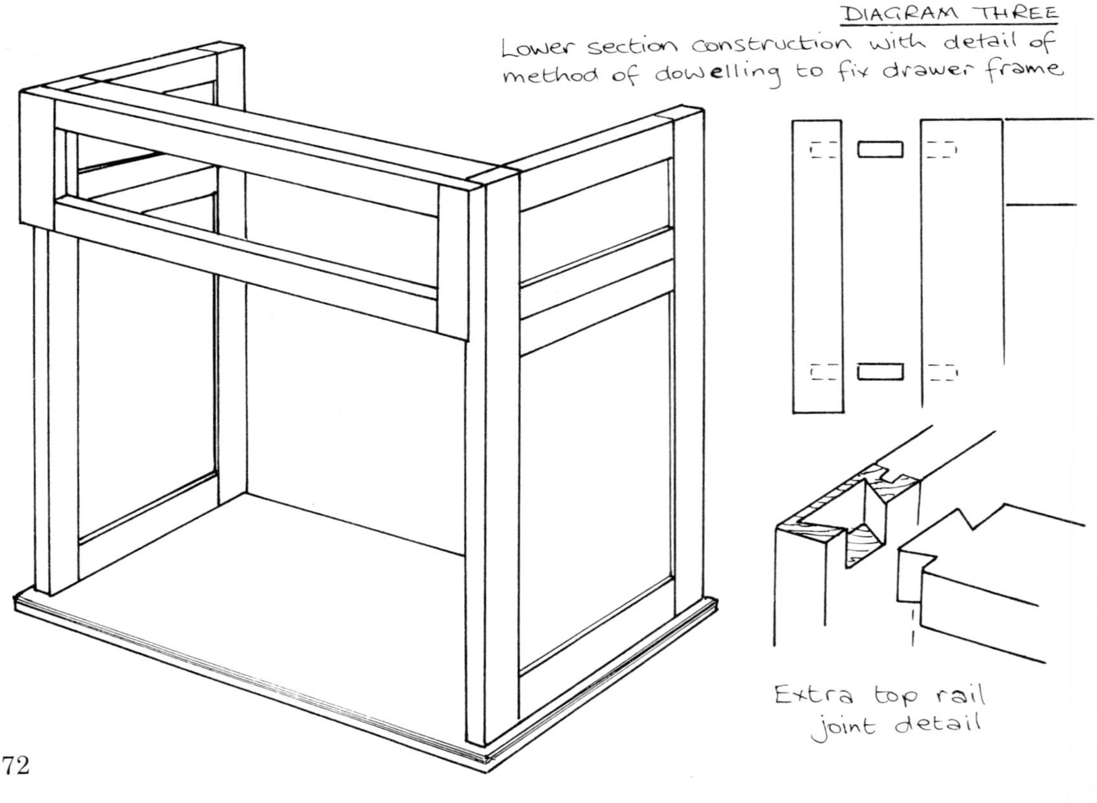
DIAGRAM THREE
Lower section construction with detail of method of dowelling to fix drawer frame
Extra top rail joint detail

hardwood could be used. The material should be well seasoned and, particularly for the long rails of the upper section and for the door uprights, straight grained so as to avoid any tendency towards twisting.

Traditional carcase-making methods as outlined on pp34–7 may be followed in the construction stages and such methods are illustrated. However, others may choose to adopt the more modern approach as was done here and this, too, is illustrated and described.

All rails are 2 × 1in initially and for the lower section these are first planed to 1⅞ × ⅞in, then cut to length. Those for the sides are slotted for the ⅜in-thick panels, the panels themselves being made up by edge gluing narrower ⅜in boards to give the required widths (see Diagram One).

The solid base of the lower section is made by edge gluing planed 1in boards to obtain the required size. Note that there is a ¾in overlap to the sides and front which has an ogee moulding worked on its top edge. This may be done by hand or with a power router.

The two side framed panels are made as shown in Diagram Two. The upright rails run through from bottom to top, but it will be noted that two intermediate rails are used. These align with the cupboard-door top rail and the drawer front bottom rail respectively and so continue this visual line around the three visible faces of the cabinet. Two separate panels are therefore used and these can be made from the same edge-glued ⅜in-thick material, cut to their separate sizes after gluing up so as to have continuity of grain and colour matching. Alternatively, the narrower top panel may be horizontally orientated to give continuity with the drawer front which is horizontal, as was done here.

Although the back is also framed, instead of having a single large panel, the infill consists of separate vertical ⅜in-thick boards as shown. These have matching rebates [rabbets] worked on their mating edges, the joint between chamfered slightly on the inside surface to emphasise the line. The boards are housed, but not glued, in grooves in the framing. All the framing for side and back panels is dowelled or mortice-and-tenon jointed and the frame edges are left square and without moulding.

The front of the lower section has an unpanelled frame made in the same way which in fact forms a surround to the inset drawer. The drawer has a solid front and, when in place within this surround, it gives the appearance of a larger framed and panelled drawer front in keeping with the cupboard doors and other panelled surfaces. This frame is dowelled to the front edges of the two side panels. Diagram Three shows this and also how an extra top rail might be added behind the frame to give additional strength.

Drawer rails and stops will need to be added as will the shelf supports. Reference should be made to the section on carcase construction (p37) for details of this work.

Plate 2 The lower section during assembly

In assembling, the back panel is inset between the side panels and dowelled into them, the extra front top rail put into place, if used, and then the front drawer frame added. All this is then checked for being square and true and put under cramping [clamping] pressure until the glue is set.

Next, the base can be added, dowelled or screwed up into the side and back panels. It will be seen that the cabinet stands on recessed bracket feet and these are made and fitted as shown in Diagram One.

A pair of cupboard doors should now be made using dimensions taken from the completed carcase frame. The doors are part

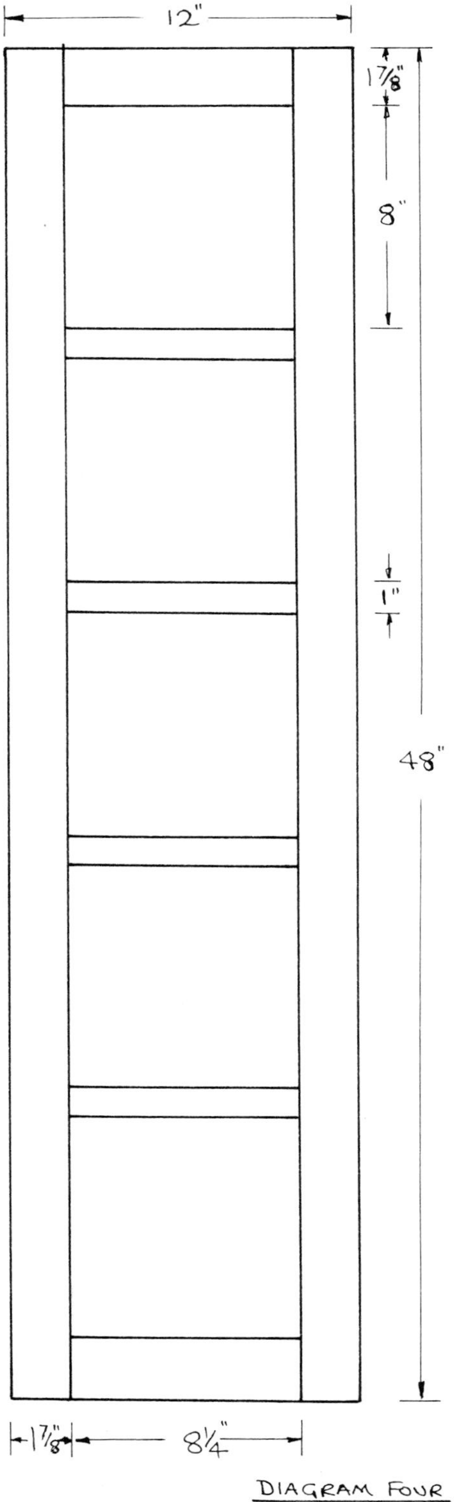

DIAGRAM FOUR
Dimensions of glazed frames

overlaid, ie they fit to the outside and overlap the edges of the side panel but fit within the base and the drawer framing. Hinges are placed to the outside edges and ball catches hold the doors shut when in the closed position. The drawer, too, can be made at this stage, again working to dimensions taken from the drawer frame opening and, as the drawer is inset, these should be taken with care and worked to precisely.

Now, work can begin on the upper section. It should first be noted that the reason for the cupboard or lower section apparently having no top is because the base of the upper section fulfils this function. It is made in exactly the same way and to the same dimensions as the lower section base. It, too, has a moulding worked on its top edge.

The glazed sections consist of four identical frames, each 48in in length and 12in wide. Their outer frame is of 2 × 1in planed to 1⅞ × ⅞in with intermediate sash bars of 1 × 1in – four bars to each frame to give five square glazed openings to each (see Diagram Four). The frames are dowel jointed together, but mortice and tenons may be used instead; use haunched mortice and tenons at the corners with stub tenons for the sash bars. The frames are rebated [rabbeted]

Plate 3 The dowel joints of the glazed frames

Plate 4 Using a router to cut the rebates [rabbets] for the glass

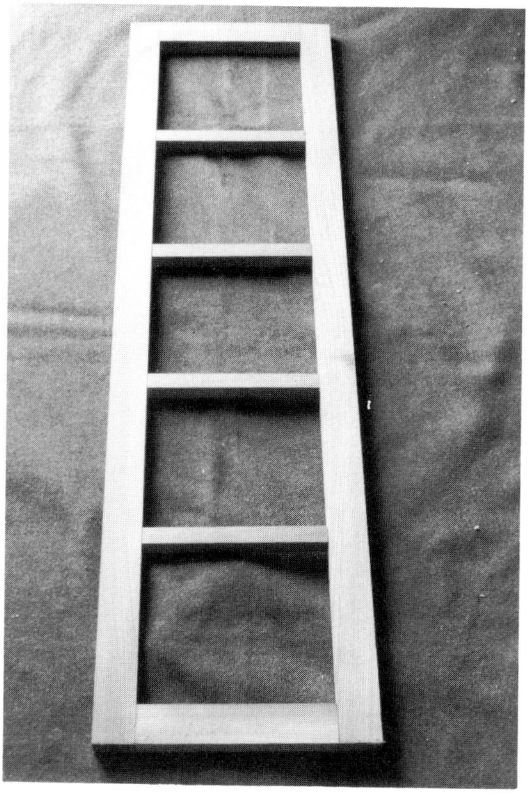

Plate 5 A completed glazed frame

on their inner edges to accept the glass and this may be done in a number of ways. With a router available, one of the simplest ways is to glue up and assemble the frame and then to rout out the rebate [rabbet] to the desired width and depth – ⅜ × ⅜in is suitable. If this method is used it will be necessary to chisel square the rounded corners which the router cutter will leave. Alternatively, the sash bars can be individually rebated on the circular saw or, by hand using a rebate [rabbet] plane, assembled into the main frame and the interrupted rebate [rabbet] on this cut in by hand.

Whatever method is used, assembly of the frames needs to be done with care. All shoulders must be square and a dry run is required to check that the whole thing goes together squarely and without twist. When all is well, glue up, check again and put into cramps [clamps] until the glue has set. The two best frames should be marked for use as doors.

The back is similar to the back of the cupboard section in that it is framed and infilled with vertical ⅜in-thick boards, but because of its extra length it has two intermediate rails across its width. These effectively divide the back into three parts of equal size. Again, the boards are rebated [rabbeted] on their mating edges and held without glue in grooves in the outer framing. For appearances through the glazed frames the boards should, ideally, be matched for grain and colour. The frame is once more dowelled together. Check for squareness and avoid twisting when gluing and cramping [clamping] up.

The top of the upper section is of solid material, like the two bases, but narrower. It has a moulding cut on its front edge which marries in with an applied moulding placed on top and held by means of glued blocks. The combined moulded edge and applied moulding forms an effective cornice to the top of the cabinet.

The entire upper section is joined together either by dowelling or with screws. First, the back is inset into the side panels or frames where it is held with dowels and glued edges, then the base is added, either dowelled and glued or, ideally, slot screwed (see Diagram Five). The top is fixed in the same way. Take care that the door opening remains square

DIAGRAM FIVE

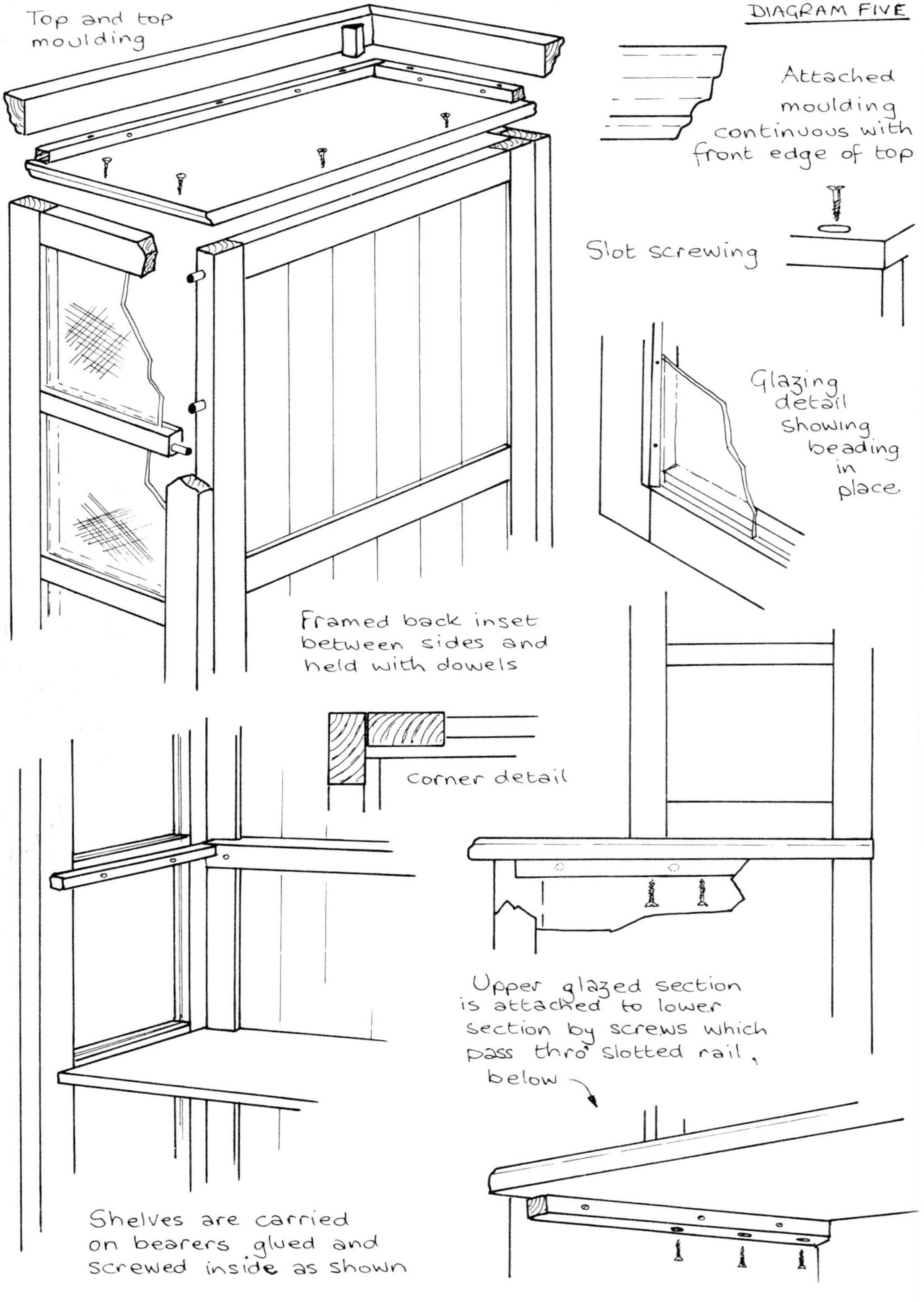
Top and top moulding
Attached moulding continuous with front edge of top
Slot screwing
Glazing detail showing beading in place
Framed back inset between sides and held with dowels
Corner detail
Upper glazed section is attached to lower section by screws which pass thro' slotted rail, below
Shelves are carried on bearers glued and screwed inside as shown

during this process and be particularly careful at the marking-out stage with this in mind. When the gluing and screwing is completed, leave in cramps [clamps] until the glue has set.

Offer up the doors to be sure they fit satisfactorily – they are again partly overlaid between the top and bottom but over the two long edges. Trim to size if necessary. For ease of working they may be glazed on the bench where they can be kept flat during the process. Glass cut to size should be ordered from a glass-supply company, but beware that there may be slight differences in the space between rebates [rabbets] (there should not be, but it sometimes happens). Measure several different ones to check this, 'just in case'. The glass is held in the rebates [rabbets] with square or triangular beading. Make it in elm to match the rest of the cabinet, but try to avoid buying beading which is sure to be made of something else, probably ramin or a softwood. The side frames may be glazed on the bench before assembly or after it. One final point about the doors: keep their lower edges just up from the base to give sufficient clearance not to scratch what is in effect the top of the cupboard section.

As a gun cabinet the upper section would be fitted with custom-made leather or green baize-lined brackets to hold its owner's guns. For use as a display cabinet or bookcase, however, shelves should be fitted; Diagram Five shows how this could be done. Obviously, the bulk of this work is best carried out before the upper section is assembled. The objective has been to keep the shelves in line with the sash bars as is normal practice, in quality furniture of this kind. Purists might like to consider this earlier and to alter the arrangement of the intermediate rails across the back to come into line with all or some of the shelves. As an alternative to the wooden shelves shown fitted, glass shelves could be used. These should be of ¼in plate glass and have all their edges ground and polished.

The upper section is joined to the lower by screws which pass up through fixing rails glued and screwed inside the top edge of the lower section and into the base of the upper section. The screws should pass through cross-grain slots rather than holes to allow for any subsequent movement of the wide boards of the base (see Diagram Five).

On completion, the cabinet was given a final light scraping and sanding, then a proprietary [commercial] clear sealer was applied inside and out and the surface lightly sanded off. Further coats of sealer or semi-matt polyurethane were applied and rubbed down, and finally the exterior was wax polished. A brass bolt was fitted to the left-hand glazed door and two good-quality locks to the other. A matching set of antique brass handles was fitted to both cupboards and to the drawer.

MATERIAL REQUIREMENTS LIST (CUTTING LIST IN INCHES)

Nº	PURPOSE	MATERIAL	INITIAL SIZES	
	LOWER CUPBOARD			
	FOR TWO SIDE PANELS			
2	LOWER PANELS	ELM	15 × 12 × 3/8	
2	TOP PANELS	"	12 × 5 × 3/8	
4	UPRIGHT RAILS	"	26 × 2 × 1	"
2	TOP RAILS	"	11¼ × 2 × 1	PLANED
4	MIDDLE RAILS	"	11¼ × 2 × 1	"
2	BOTTOM RAILS	"	11¼ × 2 × 1	"
	FOR BACK			
7	BACK BOARDS	"	24 × 4½ × 3/8	REBATED
2	UPPRIGHTS	"	26 × 2 × 1	PLANED
2	CROSS RAILS	"	20¼ × 2 × 1	"
	FOR CUPBOARD DOORS			
2	PANELS	"	15 × 12 × 3/8	"
4	STILES	"	18 × 2 × 1	
2	TOP RAILS	"	8¼ × 2 × 1	"
2	BOTTOM RAILS	"	8¼ × 2 × 1	"
	FOR DRAWER and DRAWER FRAME			
1	BOTTOM	PLY	19¼ × 14¼ × ¼	
1	FRONT	ELM	20¼ × 4¼ × 7/8	
2	SIDES	"	14 × 4½ × ¾	
1	BACK	"	20¼ × 4 × ½	
1	TOP RAIL		20¼ × 2 × 1	"
1	BOTTOM RAIL		20¼ × 2 × 1	"
2	ENDS		8 × 2 × 1	"
	Miscellaneous			
1	BASE		26 × 17 × 7/8	"
1	EXTRA TOP RAIL		24 × 2 × 1	
8	BRACKET FEET		9 × 3 × 7/8	

MATERIALS REQUIREMENTS LIST ~ continued

Nº	PURPOSE	MATERIAL	INITIAL SIZES		
	UPPER SECTION				
	FOR FOUR GLAZED PANELS				
4	UPRIGHT RAILS	ELM	48 × 2 × 1	PLANED	
4	TOP RAILS	"	8¼ × 2 × 1	"	
4	BOTTOM RAILS	"	8¼ × 2 × 1	"	
16	SASH BARS	"	8¼ × 1 × 1	"	
	FOR BACK				
7	BACK BOARDS	"	48 × 4½ × ⅜	REBATED	
2	UPRIGHTS	"	48 × 2 × 1		
4	CROSS RAILS	"	20¼ × 2 × 1	PLANED	
	MISCELLANEOUS				
1	BASE / TOP	"	26 × 17 × ⅞	"	
1	UPPER / TOP	"	25 × 13½ × ⅞	"	
	TOP MOULDING	"	1 @ 28 × 3 × 1½ 2 @ 14 × 3 × 1½		
	FOR SHELVES (WHERE FITTED)				
4	SHELVES	"	22¼ × 10 × ½	"	
	Shelf bearers ~ sufficient for all shelves. ¾ × ½				
	20 pieces 12oz glass 8¾ × 8¾. Beading for glazing & pins. Screws. 4 pairs door hinges. Door handles and locks. Pieces for glue blocks				

15

High Chair

Illustrated on page 170

One of the most endearing and enduring of family heirlooms is surely baby's first chair. Like the cradle, such chairs are used by successive children in one family, as well as being passed back and forth between related and sometimes unrelated families of the same generation, to be passed on again to the following generation for similar treatment. I know of one family which is the proud owner of a lovely old Victorian high chair; it is said to have had no less than twenty-six different babies' bottoms in it. The chair came to me recently for restoration and will now no doubt accommodate a further twenty-six babies at least.

The project described here is structurally based upon that same chair, but with one or two subtle variations designed to give it more appeal to hygiene-and-safety-conscious late-twentieth-century parents. Long-legged chairs present some problems of proportion, for the sturdy legs may easily dominate the relatively small seat and upper parts. This design appears to be satisfactory in this respect.

The original chair was in English oak and this one was made in the same kind of wood. The oak used was saved from a demolished Victorian church, which was a nice touch. New oak, bought in, would make the job somewhat expensive but well worth it. To reduce material costs beech could be used instead.

In the Materials Requirement List (p186) dimensions given for lengths are finished sizes and therefore some allowance will need to be made for waste; other dimensions are before turning or shaping and wood can be purchased cut to these sizes. If you have facilities for sawing it is often easier, and therefore usually cheaper, to buy your wood in larger, stock sizes and cut to the required dimensions yourself. For example, perusal of the Materials Requirement List will show that there are several items with one dimension of 2in; therefore it would be possible to buy sufficient of a 2in-thick board to yield the required pieces.

Make the turned components first (Diagram One), beginning with the legs. Other shapes of your own choice could be used; the important thing to remember is to keep clear and preferably at near-maximum thickness

DIAGRAM ONE

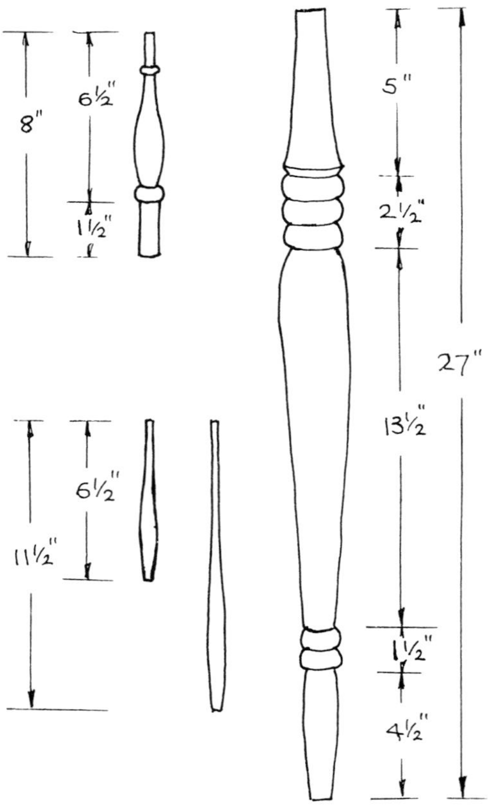

Dimensions of turned components

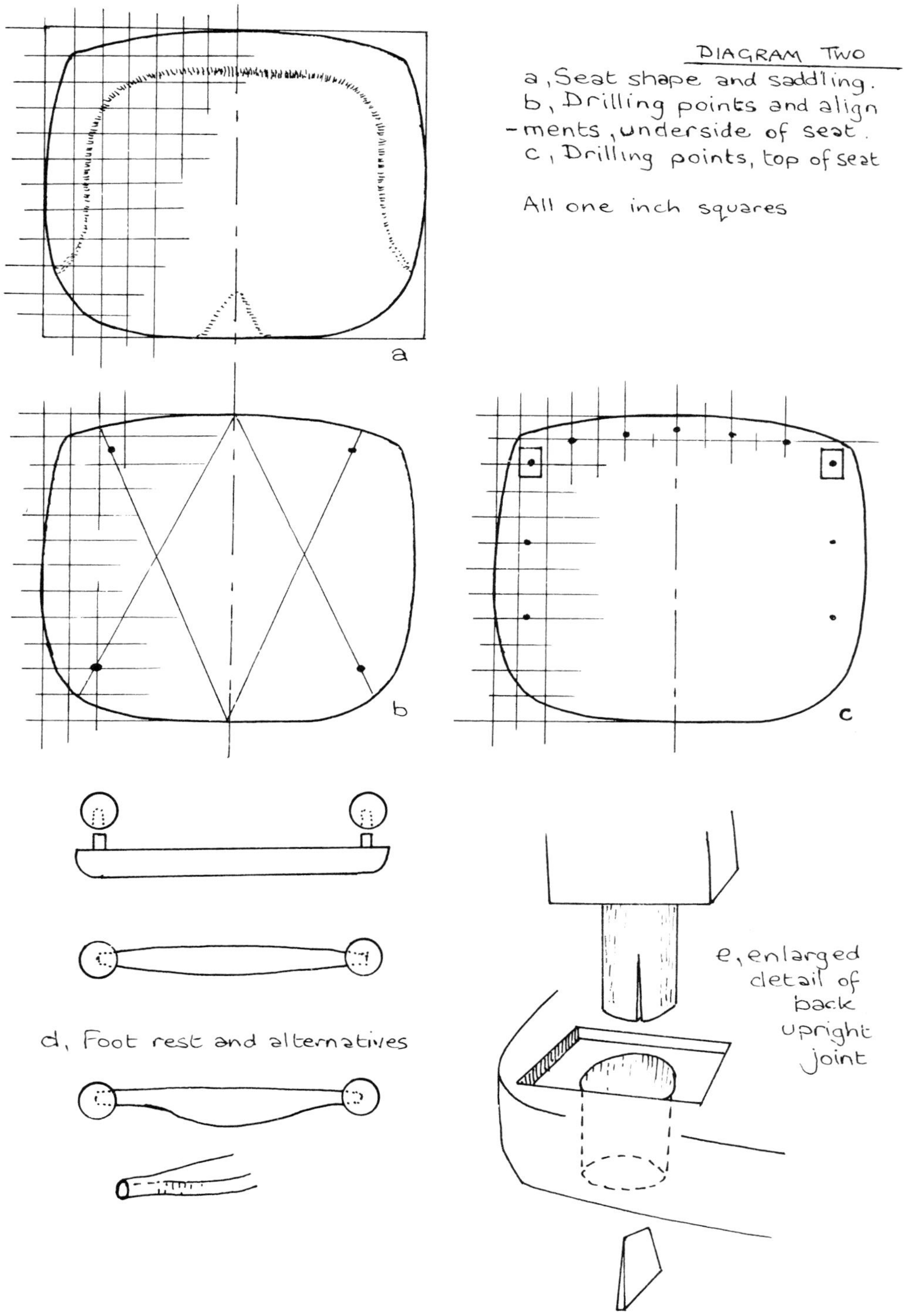
DIAGRAM TWO
a, Seat shape and saddling.
b, Drilling points and alignments, underside of seat.
c, Drilling points, top of seat
All one inch squares
a
b
c
d, Foot rest and alternatives
e, enlarged detail of back upright joint

those areas where stretchers and the foot-rest are to be fitted. And keep the top tenons a full 1in in diameter to ensure a good tight fit in the seat sockets. This is most important with legs of this length. The two front arm supports are also lathe turned; note that the bottom tenon on these goes right through the seat and is wedged from below so it will need extra length to go through and a saw cut at right angles to the grain of the seat to accommodate the wedge. The other round components, ie back and side sticks, are plain turned and tapered either in the lathe or with the rotary planes as in the rocking chair (p44).

Next, cut the seat to shape (Diagram Two, a) and, if you want to do the job properly, give the seat surface a shallow hollowing. There is no need to attempt the deep saddling of the traditional Windsor chair seat, but taking away some of the flatness and especially giving some roundness to the front edge of the seat does make for more comfort and greater contentment. Many modern baby chairs ignore this altogether and have completely flat bottoms which could perhaps explain why some babies cry a lot. This hollowing of the seat can be done with a shallow gouge or using an inshave, cleaning up with a curved scraper and glass-paper [sandpaper] to finish.

On the underside of the seat mark out the four leg sockets, (see Diagram Two, b). Using the drilling jig, drill these 1in diameter and 1in deep. Put the legs in place and, with the chair standing on its legs and being certain that the legs have gone all the way into their sockets, mark out the position of the stretcher holes and at the same time check the stretchers for true length.

The position of the foot-rest may also be ascertained at this time. The question of a foot-rest was something of a puzzle. Was one really necessary? Should it be fixed or adjustable? What form should it take? I'm still not sure that my answer was the correct one. The one used is a fixed, flat rest, held by dowels into the front legs. A simple and stronger alternative might have been to fit an extra stretcher at this point or, better still, a shaped piece held in the same way and secured against rotating by being pegged (Diagram Two, d).

Remove the legs from their seat sockets and, with the drilling jig at the same angle as that used when drilling the seat sockets, drill each of the stretcher holes in the four legs in turn, ¾in diameter, ¾in deep. Drill the foot-rest fixing points at this same time. Use a V-shaped cradle to hold the legs in place while being drilled.

Return to the seat again to mark out the position of the holes in its top surface (Diagram Two, c). There are no compound angles to worry about in this design. The five back stick sockets are ½in diameter and ¾in deep, as are those for the two short side sticks. For the front arm supports ⅞in holes are drilled right through the seat. The two back uprights are tenoned through the seat also. These can be conventional square mortice and tenons if you wish – I used a chairmaker's joint by drilling a ⅞in hole through the seat and cutting a round tenon to fit. This is done by sawing in the shoulders of the tenon and careful downward paring to the saw cut with a sharp chisel. Note the recesses in the seat surface to accommodate the rectangular end of the upright. This hides the shoulders of the tenon and makes for a neater appearance (Diagram Two, e).

The back uprights are band sawn to shape to give a slight curvature to the back, as is the top rail. These are joined with a mortice and tenon or they could be dowelled together. The arms, band sawn to the shape shown, are mortice and tenoned into the back uprights. Take care to get the correct shape to the shoulders of the tenon so that

Plate 1 The arms are morticed and tenoned into the back uprights

they mate nicely with the upright. In such cases it helps to keep the surface of the two components flat instead of slightly curved in the area where they meet. The lower joints of the back uprights are wedge jointed into the seat and will need to have saw cuts in their tenons at right angles to the grain of the seat to accommodate the wedges. All these components are shaped by spokeshave and finished with glass-paper [sandpaper] to give smooth rounded edges for safety and comfort.

Plate 2 The arm is brought down on to the arm supports

To mark the position of the holes for the arm supports in the underside of the arm, first put the arm supports, ie the turned front arm support and the short arm stick, in position, fix the back upright and arm together and enter the upright into its socket in the seat. Bring the arm down on to the arm supports and mark in the hole positions. Drill the holes at the correct angle and check by reassembling both back uprights and arms on to their arm supports following the same sequence outlined above.

If you now mark out and drill the holes for the back sticks in the top rail (½in diameter, ½in deep) the complete back and arms can be assembled dry to make sure the whole thing will go together when gluing up. If the joints you have made are good tight ones this stage of assembly will not be easy. If, on the other hand, the joints are slack you will find assembly is much simpler (and this is one of the tricks of the trade by some of those who make chair kits for self-assembly). Proceed as follows: put all back sticks and arm supports in position, fix back uprights and arms together and enter uprights into the top of the seat sockets. Place the top rail into position then, gently pushing one side a little at a time, ease the back uprights down, engaging back sticks and arm supports in their respective holes as you go. A tap or two with a soft mallet may be needed to get all the joints home, but don't overdo the tapping at this stage – you may have difficulty pulling the chair apart again for gluing. If this difficulty does arise use a short length of ¾in dowel and the mallet to tap out the front arm supports and back uprights from underneath the seat.

If all is well the chair is now ready for final assembly. Make sure all components are smooth and clean before you begin. Put glue into seat sockets and stretcher holes, assemble legs and stretchers and leave to allow glue to properly set. Glue in the foot-rest at this time, too. Then, following the procedure outlined above, assemble the back and arms. Begin by putting glue into all the holes and remember that the front arm supports and the back uprights are also wedged into their sockets. Allow glue to dry.

The removable front tray can now be made. By leaving this until the chair is completed a good matching fit is more easily obtained. Although dimensions are given (Diagram Three) it may be necessary to adjust these to suit the individual chair. Take the measurements for your tray from your chair.

It will be seen that the side rails of the tray are shaped to fit the chair arms. Cut and shape these first then, while holding the two cross rails in position on the chair, measure off their length. These are grooved along their length to accommodate the tray bottom, which in this case was ¼in solid oak (three pieces edge-joined). It could be made from veneered ply but I don't recommend it. Side and cross rails are dowel jointed – a single dowel is sufficient – and, although it is rather bad practice, the tray bottom is glued into its groove using waterproof glue. The tray on a baby chair *will* get things spilt into

ABOVE, COMPLETED TRAY

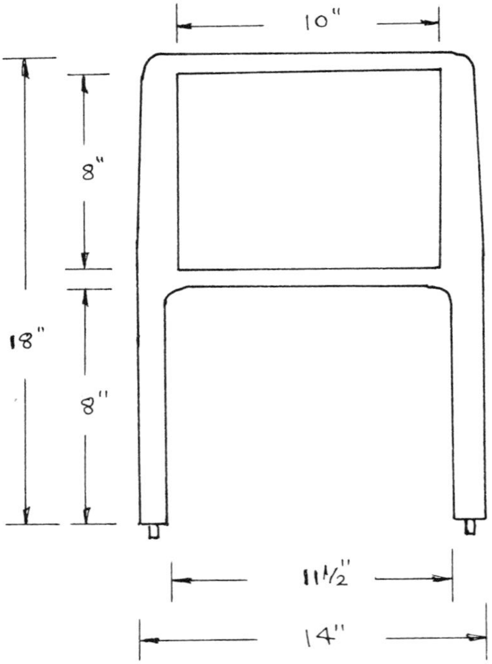

DIAGRAM THREE
DIMENSIONS OF TRAY GIVEN ABOVE. BELOW DETAIL OF FINGER BOLT AND NUT FOR ARM

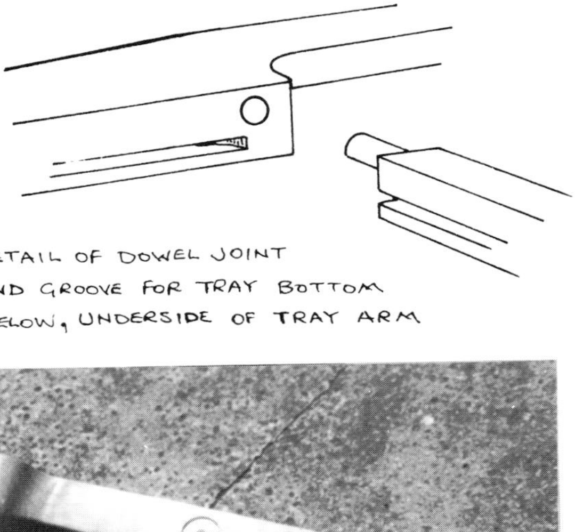

DETAIL OF DOWEL JOINT AND GROOVE FOR TRAY BOTTOM
BELOW, UNDERSIDE OF TRAY ARM

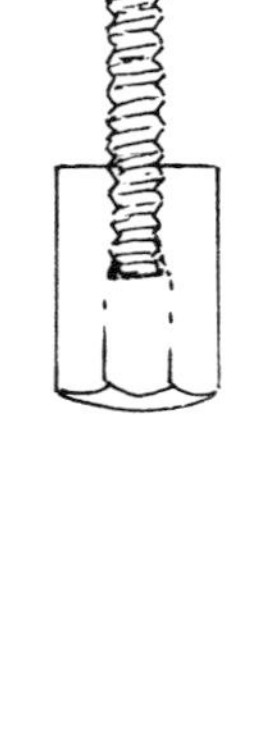

it and it is better, I believe, to combat certain problems arising from this than to make allowances for possible problems arising from shrinkage of the wood. Matters of hygiene must also be considered here: a dry assembly of the tray bottom would leave an inaccessible space in which spilt food could accumulate and germs might lurk.

The tray rests on the chair arms and is held in position by short hardwood pegs at the end of each side rail which locate into corresponding holes in the back uprights. A threaded finger bolt passing through the arm from below and into a captive nut fixed to the tray side arm secures the tray to the chair (Diagram Three, detail). To mark accurately the position of this captive nut, first drill the hole through the arm as shown and, with the tray in position, mark through on to the underside of the tray side rail. I made nuts in brass, using ¾in round bar, drilled and threaded to suit the finger bolts. These, too, were made using ¼in threaded steel rod and brass hexagon bar. The hexagon bar was drilled and threaded and the steel bar secured into it with epoxy resin (Diagram Three, detail).

The completed chair and tray need to be given a finish suited to the conditions of use. A wax finish would look well but would be rather impractical, while a high-shine lacquer, easy to wipe clean, would spoil the chair's appearance. I used several coats of thinned satin polyurethane, rubbing each coat down with flour paper and/or wire wool to seal the wood and give a pleasant wipe-clean finish.

Finally, for safety purposes, what can best be described as a crutch strap was fitted to prevent a young child from sliding forward and out of the chair. A strong but soft piece of harness leather was used, screwed to the back edge of the front tray and secured to a brass stud placed beneath the seat.

MATERIALS REQUIREMENT LIST. (CUTTING LIST IN INCHES)

Nº	PURPOSE	MAT.	INITIAL SIZES		
1	SEAT	OAK	14 × 12 × 1½	SHAPED	
4	LEGS	"	28 × 2 × 2	TURNED	
4	STRETCHERS	"	16 × 1½ × 1½	"	
1	FOOTREST	"	14 × 2 × 5/8	SHAPED	
2	BACK UPRIGHTS	"	13 × 2 × 1¼	"	
1	TOP RAIL	"	12 × 2 × 1¼	"	
2	ARMS	"	9½ × 2½ × 2	"	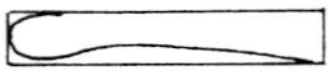
5	BACK STICKS	"	12 × 7/8 × 7/8	TURNED	
2	SIDE STICKS	"	7 × 7/8 × 7/8	"	
2	ARM SUPPORTS	"	8 × 1¼ × 1¼	"	
2	TRAY SIDE RAILS	"	16 × 2 × 1¼	SHAPED	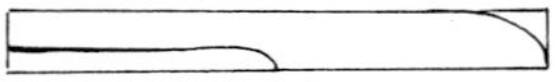
2	TRAY CROSS RAILS	"	10 × 1¼ × 1	GROOVED	
1	TRAY BOTTOM	"	10½ × 9 × ¼	3 PIECES EDGE JOINED	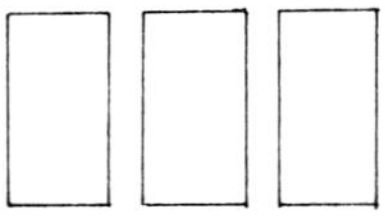
	TWO THREADED FINGER BOLTS & NUTS PIECE OF SOFT LEATHER STRAPPING				

16

Box Settle

Illustrated on page 187

Before chairs came into common use an alternative to sitting on a stool or bench was to sit on or in a settle. Early examples of these were basically chests built into an alcove or made to form an integral part of the wall panelling and the first movable versions simply a development of this. These were usually heavily built with high panelled backs and sides to match the panelled chest which formed the seat.

By the middle of the seventeenth century settles of lighter construction were in general use. The panelled back could vary from waist to head height while the sides became, in some instances, little more than shaped narrow ear pieces or were replaced altogether by open arm rests. The chest or box seat gave way in turn to an open construction consisting of four turned legs and a continuous floor stretcher supporting a wooden seat.

As the desire for greater comfort increased, wooden settles were made with upholstered seats, usually with leather, padded beneath and held in place with brass studs. Later, upholstered back panels and richer materials were introduced and in due course the settle developed into the now more familiar upholstered settee. But wooden settles continued in use especially in rural areas and are still a familiar sight in some country inns even today.

The settle described here was made in the furniture workshop of my Yorkshire friend and associate Keith Riley and the design is a return to the original box settle complete with hinged lid and panelled back but incorporating open arm rests supported on turned posts extending up from the seat (Diagram One). It is made throughout in pine but other woods would be suitable; oak would make this a very desirable family heirloom.

The two back posts are made first, from 2½in-square material. As Diagram Two shows the back slopes slightly backward for added comfort and accordingly the two back posts taper towards their tops on the front face only to provide this slope. Mark out and shape the posts as shown in the diagram and then mark out the groove for the back panelling from this tapering face to give the corresponding slope to the back panels when fitted. Note that the taper goes only to the height of the seat; below that point the posts remain parallel at 2½in square. Cut the ½in groove, using a router for preference, then mark in the position of the four mortices to receive the cross-rail tenons and deepen the groove to correspond at these places. The back posts each require a groove for the side panels and three more mortices cut into their front faces to accommodate side rails and arms. Mark and cut these as shown in the diagram.

Next, prepare the material for the back panelling which consists of two groups of four panels. Its construction is similar in part to the head panel of the four-post bed, the panels cut to size at ¾in thick and fielded to ⅜in to fit into prepared grooves in the frame. It differs in that the space below the 5in bottom rail is infilled with plain tongue and groove boards to form the back of the box seat (see Diagram Three).

When everything is cut to size and the fielded panels shaped as shown, a dry assembly of all the back components is advisable to make sure everything will go together satisfactorily. When it does it can all be glued up and put under cramping [clamping] pressure until the glue is set. Check that

(p187) Box settle *(see pp189–97)*
(opposite) Smoker's bow chair *(see pp198–206)*

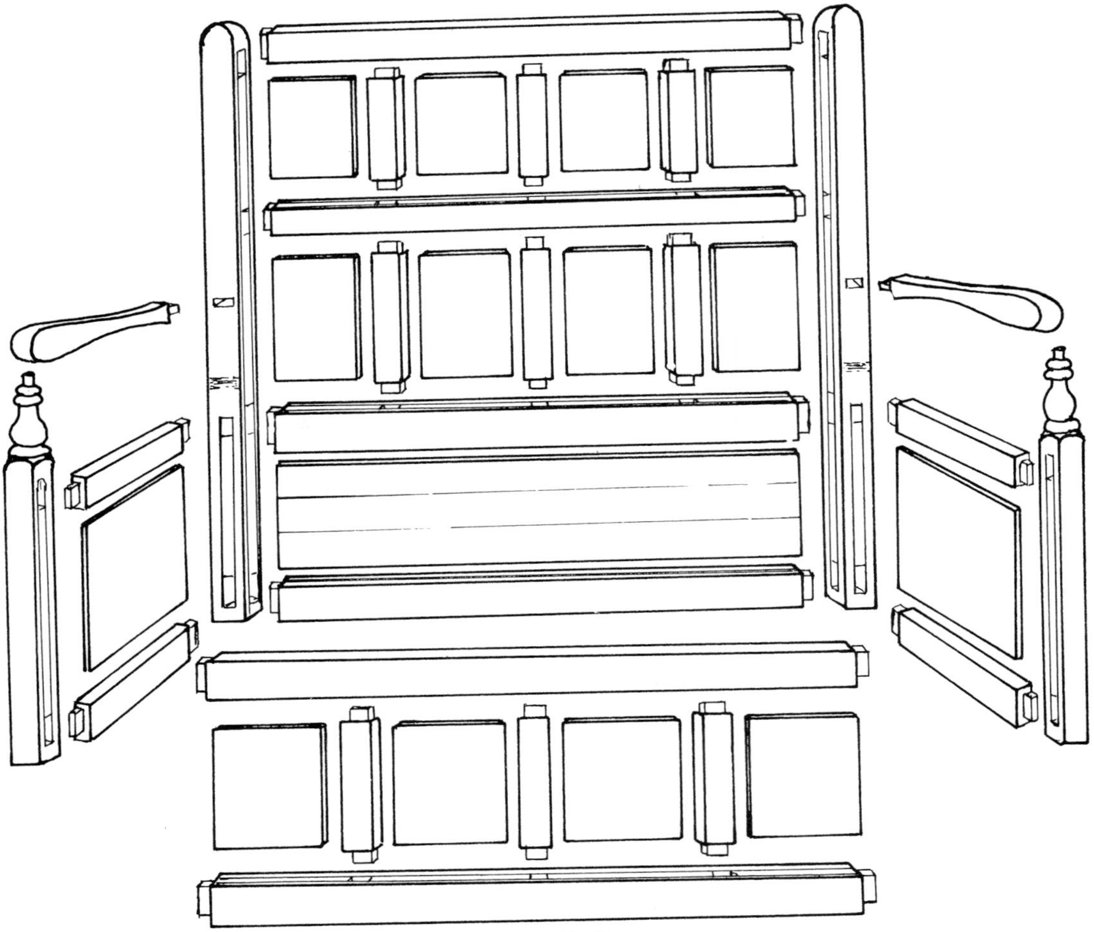

DIAGRAM ONE

Exploded view of main components of settle.
Seat is not included

Plate 1 Early stages of the frame for the back panel

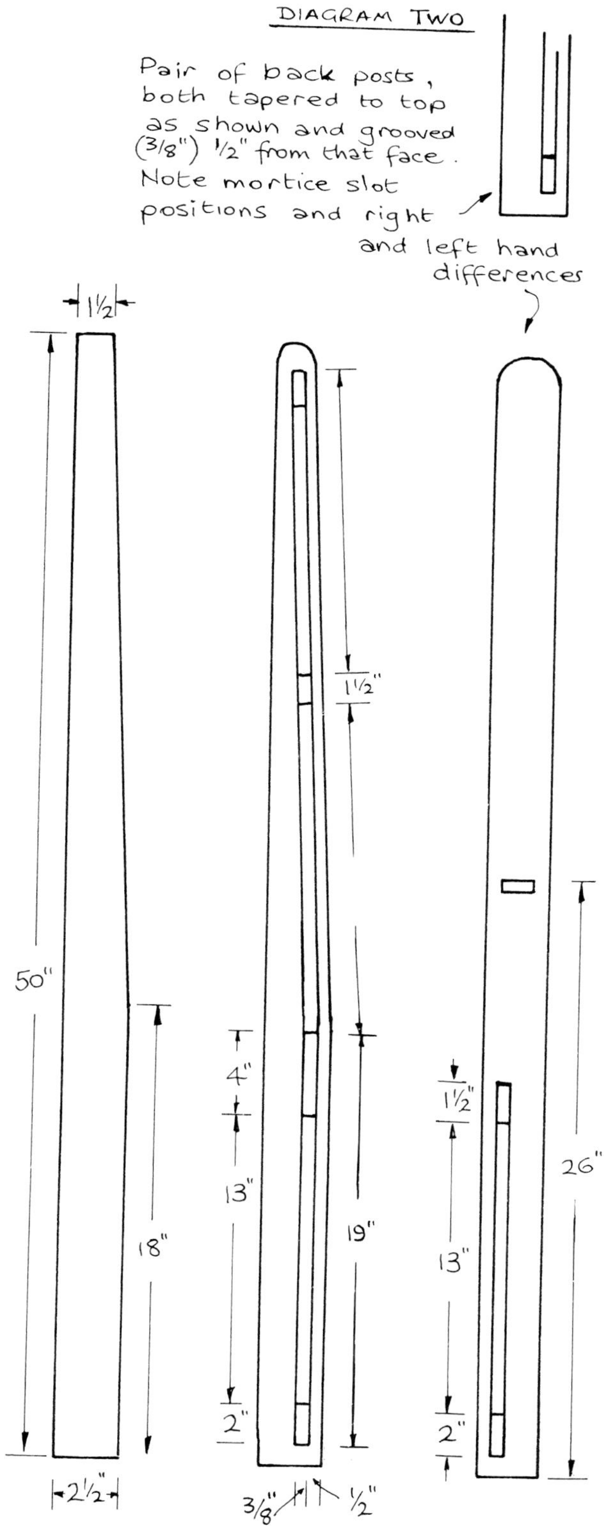
DIAGRAM TWO
Pair of back posts, both tapered to top as shown and grooved (3/8") 1/2" from that face. Note mortice slot positions and right and left hand differences
1½
50"
18"
2½"
1½"
4"
13"
19"
2"
3/8"
½"
1½"
13"
26"
2"

DIAGRAM THREE

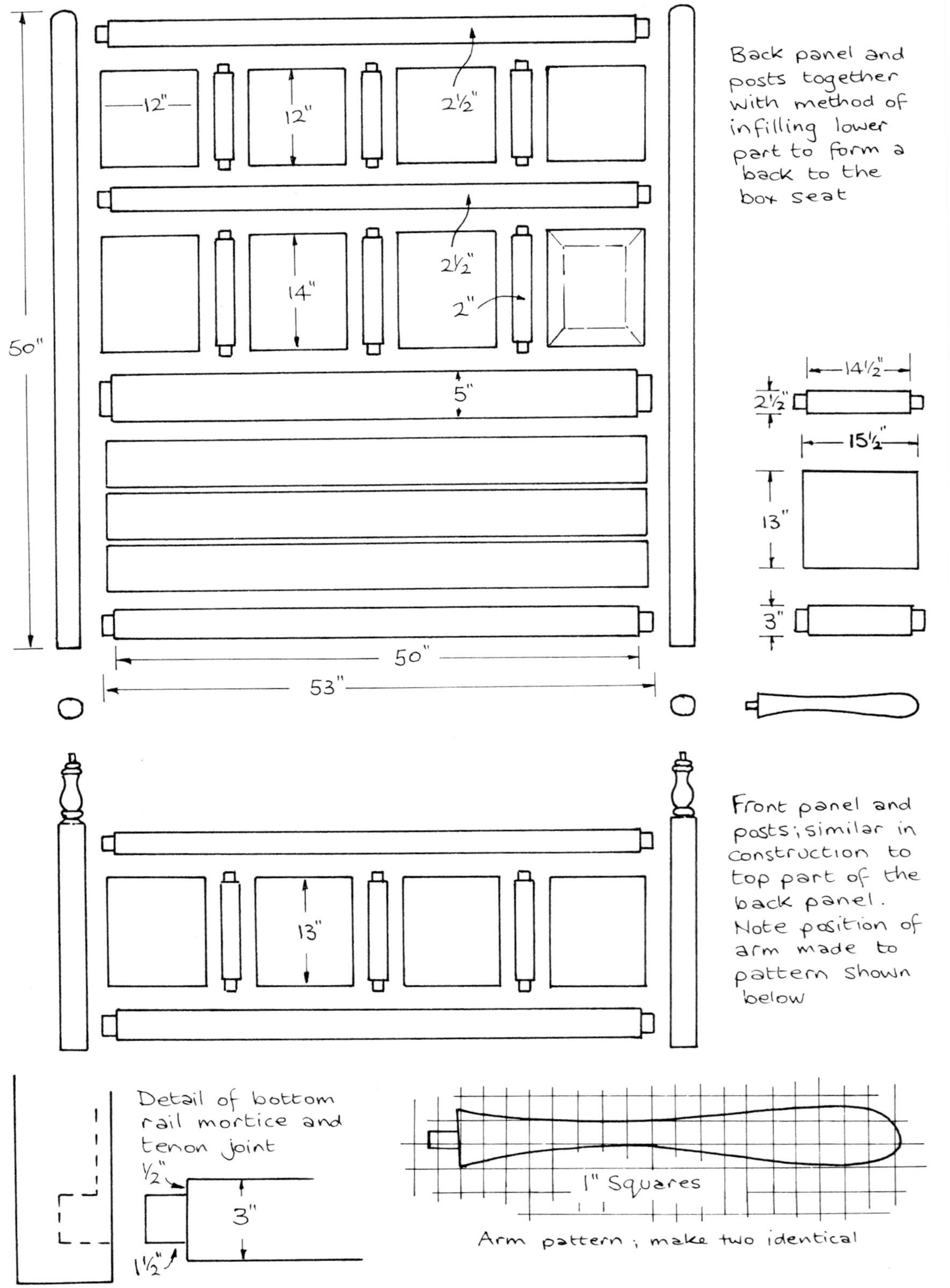
Back panel and posts together with method of infilling lower part to form a back to the box seat
12"
12"
2½"
2½"
14"
2"
5"
50"
50"
53"
14½"
2½"
15½"
13"
3"
Front panel and posts; similar in construction to top part of the back panel. Note position of arm made to pattern shown below
13"
Detail of bottom rail mortice and tenon joint
½"
3"
1½"
1" Squares
Arm pattern; make two identical

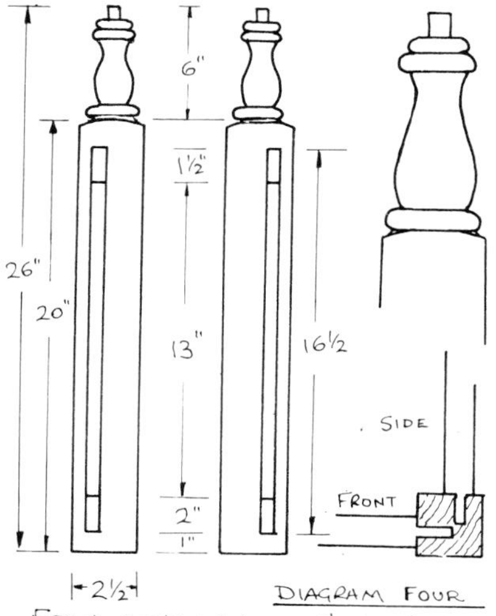

the panels and posts go together squarely and without twisting.

Meanwhile, the two front posts can be made. These, too, are 2½in square with the top 6in or so turned on the lathe to form a decorative arm support terminating in a 1in spigot which tenons into the underside of the shaped arm rest as shown in Diagram Four. After turning, mark out the grooves for side and front panels and the position of the mortices to take side and front cross rails and cut these as described.

Lack of a lathe should not deter anyone from making this settle as the turning on these posts can be omitted if required. As an alternative, simply taper or chamfer the corners of the post and cut a square tenon at its top.

The front panel is identical, apart from its vertical measurement, to the upper part of the back panel and is made up in exactly the same way. After a dry run to check that everything fits, the two front posts and the front panel may be glued up and cramped [clamped] until the glue is set.

The side rails and the single panels which form each end of the box seat section of the settle are now made and, with the cramps [clamps] removed from the back and front panels, the side rails and panels may be assembled dry into these already assembled sections. To check that all fits together correctly, stand the settle upright on its own

Plate 2 Assembling the side rails and single side panels

Plate 3 Using the spokeshave to shape the arm. Note the tenon on the end

Plate 4 Checking the fit of the arm and ends ready for final assembly

Plate 5 The assembled settle in cramps [clamps] after gluing up

feet, put under cramping [clamping] pressure and check especially at this stage that everything goes together square.

Arms shaped as in Diagram Three are made from 2½in square material and have a tenon cut at the end to correspond with the mortice already cut in the back post. Note that the shoulders of these joints are not quite square but are at a slight angle to follow the taper of the back post. A careful measurement taken from the back post to the centre of the spigot or tenon on the top end of the front post while the settle is in cramps [clamps] will give the position to drill or cut the mortice in the underside of the arms. Now remove the cramps [clamps], glue up all the end and arm joints and join up ends and arms with back and front sections. Drill and peg the front arm joints, then position cramps [clamps] to give pressure front to back and leave until the glue is set.

The box section of the settle requires a bottom or base and this consists of short lengths of tongue and groove boards laid across the width of the box and resting on a pair of rails glued and screwed to the inside faces of the back and front-bottom cross-rails. The two end boards of this base will require shaping to fit around the corner posts inside the box.

All that remains now is to fit the hinged lid. Because of the intervention of the arms this cannot be to the full width of the seat, therefore a narrow fixed board is placed at each end of the seat, shaped to fit between the corner posts. First, a 2 × 2in rebated [rabbeted] rail is glued and screwed to the middle back-rail, positioned so that the bottom of the rebate [rabbet] is in line with the top edge of the side and front top rails. The rebate [rabbet] itself is equal to the thickness of the hinged seat and to the side pieces so that on completion all lie flush and level. The ends of this rebated [rabbeted] rail are cut away to accommodate the end pieces which should be cut out according to Diagram Five. But check the measurements given against measurements taken on the job in case there are some slight discrepancies. For a neat appearance these end pieces need to be a good fit. They are glued and pinned into position, the pins punched below the surface and suitably filled. The outward-facing edge of each piece is rounded over and

DIAGRAM FIVE

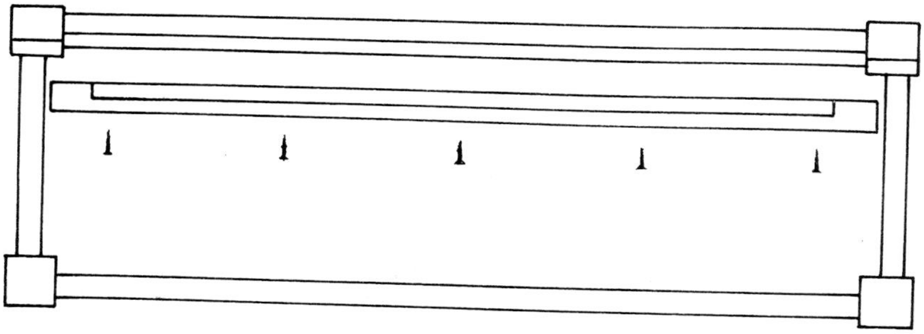

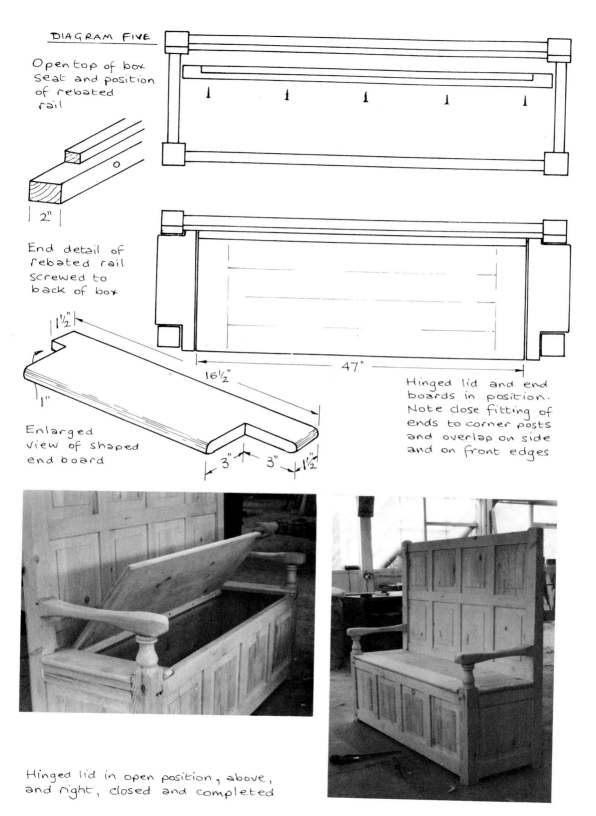

Open top of box seat and position of rebated rail

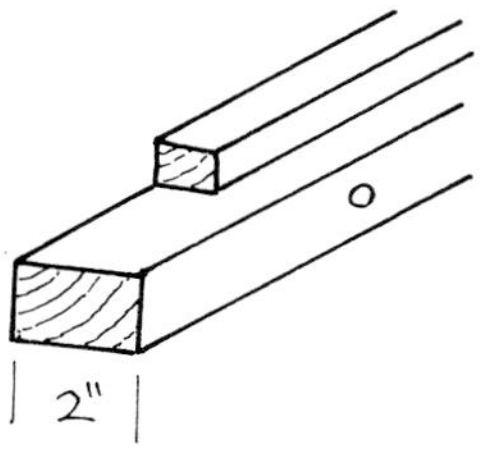

End detail of rebated rail screwed to back of box

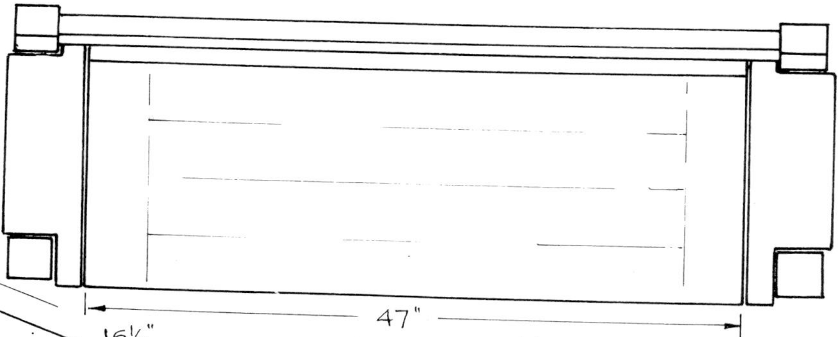

Hinged lid and end boards in position. Note close fitting of ends to corner posts and overlap on side and on front edges

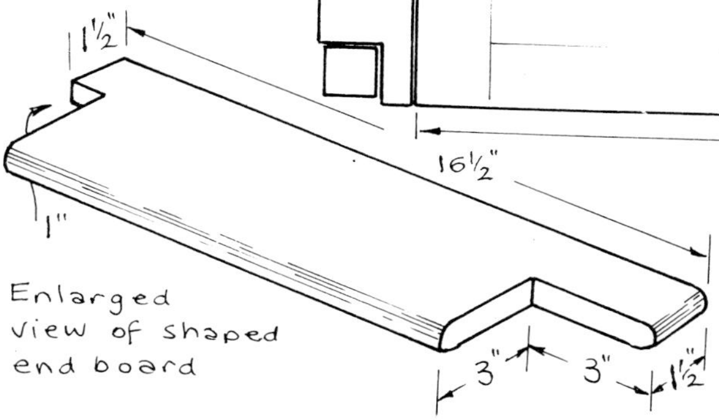

Enlarged view of shaped end board

Hinged lid in open position, above, and right, closed and completed

glass-papered [sandpapered] smooth.

The hinged part of the seat is made up of edge-jointed boards to make the required width and to include an overlap of ½in at the front edge. It is strengthened by having two bracing pieces tongued and grooved and glued at right angles across each end. Measure the space between the two end pieces and then cut the lid to fit nicely between. It is hinged by means of a pair of ordinary butt hinges, fitted as described in the chapter on Fixings and Fittings. Its front edge is rounded over in line with the end pieces and to avoid a sharp edge which would prove uncomfortable to the sitter.

After a final light sanding all over, the settle is ready for finishing. This is again left to individual choice; the one illustrated was stained and polished to produce the 'stripped pine' effect used elsewhere.

	MATERIAL REQUIREMENTS LIST. (CUTTING LIST IN INCHES)				
Nº	PURPOSE	MATERIAL	SIZE		
2	ARMS	PINE	20 × 2½ × 2½	SHAPED	
	FOR FRONT				
2	FRONT POSTS	"	26 × 2½ × 2½	PLANED & TURNED	
1	TOP RAIL	"	53 × 2½ × 1⅛	PLANED	
1	FOOT RAIL	"	53 × 3 × 1⅛	"	
3	UPRIGHTS	"	15 × 2 × 1⅛	"	
4	PANELS	"	13 × 12 × ¾	FIELDED	
	FOR SEAT				
3 OR 4	¾in. BOARDS	"	39in. long to cover 16½in. wide	EDGE JOINED	
2	CROSS PIECES	"	16½ × 4⅛ × ¾	GROOVED & TONGUED	
2	END BOARDS	"	16½ × 4½ × ¾	SHAPED	
1	BACK RAIL	"	50 × 2 × 2	REBATED	
	FOR BASE				
9 OR 10	½in. BOARDS	"	15in long to cover 51in wide	EDGE JOINED	

No	PURPOSE	MATERIAL	SIZE		
	FOR BACK				
2	BACK POSTS	PINE	50 x 2½ x 2½	PLANED & TAPERED	
1	TOP RAIL	"	53 x 2½ x 1⅛	PLANED	
1	MIDDLE RAIL	"	53 x 2½ x 1⅛	"	
1	LOWER RAIL	"	53 x 5 x 1⅛	"	
1	FOOT RAIL	"	53 x 3 x 1⅛	"	
3	UPRIGHTS	"	14 x 2 x 1⅛	"	
3	UPRIGHTS	"	16 x 2 x 1⅛	"	
4	TOP PANELS	"	12 x 12 x ¾	FIELDED	
4	LOWER PANELS	"	14 x 12 x ¾	"	
3 OR 4	½ in. BOARDS		51 in. long to cover 13 in. wide	EDGE JOINED	
	FOR SIDES				
4	TOP RAILS	"	17½ x 2½ x 1⅛	PLANED	
4	FOOT RAILS	"	17½ x 3 x 1⅛	"	
2	PANELS	"	13 x 15½ x ¾	FIELDED	

17
Smoker's Bow Chair

Illustrated on page 188

The style of low-back Windsor chair described here dates from about 1830. It is thought to have been a development from the earlier scroll-back chairs, of which there were a number of varying types, influenced by both the Philadelphia low-back, popular in the USA from around 1750, and the heavily built eighteenth-century Lancashire or Yorkshire Windsors. Characterised by sturdy construction and the continuous line of armbow and back scroll supported on a number of turned spindles, the smoker's bow, hybrid though it may be, was to become one of the most popular chairs for use in public places and for office as well as domestic purposes. It has appeared in other forms only slightly different from the original and under other names, typical among these being the Victorian berger or bergere bow with its high curved back and pierced splats and the so-called captain's chair popular in the pilot houses of Mississippi steam boats. The latter has narrower arms which curve downwards and socket into the seat.

Made in my own workshop, this chair is based on a traditional smoker's bow design. Elm was used for the seat and for the arm bow because of the strength imparted by its interlocking grain, with beech for all the

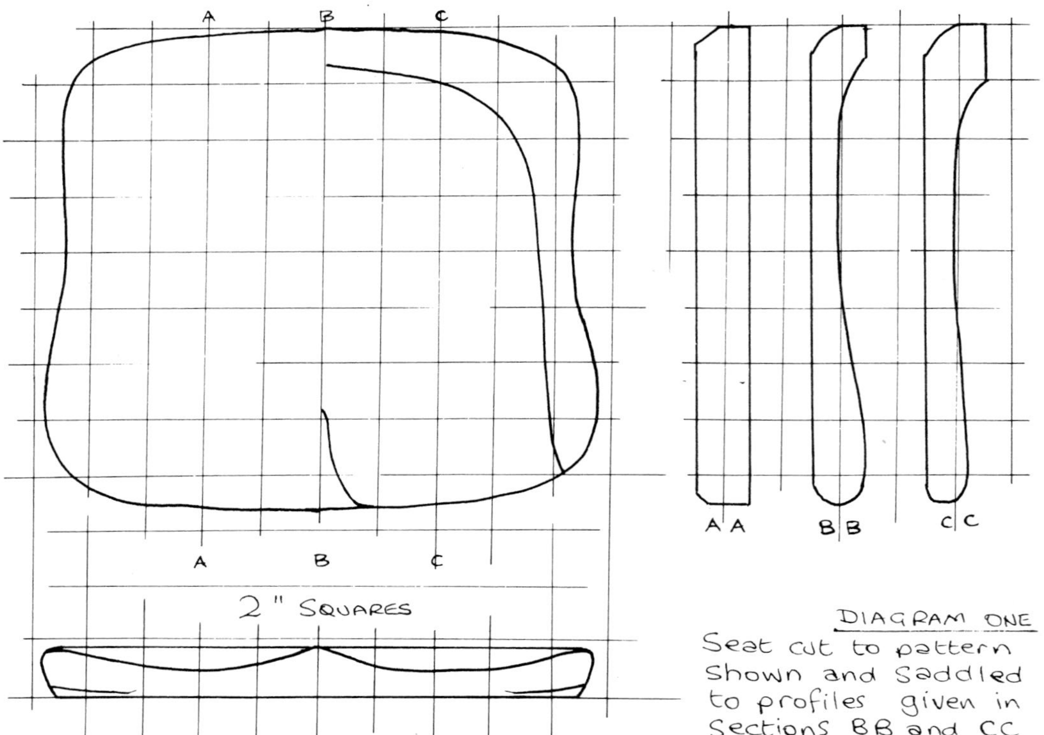

DIAGRAM ONE

Seat cut to pattern shown and saddled to profiles given in Sections BB and CC turned spindles. All the material used should be thoroughly dry and the beech straight grained.

Shaping the elm seat is as good a place as any to begin with. It is first band sawn to the outline given in Diagram One, after which it is saddled, ie the top surface hollowed out as with other Windsor chair seats. This can be done, as is described later for the Windsor rocking chair (p219), using the mallet and gouge method or with the tool known as an inshave. Work across the grain and notice that the grain in this case runs across the seat and not front to back as with the rocking chair. The choice of grain direction is entirely arbitrary, although some would argue differently. For me it is most often decided by the width of the board from which the seat is cut as seats are usually wider across than they are from front to back. If I have a wide enough board I cut seats with the grain running back to front or fore and aft – it's a matter of personal choice.

Pay particular attention to getting the front edges between the so-called 'cod-piece' nicely rounded over for maximum comfort. A sharp edge at these points would result in a pressure area to the underside of the thigh of the sitter which could be most uncomfortable and might lead to cramping of the lower limbs.

Chamfer the edges of the seat all round, top and bottom, then finish the hollowing with a curved steel scraper and finally with glass-paper [sandpaper].

Plate 1 Finishing the seat with a steel scraper

Still working with elm the chair arm bow can now be made. It is built up from three parts as shown in Diagram Two and these are sawn to shape using the patterns given. The two arm pieces come from a 1¼in-thick board; the centre piece, which is known as the scroll or crest, is made from a piece which must be 4 × 3in in section in order to obtain the required contoured shape. Note carefully the grain direction of the material used for the two arm pieces and for maximum strength cut these so as to retain as near to straight grain as possible, especially through their forward ends. To ensure a close fit between arms and scroll the mating surfaces of each should be planed and this is perhaps easiest done before cutting to shape.

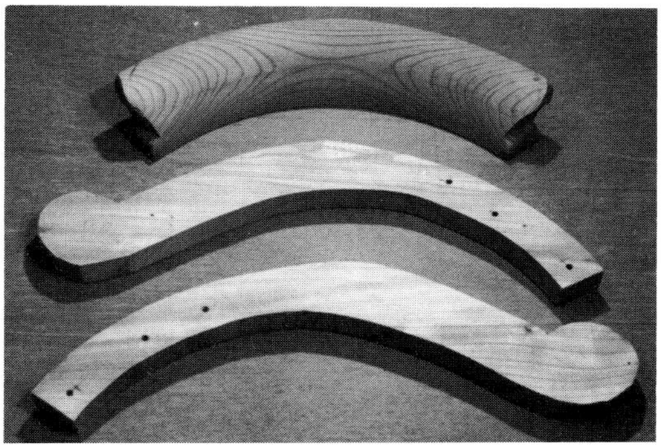

Plate 2 The three separate parts of the arm bow

After planing and sawing to pattern, some preliminary shaping of the scroll may be carried out, but do not attempt a finished shape at this stage; this is achieved after the three separate parts have been joined together.

The simplest and safest way of making sure that the three parts go together right so that you have an arm bow of the correct size and shape is to make a full-size paper pattern as shown in Diagram Two and lay the parts out on this. In particular, the junction between the two ends of the separate arm pieces must be correctly made and aligned otherwise the arms will spread either too little or too much and will not match up with the spindles rising from the seat. This junction must also be made a close fit as an

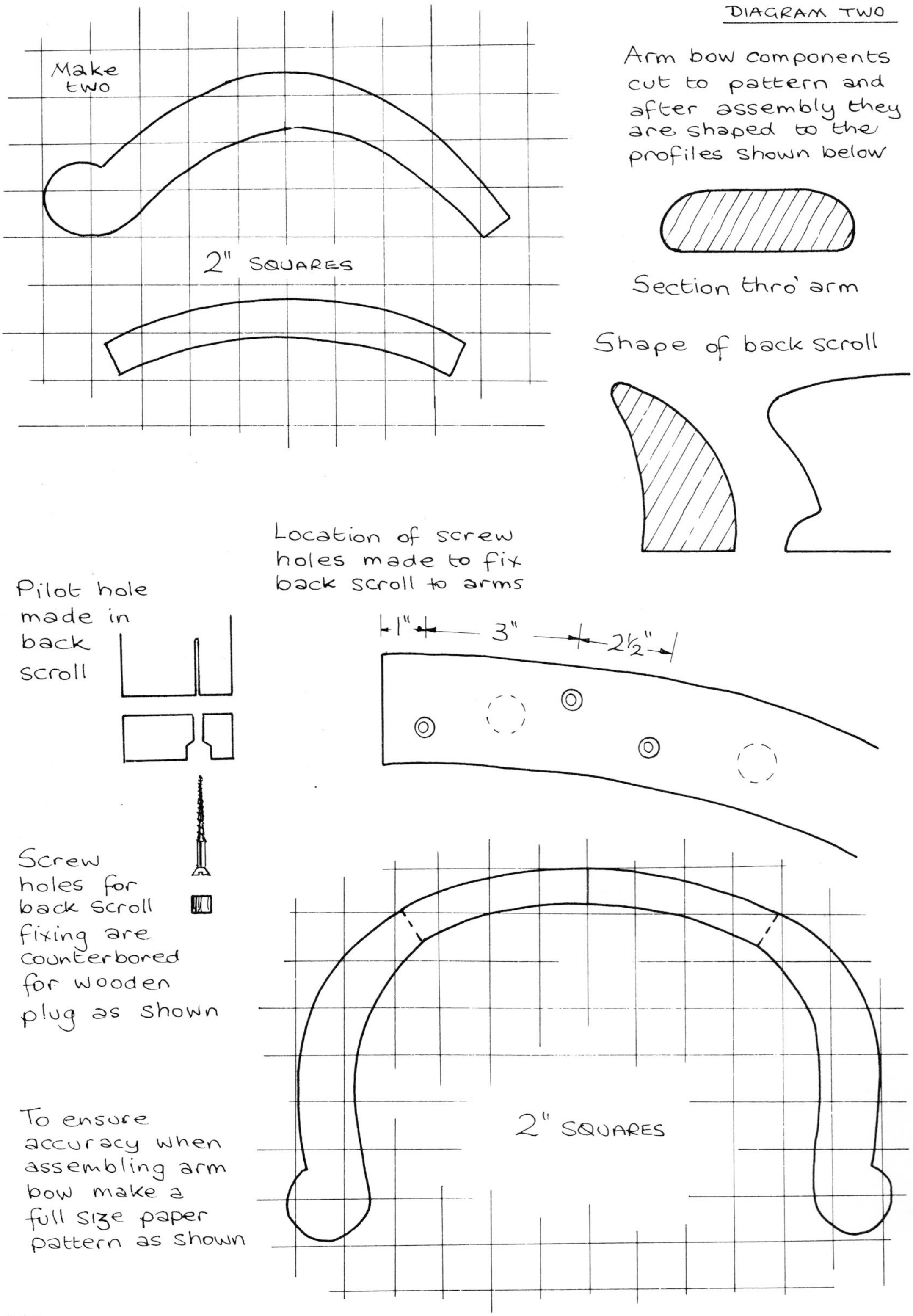
DIAGRAM TWO
Make two
2" SQUARES
Arm bow components cut to pattern and after assembly they are shaped to the profiles shown below
Section thro' arm
Shape of back scroll
Location of screw holes made to fix back scroll to arms
1"
3"
2½"
Pilot hole made in back scroll
Screw holes for back scroll fixing are counterbored for wooden plug as shown
To ensure accuracy when assembling arm bow make a full size paper pattern as shown
2" SQUARES

unsightly gap at this point would spoil the finished appearance of the chair.

The scroll, placed centrally over this junction, is fixed to the arm pieces by means of glue together with long screws. Drill three holes in each arm piece as shown in Diagram Two (these are strategically placed so that they do not interfere with the holes drilled later to accommodate the seat spindles), locate the position of these screw holes on the undersurface of the scroll and drill pilot holes of adequate diameter and depth. Then liberally coat the mating surfaces with glue, not forgetting the end-to-end junction of the two arm pieces; place the parts together and screw up tightly. Wipe off the surplus glue squeezed from the joint and leave to set.

When the glue is properly set the arm bow may be fashioned to its finished shape using spokeshave and scraper. First, shape the edges so that the scroll and arm pieces all 'marry' together nicely, then turn your attention to top and lower surfaces. The underside remains flat, only its corners being lightly chamfered. The top surface of the arms also remains fairly flat, but their corners are more softly rounded over to give a comfortable feel. The scroll is contoured to

Plate 3 Assembling the separate parts of the arm bow

Plate 4 The assembled joint of the arm bow before cleaning off surplus glue

Plate 5 Shaping the arm bow with a spokeshave

the section given in Diagram Two, the slightly concave surface at the back being made with a round-bottomed spokeshave and a curved scraper.

The remaining parts, legs, stretchers and spindles, are all made on the lathe. The legs are turned from 2½in material; the stretchers which form the underframing from 1¾in stuff. The type of underframing used in this chair is known as a double H-stretcher as it is stronger than the more normal H-stretcher which has only a single cross-piece. The spindles, eight in all, consist of six identical side and back spindles and two of a different shape and stronger which

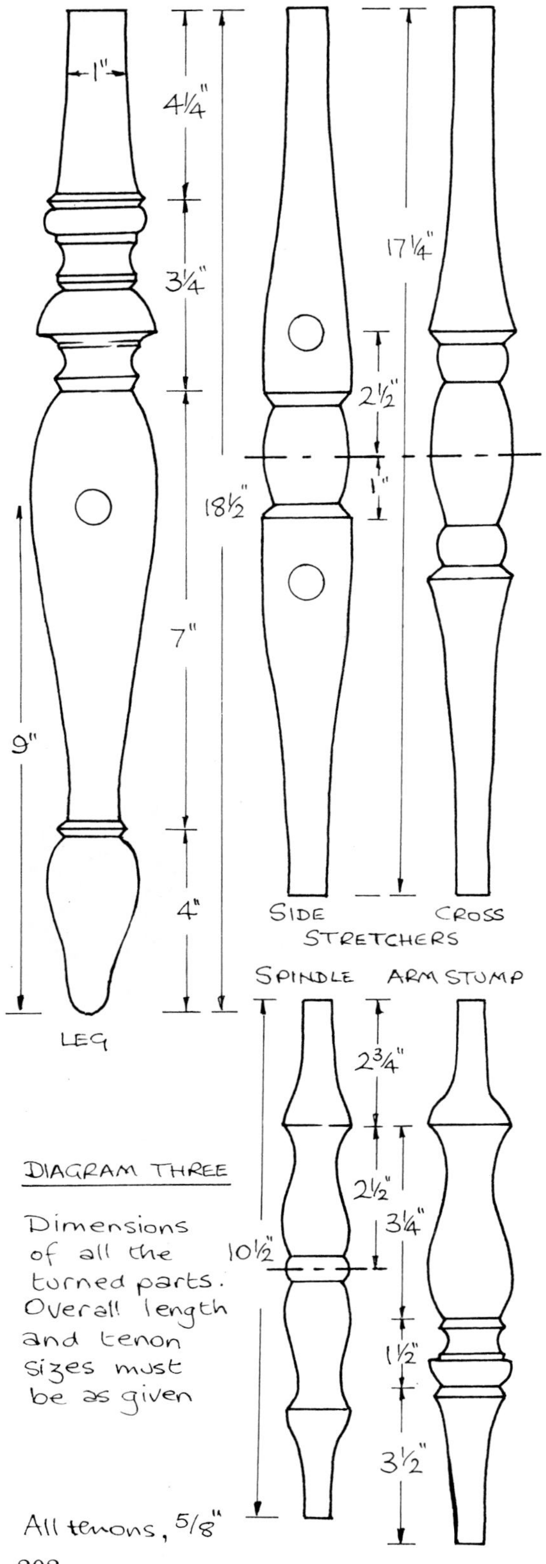

DIAGRAM THREE

Dimensions of all the turned parts. Overall length and tenon sizes must be as given

All tenons, 5/8"

form the front spindles, or arm stumps as they are sometimes described.

The designs given for these turned parts in Diagram Three need not be strictly adhered to; there is opportunity here for some individuality. But finished overall lengths and tenon sizes must be as given and I emphasise again the essentiality of tenons being a good fit in their respective sockets. Use glue but do not rely on it to fill gaps in loose-fitting joints. If a joint is loose because the tenon is too small, or the socket hole too big, make a replacement part.

The turned parts may be polished while in the lathe, a technique known as friction polishing. Turn each component to a smooth surface, preferably from the bevel of the turning tool, and bring to a fine finish by sanding and finally burnishing with a handful of shavings. Then, with the lathe running, apply a proprietary [commercial] polish and burnish this with a soft cloth. Avoid getting polish on the jointing surfaces at the ends of each component as this will seriously inhibit the adhesion of the glue used in jointing later.

With all the parts of the chair made, attention can now be turned to drilling holes in most of them, each one in its proper place and at its correct angle. Traditionally, this would often have been done by hand with a brace and bit, but here I have tried to simplify the task, especially that of obtaining correct angles, by the use of a simple jig used in conjunction with a pillar drill [drill press] or an electric hand drill in a pillar or drill press attachment. Forstner-type toothed bits are recommended for the drilling as these produce accurate, parallel-sided flat-bottom holes. Refer to the section on chairmaking, p44, for full details.

Begin with what in fact forms the 'foundation' of the chair, ie the seat, and mark this out on its underside as in Diagram Four to locate the position and sight lines of the leg holes. Noting that the drilling angle is different for front and back legs, set the drilling jig or sloping platform to the required angle for the front legs, in this case 12°, line up sight lines and centre lines on the jig and, after setting the depth stop on the machine, drill the front seat holes 1in in diameter. With the drilling jig at this same angle and using the V-shaped cradle, drill two of the

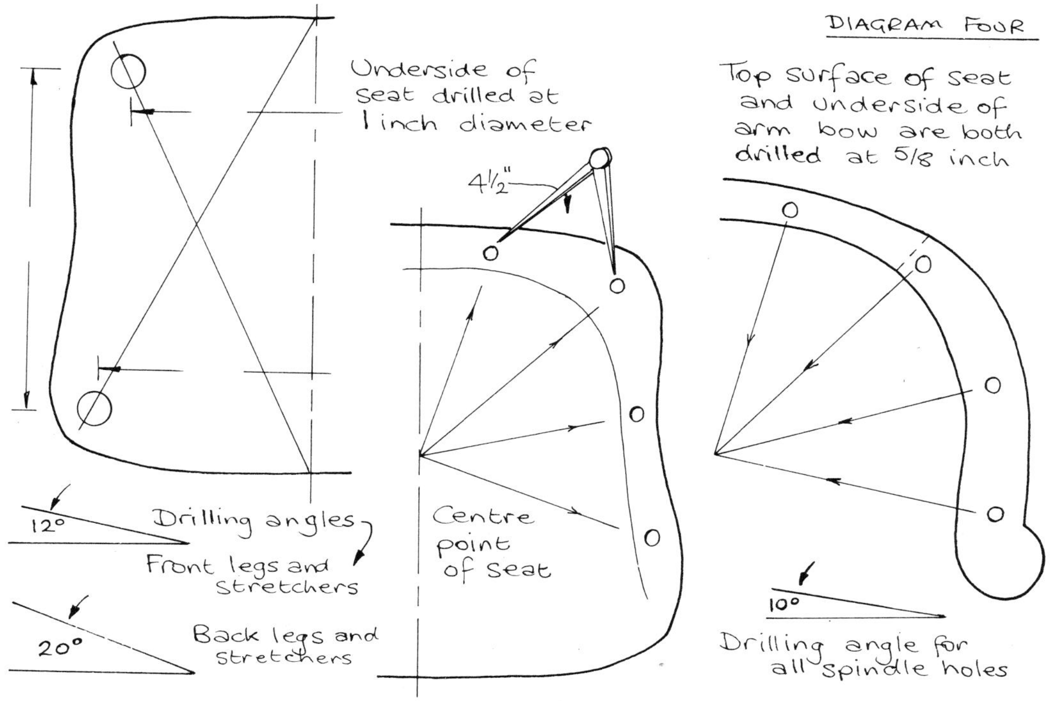

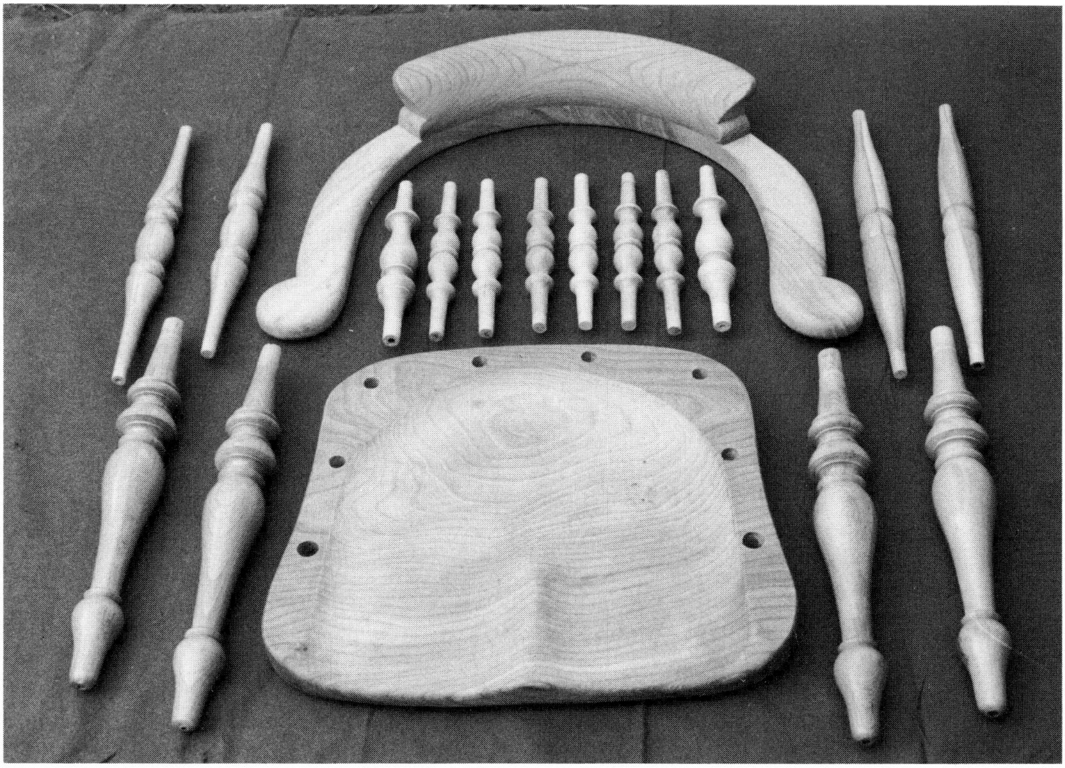

Plate 6 All the parts of the chair

prepared legs as shown to take the side stretchers of the underframing. Mark these two legs as front legs. Now alter the drilling jig to the required angle for the back legs, 20°, line everything up and drill these holes as before. Repeat the procedure just described to drill stretcher holes in the two remaining legs and mark these as back legs. The different angles of the stretcher holes will not allow front and back legs to be interchanged.

Fit the side stretchers into the legs dry, ie without glue at this stage, then fit legs into the seat to make sure everything goes together correctly. While these parts are together, ascertain the position, drilling angle and actual length of the two cross stretchers which complete the underframe – do this simply by placing them across the top of the two side stretchers and taking or marking in the required measurements. Dismantle the assembled parts, drill the holes for the cross stretchers, then have another dry assembly of the complete underframe and seat. Some minor adjustments may be required, but when all is satisfactory dismantle again so that work may be continued on the seat.

Mark out the top surface of the seat according to Diagram Four to give the positions of and the sight lines to the spindle socket holes. Using the drilling jig at the required angle of 10°, the spindle and arm stump holes are drilled at ⅝in diameter. The two front holes are drilled to the fullest depth possible, somewhere between 1¼in and 1½in in this case, or they may be taken straight through and the spindles wedged from below. If this is done the two front components will need to be made extra long. The six spindle holes should be drilled to a depth of at least 1in.

The underside of the arm bow should be marked out as shown in Diagram Four to give the position of the socket holes to accommodate the spindles rising from the seat. However, the bow should be put in place on the ends of the uprising spindles and the relative position of marks made and the actual placement of the spindles checked. If any adjustments are required they are best done before drilling the holes.

All the holes in the bow are ⅝in in diameter and they are drilled with the drilling jig set as for drilling the spindle holes in the seat top. Set the depth stop on the drill carefully so that the drilled holes are not made too deep with the resultant risk of breaking out on the top surface of the arms. Drill only to a depth which leaves at least ¼in of solid wood remaining. The two back-centre spindle holes may be made deeper as these can go up into the scroll if required. A dry assembly of bow on to spindles should be made at this stage to make sure that all goes

Plate 7 Checking the spindles and arm stumps for fit in the holes drilled in the seat surface

Plate 8 Dry assembly of the bow on to the spindles

Above, a peg in place

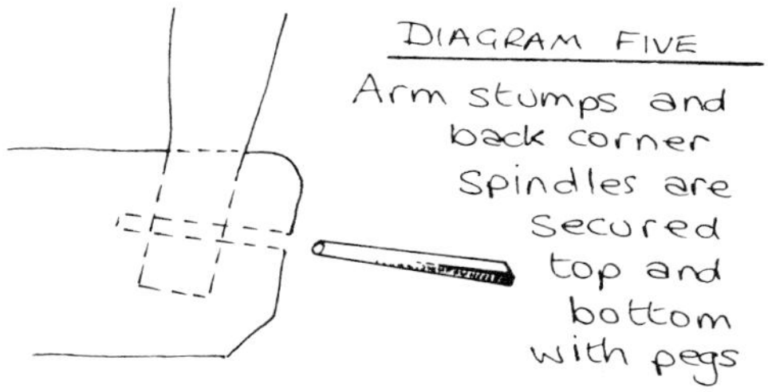
DIAGRAM FIVE
Arm stumps and back corner spindles are secured top and bottom with pegs

together nicely. Make sure that all the spindles and especially the two front ones go to or close to their full depth in the arm bow sockets to obtain the maximum gluing area for maximum security at these points.

After sanding, clean the seat and arm bow to remove any handling marks and all pencilled marks made during drilling, etc after which the chair may be glued up and assembled. Before this is done both the seat and arm bow may be given a coat of sanding sealer or varnish and rubbed down, but avoid getting sealer in the socket holes. Begin the assembly with the underframe; put glue into socket holes and insert the cross-stretcher tenons to their full depth. Fit stretchers to legs, put glue in leg sockets and insert the legs into their respective holes in the seat using a soft mallet or a hammer and a block of softwood to persuade tight joints to fit. Then set the chair up on its four legs, put glue in the spindle socket holes and put each of the spindles and the front arm stumps into their respective holes. Now put glue in the holes in the arm bow and bring this down on to the spindles, starting from the back, entering each spindle into its corresponding hole. Press the arm bow down into position and, if necessary, use the soft mallet to ensure that all the spindles are entered to the required depth, especially the two front ones. Check that the top of the arm bow is at the correct height of 9½in. A slight deviation from this measurement is of little consequence; what is more important is that the arm bow should be parallel to the top of the seat surface. Clean off any surplus glue.

Certain of the spindle joints are further secured by wooden pegs as Diagram Five shows. Do this preferably before the glue has set by drilling 3/16in holes at the points shown and hammer in square pegs whittled to a slightly tapered round along about two-thirds of their length. A little glue may be placed in the drilled holes before inserting the pegs. Clean off the top of the pegs flush with the surface and leave for all the glued joints to set.

If the seat and arm bow were sealed before assembly and with all the turned parts already polished, all that remains now is to give seat and arm bow two or three applications of wax polish. The chair illustrated was finished in this way.

Plate 9 Assembling the chair; persuading the legs to fit using a hide mallet

MATERIALS REQUIREMENTS LIST. (CUTTING LIST IN INCHES)

No.	PURPOSE	MATERIAL	INITIAL SIZES.		
1	SEAT	ELM	19 × 17½ × 1¾	SHAPED	
2	ARMS	"	20 × 8 × 1¼	"	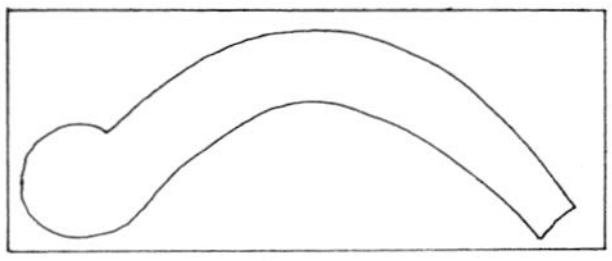
1	BACK SCROLL	"	15 × 4 × 3½	"	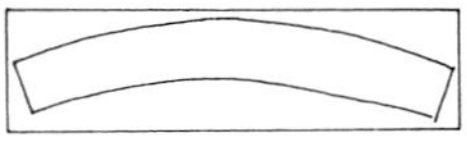
4	LEGS	BEECH	19 × 2½ × 2½	TURNED	
2	SIDE STRETCHERS	"	17½ × 1¾ × 1¾	"	
2	CROSS STRETCHERS	"	17½ × 1¾ × 1¾	"	
2	ARM STUMPS	"	11½ × 1¾ × 1¾	"	
8	SPINDLES	"	11 × 1⅜ × 1⅜	"	

18
Spinning Wheel

Illustrated on page 83

Before the invention of the spinning wheel fibres were spun on a simple spindle – little more than a weighted stick – suspended vertically from the hand. The spindle is normally revolved clockwise and as it rotates it imparts twist to the drawn-out fibres. At intervals, the rotating spindle is stopped so that yarn can be wound on to it. The process was partially mechanised, probably in the Far East, when the spindle, attached to a post in a horizontal position, was revolved by means of a wheel. In turn this gave rise to the European spinning wheel, known generally as the Great Wheel, which, as its name implies, employed a large wheel, pushed round by hand which, by means of a cord, was made to drive a much smaller wheel attached to a horizontal spindle. This caused the spindle to revolve at high speed and so increased considerably the rate of spinning.

Twisting and winding on were still two separate actions until, in the sixteenth century, the clever mechanism known as the flyer was introduced to combine these two parts of the spinning process. Now the twisting and the winding on were done simultaneously with the spun fibres collected not on the spindle itself but on a bobbin easily slipped off and replaced when full. The addition of the treadle to drive the wheel further increased its efficiency. The majority of spinning wheels in use today adopt this principle although there are many, usually regional, variations.

The wheel described here was made by Spock Morgan, a woodcarving, woodturning, jazz-saxophone-playing friend of mine from Selly Oak, Birmingham. Basically, the wheel is a traditional Saxony double-cord type but with a number of features which may or may not be strictly traditional but which, nevertheless, produces a well constructed and very usable wheel. The wheel is made throughout in seasoned beech, chosen because of its suitability for wooden 'engineering', and for its pleasing soft tones when brought to a fine finish and polished. All the turned parts were wax-friction polished in the lathe – the other components waxed by hand – as the work progressed.

Arguably, it may be said that the most difficult part in making a spinning wheel is the making of the wheel itself. The greatest problem lies not just in the method and processes involved in producing a wooden wheel but in how to make that wheel not only concentric but properly aligned so that in use it runs absolutely true. A wheel off-centre would be out of balance; it would set up unwanted vibrations and gyrate from side to side – in other words, it would wobble, it would be difficult to turn with ease and it would not spin satisfactorily. If one only wants a working model of a spinning wheel that would be quite acceptable, but if a spinning wheel is to spin well a first principle is that its wheel must run true and easy.

It should also be said that there are several different ways of making a spinning wheel correctly. Some ways are better than others and some ways are better for others. Certainly, each published description seems to prescribe a different approach to the problem so that in the end you can only choose one and try it.

Start with the hub of the wheel, mark this out oversize with compasses and band saw or otherwise cut roughly to size. Then turn the hub in the lathe by the method shown in Diagram One. By centring the hub in this way it ensures that the completed hub is concentric to the spindle hole.

Next, mark out the spoke holes on the hub's perimeter. The wheel has a rim consisting of four felloes (pronounced to rhyme

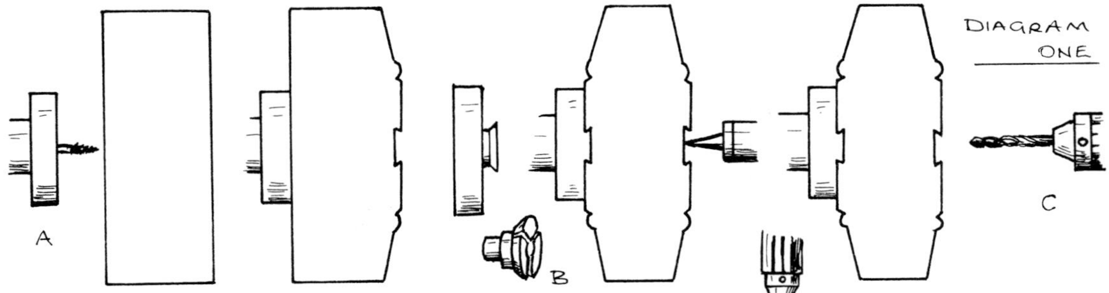

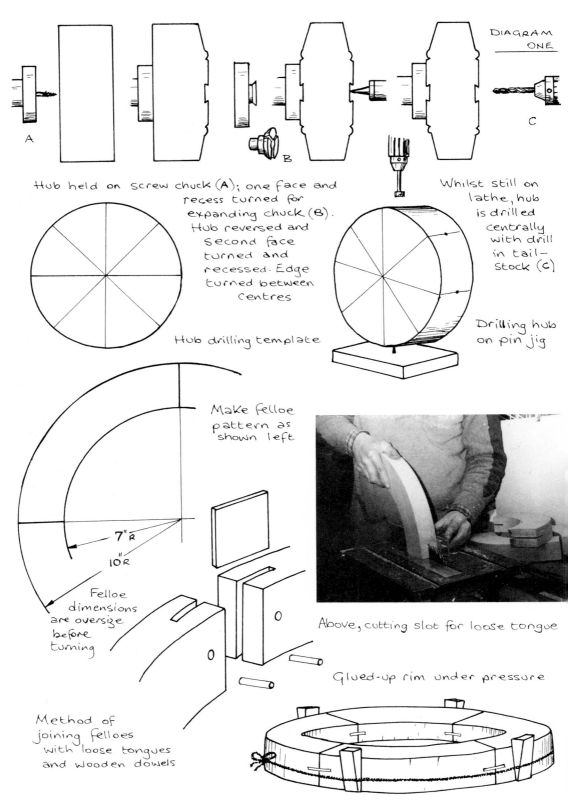

Hub held on screw chuck (A); one face and recess turned for expanding chuck (B). Hub reversed and second face turned and recessed. Edge turned between centres

Whilst still on lathe, hub is drilled centrally with drill in tail-stock (C)

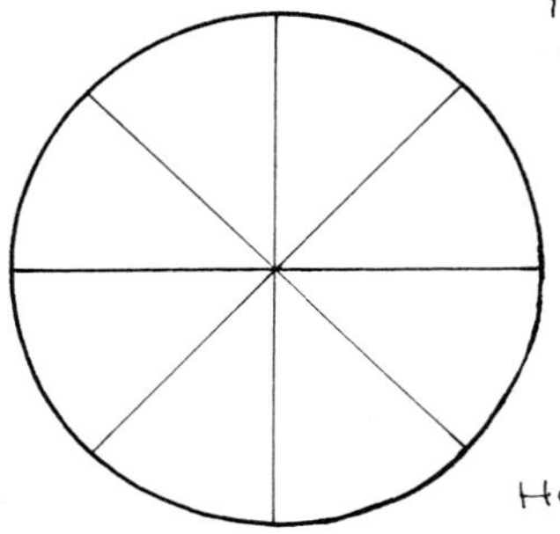

Hub drilling template

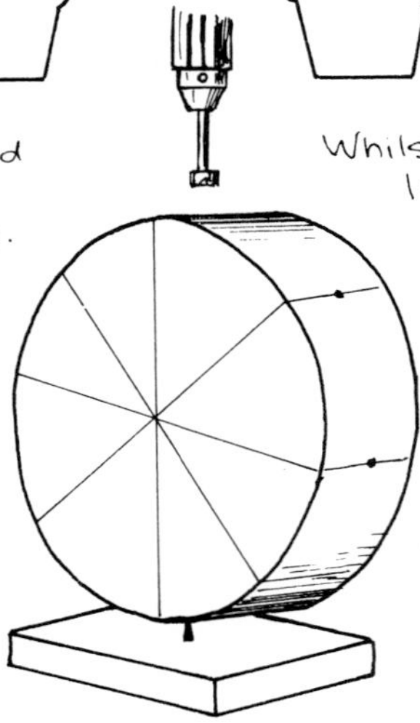

Drilling hub on pin jig

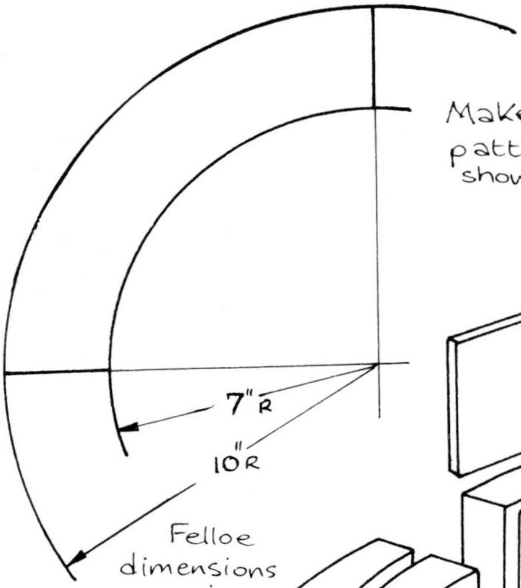

Make felloe pattern as shown left

Felloe dimensions are oversize before turning

Above, cutting slot for loose tongue

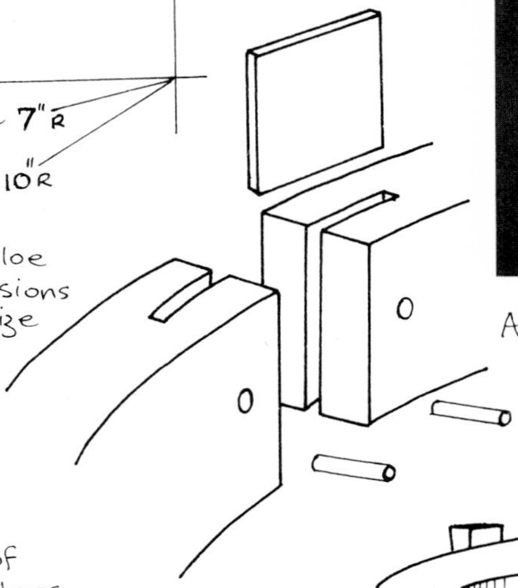

Method of joining felloes with loose tongues and wooden dowels

Glued-up rim under pressure

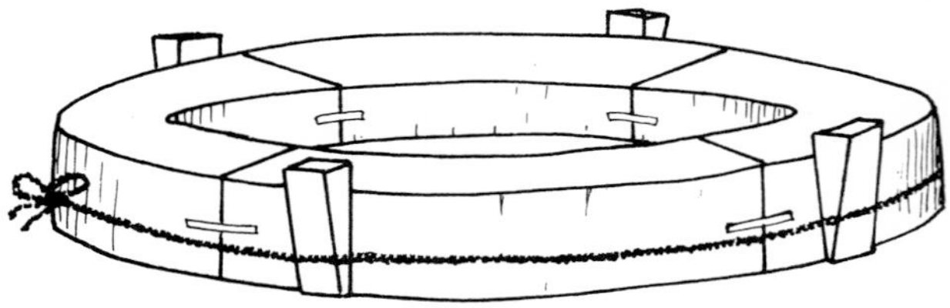

with bellies) and, as there are normally two spokes to each felloe, this means eight spoke holes in the hub. Complicated jigs are sometimes recommended for this operation but careful marking out and a pillar drill [drill press] are quite adequate, or the simple 'pin' device can be made and used as shown in Diagram One. For marking out, draw the 'Union Jack' template shown, centre the hub on this and mark in the points; or, if you are mathematically minded, it can be done by calculation and a pair of dividers. Mark the drilling points along a centre line scribed into the hub's perimeter.

For drilling, the pin device works well. Make it by first fixing a piece of softwood to the table of the pillar drill. Put a small drill in the machine and bring its point down to just touch and mark the surface of the wood. At this point hammer in a panel pin and cut off its head to leave approximately ⅛in protruding. Centre a point marked on the hub on this pin and drill its opposite point to the required depth. When four holes have been drilled in this way it will be necessary to fill each one temporarily with a centred dowel in order to drill its opposite hole. Remove the plugs on completion.

Now the rim of the wheel can be made. The finished diameter is 19½in with a rim depth of 2¾in. Cut each of the four felloes to the pattern given in Diagram One. Make this on card or thin ply which can be easily

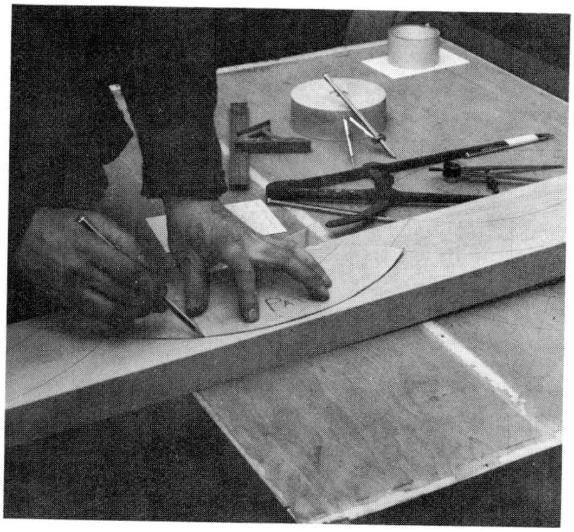

Plate 1 Using a pattern to mark out felloes for the wheel

cut. Cut out this pattern and use it to mark out the felloes and saw these to shape.

Felloes are frequently joined end-to-end with dowels; this jointing method is quite satisfactory and has the advantage of being invisible on completion. However, it can be problematic, especially at the marking-out stage. The loose tongue method shown in Diagram One may prove easier for some. Holes, which serve a double purpose, are drilled through at each end of each felloe and pass through the loose tongue; tapered wooden pegs driven in when gluing up keep the joints under pressure until the glue sets. Additionally, pressure may be applied by means of a Spanish windlass and wedges as shown in the diagram.

Plate 2 Turning the rim of the wheel

When the glue is properly set the pegs are removed and the holes counterbored each side, ½in in diameter, to a depth of approximately ½in. Then, by means of woodscrews through these holes, the built-up rim is mounted as near central as possible on a disc of ply or blockboard which has been centred and fixed to the largest face plate available. Then, with the lathe at its slowest speed – remember the peripheral speed of the rim will exceed the spindle speed by a factor of twenty, ie 600 rpm (say 30 ft per second) at the spindle means 600 fps for the rim – true up the outside face and mark it with any decorative lines. Remove from the wood disc 'face plate', turn it over and, using the same screw holes, remount it on the lathe. Again,

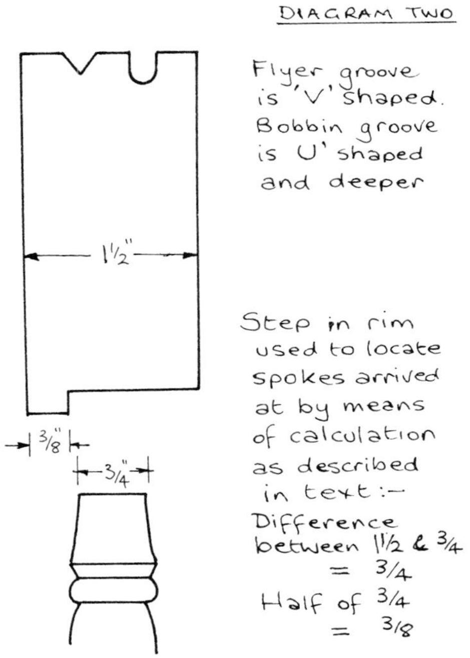

true up the outside face, then proceed to turn the inside and outside edges.

DIAGRAM TWO
Flyer groove is 'V' shaped.
Bobbin groove is U' shaped and deeper
1½"
Step in rim used to locate spokes arrived at by means of calculation as described in text:-
Difference between 1½ & ¾ = ¾
Half of ¾ = 3/8
3/8"
3/4"

When these are completed the outside surface has two cord grooves cut into it. These should differ in respect of the different functions which they serve; a) to drive the flyer; b) to drive the bobbin. The flyer groove should be V-shaped; the bobbin groove U-shaped and deeper than the flyer groove. The inside surface is not left plain either; it has a step of about ⅛in high cut into it, equal in width to half the difference between the thickness of the rim and the diameter of the end of a spoke. This step helps locate the spokes when fitted later. (Diagram Two will explain the method.)

The eight spokes can now be turned. Any design may be followed, but they should all be of equal size and weight so that the wheel is not unbalanced and tenon sizes and initial length should be as given. Check this initial length against the inside diameter of your rim – spokes should be a little overlength at this stage. Glue each finished spoke into a hole already drilled in the hub, making sure each goes in to its full depth, and allow to set.

The careful work of matching spokes to rim is the next task and use is made of the

Plate 3 (*below*) Completed rim and hub with spokes

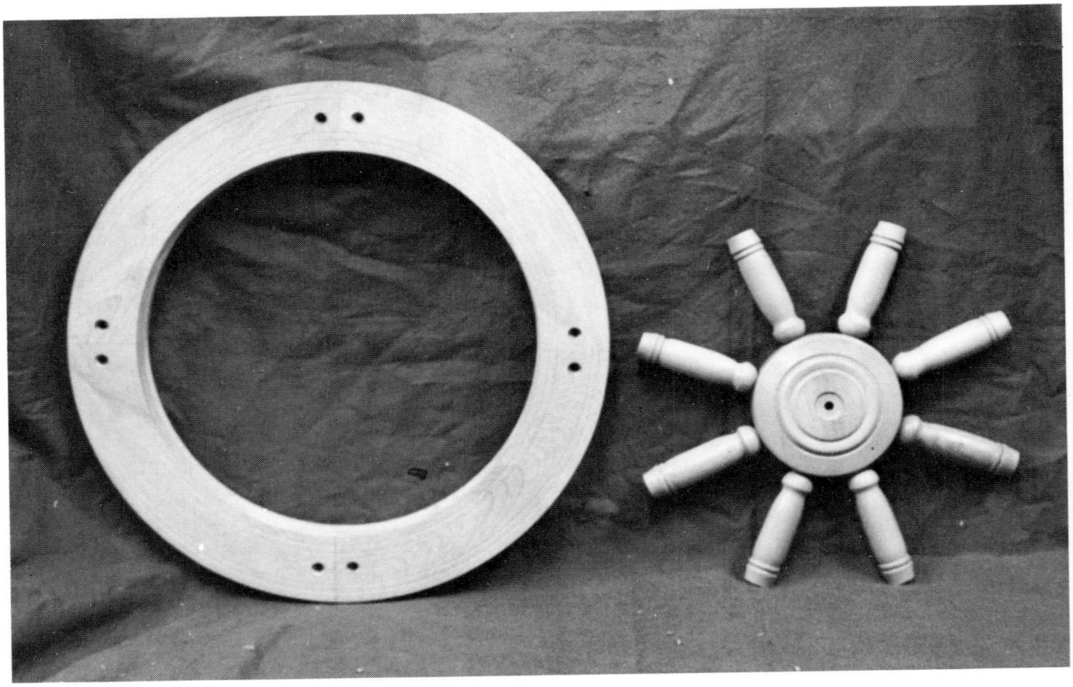

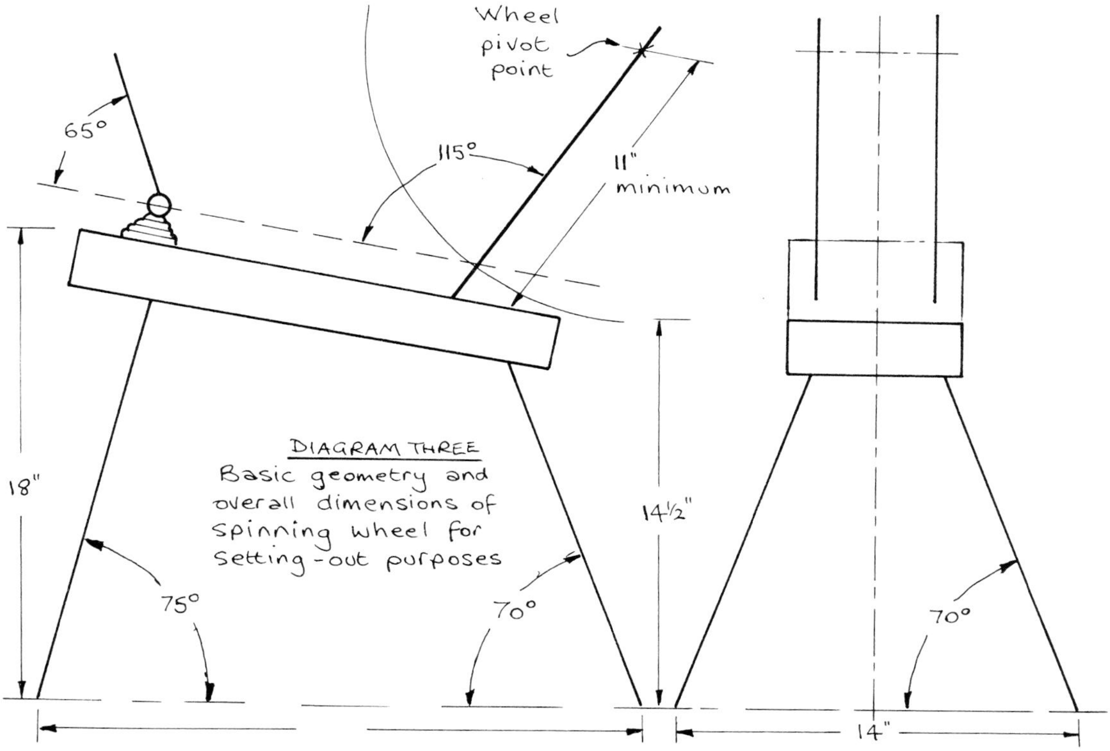

Plate 4 Matching up spoke length on the lathe

lathe in what may seem a somewhat unorthodox manner. A sanding disc, mounted on a face plate, is used to trim the ends of spokes which are rotated against it, as illustrated in Plate 4. The hub is set up to be a running fit on a short length of metal rod held in the lathe's tool post for this purpose. Making sure each spoke is treated equally, take a little off at a time, until the hub and spoke assembly are a snug fit within the rim. Raise the rim off the bench on blocks while doing this to clear the hub if it protrudes. When a nice fit has been achieved – and it is not as difficult as it may seem – put glue on the end of each spoke and leave to set. Then drill ⅛in holes through the edge of the rim into the spoke ends and tap in a hardwood peg. The result is an absolutely concentric wheel.

This rebated [rabbeted] rim and pin method is not new; a similar technique has been in use for many years and has proved itself to be totally satisfactory. As stated, there are other ways of making a wheel. By all means, try one, or some, of the others.

Plate 5 The completed wheel – the holes are dowelled through later

Plate 6 Close view of the flyer/bobbin assembly mounted in the mother-of-all

With the wheel completed now you can begin on the easy parts! Concentrate next on making the base, platform, stock or table – it has been given all these different names. Like a chair seat this part is the foundation of the construction and is carried on three legs, well splayed out to give the necessary stability. In this type the table has a pronounced downward slope to give adequate clearance to the wheel which is carried on two wheel uprights socketed into the top of it. At the opposite end is an arrangement known as the mother-of-all which, as its name suggests, carries all the working parts. This in turn is carried, not by direct fixing to the table, but into a sliding block, adjustable by means of a threaded screw by which means tension may be applied to the drive cord between the wheel and the working parts.

Rising up from the mother-of-all bar are two turned pieces known as maidens and between these, mounted in bearings, is the arrangement known collectively as the flyer mechanism, but which actually consists of the separate flyer, bobbin and pulley whorl, all carried on a steel shaft. Located to one side is the distaff, used when spinning flax but otherwise not essential.

Below the table is the treadle, fixed to a bar free to pivot between two of the legs. Treadle motion is transmitted through a rod

Plate 7 Close view of the footman attached to the eccentric crank

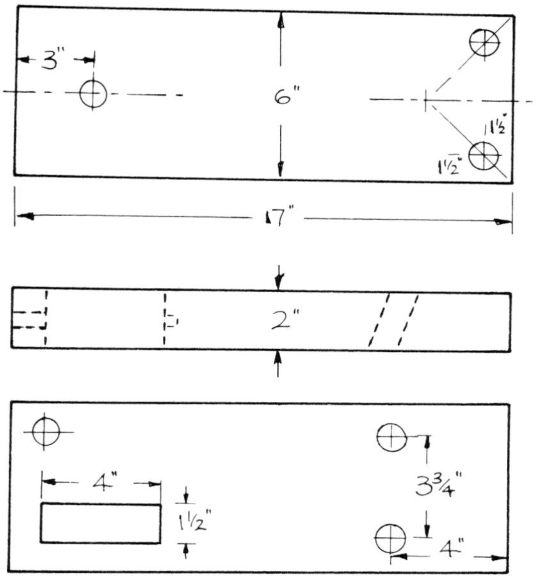

DIAGRAM FOUR
Table dimensions and setting-out

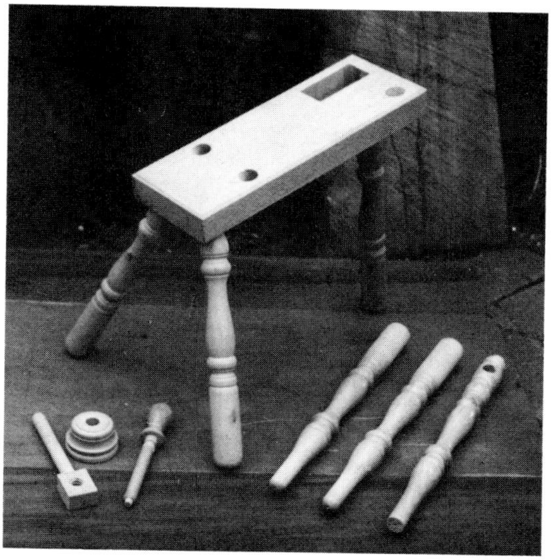

Plate 8 Trial assembly of the table and legs; other completed components are shown in the foreground

known generally as the footman or pitman which has its upper end connected, via an eccentric crank to give turning motion, to the wheel.

Begin by setting out the position of all socket holes, etc, in the table, top and bottom, as shown in Diagram Four, and drill the holes at the correct diameters and at the appropriate angles. The techniques for angle drilling described for chairmaking (p44) are appropriate here, too. Note that leg-socket holes are 'blind' but that the two wheel upright sockets go right through. The rectangular slot into which fits the sliding tensioning block can also be cut.

Now, all the turned parts and other components can be made beginning with the three legs. Only these are glued in and their joints are straightforward parallel round tenons. All the other joints between components are not glued but are taper-fit dowels, some of them held with retaining pegs where necessary. This is done principally to allow adjustments to be made to the precise positioning of these parts during the spinning process – the proper function of the wheel depending upon quite subtle changes in orientation, determined by the experienced spinner.

The aforementioned taper dowels, and their sockets, should not cause any undue alarm; the taper needs only to be a very gradual one – similar to the engineer's Morse taper. As a consequence, socket holes can be drilled parallel, in a size which corresponds to the diameter approximately half way along the taper. The application of a little rosin helps the friction fit.

Reference to Diagram Five will show that the two wheel uprights have slots cut into them for the wheel axle. These are lined with thin leather to give an improved bearing surface and are capped and pegged to prevent the wheel from jumping out when in motion. Both maidens have small slots in them to take the leather bearings for the flyer/bobbin spindle; the bearings themselves are cut from ¼in-thick shoe-sole leather. The three ¾in holes in the mother-of-all bar are carefully drilled at the correct angles using the chairmaker's V-shaped cradle and drilling jig.

The tension screw and its sliding block are first turned to size and then threaded using a wood-thread-forming tap and box. Where these are not available threaded metal components make an aesthetically poor but mechanically fair substitute.

Bobbin and spindle whorl are turned to the dimensions given, while the flyer is cut from ¾in-thick beech to the pattern shown.

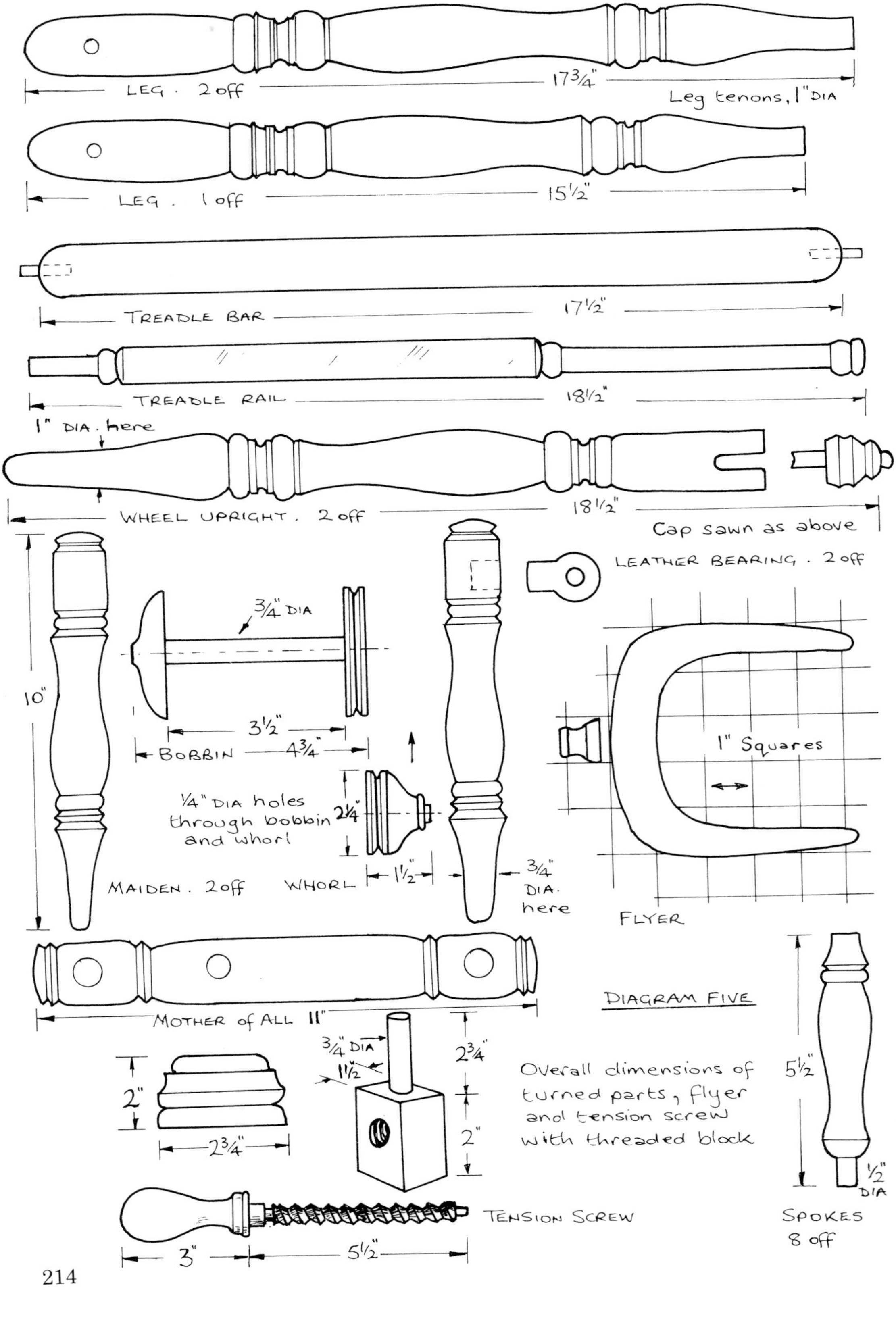
LEG . 2 off
17¾"
Leg tenons, 1" DIA
LEG . 1 off
15½"
TREADLE BAR
17½"
TREADLE RAIL
18½"
1" DIA. here
WHEEL UPRIGHT . 2 off
18½"
Cap sawn as above
LEATHER BEARING . 2 off
¾" DIA
10"
3½"
BOBBIN
4¾"
¼" DIA holes through bobbin and whorl
2¼"
1" Squares
MAIDEN . 2 off
WHORL
1½"
¾" DIA. here
FLYER
MOTHER of ALL 11"
DIAGRAM FIVE
¾" DIA
1½"
2¾"
2"
2"
2¾"
Overall dimensions of turned parts, flyer and tension screw with threaded block
5½"
½" DIA
TENSION SCREW
SPOKES 8 off
3"
5½"

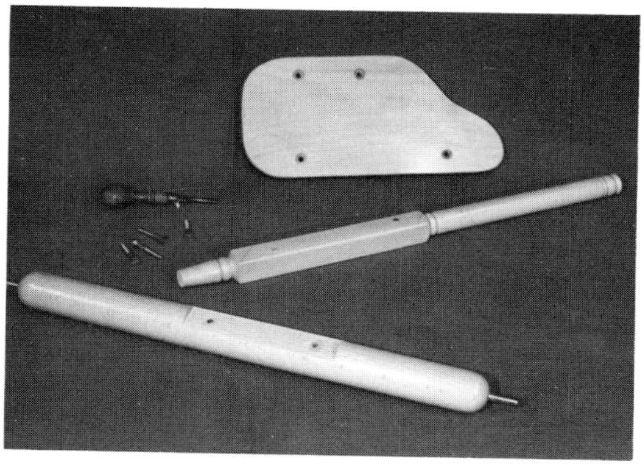

Plate 9 Treadle parts ready for assembly

The grain direction should follow the arrow in the diagram. The small collar is turned separately.

The treadle bar has metal pins inserted at each end and these locate in the holes drilled into two of the legs. It has a flat cut on one edge and is drilled at an acute angle to take the end of the treadle rail. The treadle itself, cut from ½in beech, is screwed across the two (see Plate 9). The free end of the treadle rail should be below the crank of the wheel axle. A leather thong looped through a hole ties it to the bottom end of the footman, the other end being attached to the axle crank in a keyhole slot (Diagram Six).

With all the components now made, fit together first the legs and treadle assembly into the table, then fit the top components, tension block and screw, mother-of-all and maidens and then the wheel uprights. Finally, fit the wheel.

Meanwhile, work on the flyer/bobbin assembly can be completed. The flyer is fixed to a ¼in steel shaft, the outboard end of which has a short piece of hollow tube silver soldered (or use epoxy resin) to it. A turned wooden collar is fitted over the joint and a ¼in hole drilled through it and into the tube to form the orifice through which the yarn passes when spinning. The bobbin should be a nice running fit on the shaft, free to rotate independently but without wobble. The separate spindle whorl has to drive the spindle and flyer but has to be detachable so that bobbins can be interchanged. Accordingly, a square is filed on the shaft to match a

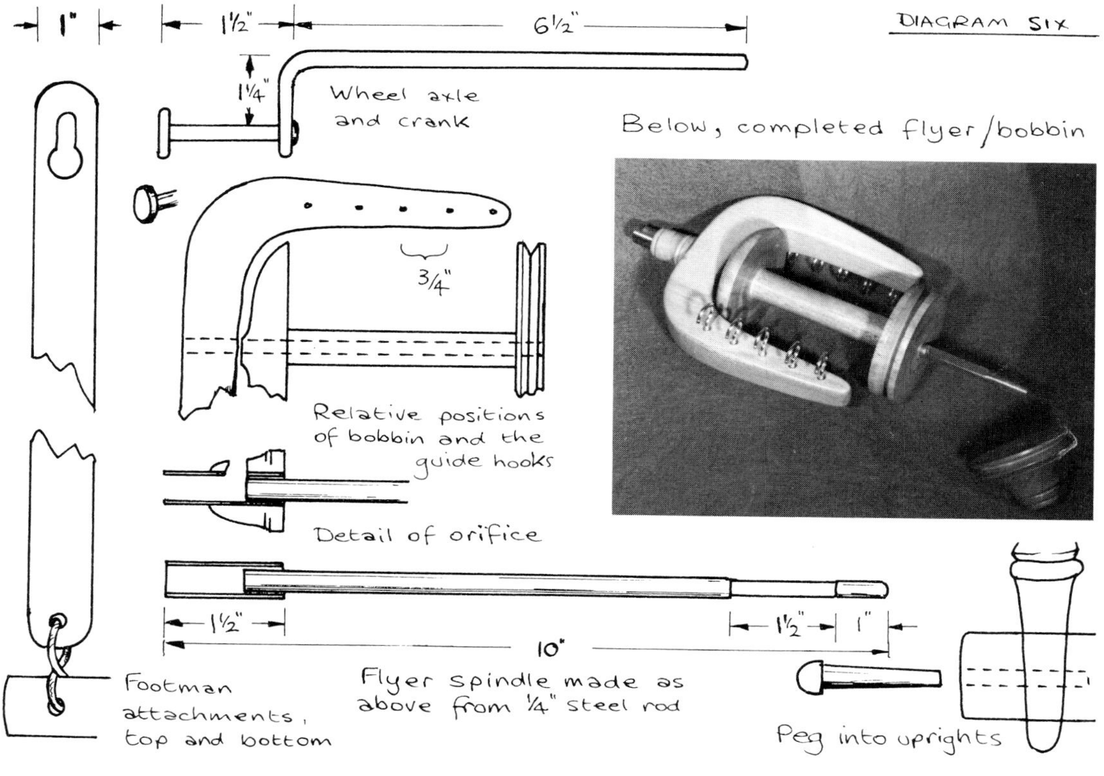

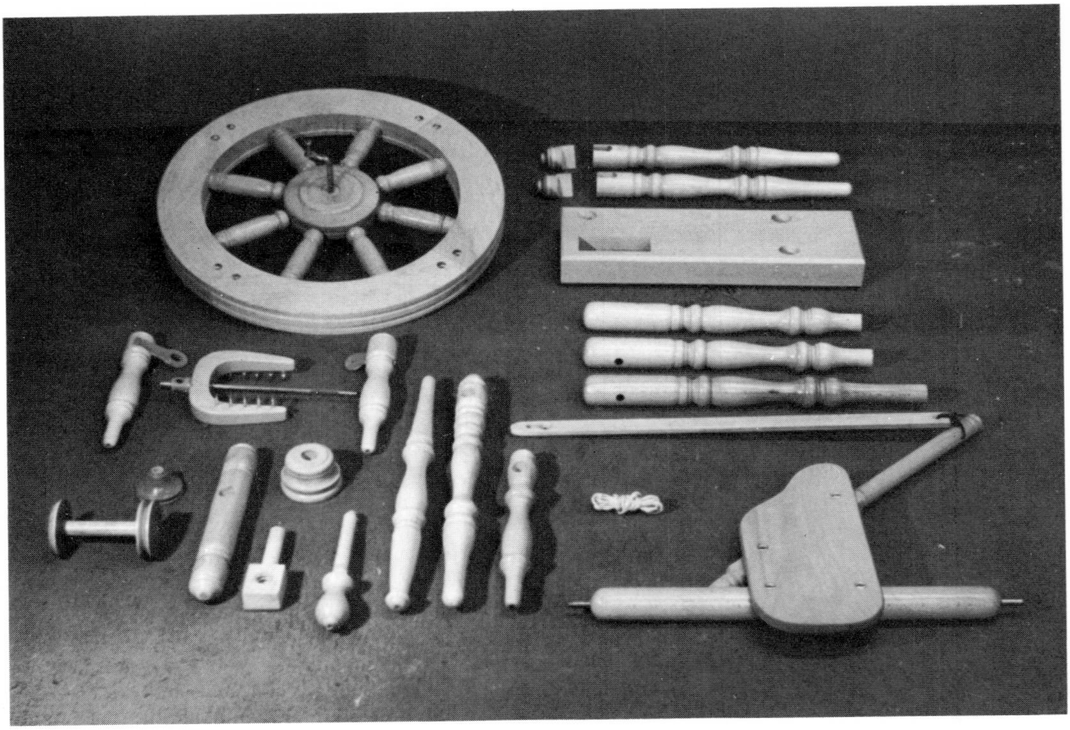

Plate 10 (*above*) All the wheel components on display

Plate 11 Trial assembly of the main components

Plate 12 Work in progress on the flyer and bobbin

square hole in the whorl. Finally, screw in a row of small brass guide hooks on opposite sides of each arm of the flyer. Space these about ¾in apart, positioned to match up with the bobbin. These serve to distribute the spun fibres equally along the length of the bobbin (see Diagram Six).

The flyer/bobbin assembly can now be mounted in its leather bearings and the wheel fitted in its bearings in the uprights. With the double drive cord loosely in place, the wheel should be revolved and 'sighted' for being in line with the bobbin and spindle whorls. Uprights and maidens should be adjusted until they are. When everything is satisfactory, holes are drilled through the side of the table into the wheel uprights and wooden pegs fitted. The maidens are not pegged but left free for adjustments by the spinner. Then, with the footman connected, revolve the wheel again by hand to start it and check the treadle action.

If all parts were waxed as they were produced all that is needed now is a final loving polish and you are ready to begin spinning, or learning how to.

	MATERIALS REQUIREMENTS LIST		(CUTTING LIST IN INCHES)		
Nº	PURPOSE	MATERIAL	INITIAL SIZES		
1	TABLE	BEECH	17 × 6 × 2	PLANED	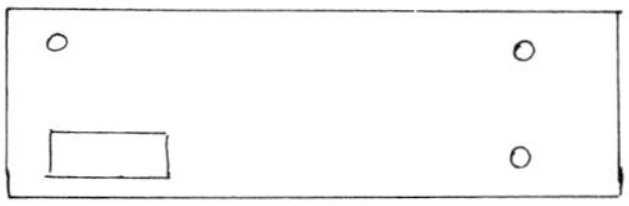
4	FELLOES	"	14 × 6 × 2	SAWN & TURNED	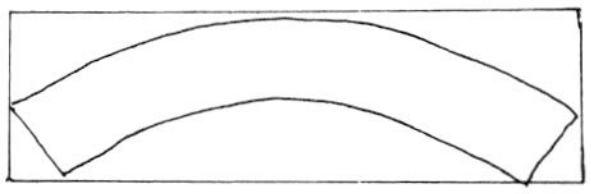
1	HUB	"	6 × 6 × 2	"	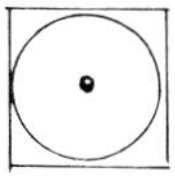
8	SPOKES	"	6 × 1½ × 1½	TURNED	
2	LEGS	"	16 × 2 × 2	"	
1	LEG	"	18 × 2 × 2	"	
2	UPRIGHTS	"	18 × 1¾ × 1¾	"	
1	MOTHER-OF-ALL	"	12 × 1¾ × 1¾	"	
1	" " " BASE	"	3 × 3 × 2	"	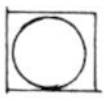
2	MAIDENS	"	11 × 1¾ × 1¾	"	
1	TENSION SCREW	"	9 × 1¾ × 1¾	TURNED & THREADED	
1	" BLOCK	"	5 × 2 × 2	SHAPED & THREADED	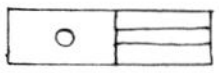

MATERIALS REQUIREMENT LIST. continued

Nº	PURPOSE	MATERIAL	INITIAL SIZES		
1	FLYER	BEECH	6 × 6 × 3/4	SHAPED	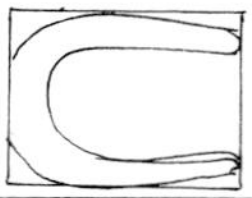
(3) 1	BOBBIN	"	5 × 3 × 3	TURNED	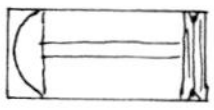
1	WHORL	"	2½ × 2½ × 2	"	
2	DISTAFF	"	17 × 1½ × 1½	"	
1	DISTAFF	"	10 × 1½ × 1½	"	
	¼" STEEL ROD, 2 pieces 10" long. ¼ I.D. STEEL TUBE. 1 piece 1½" long 10, ½" BRASS HOOKS. LEATHER FOR BEARINGS. CORD				
1	TREADLE BAR	"	17½ × 1½ × 1½	TURNED	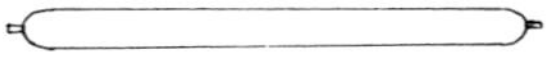
1	TREADLE RAIL	"	18½ × 1½ × 1½	"	
1	TREADLE	"	10 × 5½ × ½	SHAPED	
1	FOOTMAN.	"	22 × 1 × 3/8"	"	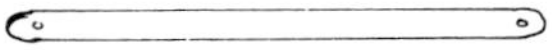
	¼" STEEL ROD – 2 pieces 1½" long. 4 BRASS SCREWS, 8's 1½" long.				

19

Double-bow Windsor Rocking Chair

Illustrated on page 221

The double-bow Windsor rocker is a typical example of what might be called a desirable heirloom. Many of those nice old ones still around today, probably made during the late nineteenth century, are among the best examples of the fine craftsmanship of the period. Time has given them a warm patina unobtainable from a tin of spray-on lacquer and even after years of use – and sometimes misuse – most are still as sturdy as the day they were made. Honestly built in sound and suitable materials they have served several generations already and should serve several more.

By using the same materials and similar methods of construction it is possible still to produce such a chair – not a 'reproduction' (how I hate that word) but an honest, late-twentieth-century version of this classical design.

Materials are all-important in this project, so first obtain your wood: elm for the seat, ash or beech for all else, or yew if you can obtain it. Choose your wood carefully and from a reliable source. For the seat use a nicely grained piece of dry elm, and I do mean really dry – air dried for preference but it may have to be kiln dried to be sure. I use ash with the elm seat, cut from a Lakeland coppice, cleft with the axe and roughly shaped before seasoning until dry. Cleaving the ash ensures straight grain, important for strength and essential for the steam bending of the two bows. It is possible to use sawn material provided it is truly straight grained, but I must emphasise, choose carefully.

Gather together all the wood you are going to need (see Materials Requirement List, p229) plus some extra in case of accidents. This applies especially to the pieces which are to form the bows. Select for matching grain and colour if you intend to clear wax the finished chair; if staining, this is obviously less important. Don't be in too big a hurry at this, or for that matter, any other stage; the finished chair will last for a hundred years or more – if it takes a hundred hours of work spread over a hundred days or more to finish it then it will be all the better made because of this.

As an initial step, cut out the seat shape to the pattern given (Diagram One). This sawn shape is first used as the former [form] around which the two bows are bent after steaming (described earlier, p42). Clamp the temporary former with cramps [clamps] as shown.

Bend the arm bow first and, with the bending strap still in place and held with a sash cramp [clamp], ease the bow off the former [form] and give the cramp [clamp] screw several more turns so as to 'overbend' the bow. This compensates for the inevitable small amount of springback which will occur when the bow is dry and the clamping pressure is released. With the former now available, again bend the back bow but leave this in position on the former to dry out and set.

With the two bows bent successfully – and be prepared for possible disappointments at this stage – give yourself a pat on the back, for this is, technically, the most difficult part of the work. If you have got this far the rest is all plain sailing – well, almost!

Now, let's turn to turning. The four legs and the two front arm-supports are lathe turned from dimensioned stock as given in the Materials Requirement List. The designs shown are arbitrary; choose whatever pleases you to give your chair some individuality, but adhere to the finished overall lengths and tenon sizes as given. The tenons must all be a really good interference fit in their respective mortice holes. Do not rely on plenty of glue as a filler in these joints. If the tenon is at all loose consign the

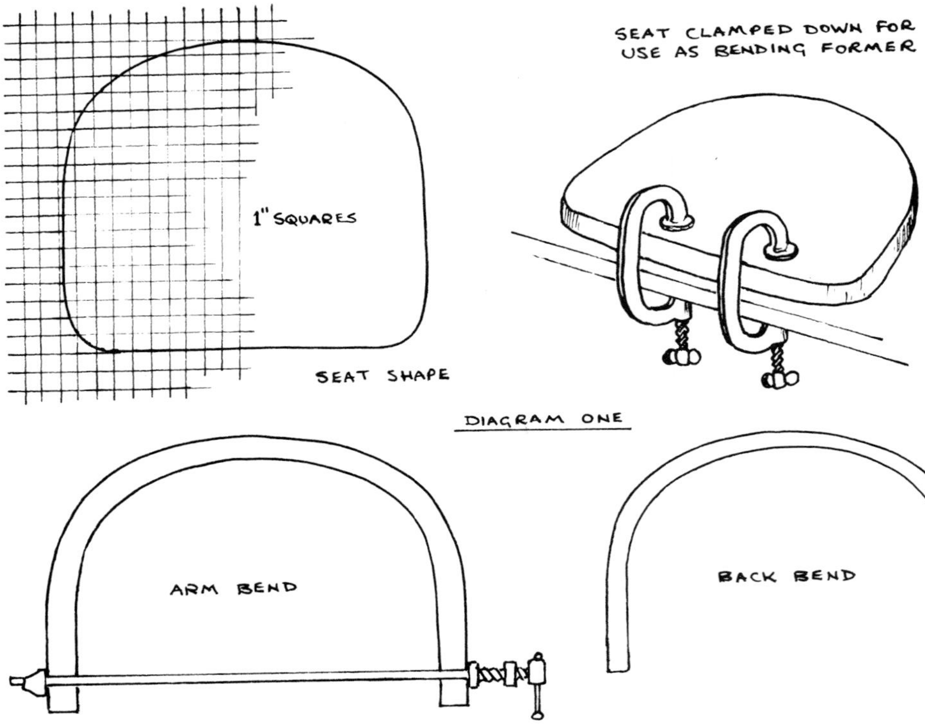

piece to the waste bin and make a replacement.

The other turned pieces, sixteen in all, consist of the two stretchers to the legs, eight long back sticks and six short side sticks (see Diagram Two). These are all plain turned and tapered on the lathe or by using the rotary planes described on p44.

The back sticks in particular need to be made from straight-grained material. Although turned to a diameter of $\frac{3}{4}$in to begin with, they taper at their top ends to only $\frac{3}{8}$in in diameter, and so need to be strong yet resilient. In working the taper on these components ensure that at the point where they pass through the back bow – approximately 9in from their bottom end – they have a $\frac{1}{2}$in parallel diameter. The holes through which they pass in the arm bow are $\frac{1}{2}$in in diameter and this parallelled portion on the back sticks allows the bow to go down far enough without leaving unsightly gaps around the holes on the top edge. Use a simple sizing stick during turning to help in achieving this. Again, keep the round tenons at each end of each component full size to ensure the essential tight joints.

The centre splat (Diagram Three) in this particular design is made in two pieces and does not pass through the arm bow. It is held in mortice slots and the ends of the splat parts are taper tenoned to fit. The shape of the splat, within the limitations of the design, can be altered to suit individual choice, as can the centre decoration. I chose to carve the Tudor rose which is the emblem of the county of Lancashire, in which I was born, but it could, for example, be a pierced design such as the traditional wheel back. Initials or even a family crest are alternative suggestions. The splat shape is sawn using either a powered fret saw or with a hand-held tool such as a coping saw. Small files are useful for cleaning up, especially where pierced shapes have been hand sawn.

The two rockers are hand or band sawn to shape to the radius given in Diagram Three. After sawing they may be cleaned up using spokeshaves and glass-paper [sandpaper].

By this time the seat should no longer be needed as a bending former [form] and it can be shaped or bottomed, as the process is

(*opposite*) Double-bow Windsor rocking-chair
(*overleaf*) Tambour-top desk (*see pp230–43*)

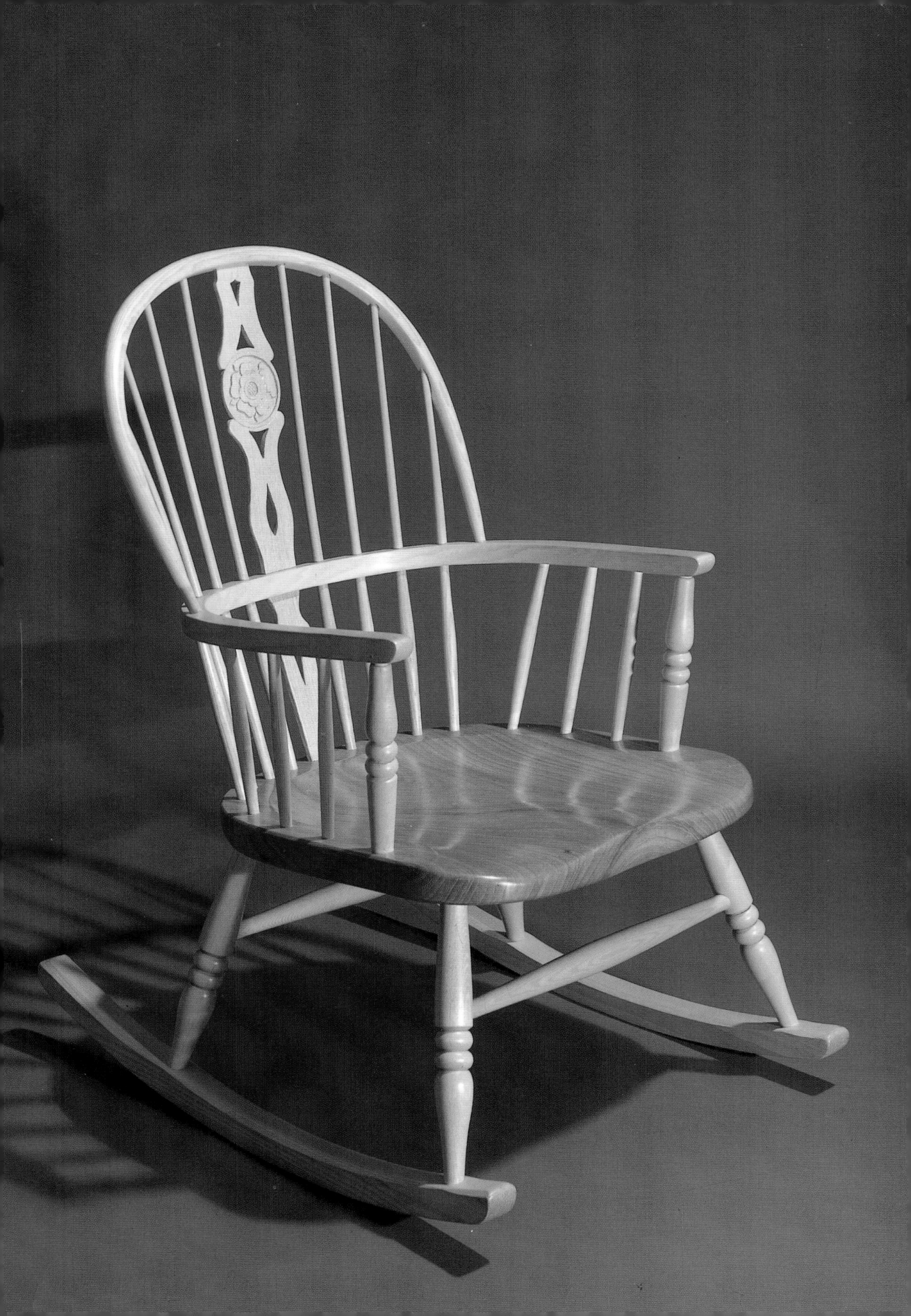

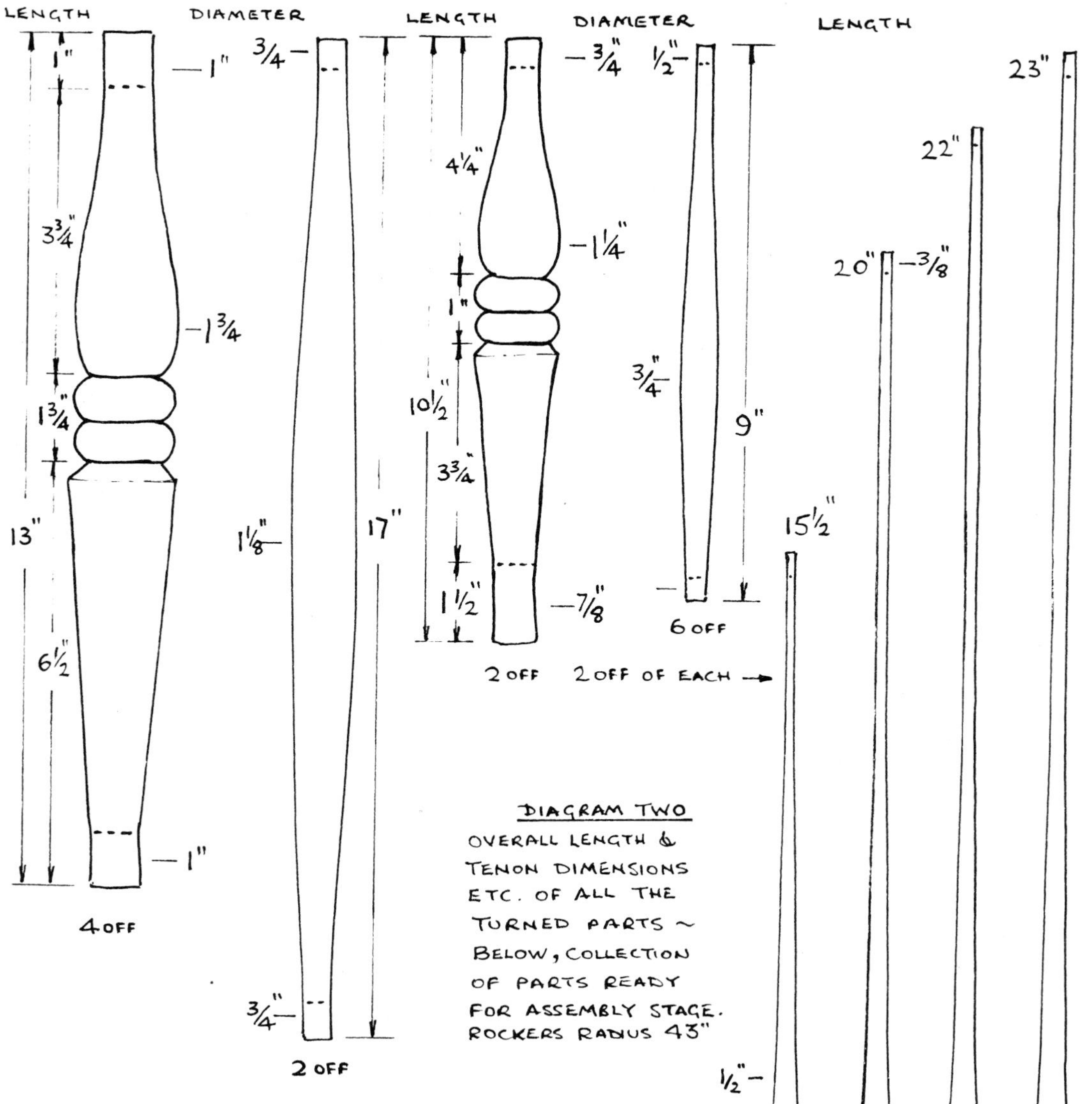

DIAGRAM TWO

OVERALL LENGTH & TENON DIMENSIONS ETC. OF ALL THE TURNED PARTS ~ BELOW, COLLECTION OF PARTS READY FOR ASSEMBLY STAGE. ROCKERS RADIUS 43"

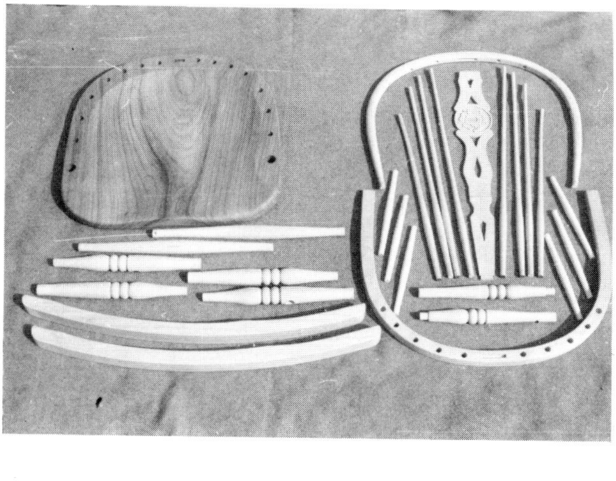

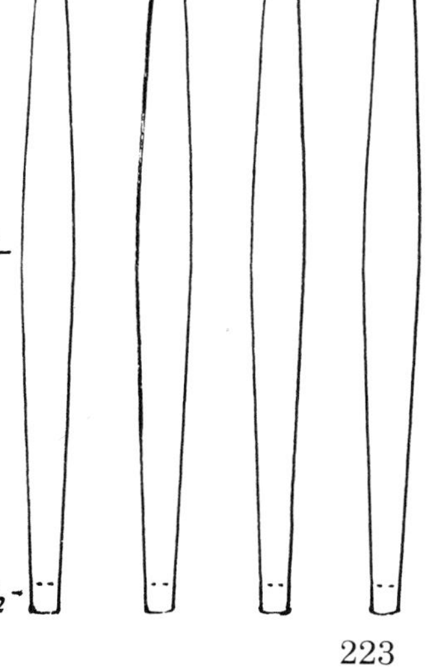

DIAGRAM THREE

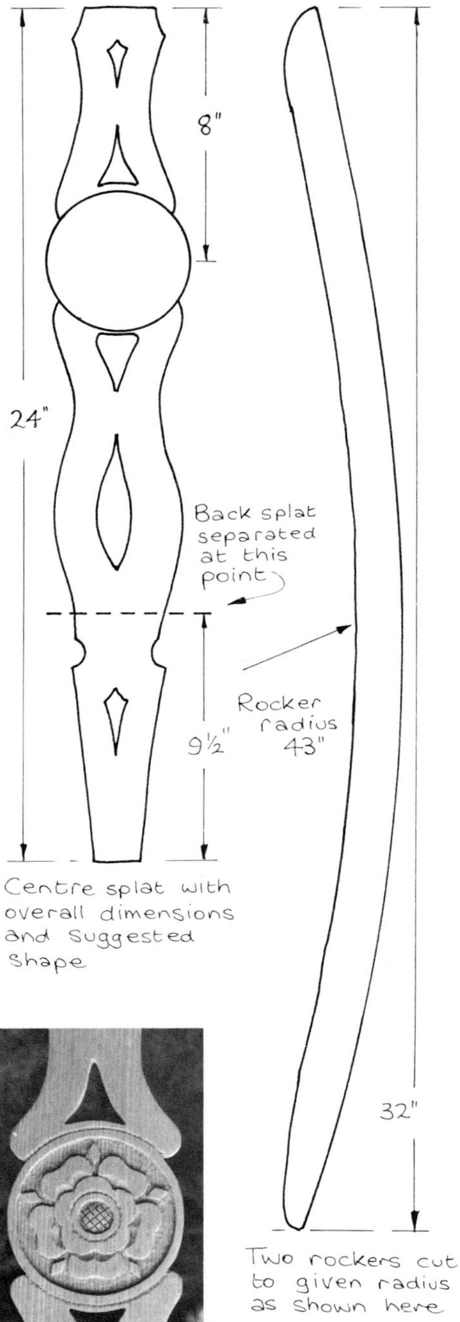

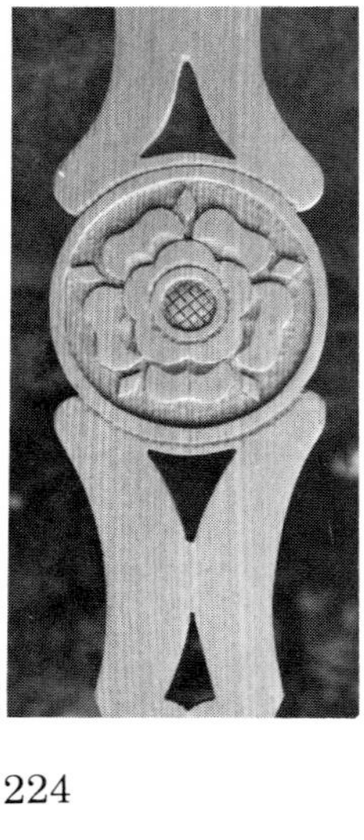

Plate 1 Using an inshave to hollow the chair seat

traditionally known. The deep hollowing of the seat is what makes the Windsor-style chair so comfortable and it was always done by hand using a long-handled curved adze. For those without an adze or the expertise to use one, other methods of bottoming can be used. By treating the seat as a shallow bowl, for example, a gouge and mallet will remove the bulk of the waste wood. I use a tool called an inshave – a type of curved draw-knife tool – either to do all the hollowing or mainly for cleaning up purposes. Whatever method is used, for the best results work across the grain of the seat, and for a good finish, use shaped steel scrapers before resorting to glass-paper [sandpaper]. This part of the task is hard work, but remember the old adage, 'nothing without effort'. Finally, clean up and bevel the edge of the seat, top and bottom.

With all the chair parts now made, the next job is to drill holes in or through most of them – a total of fifty-four holes to be exact – each in its own particular place and at its particular angle. A brace and bit was the traditional tool for this job, the correct angle the product of experience and eye judgement. Here I have tried to regularise the drilling by means of simple jigs and templates. They are intended for use in conjunction with a pillar drill [drill press] or in an electric hand drill on a pillar attachment [with a drill press attachment]. For accurate parallel-sided holes use Forstner-type toothed bits. Begin with the seat which forms the 'foundation' of the chair. Mark out the

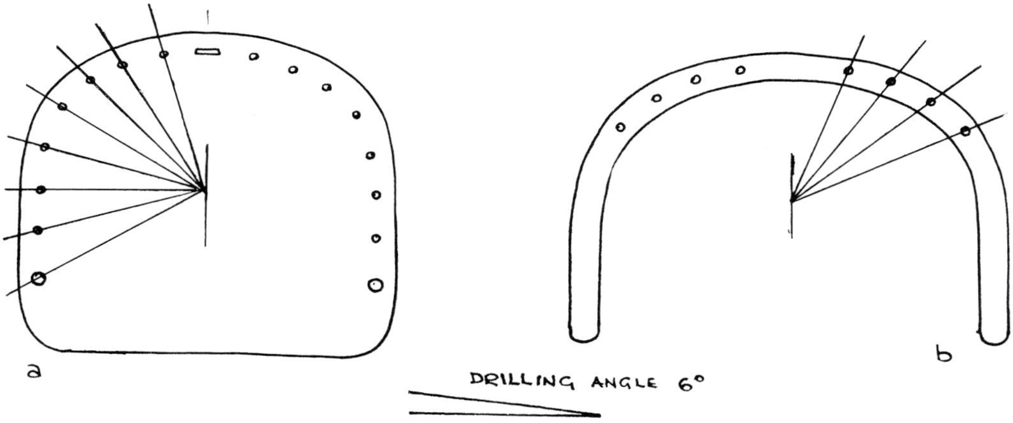

DIAGRAM FOUR

DRILLING ANGLES AND ALIGNMENTS FOR USE IN CONJUNCTION WITH THE DRILLING JIG AND PILLAR DRILL. ALL BASED ON CENTRE POINT OR LINE OF CHAIR SEAT SHAPE EXCEPT FOR d AS SHOWN.

BELOW, ARM AND BACK BEND SET-UP FOR CHECKING TRUE ANGLES

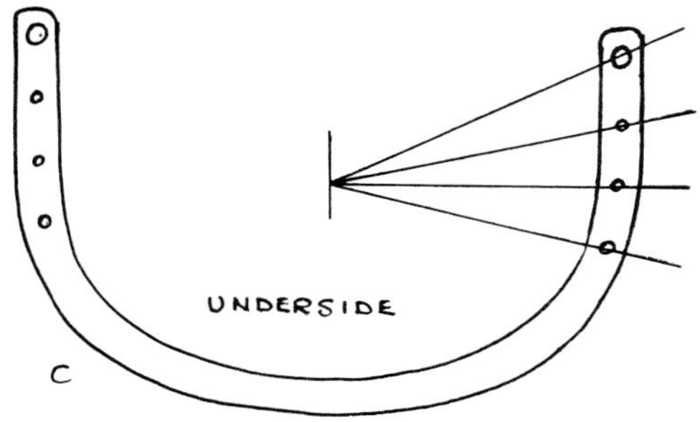

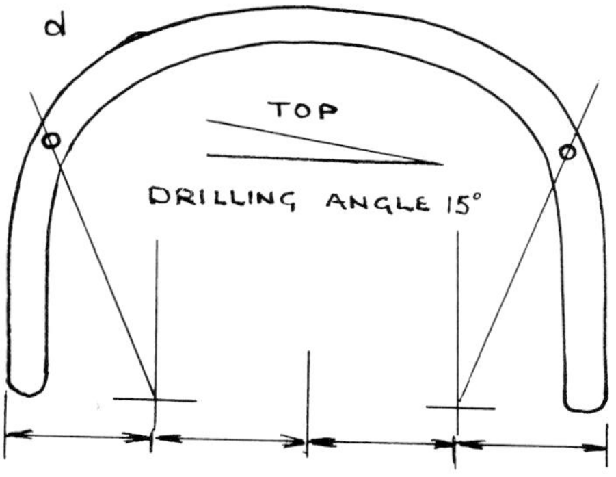

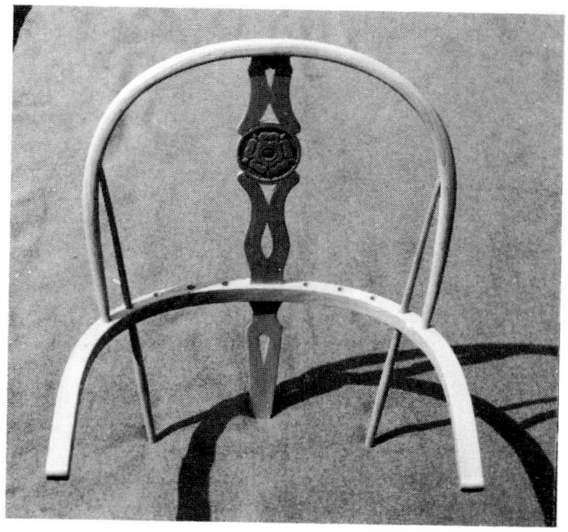

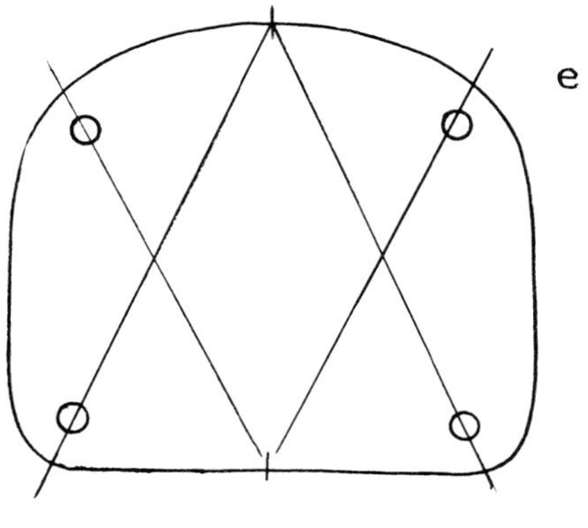

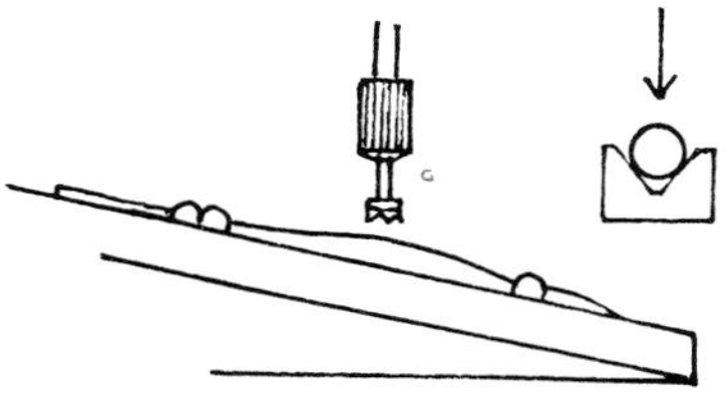

METHOD OF DRILLING LEGS

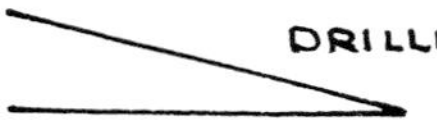

top surface of the seat (Diagram Four, a) and, after setting the drilling jig to the correct angle, drill all the holes required. All are ½in in diameter and ¾in deep, except the two front arm-rest holes which are ⅞in in diameter and go right through the seat. Then, without altering the angle of the drilling jig, put the arm bend into place and drill the eight ½in-diameter holes for the back sticks through the bow. Mark on and drill from the bow's top surface (Diagram Four, b). Keeping the same angle, turn the arm bow over and, after marking out, (Diagram Four, c) drill the six ½in-diameter holes to accommodate the short arm sticks and the two ¾in-diameter ones for the front arm supports. All these holes are ¾in in depth.

Two further ½in holes are needed in the top surface of the arm bow – those which accommodate the ends of the back bow. These are at a different angle from the rest of the arm-bow holes, so reset the drilling jig and drill these ⅞in deep (Diagram Four, d). Check that the resulting holes are correct by placing the back bow into place in the holes – it will need to be sprung into position against the tension of the curve – making sure that each end goes to its full depth in the arm bow. Pencil a depth mark on each as a check for use during final assembly later.

Next, turn your attention to the underside of the seat and the underframing, ie legs and stretchers. Mark out the four leg holes in the seat (Diagram Four, e) and with the drilling jig at its correct angle drill these 1in in diameter and 1in deep. With the same angle on the drilling jig now drill each of the four legs as shown to take the stretchers, ¾in in diameter, ¾in deep. Use a simple V-shaped cradle to hold the legs while drilling. On completion, try legs and stretchers for fit into the seat.

The way to mark out the position of leg holes in the rockers is to assemble the legs and stretchers into the seat, without glue at this stage. Then, on a level surface, stand the chair on both rockers and mark the respective position for each hole. Drill the holes with the drilling jig at the same angle as above. Try the rockers for fit, then dismantle the whole underframing and put to one side. It is easier to do the next stage with the chair, but not the chairmaker, legless.

Plate 3 Marking the back stick positions on the back bow prior to drilling

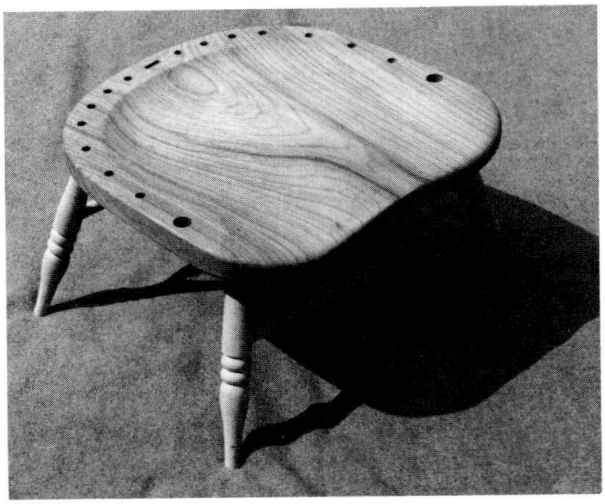

Plate 2 Legs assembled into the seat

A dry assembly of the arm and back parts into the seat is now required, mainly to set up the back sticks and centre splat and to mark their positions on the back bow so that this can be correctly drilled. First, put all back and arm sticks and the short half-splat into their appropriate holes and then drop the arm bow over the long back sticks and down on to the short side sticks and half splat and front arm supports. Manipulate these into their respective holes. The lower edge of the arm bow should be 8½in above and parallel to the upper seat surface. The

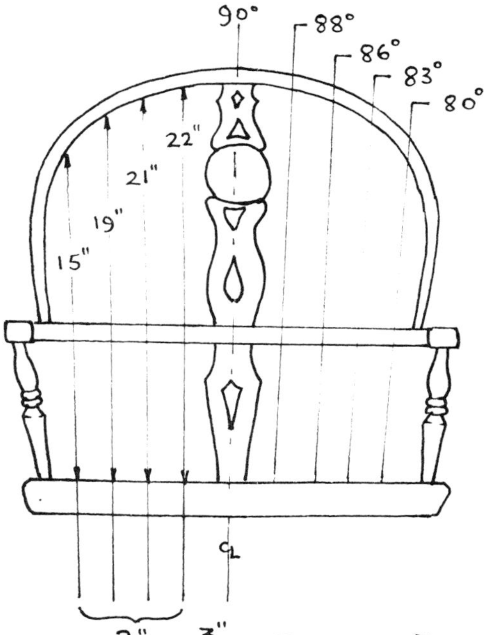

DIAGRAM FIVE

Position, true length and angle of back sticks and centre splat

arm sticks, etc, may need some adjustment to achieve this.

Next, spring the back bow into position, making sure its ends go all the way down into the back-bow holes. Put the top half of the splat in place. It will be found that the long back sticks and splat lie naturally either to front or to back of the back bow; these, too, will be sprung into position during final assembly.

Measure round the arch of the back bow with a flexible tape to find its mid-point and arrange the centre splat equally to each side of this point and mark its position. Check that the long back sticks can be arranged equidistant apart on either side and mark in their position, true length and angle (Diagram Five). The diagram shows what these measurements should be, but be prepared to make minor adjustments if necessary.

Remove the back bow and cut the slot for the splat, then drill the back stick holes, 3/8in diameter and between 3/8in and 1/2in deep. The drilling table is placed in the horizontal position for this operation. A small machine vice or something similar is useful to hold the bow in place, or a small cramp [clamp] and two wooden blocks makes a good substitute. If difficulty is experienced – the handle of some drilling machines may get in the way – hold the bow in a bench vice and drill with a hand drill. Difficulty will be experienced in starting the two outer holes because of the angle; cutting a small U-shaped step with a small carver's gouge into the back bow at the points marked for drilling will overcome this problem.

Now, reassemble back bow and arm bow together with the back sticks and centre splat; do this, initially, separately from the seat as illustrated. The dimensions given in Diagram Five should allow the ends of the back bow to just enter into place in the arm bow while each back stick and finally the splat are manipulated into their respective places. Again, some adjustment to the length of back sticks and splat may be needed. In fact, a number of 'dry runs' may be necessary before you are satisfied that the back components are ready for assembly into the seat and gluing up. It is a good plan to number components and their appropriate holes so as to avoid mistakes later.

Plate 4 Back components assembled for checking

When satisfied, clean up all the parts with scraper and glass-paper [sandpaper], then tidy up the bench and prepare for gluing. Of the modern adhesives, one of the urea formaldehydes such as Cascamite or Aerolite is recommended, or you may prefer to use hot animal glue as was done in the past. Do the gluing up in three main stages.

First, assemble and glue in the legs and stretchers but do not add the rockers at this stage. It is easier to assemble bows and sticks, etc, before the chair becomes a rocker. Leave to allow the glue to set properly.

Next, glue and wedge into place the two front arm supports. Remember that the wedges must be at right angles to the grain of the seat. Then, put glue into all the remaining holes in the top of the seat and place all the upright components into their appropriate holes. Put glue into the eight holes drilled into the underside of the arm bow and into the slot for the splat but do not put glue into the eight holes which go right through the bow. Place the bow over the long back sticks and down on to the short components. If the arm bow needs any 'encouragement' to go properly into place use a padded mallet but make sure each short stick, etc, is going into its hole. Again, leave to allow the glue to set.

Fitting the back bow is the final stage in this main assembly stage. Put glue into the two holes in the upper surface of the arm bow which take the back bow and into the slot for the splat. Also put glue into each of the holes and the slot in the back bow. Spring the back bow into place and fit the lower end of the splat into its slot. After arranging the top end of each back stick and the top of the splat into their respective holes, press the whole back assembly into place using the weight of the body (avoid cracking a rib as the author once did!) or use a padded mallet to persuade it into position. It is most important to check that both ends of the back bow are down all the way into their holes in the arm bow.

These two joints are secured by wooden pegs or pins. From the back of the chair drill a $^{3}/_{32}$in hole into the arm bow to pass through each end of the back bow but not out to the front of the chair. Into this hole drive a square $^{1}/_{8}$in peg and trim flush. Taper one end of the peg slightly to aid entry and smear with a little glue. Similarly, secure the top end of each of the front arm supports by the same method. Check that the chair back is symmetrical and leave for the glue to set before fitting the rockers.

Fitting the rockers is most easily done with the chair lying on its side on an old blanket or rug placed on the floor. Fit the uppermost rocker, glue in the hole not on the leg, then turn the chair over and repeat.

If you think the chair is now finished, think again! Finishing, ie final cleaning up, rubbing down and polishing, has still to be done. Done properly it is quite a long job but a satisfying one. And it is important to have a really good surface to the wood before applying the final polish, if the high standard of finish which this chair deserves is to be obtained.

Any glue which has been allowed on to the wood must first be cleaned off carefully, as this will reject polish and leave unsightly blemishes. Use a steel scraper followed by glass-paper [sandpaper] in progressively finer grades. When the surface is smooth, apply a coat of sanding sealer, allow to dry and rub down with either fine steel wool or a flour-grade glass-paper [sandpaper]. Feel the surface smooth with the fingers and if it does not give pleasure rub again until it does. Finally, remove all dust from the surface with a soft brush or cloth.

When the dust has settled apply a good-quality beeswax polish; do this to a small area at a time and buff that area before applying more polish elsewhere. When the entire chair has been waxed and buffed, wax it and buff it all over again.

MATERIALS REQUIREMENT LIST. (CUTTING LIST IN INCHES)

Nº	PURPOSE	MATERIAL	INITIAL SIZES		
1	SEAT	ELM	21 x 19 x 1¾	SHAPED	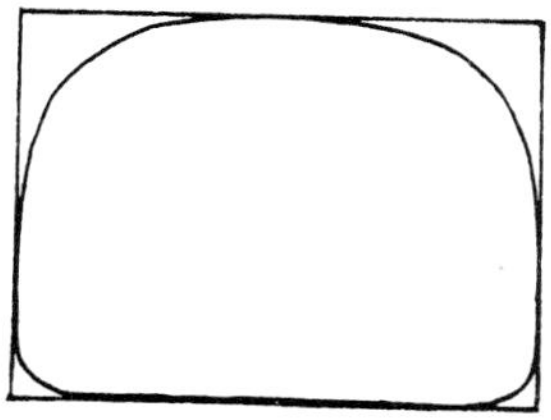
4	LEGS	ASH OR BEECH	14 x 2 x 2	TURNED	
2	STRETCHERS	"	18 x 1¼ x 1¼	"	
1	ARM BOW	"	50 x 1½ x 1½	BENT	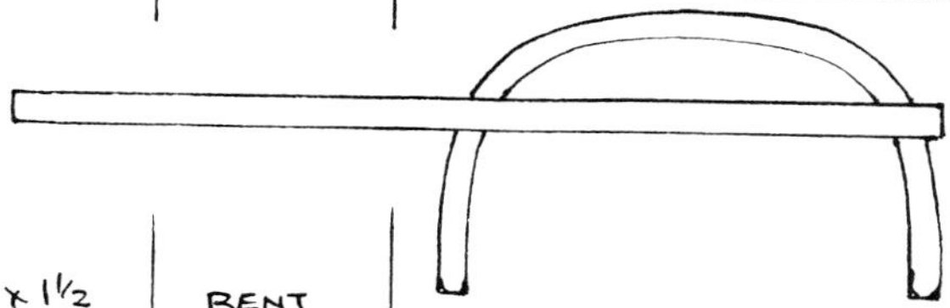
1	BACK BOW	"	48 x 1 x 1	BENT	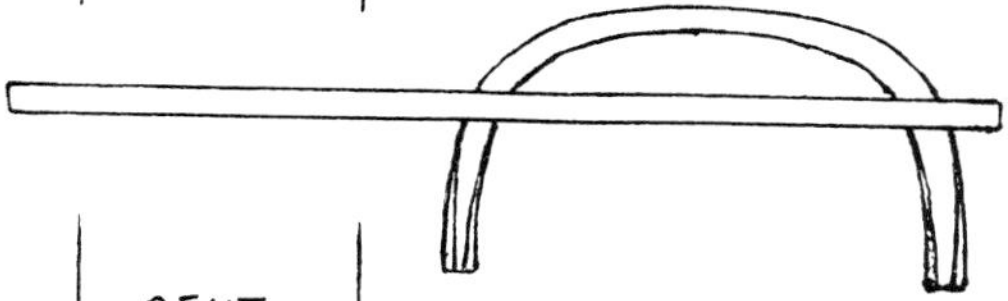
2	ARM SUPPORTS	"	12 x 1½ x 1½	TURNED	
6	SHORT ARM STICKS	"	10 x ⅞ x ⅞	"	
8	LONG BACK STICKS	"	24 x ⅞ x ⅞	"	
2	ROCKERS	"	32 x 3½ x 1½	SHAPED	
1	CENTRE SPLAT	"	24 x 4 x ½	SHAPED	

20

Tambour-top Desk

Illustrated on page 222

The pedestal form of writing table or desk came into vogue during the reign of George I. In its original form it consisted of a flat top over a single-drawer apron supported by a pair of pedestals containing three or four more drawers. More commonly known as a knee-hole desk, this item of 'writing furniture' is one of several pieces which were developed, so it is said, along with the establishment of postal services and a greater interest in letter writing. Other types, not of the knee-hole variety, included cupboards above the writing surface, while some, instead of a flat top, had a sloping or slanting writing surface. This type, the bureau, later had what became known as a fall front, hinged at its lower edge which, when opened, was supported on sliding bearers to become the writing surface and reveal an interior fitted with small drawers, shelves and niches intended for writing materials.

Variants of the fall front were those desks or writing tables in which the slanting lid lifts up to slide partially or wholly into the back part of the fitted section. Many were flat fronted, but in some the sliding lid is curved and these are known as cylinder fall fronts.

An alternative to the rigid cylinder fall front was the tambour front or simply tambour, a French idea introduced into England in the late eighteenth century and used originally, I believe, on the very elegant Carlton House writing table around 1790. The tambour consists of a flexible shutter made up of narrow strips of wood placed horizontally and glued to a backing, usually of canvas, which runs in grooves in each end of the desk's top section.

The combination of pedestal desk and tambour top took place some time during the nineteenth century and desks of this type became firm favourites in homes and offices in both England and the United States of America where it is better known as the roll-top desk.

Designed and made by Ian Massey, this desk was constructed throughout in American red oak. Only for the drawer bottoms was veneered ply used – the remainder was all solid timber. Obviously, material costs could have been reduced by using oak-veneered panels, either just in the back or throughout; however, you will probably only make one of these, so why not make it in the best materials possible? The price of English oak was, simply, prohibitive.

Although the style is strictly traditional, the method of construction is not entirely so. Its basic structure consists of a series of dowel-jointed, framed panels joined together by means of either screwed rails or further dowelling where appropriate. The two pedestals containing a cupboard and a drawer are made as two separate, open-backed units linked together by the full-width panelled back and to this is added the solid desk top. The upper section, consisting of a divided compartment section, two side pieces, a top piece, tambour and separate panelled back comprise a third unit secured to the desk top by screws which pass up through it.

This 'box' or unit construction using sound materials gives the necessary rigidity to the structure as a whole, while at the same time not only is the making more straightforward and therefore easier but it provides a partial 'knock-down' facility should this ever be required. A feature of the design is that the back is as well made and attractive as the remainder so that the desk can be used free-standing or end-on to a wall with the back panels fully on view and not required to be concealed forever. All the panel frames are lightly moulded on their inside edges and

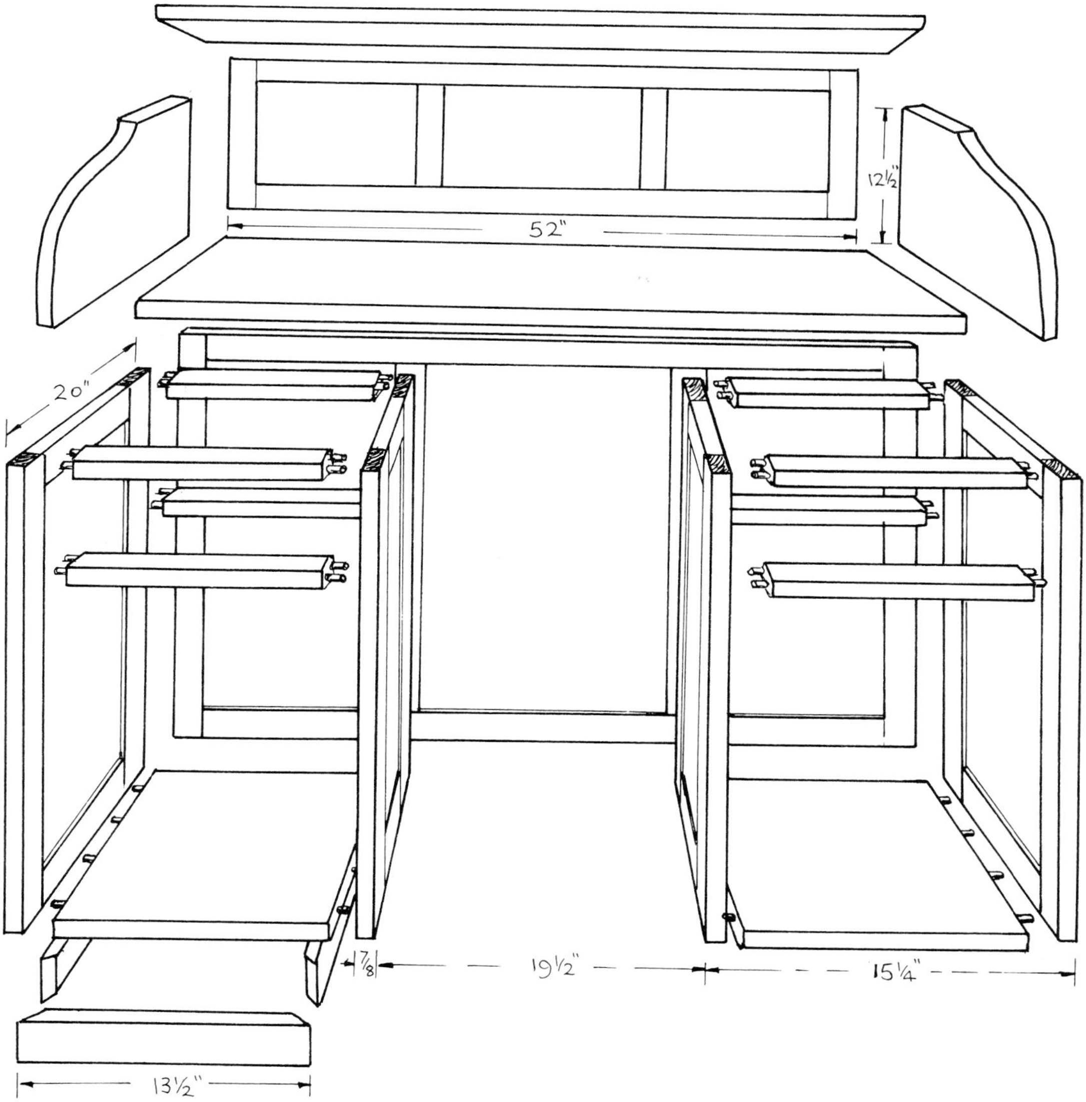

DIAGRAM ONE

Exploded view of main carcase components showing method of assembly and some dimensions

Partially assembled desk

Plate 1 A book matched panel

Diagram Two shows how this is cut to form a mitred corner.

First, select the material to be used for the top of the desk. Three or four nicely grained boards, 52in long to make up the 22in-wide surface are required and it makes sense to choose these initially, to mark them accordingly and to stack them, preferably, in conditions similar to those where the desk is to be used. It may also be found advantageous to do this for the material for the two shaped side pieces and for the top piece. Side pieces will need edge gluing to obtain the necessary width, but a single wide board is preferable for the top piece. Next, the panel material should be selected for compatibility, ie the two cupboard door panels should be close relatives as regards figure and colour and the back panels as close a match to each other as possible. As each of the separate panels will have to be made up of two or perhaps three pieces, edge glued to provide the necessary width, matchability needs further consideration when this is being done. If, say, 1in-thick boards are deep sawn to provide the ⅜in material of the panels then 'book matching' is an attractive possibility. (Book matching is where two adjacent sawn faces are used like the pages of an open book to make a single panel [see above].)

All the rails used in making the framed panels are 2⅛ × ⅞in cut from the 1in-thick boards and planed to these finished dimensions. These are cut to length to make, first, the four identical frame panels which make up the sides of the two pedestals. Slot the rails, ⅜in to accept the panels, work the moulding on the inside edge of each rail by hand or with a power router, and cut the mitres as in Diagram Two. Make up the panels by edge gluing where solid timber is used, and cut these to size. Dowel joint the rails and after a trial 'dry run' to make sure everything fits snugly, glue up and put into cramps [clamps]. Do not glue the panels into the slots but leave dry to allow for any movement of the wood. Check that the panels are square and not in twist and leave until the glue sets.

The two back panels, lower and upper, are made in the same way, each one consisting of three adjoining panels separated by vertical rails, or muntins as they are correctly known. Make absolutely certain when gluing and cramping [clamping] up that these framed panels, especially the lower and larger of the two, remain square and out of twist.

Doors to each of the pedestals are also framed up in a similar fashion, but, as these are best made after the pedestals are assembled using measurements taken directly from the door openings, they are not made at this stage.

The base or floor of the pedestals is of solid construction and is made up of ¾in edge-jointed boards to give the necessary

Plate 2 Close up of the pedestal corner joint

DIAGRAM TWO

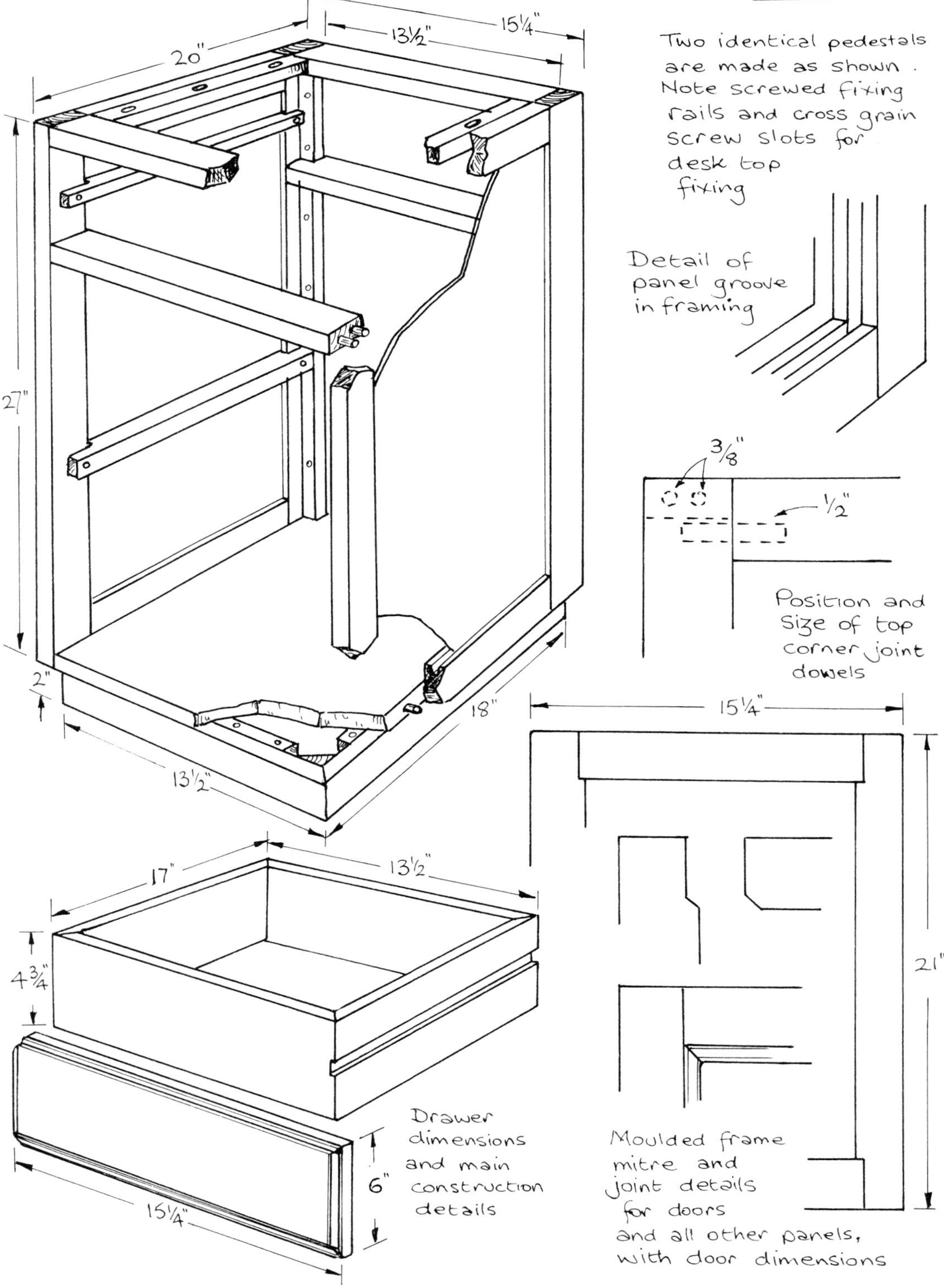

Two identical pedestals are made as shown. Note screwed fixing rails and cross grain screw slots for desk top fixing
20"
13½"
15¼"
27"
2"
13½"
18"
Detail of panel groove in framing
3/8"
½"
Position and size of top corner joint dowels
15¼"
21"
17"
13½"
4¾"
6"
15¼"
Drawer dimensions and main construction details
Moulded frame mitre and joint details for doors and all other panels, with door dimensions

width. Below the base a separate plinth is added to raise the pedestals off the floor. This plinth has glued, mitred corners further secured by glued blocks inside each corner angle.

In assembling the pedestals, front and back top rails, front and back drawer rails and the solid base are dowelled across the two side panels as shown in Diagram Two. Note in the detail how the dowels are arranged for maximum strength. Cramp [clamp] up each separate unit, check that all remains square and leave for the glue to set. Then each plinth can be added, screwed up through blocks glued and screwed to the inside edges of the plinth sides. Finally, the back is added to join the pedestals together using screws from the inside through the fixing rails.

The pieces chosen for the desk top can now be trued up along their edges and dowelled and glued together. After wiping off surplus glue top and bottom, these are placed under pressure using at least four sash cramps [clamps], checking that the top is lying true and flat, and left for the glue to set. When dry, the top surface is scraped and sanded smooth and the top edge rounded over or chamfered just slightly to take off the feel and the appearance of the sharp edge.

The top is fitted to the pedestals by means of screws which pass through blocks or

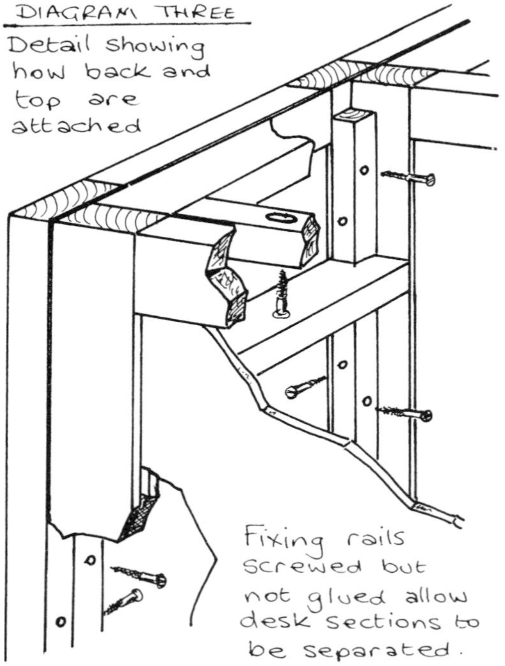

fixing rails glued and screwed inside the top rails of the pedestal panels (see Diagram Three). To allow for movement of the wood used in the top these screws pass through slots and not holes in the fixing rails, which reduces the risk of problems caused by opening joints, splitting or distortion.

DIAGRAM THREE
Detail showing how back and top are attached
Fixing rails screwed but not glued allow desk sections to be separated.

Plate 3 Side pieces and top before shaping

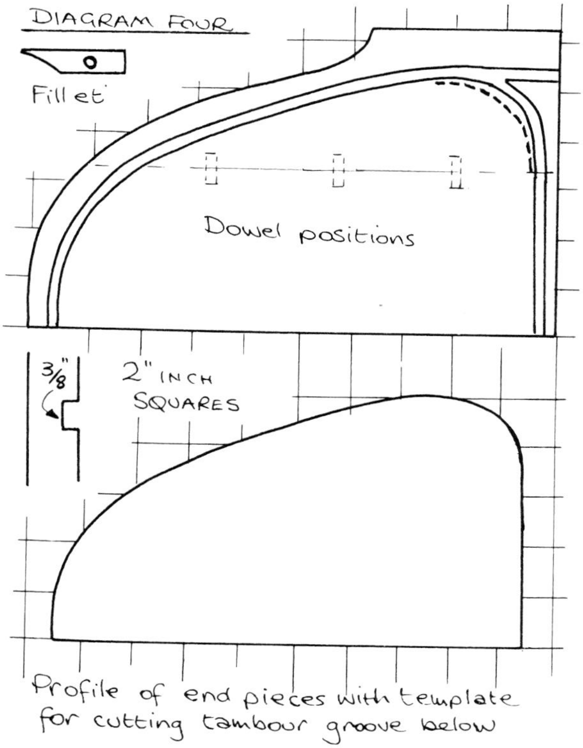

Using the same thickness material, the two shaped side pieces and the top piece are now made. The top piece is simply cut to size and planed and has its top edge rounded over or chamfered to match the edge of the desk top. The two side pieces are made up from two pieces of suitable length, edge glued and dowelled to give the required width. Position the dowels so that none is revealed when the side pieces are cut in their final shape and grooved (see Diagram Four). Cut to the profile shown in this diagram. The groove in which the ends of the tambour rails fit is cut in with a router.

To do this a template is needed to guide the router. Cut this to the pattern given in the diagram. Secure the template to the work piece with G-cramps [C-clamps] – or it can be lightly panel pinned into place where the pin holes will not show – and follow this with the router guide. Aim to get a continuous free-flowing curve of constant depth otherwise the sliding shutter of the tambour top will not slide with ease. Relieving the inside of the curve just slightly on the inside of the sharp bend, as indicated with the dotted line in Diagram Four, helps the tambour negotiate the bend more easily. The cut-out slot into the groove is to allow entry of the tambour and a fillet shaped to fit closely in the slot and to follow the line of the curve is screwed in after the tambour is fitted.

The top piece is fixed to the side pieces by means of dowels and these in turn are fixed to the desk top using wood screws. These screws pass up through cross-grain slots in the desk top in accordance with the allowance made for movement outlined earlier. Accurate positioning of the two side pieces is important, for this will affect the action of the tambour top fitted later. The two side pieces must be square and perfectly parallel to each other to allow free movement of the tambour strips.

The two cupboard doors can now be made and fitted. They are laid on, that is, fitted to the outside of the carcase frame by a pair of brass hinges. The two drawers may also be made now and the instructions for drawer making given on p37 can be followed for this. These drawers have overlaid fronts, the drawer frames in this case being mitre jointed. Solid, moulded edge fronts are glued and screwed on from inside. The drawers slide on central runners as shown in Diagram Two and for this grooves are cut each side of each drawer to suit the rail or runner screwed inside the carcase frame.

The divided compartments section or, more simply, the pigeon holes, are made up

Plate 4 Drawer and solid drawer front ready for fitting

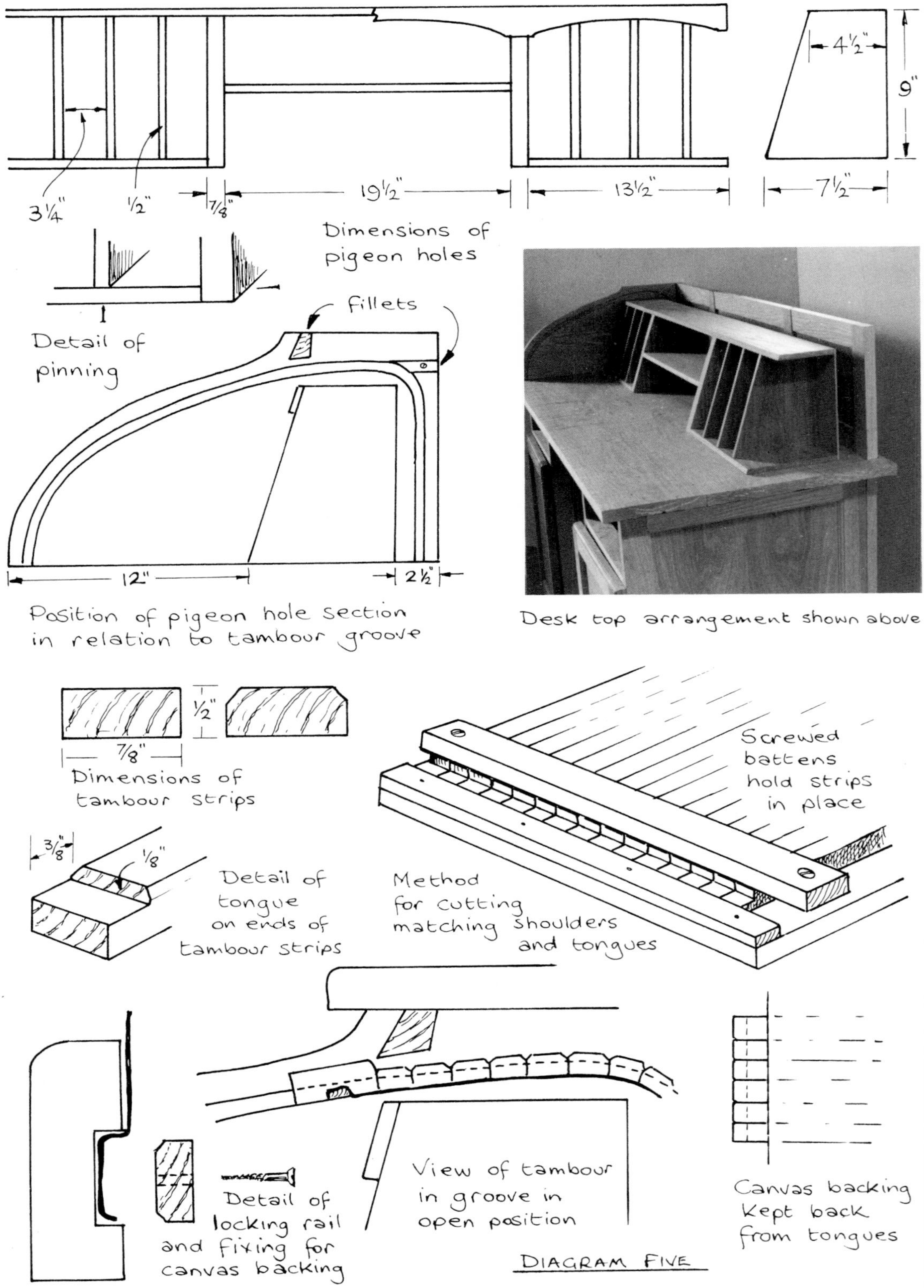
3¼"
½"
⅞"
19½"
13½"
4½"
9"
7½"
Dimensions of pigeon holes
Detail of pinning
Fillets
12"
2½"
Position of pigeon hole section in relation to tambour groove
Desk top arrangement shown above
½"
⅞"
Dimensions of tambour strips
Screwed battens hold strips in place
⅜"
⅛"
Detail of tongue on ends of tambour strips
Method for cutting matching shoulders and tongues
Detail of locking rail and fixing for canvas backing
View of tambour in groove in open position
Canvas backing kept back from tongues
DIAGRAM FIVE

Plate 5 Pigeon holes section in place

as a separate unit as shown in Diagram Five. Note that the dimensions of this make it a tight end-to-end fit but allow sufficient space above and behind it for the movement of the tambour. It is for this reason that the pigeon holes must have both a top and a back so that this space is totally enclosed and the tambour concealed in its open position. As the amount of space is critical, work closely to the dimensions given.

Incidentally, veneered ply could have been satisfactorily used for the back of the pigeon holes, but as there were sufficient short off-cuts [cutoffs] available these were used instead, invisibly edge jointed to correspond with the vertical partitions of the pigeon holes. The shaped front top rail was cut with a coping saw and cleaned up by sanding with a curved block and the various parts simply glued and panel pinned together – quite adequate for the particular job. On completion, the pigeon holes section should be tried for fit and a little trimmed off the ends if oversize. It is then put aside while the tambour is made and fitted.

The tambour has been described as a wooden but flexible sliding shutter and this is precisely what it is. Its unique feature is that it is flexible in one plane only, ie from front to back; across its width it remains quite rigid. This is due to its method of construction. Horizontal strips of wood, each one stiff along its length, are glued edge-to-edge to a canvas backing to give the appearance of a continuous, ribbed surface. The ends of the strips are housed in grooves which permit the shutter to travel, ie open and shut, but which also restrain the individual strips and control their movement.

The point about the careful positioning of the two end pieces into which the grooves are cut and the need for the groove to be a free-flowing curve of constant depth has already been made and it will be seen now how important these factors are. If the end pieces are out of square or the grooves obstructive in any way the tambour will not work successfully.

The individual strips used measure $7/8 \times 1/2$in, but these precise dimensions are fairly arbitrary; if strips narrower than the seventeen mentioned here are used, then more will be needed to fill the space. What is more important is that the total length of the strips is the exact measurement across the opening plus the depth of the two grooves minus a tiny bit – say a bare $1/16$in to just give clearance to the strips in the groove. When sufficient strips have been cut their top edges are lightly chamfered as shown in the diagram and then arranged on a flat surface to be matched for figure and colour. It is essential to number them so that this arrangement may be retained.

The front edge of the tambour has a piece thicker and wider than the strips which is known as the locking rail. This is made more substantial to carry a lock and handle (or handles) to stop the tambour going back too far and to give a neat appearance in the open position where it comes up against the front cover fillet (see detail in Diagram Five).

In the best work the strips are shouldered and this detail is shown in Diagram Five. In the same diagram a method of forming identical shoulders on the strips is shown. The screwed batons placed exactly on the shoulder line hold the individual strips together and a fine tenon saw is used to cut the shoulders in. Matching tongues are then formed by planing down to a template of the required thickness pinned alongside. A shoulder plane is best for this and don't forget to punch the pins holding the template down below the surface before planing. A power router can be used instead of the saw and plane. Some like to make first a single trial strip which can be tested for fit and travel in the groove and to use this as a pattern for the others. The size of the tongue is directly related to the width and depth of the groove and the dimensions given in the diagram may be strictly adhered to or changed to suit the size of router cutter available. A final important point is to have the tongues just undersize in the grooves to give free running and to keep the shoulders just back from the groove for the same reason and to avoid a surface rub mark parallel with the groove.

The canvas back can now be glued on. It is a good idea to apply a finish to the top and edges of the strips at this stage – polish applied now will prevent glue adhesion and make final finishing much easier. The adhesive used should be semi-flexible glue such as PVA. The backing should extend across the strips but be kept back from the tongues by about 1/4in on each side and long enough to include the locking rail. With the strips on a level surface, face down, and held in close contact with each other – the screwed batten jig used in cutting the tongues can be used – glue is applied to the back of the strips and the canvas smoothed down on to them by the pressure of the hand. The locking rail is kept separate for the time being. Leave to set then, after rubbing the tongues with a candle for lubrication, feed the tambour into the groove via the slot cut specially for this purpose (see Diagrams Four and Five), fill the slot with a shaped fillet and test the movement of the tambour. If all is well, the locking rail can be attached by means of screws holding a fillet of wood (a spare tambour strip) to trap the end of the canvas backing as shown in Diagram Five. Now the back can be fitted, screwed from inside through the fixing rails as shown, after which the pigeon holes can be replaced.

Plate 6 The completed tambour

American red oak, if well finished by scraping and fine sanding, may be clear-wax polished after the application of a suitable sealer, either a proprietary [commercial] sealant or clear matt polyurethane, or stained before polishing. The desk illustrated was stained to give the wood a slightly darker colour and to enhance the figure. A combined sealer and stain was used, two coats lightly rubbed down with wire wool. Stain was not applied to the interior behind the tambour; this was clear-wax polished to provide a contrast when the tambour is open. After staining and sealing the exterior of the desk was also clear-wax polished.

(*opposite*) Back: rocking horse (*see pp244–52*); front: decorated and undecorated doll's houses (*see pp132–41*)
(*overleaf*) Four-poster bed (*see pp253–61*)

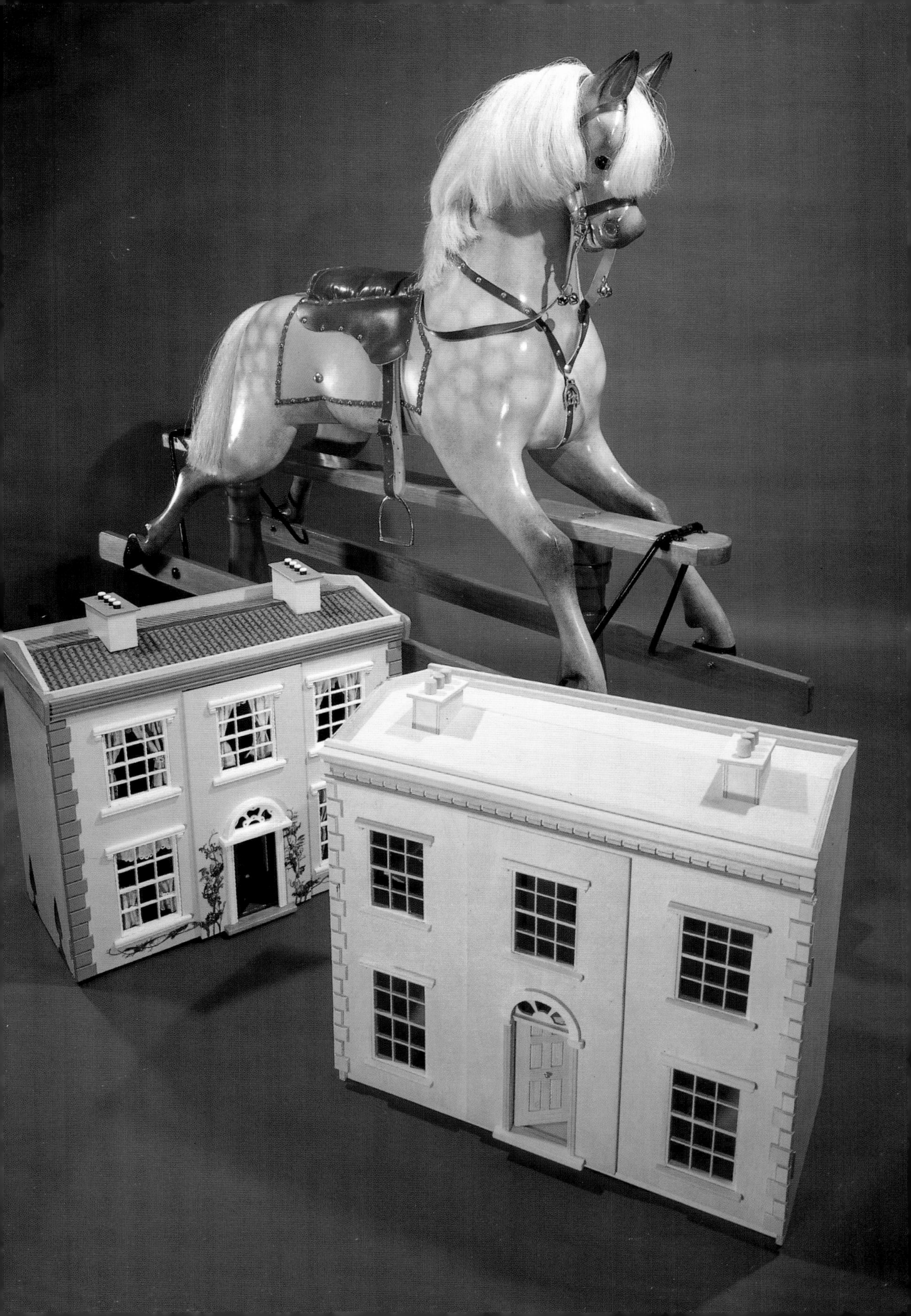

MATERIALS REQUIREMENTS LIST (CUTTING LIST IN INCHES)

No.	PURPOSE	MATERIAL	INITIAL SIZES
	FOR FOUR FRAMED PANELS		
4	PANELS	AMERICAN RED OAK	23½ x 16½ x 3/8
8	UPRIGHTS	"	27 x 2¼ x 1
4	TOP RAILS	"	15¾ x 2¼ x 1
4	BOTTOM RAILS	"	15¾ x 2¼ x 1
	FOR JOINING RAILS and BASES		
2	BASES	"	20 x 13½ x 1
2	BACK TOP RAILS	"	13½ x 2¼ x 1
2	FRONT TOP RAILS	"	13½ x 2¼ x 1
4	DRAWER RAILS	"	13½ x 2¼ x 1
	MISCELLANEOUS		
2	SHELVES	"	18 x 13½ x ¾
4	BACK FIXING RAILS	"	27 x 1 x 1
4	TOP FIXING RAILS	"	15¾ x 1 x 1
4	DRAWER RUNNERS	"	20 x 7/8 x ¾
4	SHELF RAILS	"	20 x 1 x ¾
	FOR TWO PLINTHS		
4	PLINTH SIDES	"	18 x 2 x 1
4	PLINTH ENDS	"	14 x 2 x 1
	SHORT PIECES FOR CORNER BLOCKS and FIXING RAILS		
	FOR CUPBOARD DOORS		
4	PANELS	"	17½ x 11¾ x 3/8
2	UPRIGHTS (STILES)	"	21 x 2¼ x 1
2	TOP RAILS	"	11 x 2¼ x 1
2	BOTTOM RAILS	"	11 x 2¼ x 1
	MISCELLANEOUS		
2	SHAPED PIECES		19½ x 2¼ x 1

MATERIALS REQUIREMENTS LIST — continued

No.	PURPOSE	MATERIAL	INITIAL SIZES
	FOR TWO DRAWERS		
2	BOTTOMS	PLY	16 × 13 × 1/4
4	SIDES	OAK	17 × 4 3/4 × 3/4
4	ENDS	"	14 × 4 3/4 × 3/4
2	FRONTS	"	15 1/4 × 6 × 7/8
	TOP SECTION		
1	DESK TOP	"	52 × 22 × 1
1	TOP PIECE	"	52 × 8 1/2 × 1
2	SIDE PIECES	"	20 × 12 1/2 × 1
	FOR TAMBOUR		
1	LOCKING RAIL	"	49 × 2 × 1
17	STRIPS	"	49 × 7/8 × 1/2
1	FILLET	"	49 × 7/8 × 1/2
	PIECE OF CANVAS, 48 INCHES WIDE, 18 INCHES LONG		
	FOR PIGEON HOLES		
2	BOTTOM PIECES	"	14 1/2 × 7 1/2 × 3/8
1	MIDDLE SHELF	"	20 × 6 × 3/8
6	INTERMEDIATES	"	8 1/2 × 7 1/2 × 3/8
2	CENTRE PIECES	"	9 × 7 1/2 × 3/8
1	TOP PIECE	"	48 1/2 × 4 1/2 × 3/8
1	SHAPED RAIL	"	48 1/2 × 1 1/2 × 3/8
1	BACK	PLY	48 1/2 × 9 × 1/4

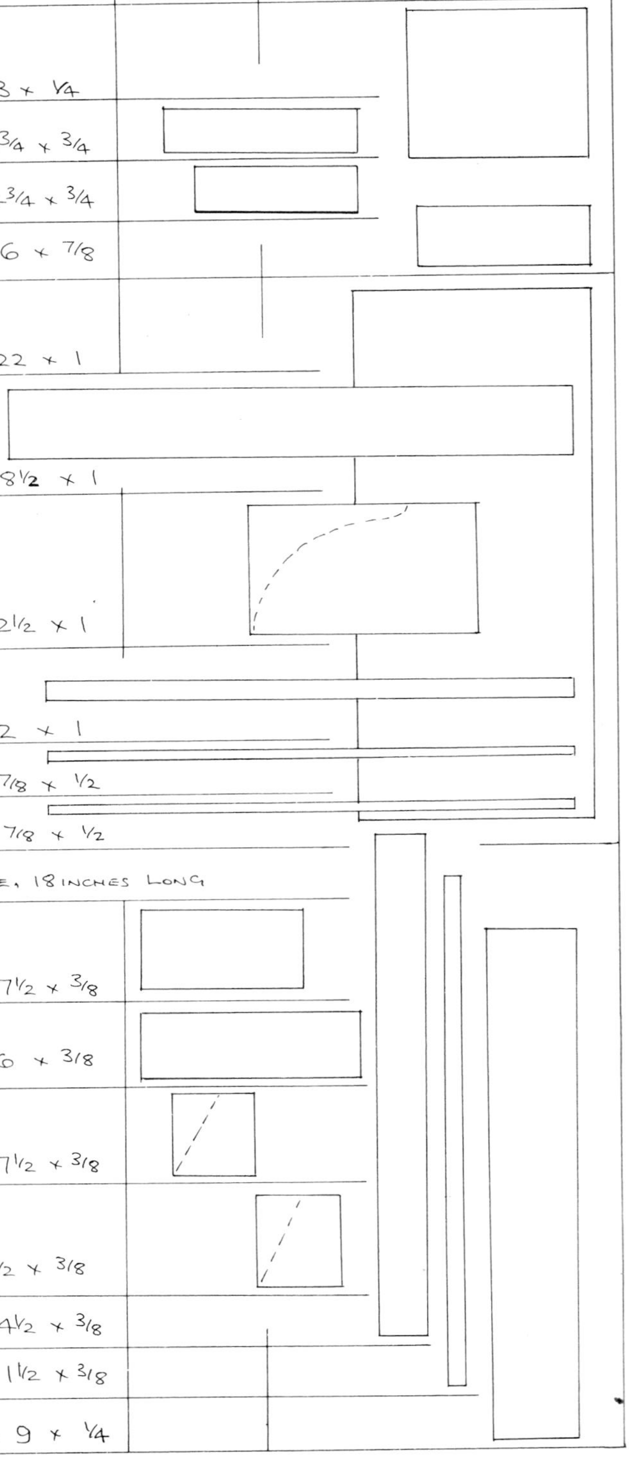

MATERIALS REQUIREMENTS LIST ~ continued

Nº	PURPOSE	MATERIAL	INITIAL SIZES
	FOR LOWER BACK PANEL		
1	PANEL	OAK	23½ x 20 x 3/8
2	PANELS	"	23½ x 12¼ x 3/8
2	LONG RAILS	"	50 x 2¼ x 1
2	END RAILS	"	27 x 2¼ x 1
2	MUNTINS		22¾ x 2¼ x 1
	FOR TOP BACK PANEL		
1	PANEL	"	20 x 9 x 3/8
2	PANELS	"	12½ x 9 x 3/8
2	LONG RAILS	"	50 x 2¼ x 1
2	END RAILS	"	12½ x 2¼ x 1
2	MUNTINS	"	8¼ x 2¼ x 1
	SIX BRASS DROP HANDLES TWO CUPBOARD DOOR BALL CATCHES BRASS HINGES (2 PAIRS) BRASS SCREWS		

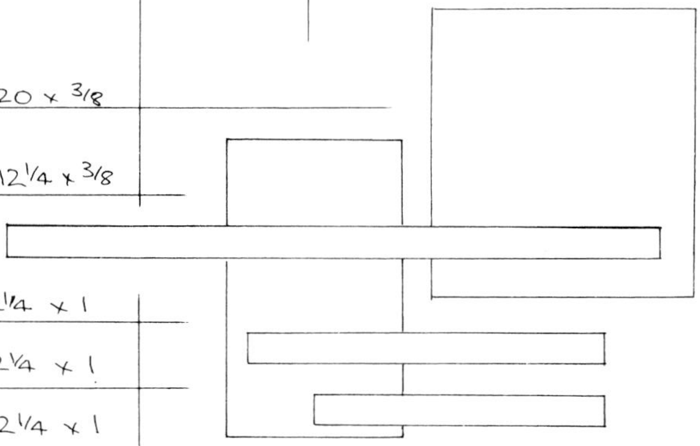

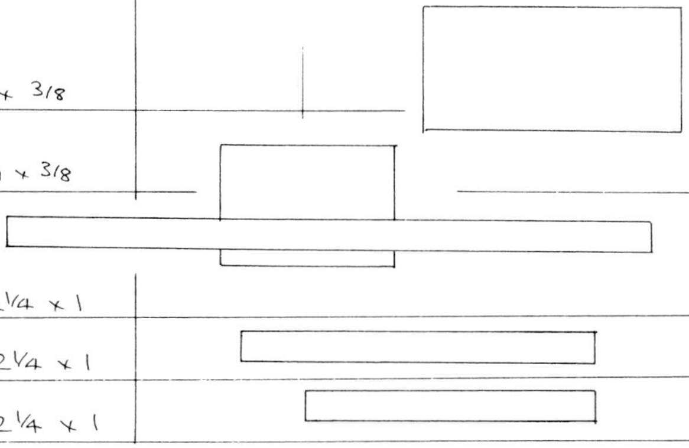

21

Rocking horse

Illustrated on page 239

Rocking horses have been around in one form or another for hundreds of years. A popular nursery toy from early in the seventeenth century, it consisted then of little more than a wooden seat mounted on a pair of crescent- or bow-shaped rockers. Examples of early wooden representations of real horses are rare and the most popular conception of a traditional rocking horse is the Victorian hand-carved horse painted dapple-grey. Built up and carved from yellow pine with legs of beech, these were fitted with mane and tail made from real horse hair and had leather saddle and harness. Originally on bow rockers, these nineteenth-century horses held pride of place in the Victorian nursery.

Around the turn of the century the bow rockers were largely replaced by the safety type of underframe which, while still producing the rocking motion, was much safer in use and, incidentally, occupied less space. Since that time rocking horses have been mass-produced in wood, pressed steel and rubber and, more recently, in plastics and fibreglass, the latter often seen covered in fur fabric and resembling large stuffed toys.

Despite changes in materials and manufacturing methods, the carved wooden horse is popular still. Old ones are being brought out of attics and restored to former glory and new ones are being hand carved and painted by traditional methods by a few specialist craftsmen. One such craftsman is John Wood of Westhoughton in Lancashire. He and his wife both restore old horses and make new ones, hand built, carved and painted to the true Victorian style.

The horse described here is next to the largest in a range of five which they make. Its overall length, including the underframe, is approximately 6ft, the height to saddle 39in and to top of head 54in. Yellow pine can be used throughout; it carves well and is available in large sizes, but a stronger horse results if the legs are made in beech with yellow pine for all else. Alternatively, red deal may be used.

It is important to build a horse as large as this over a period of time; don't rush into it and try to have it ready next week. Large sections of timber are involved and it needs time to 'settle down'. Spread the work out over several weeks – two or three months maybe; cut out the separate parts and leave them to one side indoors and preferably move them gradually into a warm room. Make the box section which forms the body, build up and part carve the head section and round up the legs and leave again. Then assemble head and legs to body and leave again. Later, add the pieces which will build up the 'muscled' areas. If large cracks appear in the wood, fill them with fillets of wood; fill small ones with a good wood filler. Complete the shaping, smooth down, go on holiday for two weeks and, on your return, begin the painting. Between-times you can make the tack, ie saddle and harness, and construct the underframe. Take it easy – make it a labour of love.

But to begin at the beginning. The body is constructed as a box as shown in Diagram One. All the material used is 2in in thickness. Note the extra thickness built up on each end of the box; these solid areas provide for secure anchorage of head and legs and also allow for the rounding over of the rump and the carving of the chest muscles which takes place later. The box is glued together and cramped [clamped] up to dry. Alternatively, the box parts may be glued and screwed together, but when the glue is dry the screws are removed before the jointing and carving begins.

Two front and two back legs are next cut

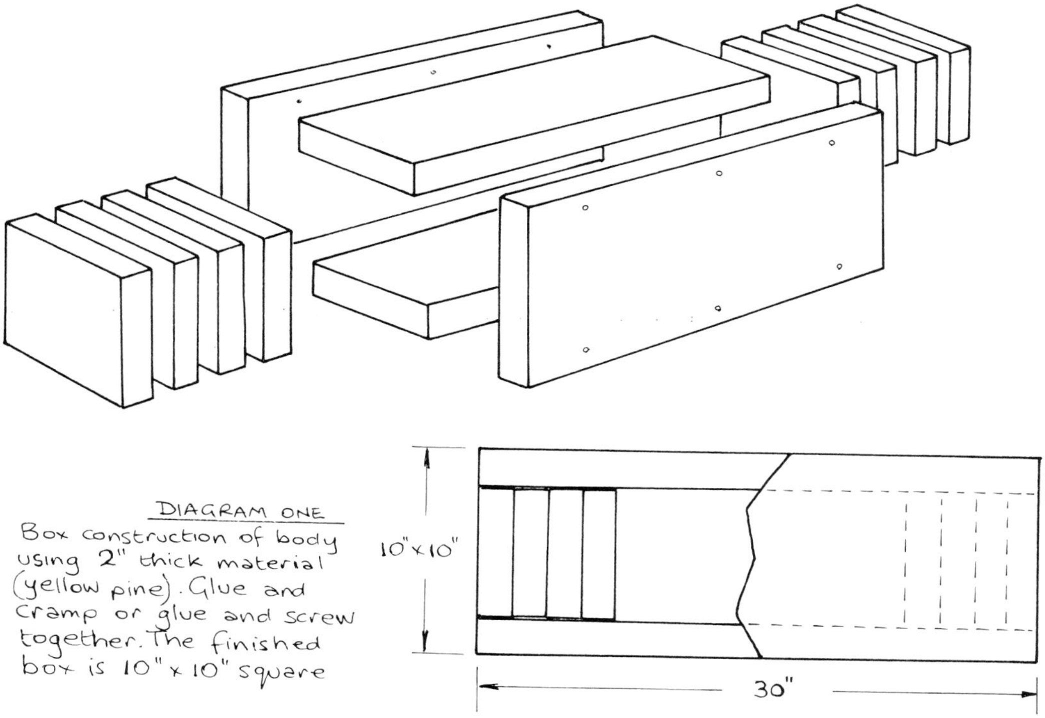

DIAGRAM ONE
Box construction of body using 2" thick material (yellow pine). Glue and cramp or glue and screw together. The finished box is 10" x 10" square
10"x10"
30"

Plate 1 The head in place on body

to the patterns given in Diagram Two. Again, 2in-thick material is used and, remember, beech is best. The basic shape of the head is also made from 2in material (yellow pine preferred) and this consists of a sandwich of two 2in pieces glued together and cut to the profile shown in Diagram Two. Where 2in material is in short supply a head may be built up by laminating a number of smaller or thinner pieces; offset and overlap small pieces to retain strength and, while the glue dries, screws may be used instead of cramps [clamps] to hold the head parts together. As with the body, screws are removed before carving begins. Screw holes are filled with short lengths of glued dowel or whittled pegs.

So far everything will appear square and flat and very basic, the real shape of the horse not emerging until later. This is achieved by building up certain areas either before or when the basic parts are assembled and then carving and shaping these areas to give the muscle effect and contours of a real horse. Some shaping is best carried out before assembly; the separate parts are easier to handle and may be held on the bench or in a vice. The rear end of the body can be rounded off to form the rump and the top edges rounded over also to give some shape to the back, but leave the front area flat. The legs, held in the vice, are shaped to a smooth roundness mainly by means of a wood rasp or a Surform tool. Keep the joint areas square. The head, but not the neck, is carved almost to its finished stage while held in the vice. Before carving, broaden the upper part of the head and ears by gluing a piece of

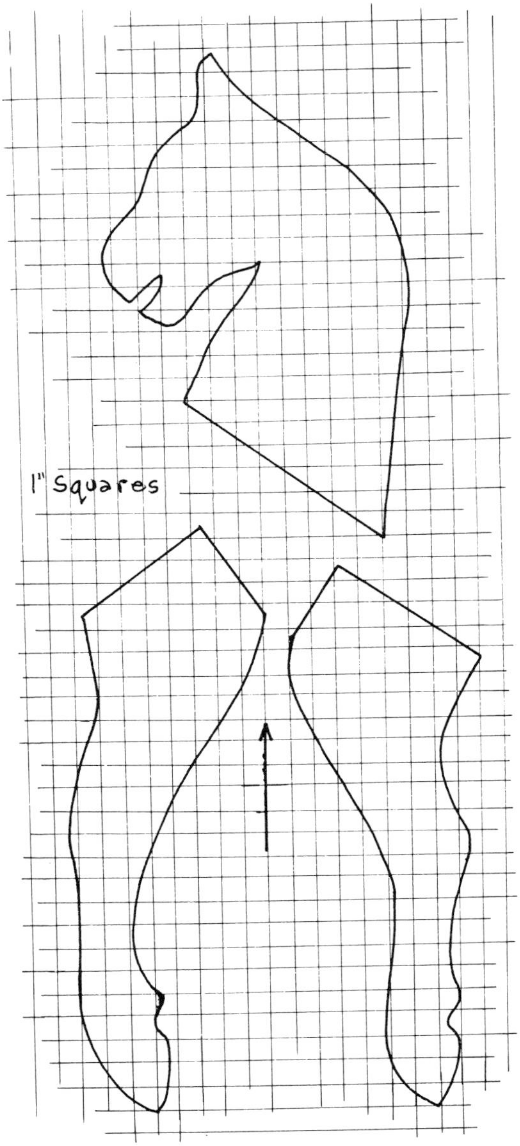

DIAGRAM TWO

Head and legs are cut from 2" thick material to these patterns. Cut two of each shape to make double thickness head and a matching pair of each leg. Grain of wood used should follow direction of the arrow

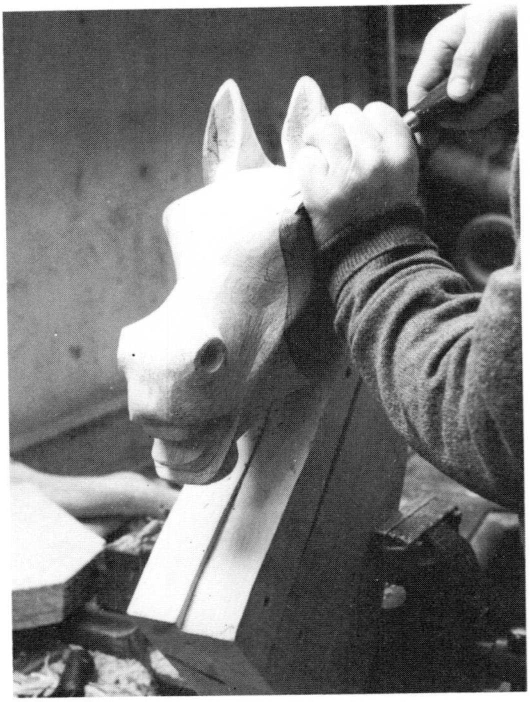

Plate 2 Close-up of carving the head

Plate 3 Details of the carved head after fitting to the body

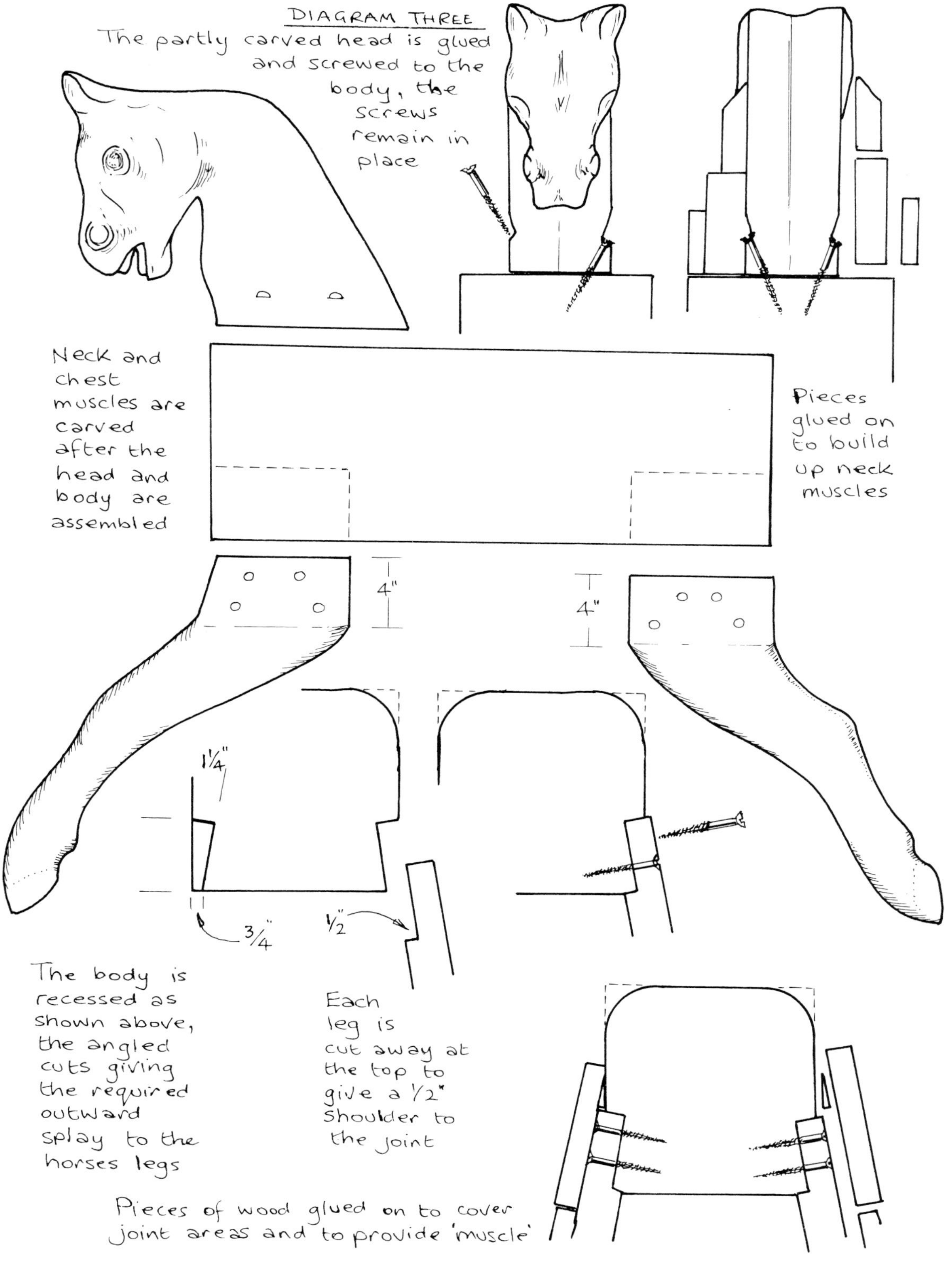
DIAGRAM THREE
The partly carved head is glued and screwed to the body, the screws remain in place
Neck and chest muscles are carved after the head and body are assembled
Pieces glued on to build up neck muscles
4"
4"
1¼"
¾"
½"
The body is recessed as shown above, the angled cuts giving the required outward splay to the horses legs
Each leg is cut away at the top to give a ½" shoulder to the joint
Pieces of wood glued on to cover joint areas and to provide 'muscle'

wood about 1in in thickness to both sides of the cut-out shape. A good shape to the head gives the finished horse its character; this will vary according to the carving skills of the individual maker.

The first stage of assembly is to fit legs to the body – one at each corner as in a real horse. The traditional method was to tenon the legs into mortices in the body, but experience has shown that most repair work on old horses is due to the failure of this type of joint, particularly when the legs are of yellow pine. If mortice-and-tenon joints are insisted upon, then beech must be used for the legs, but the jointing method described here is strong and adequate, and it is much easier. It is suitable for legs of beech or yellow pine.

Mark out on the body the joint areas and recess these as shown in Diagram Three. The wood cut away is in the solid section of the box so there is no weakening of the structure at these points. The slope of the recess gives the required splay to the legs. The joint areas of the legs themselves are also cut away slightly to give a ½in shoulder at the joint. Check for fit, then drill and countersink screw holes in the leg joint areas, apply glue to the joints, screw each leg into place and leave to set. These screws are left in place as later they will be entirely covered over by pieces of wood used to build up the areas of 'muscle'. Stand the headless horse on its feet and demonstrate the confidence in your workmanship by sitting astride it!

The head is simply glued and screwed to the body. Some Victorian horses had large mortice and tenons while others were secured with large dowels and this latter method might easily be followed. However, the method described here has certain advantages, the main one being that it does not require cramping [clamping] while the glue sets – a very awkward business once the head is shaped. Make sure that the mating surfaces between body and neck are flat and true, drill screw holes at an angle down through the lower part of the neck as shown in Diagram Three, glue up and screw down. These screws also remain in place and are covered over.

Much of the horse is still rather angular and in order to give it more roundness and a more muscled shape, pieces of wood are glued into place in the neck and upper leg areas to cover joints and to provide extra material for carving and shaping. The sections given in Diagram Three show this in some detail. The pieces used can be scrap material, offcuts [cutoffs] from the yellow pine from which head and perhaps legs were cut. Secure these added pieces with screws until the glue is set, but these screws must be removed and the holes filled before carrying out any shaping.

Plate 4 John Woods carving the horse in his workshop

As in carving the head, the shaping of the muscles and the contours of the horse's body will depend very much upon individual skills in this type of work. The rocking horse is of necessity a somewhat stylised version of a real horse so don't attempt a perfect horse 'sculpture'. More important is to aim to get the proportions right and to achieve continuous contours over the horse as a whole.

When satisfied with the general shape, fill any screw holes, gaps or surface cracks in the wood with wood or wood filler and give a final smoothing over with the rasp and with increasingly smoother grades of glass-paper [sandpaper]. Traditional rocking-horse makers used gesso – a mixture of plaster of Paris and size – to finally smooth over their horses. Instead, two coats of grey undercoat, both well rubbed down, should be applied as preparation for final painting.

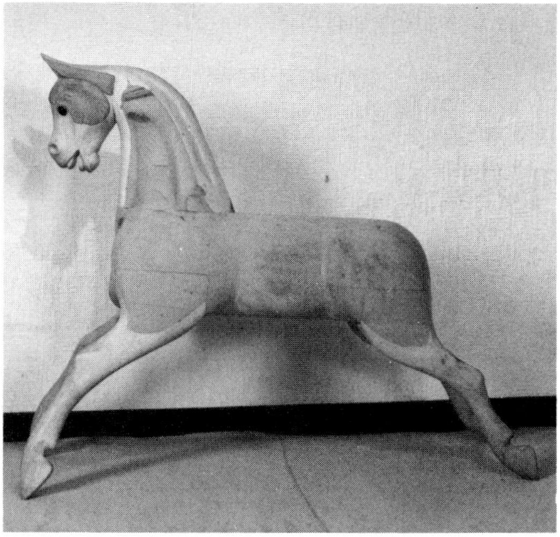

Plates 5 and 6 Shaping and carving completed – 'proportions and continuous contours' on display

The final paint finish is left entirely to choice. Traditional Victorian rocking-horse makers seem to have favoured the dapple-grey and this is still popular today. It requires skill to do well and some may prefer to settle for an all-over colour in white, grey or perhaps chestnut. Use a good-quality lead-free paint and finish with a coat or two of copal varnish to mimic the sheen of a healthy horse.

Essential finishing touches to the horse now are to fit eyes, mane and tail and to make up and fit the saddle and harness. For those who have difficulty in obtaining suitable materials to make these, all the items may be obtained ready made from the address given in the Appendix. The glass eyes are fitted into sockets cut in to the head and secured in place with epoxy resin glue. To fit the mane, which should be of real horse hair, to the head, a groove of 3/8in deep and wide is cut along the back centre of the neck. Glue is placed into this and the ends of tufts of horse hair laid along the groove to hang back and down over the horse's neck. The tail, also of horse hair, is held in a 1in hole drilled 3in deep into the upper rump of the horse. Glue is placed in this hole, the end of a thick bundle of horse hair is pushed into the hole and held with a tapered dowel hammered into the hole. When the glue is well set mane and tail may be combed and brushed to improve their appearance (see Diagram Four).

The saddle may be a simple shape cut from leather or a more elaborate padded version just like the real thing. John Wood's saddles

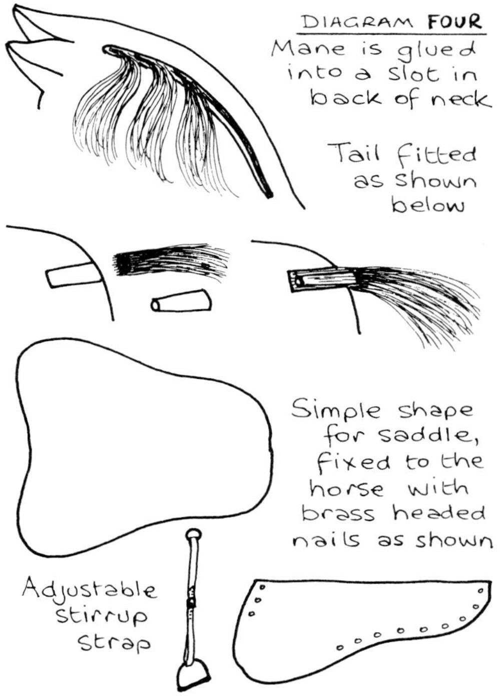
DIAGRAM FOUR
Mane is glued into a slot in back of neck
Tail fitted as shown below
Simple shape for saddle, fixed to the horse with brass headed nails as shown
Adjustable stirrup strap

are built up and padded and are very comfortable. The adjustable stirrup straps hang from screw attachments concealed by the loose skirt of the saddle. The imitation saddle blanket and the saddle itself are fixed to the horse by means of brass-headed upholstery nails. The head harness and reins are leather straps and these, too, are fixed to the horse with brass upholstery nails.

With the horse itself completed a frame must now be made upon which it can be mounted to give the required rocking motion. This must adequately and safely carry not only the weight and movement of the rocking horse but also children of indeterminable size and disposition, so it must be well made. It consists of two turned pillars fixed rigidly to a solid base. These support a cross bar which carries the moving parts of the frame to which the horse is attached. The moving parts are two U-shaped metal hanger brackets linked to a pair of rails which support the horse. The fixed parts of the frame may be of softwood but the two supporting rails must be of a strong hardwood, such as ash or beech. The hanger brackets are free to pivot at the points where they attach to the cross bar and to the supporting rails; the horse is held to these rails by means of coach bolts, the inside of the hoof being recessed to fit over the rail. Diagram Five gives all the necessary constructional details for making the frame. All the metal components required are obtainable ready-made from the address in the Appendix. A suitable finish for the frame is to use a clear varnish on the wood with black gloss paint for the metalwork.

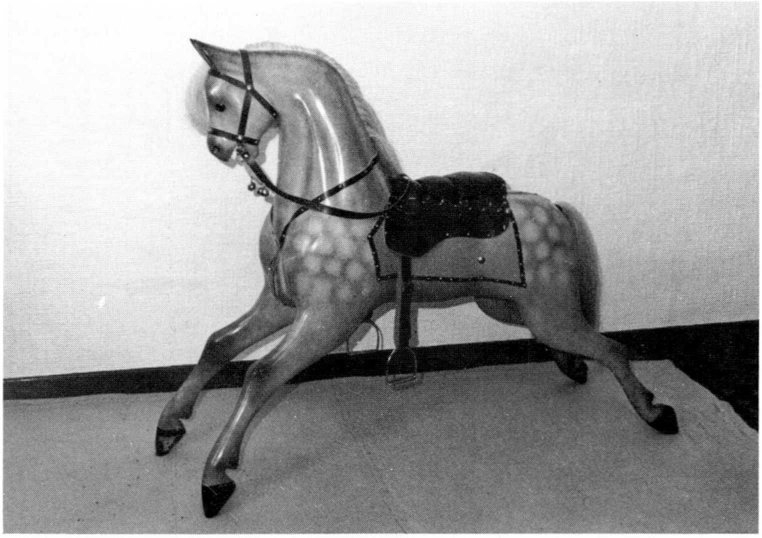

Plate 7 Completed horse after painting, etc

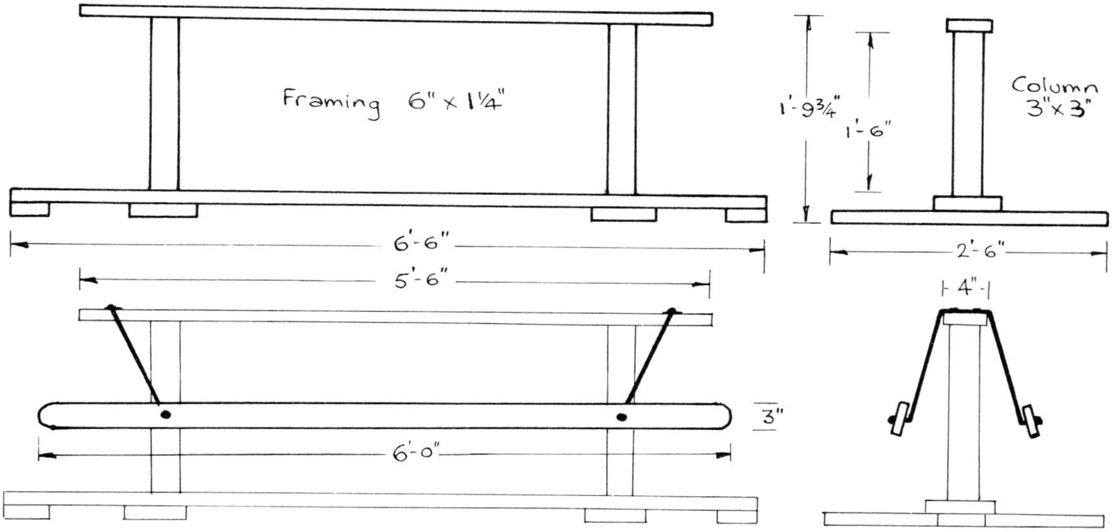

DIAGRAM FIVE
Overall dimensions and construction details for rocking horse frame

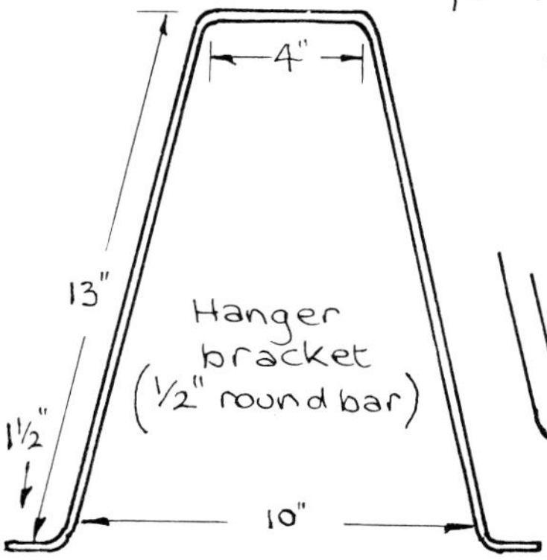

Hanger bracket (½" round bar)

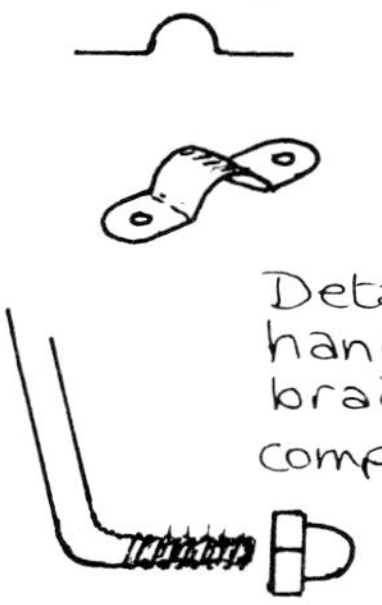

Details of hanger bracket components

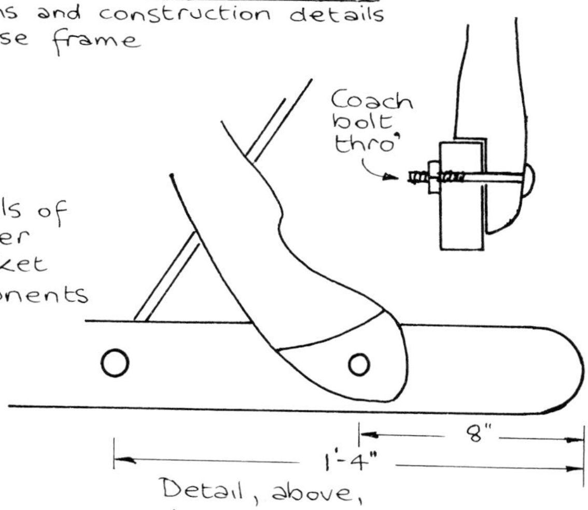

Detail, above, showing how horse is attached to frame

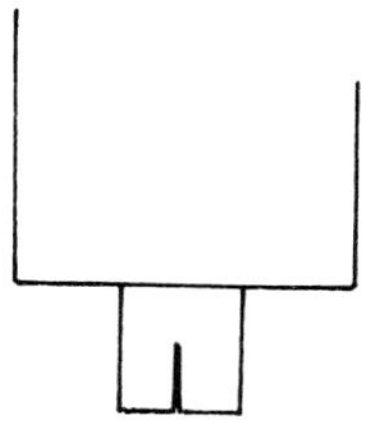

Turned spigot on column and wedged joint fixing

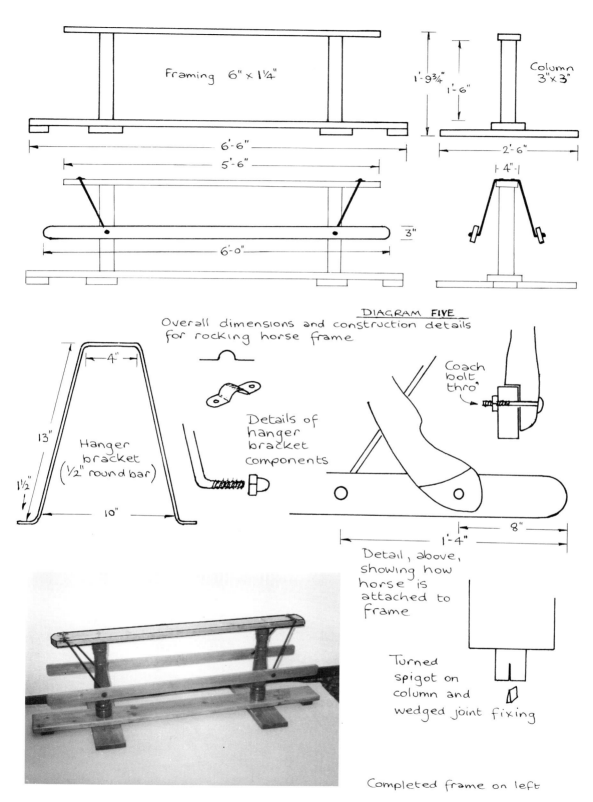

Completed frame on left

MATERIALS REQUIREMENT LIST. (CUTTING LIST IN INCHES & FEET.)				
№	PURPOSE	MATERIAL	INITIAL SIZE	
	HORSE			
2	BODY SIDES	YELLOW PINE	30" × 10" × 2"	
2	"	"	30" × 6" × 2"	
8	ENDS	"	6" × 6" × 2"	
2	HEADS	"	22" × 13" × 2"	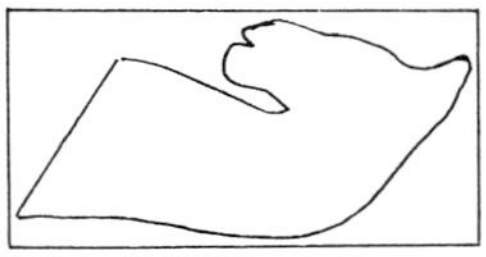
4	LEGS	BEECH	26" × 9" × 2"	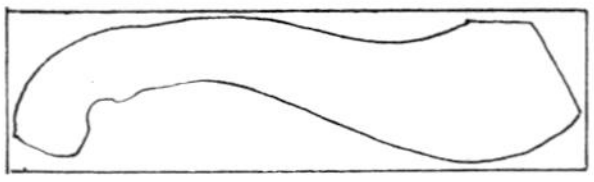
PIECES OF PINE TO BUILD UP MUSCLE AREAS. 4" WOODSCREWS. GLUE.				
LEATHER, ETC. FOR SADDLE, HARNESS, ETC				
HORSE HAIR FOR MANE AND TAIL. PAIR OF LARGE GLASS EYES.				
	FRAME			
2	COLUMNS	PINE	20" × 3" × 3"	
1	BASE	"	6'-6" × 6" × 1¼"	
2	CROSSPIECES	"	2'-6" × 6" × 1¼"	
1	TOP PIECE	"	5'-6" × 4" × 1¼"	
2	SUPPORT RAILS	BEECH	6'-0" × 3" × 1¼"	
TWO HANGER BRACKETS. 4 ACORN NUTS. 4 CLAMPS. 4, 2½" × 3/8" COACH BOLTS				

22

Four-poster Bed

Illustrated on page 240

The four-poster bed enjoyed its zenith of popularity among the wealthier classes during the late-Tudor to Elizabethan period, replacing the more widely used hung bed of earlier times. The hung bed, itself a development from the earlier simple bedstock or frame supporting a rudimentary mattress, had been concealed with curtains which were hung either from the ceiling or from horizontal rails projecting from the wall. As early as the thirteenth century free-standing columns supporting curtain rails were in use and later these gave way to a light wooden framework or tester to which hanging draperies and a canopy were attached. In the opening years of the sixteenth century the drapery at the head of the bed was replaced by wooden wainscot panelling and the head posts incorporated with this but, at first, the foot posts remained separate. A heavy wooden tester in turn replaced the canopy draperies on some beds and the foot posts became part of the bed frame.

In various forms, heavy and ornately carved, higher and elegantly draped, the four-post bed has remained a prestigious piece of furniture even up to the present time. Some early examples were so large that clearly they must have been built inside the room in which they were used and modern bedrooms are now often so small that without some kind of 'knock-down' method of construction the same could still apply.

Designed and made in the workshop of Yorkshire furniture maker Keith Riley for a firm of bed specialists intriguingly named 'And So To Bed', the four-poster described here is constructed with this in mind. It is made throughout in pine and, as the Materials Requirement List shows, p260, it is a large bed, strongly made and therefore requiring a lot of timber, much of it of large proportions. The four posts are lathe turned from 4 × 4in material while the main framing is mainly 1½in thick, with the two side and two end lower rails measuring 8in across their width. The eight fielded panels in the headboard begin as ¾in-thick boards. These are housed in slotted rails which are in turn mortice and tenoned into the main frame and into the four corner posts.

The bed measures overall 7ft 2in long, 5ft 2in wide, and 7ft 6in high and is made to accept a British Standard mattress of 5ft width, 6ft 6in length. Measurements of the bed will have to be altered to suit a mattress different in size.

The availability of a long-bed lathe made it possible to turn each of the posts used in the bed illustrated in one continuous piece, but as it is appreciated that not everyone has a lathe capable of accepting 7ft 2in between centres, instructions are given here for making the posts from joined sections. Beginning with the two head posts, it will be seen that these remain square over most of their length anyway and it is only necessary to turn, separately, the ball foot and the short turned top section. As Diagram One shows, spigots or round tenons are turned on these sections and these are glued into matching holes drilled into the end of the mating pieces to make up the required continuous length.

The two foot posts require a slightly different approach for they have only a short square section, and in the design illustrated, a long plain tapered section not suitable for concealed jointing. To be unseen joints must be made at lines of junction between beads, etc, in turned sections of the posts. The lower part of the post presents no problem; turn the ball foot at one end and a short turned section to a bead at the other end of the portion left square, not forgetting to drill out the top end for the joining spigot. The design of

DIAGRAM ONE

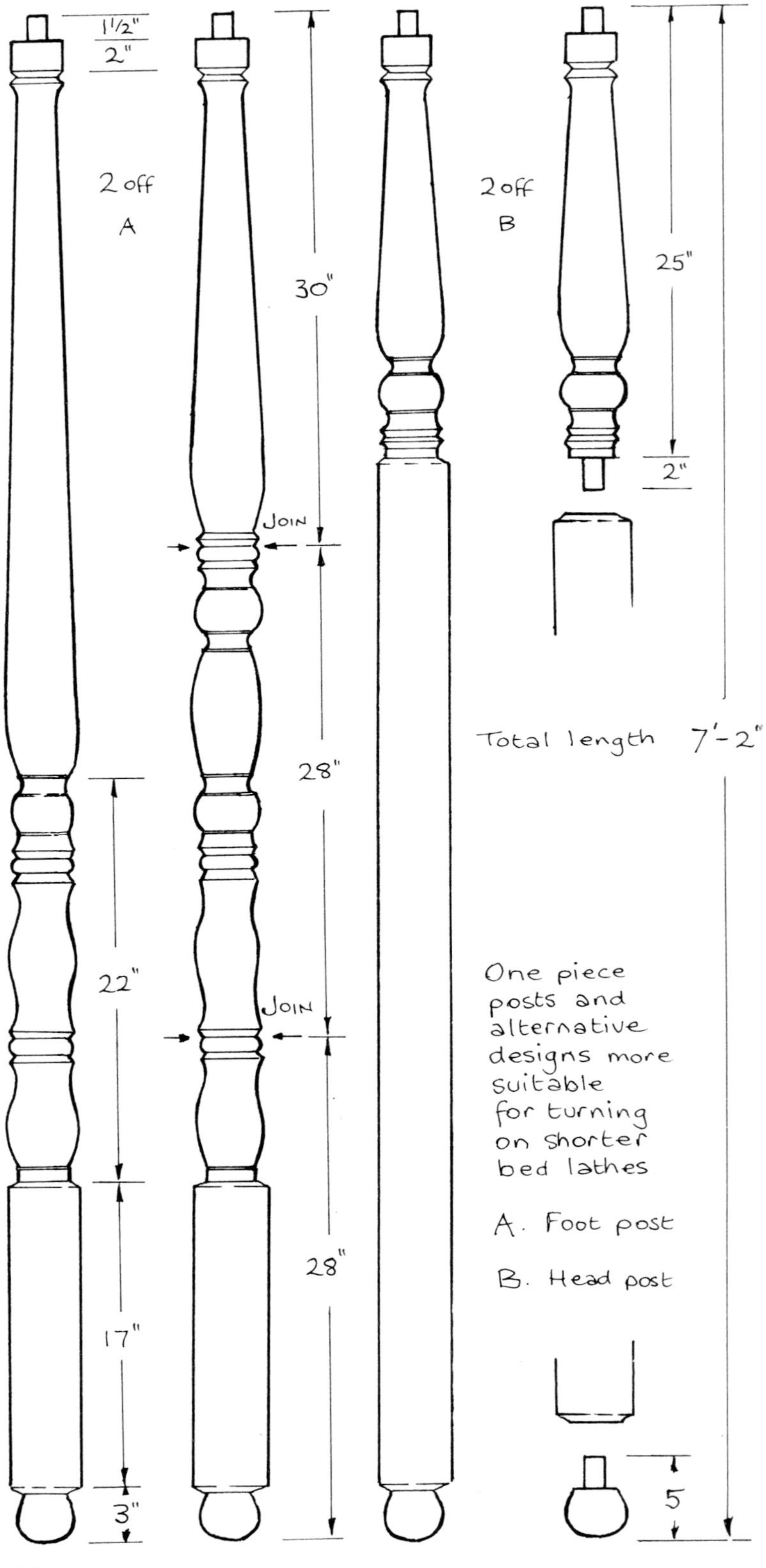

Above,
Showing method of joining separate parts to make up long corner post

DIAGRAM TWO

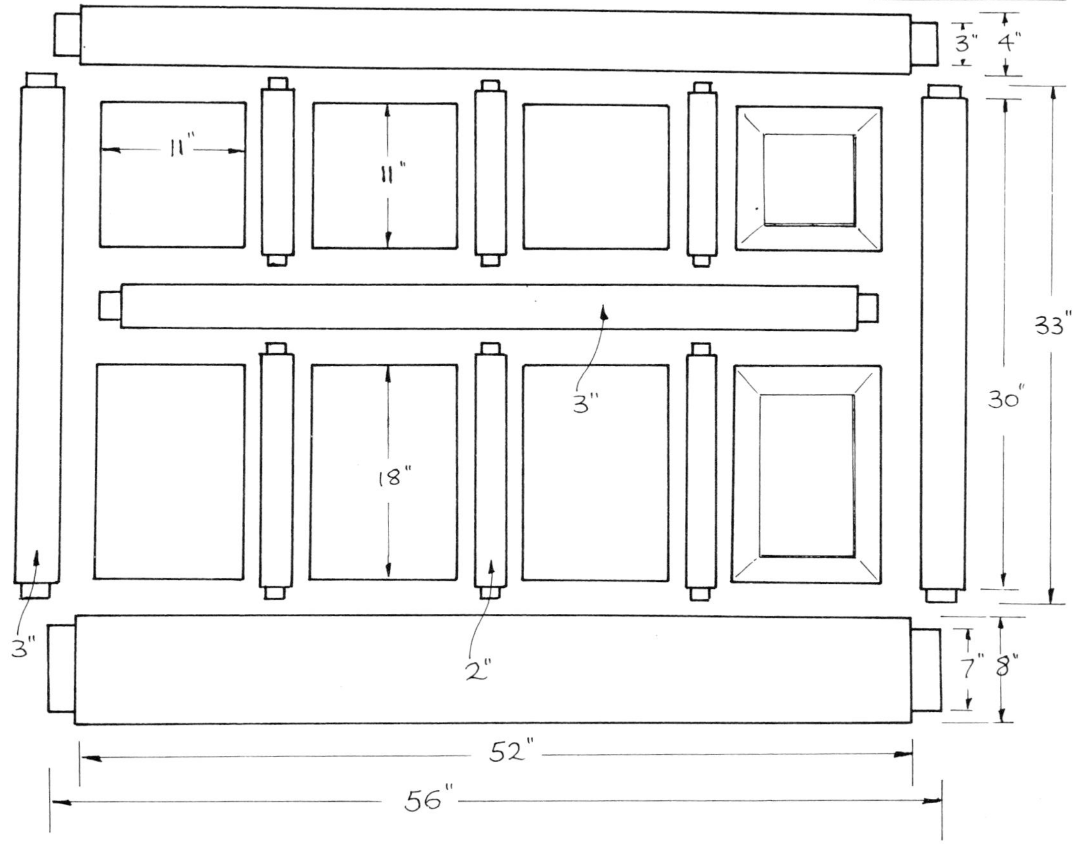

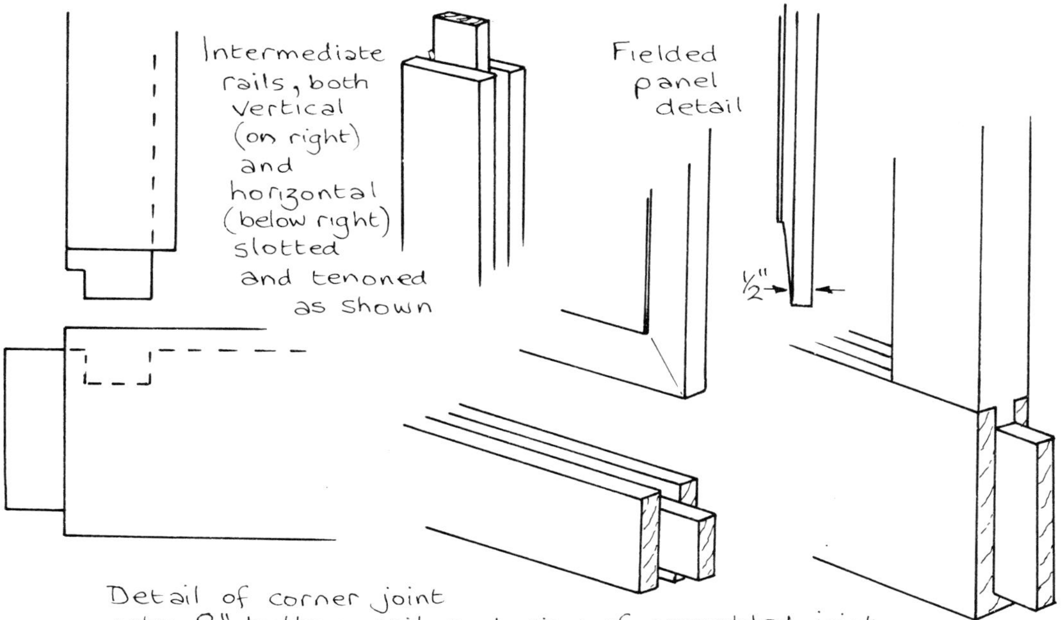

Detail of corner joint into 8" bottom rail and view of assembled joint

the remaining part may have to be altered to suit individual lathes by lengthening the centre turned section, thus making the plain tapered part shorter or by introducing an extra beaded area part way up the tapered section where a joint can be made. Diagram One shows these alternatives and the method of joining the post sections. Do not forget to include spigots for jointing when turning these parts. To ensure a good matching fit for these joints, socket holes are best drilled on the lathe using a suitable Forstner-type bit.

It will be obvious that the areas left square on the corner posts are there to accommodate the mortice-and-tenon joints with which the side, end rails and headboard are joined to them. Do not make the mortices in the posts until the rails and headboard are completed. The turned spigot at the top end of each post locates in the canopy which surrounds the top of the bed.

The headboard is made as shown in Diagram Two, the framing being all 1½in in thickness. Top and bottom rails have tenons which fit into mortices to be later cut in the corner posts. All the slotted edges and end tenons may be marked out with the marking gauge at one setting, which is ½in, the tenons themselves being 2in long where they enter the corner posts and 1½in long at the intermediate joints.

Cut the slots first, to a depth of ½in either on a circular saw or by hand with a router,

Plate 1 Dry assembly of the frame

Plate 2 Panel ready for fielding with the rebate frame

then deepen them at the points where the mortices occur to accommodate the cross-rail tenons. Saw the tenons next, making sure they are square at the shoulders. A dry assembly of the frame at this stage will enable minor adjustments to be made so that it all goes together easily at the final assembly stage. Pencil identification marks on each rail and its mating piece.

The eight headboard panels are cut from ¾in boards edge glued to make up the required width of 11in. Glue up four of these, each initially 30in long, sufficient to make a pair of panels, ie a top and a lower, with some continuity of grain. Cut the two panels from each to finish square at 11 × 11in and 18 × 11in respectively. Mark out for fielding as shown in Diagram Two and carry out the fielding using a suitable plane. Test each for fit in the rail slots and pencil identification marks on to each so that it goes back in its proper place.

The headboard can now be assembled and glued up. Plate 3 shows this in progress. Start with the bottom rail on the bench, put glue in the mortices and insert the tenons of the upright rails. Then slot in the four lower panels. Do not use glue as the panels should be free to move to allow for any movement, ie shrinkage of the wood. Next, put the centre rail in place, put glue in the mortices and add the four top panels, without glue, put the top rail into place and finally add the two end uprights. The whole

Plate 3 Gluing up the headboard

assembly is then cramped [clamped] up and this is easiest done flat on the floor. Check that it lies flat and square and allow the glue to dry. While it is flat on the floor and under cramping [clamping] pressure the mortice-and-tenon joints in the main outer frame may be drilled and pegged for added security.

This bed does not have a foot board, but instead has a foot rail identical in section and every other respect to the side rails. These are all 8 × 1½in similar to the bottom rail of the headboard. Shoulder-to-shoulder length of the side rails is calculated from the length of the mattress, plus 1in which, with 2in tenons at each end makes a total rail length of 6ft 11in. The foot rail length must match the width of the head rail, also determined by the width of the mattress, in this case 5ft giving a total rail length of 4ft 8in.

The 2in-long tenons, ½in thick, are marked out and cut on all three rails, and the position of the mortices in the four posts marked out, using measurements taken from the headboard and rails. All the mortices are then cut and their respective tenons fitted dry or trimmed to fit where necessary. Mating pieces should be given identificaion marks and these may be of a permanent nature, ie, either scribed or chiselled on inside surfaces

Plate 4 Marking out the mortices on the corner posts

Plates 5 and 6 Fitting side and end rails to the corner post using threaded studding for knock-down purposes

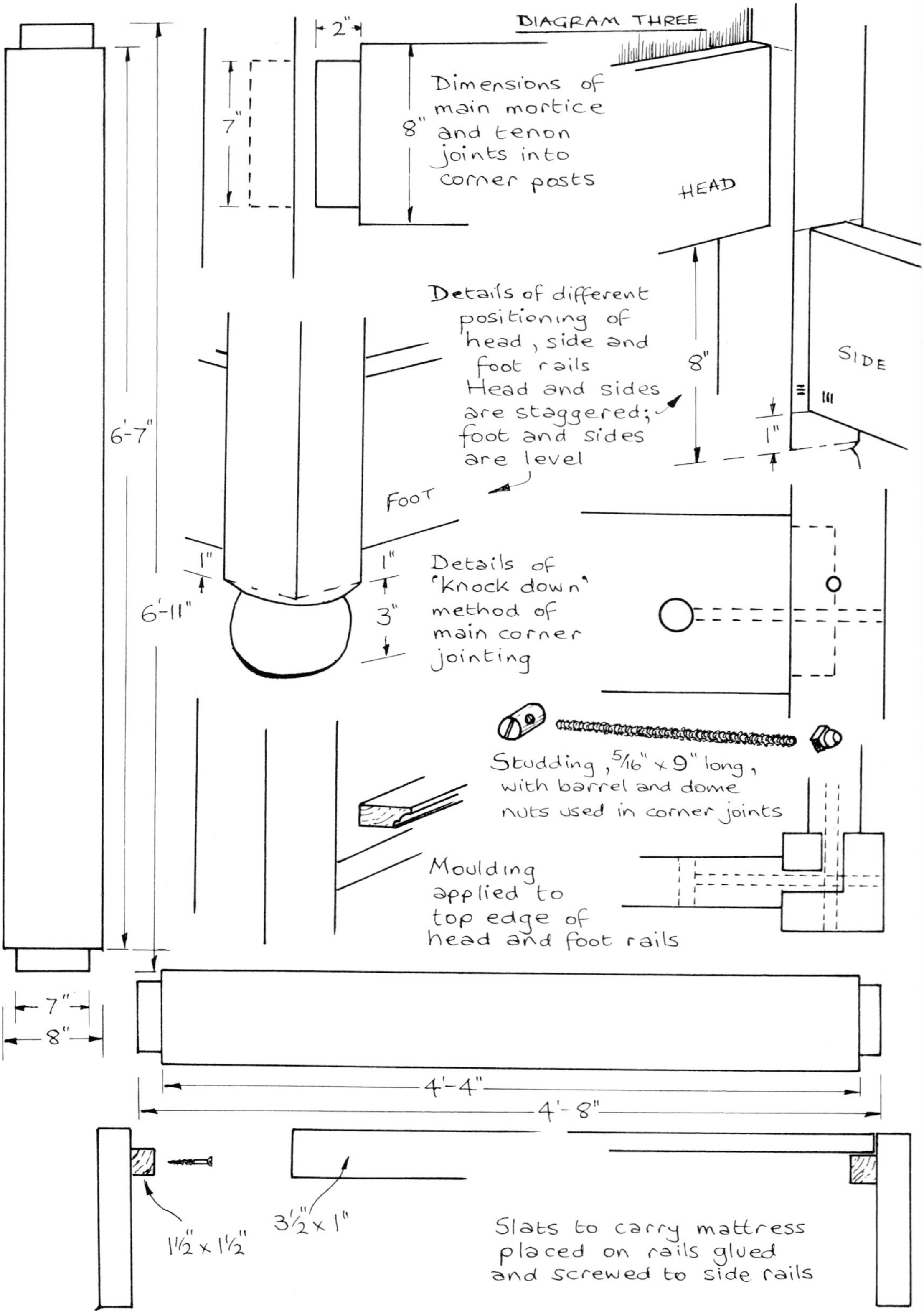
DIAGRAM THREE
2"
7"
8"
Dimensions of main mortice and tenon joints into corner posts
HEAD
Details of different positioning of head, side and foot rails
Head and sides are staggered; foot and sides are level
8"
SIDE
1"
6'-7"
FOOT
1"
1"
6'-11"
3"
Details of 'knock down' method of main corner jointing
Studding, 5/16" x 9" long, with barrel and dome nuts used in corner joints
Moulding applied to top edge of head and foot rails
7"
8"
4'-4"
4'-8"
1½" x 1½"
3½" x 1"
Slats to carry mattress placed on rails glued and screwed to side rails

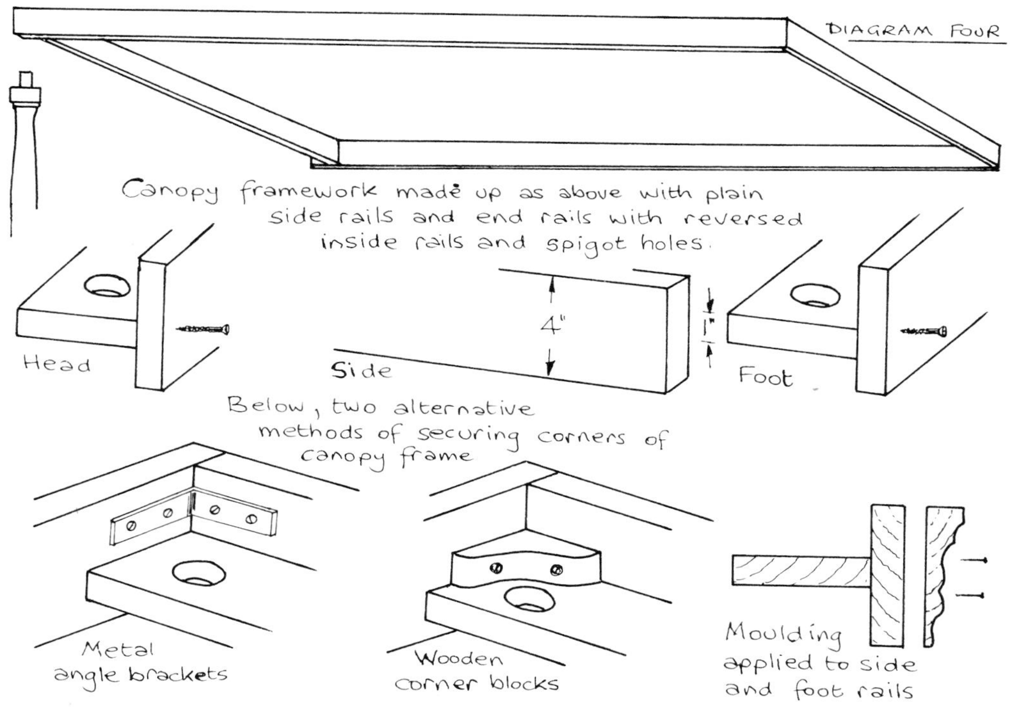
DIAGRAM FOUR
Canopy framework made up as above with plain side rails and end rails with reversed inside rails and spigot holes.
4"
1"
Head
Side
Foot
Below, two alternative methods of securing corners of canopy frame
Metal angle brackets
Wooden corner blocks
Moulding applied to side and foot rails

as the bed may be assembled on the 'knock-down' principle if required for removal and transport purposes. Permanent marks could thus prove helpful.

The knock-down system means that these major corner mortice and tenons are not normally glued. Instead they are secured by means of a length of 5⁄16in threaded studding fitted with a dome-headed nut which passes through the tenon and is screwed into a barrel nut located in the rail as shown in Diagram Three. Correctly fitted, this has the effect of pulling the joint up really tight yet allowing it to be dismantled if and when required. Success lies in accurate joint making, especially with regard to square shoulders to the tenons. Of course, the bed can be permanently glued up but it will have to be assembled inside the room in which it is to be used and will probably have to remain there.

With the four posts, headboard, and side and foot rails assembled, work can begin on making the canopy. This consists of four separate rails which, when in position, form a continuous open framework around the top of the bed from which are hung the curtains or drapes. The two side rails and the rail at the foot of the bed have applied moulding on their outside surfaces but the head of the bed is left plain. This end is usually up against a wall and so is not seen. The canopy is held in position on the spigots turned on the ends of each of the corner posts.

To determine the true length of each canopy rail and the correct centre for drilling the spigot hole, take measurements low down on the bed (higher up may prove inaccurate owing to any splay or slight bowing of the corner posts). The distance from the outside edge of one post to the inside edge of the opposite one will give the spigot hole centre, and adding 2¾in twice to this measurement will give the overall length of each canopy rail.

Head and foot ends are dealt with rather differently as Diagram Four shows. Both have an inside rail screwed on as shown, one being the reverse of the other. It is these rails which are drilled to accept the spigots rising from each corner post. Corner joints between end and side canopy rails may be strengthened by either of the two methods illustrated.

One final job is to make provision for the

mattress. This is placed on substantial slats which cross the bed and are carried on a pair of rails glued and screwed to the inside of the two side rails.

The completed woodwork may be finished in a variety of ways to give either a clear polished or semi-matt surface, or it may be stained to the colour of your choice before polishing. This bed was stained and wax polished to give an authentic, 'stripped pine' effect. It was subsequently fitted with a suitable mattress and then dressed overall with specially designed draperies and matching bed linen made by 'And So To Bed'.

MATERIALS REQUIREMENT LIST. (CUTTING LIST IN INCHES)

Nº	PURPOSE	MAT.	INITIAL SIZES		
4	POSTS	PINE	7'-3 × 4 × 4	TURNED	
2	SIDE RAILS	"	6'-11 × 8 × 1½	PLANED	
1	FOOT RAIL	"	4'-8 × 8 × 1½	"	
	FOR HEAD PANEL.				
1	HEAD RAIL	"	4'-8 × 8 × 1½	"	
1	TOP RAIL	"	4'-8 × 4 × 1½	"	
1	MIDDLE RAIL	"	4'-8 × 3 × 1½	"	
4	TOP PANELS	"	11 × 11 × ¾	FIELDED	
4	LOWER PANELS	"	18 × 11 × ¾	"	

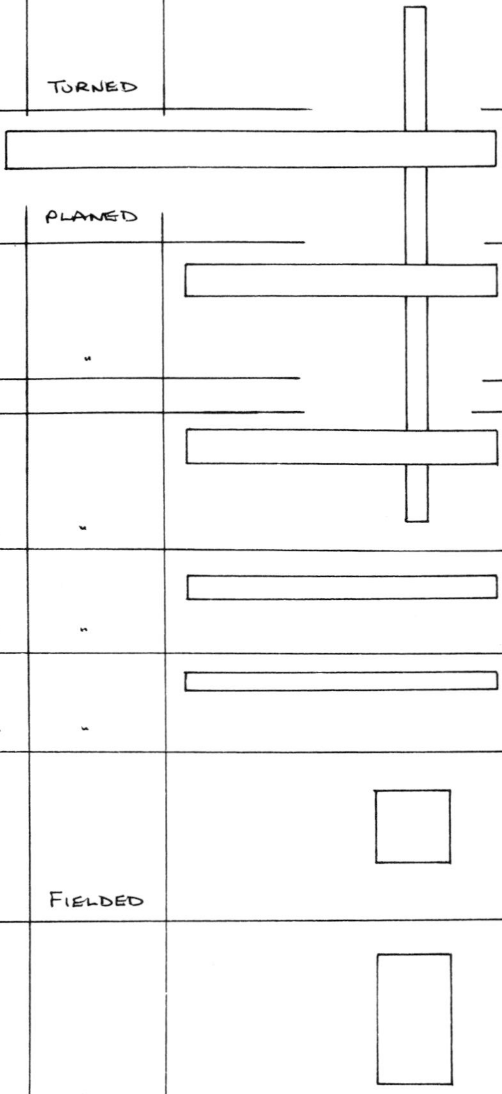

Nº	PURPOSE	MAT.	INITIAL SIZES		
2	END UPRIGHTS	PINE	33 × 3 × 1½	PLANED	
3	INTERMEDIATE UPRIGHTS	"	13 × 2 × 1½	"	
3	INTERMEDIATE UPRIGHTS	"	20 × 2 × 1½	"	
20	MATTRESS SLATS	"	4'-6½ × 3 × 1	"	
2	RAILS (FOR ABOVE)	"	6'-7 × 1½ × 1½	"	
	FOR CANOPY				
2	SIDES	"	7'-0 × 4 × 1	"	
2	ENDS	"	5'-6 × 4 × 1	"	
2	INSIDE ENDS	"	5'-6 × 4 × 1	"	
2	SIDE MOULDINGS	"	7'-3 × 4 × 1½	MITRED	
1	FOOT MOULDING	"	5'-9 × 4 × 1½	"	
2	HEAD & FOOT MOULDINGS		4'-4 × 1¾ × 1	"	
	THREADED STUDDING WITH SUITABLE END NUTS				

23

Contemporary Rocker

Illustrated on cover

Finally, we come to the piece of furniture which forms the subject of the jacket of this book. The chair shown is a contemporary interpretation of a traditional style and it is made in the traditional way. It is, I believe, a true heirloom in the sense that while it holds elements of the past it embraces the present and will go on into the future, cherished in ownership, to be passed on with love into the care of others.

For all the furniture and other items in the book an approximate date can be given for their style or period; a sixteenth-century chest, an 1850s table, and so on – each one basically a copy from an earlier time. Family heirlooms, by definition and certainly in practice, are and are seen to be things from the past. In contrast, this chair is of the present; if dated, it can only be described as being a 1980s style. Therefore, any suggestion that it is an heirloom can only be a projection into the future; in fact, it is a future family heirloom.

I designed the chair for an American lady now domiciled in Devon, England, and made it mainly in ash which I cut from a hillside coppice in the Cumbrian Lake District. The seat is a solid piece of English elm, its shape and the manner in which the legs socket into it following closely the traditional Windsor

Plate 1 The design stage – parts in preparation

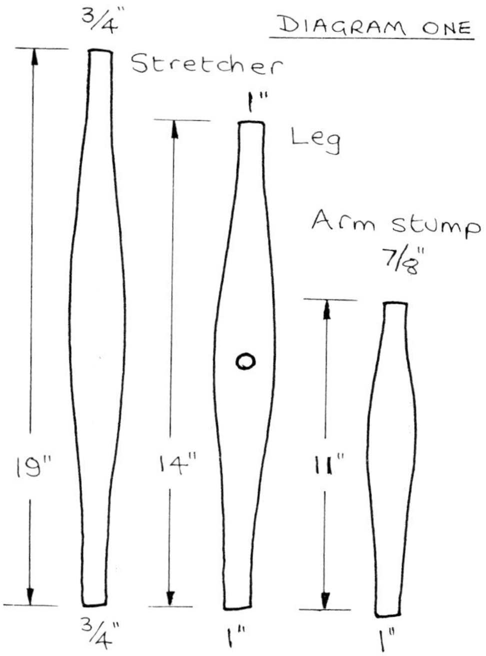

method of construction. However, the legs and the cross stretchers are plain turned, without ornamentation, with plain, substantial rockers to complement them. The main back stiles are continuous with the curved arms, being bent to that shape in a rather special way and inserted into the shaped comb or cresting rail so that this continuity is retained across the back of the chair. The forward ends of the curved arms are supported on plain turned arm stumps securely socketed into the seat; intermediate arm supports are omitted without loss of strength. The seven back sticks are tapered in their length and are curved to follow the contours of the sitter's back. The chair's simple lines and plain turnings relate to my interest in American Shaker styles, while its shape and dimensions owe much to a brief study of anthropometrics.

The ash for legs, stretchers and arm stumps was cleft and not sawn so as to retain the maximum strength and resilience of the wood. Components were rough shaped with a draw-knife and then turned to the sizes shown in Diagram One with the rotary planes described elsewhere. A conventional lathe could have been used – the back sticks,

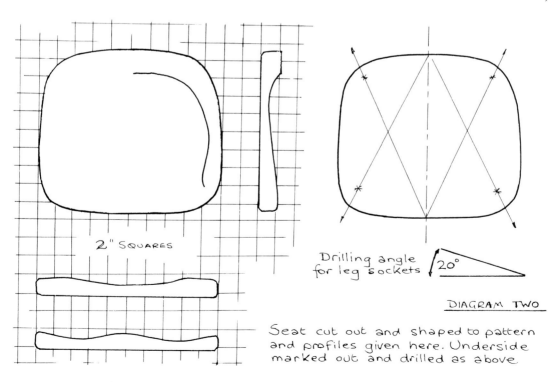

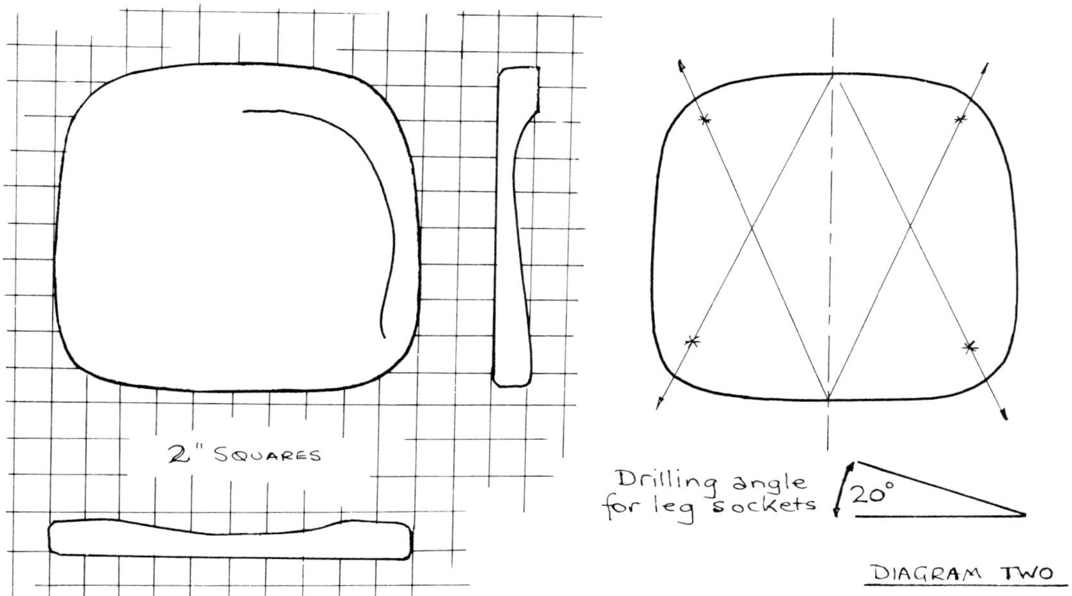

Seat cut out and shaped to pattern and profiles given here. Underside marked out and drilled as above

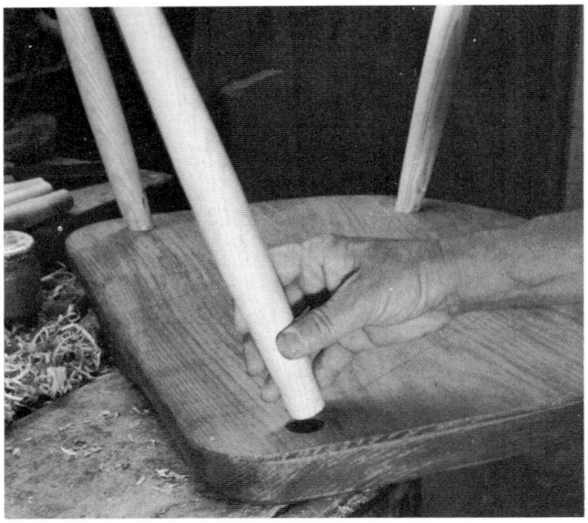

Plate 2 The legs being fitted

which were also cleft, raising the usual problems with turning long thin sections. All other material was sawn.

The seat was cut to shape and the top surface hollowed or saddled as shown in Diagram Two. The underside was marked out and drilled for the leg sockets as shown in the same diagram, this work following quite closely that described earlier for the Windsor rocking chair. Legs were temporarily fitted to enable measurements to be taken for the cross stretchers and these were cut to length and the respective socket holes drilled. With a pair of rockers band sawn to shape and smoothed with the spokeshave,

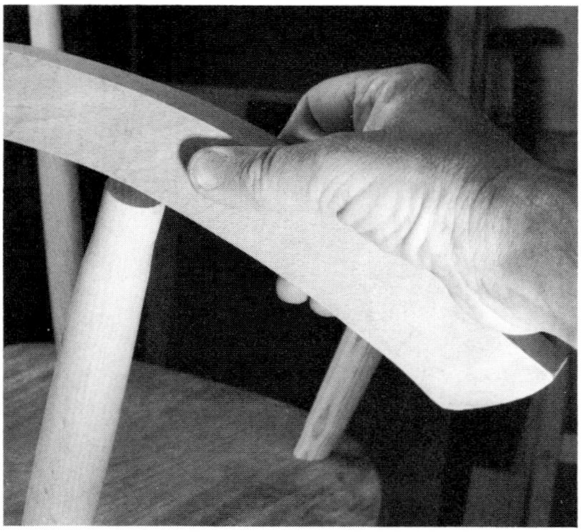

Plate 3 Checking the fit of the rockers

legs were again temporarily inserted into their seat sockets and the rockers offered up and marked out for drilling. The rockers are best fitted at a later stage.

The upper surface of the seat was marked out and drilled for arm stumps and back sticks, the former going right through the seat so that they could be wedged in for added security. Note that the drilling angle for the back sticks appears odd in that they angle forward rather than backwards, as seems more correct. This forward angle is due to the lumbar curve of the back stick, described later (see Diagram Three).

DIAGRAM THREE

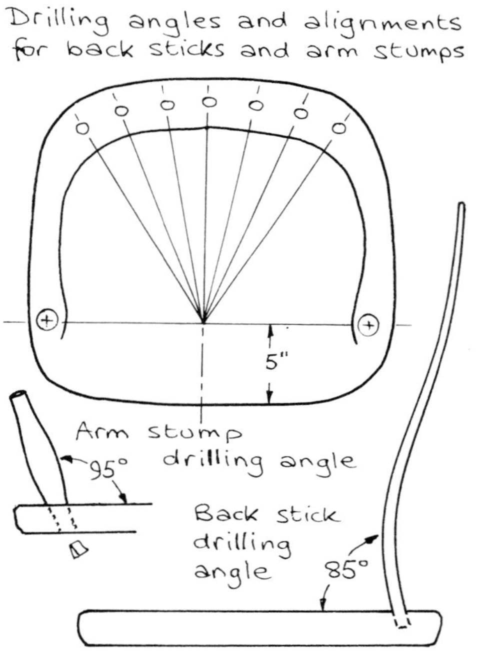

In making the two continuous arms and back stiles a combined technique utilising steam bending and laminating methods was used. Instead of making each bend in the solid or of alternatively using thin veneers, a piece of straight-grained ash was cut into three ½in-thick strips, 2in wide, and the pieces marked so they stacked together as cut for grain matching. These were steamed for approximately 30 minutes, then bent on a prepared former [form], and held there under pressure until set. This took three days

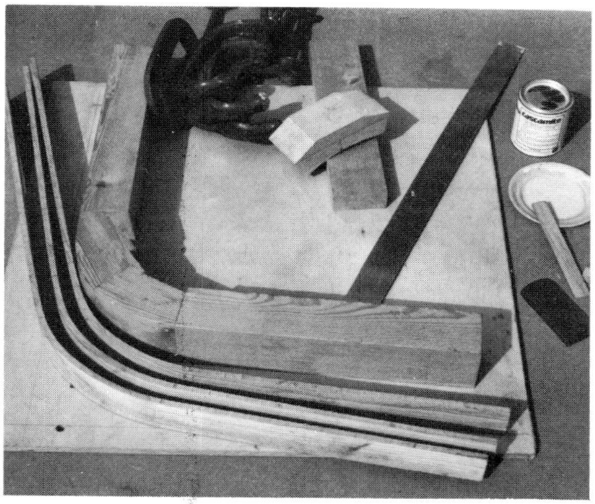

Plate 4 The bend ready for gluing up

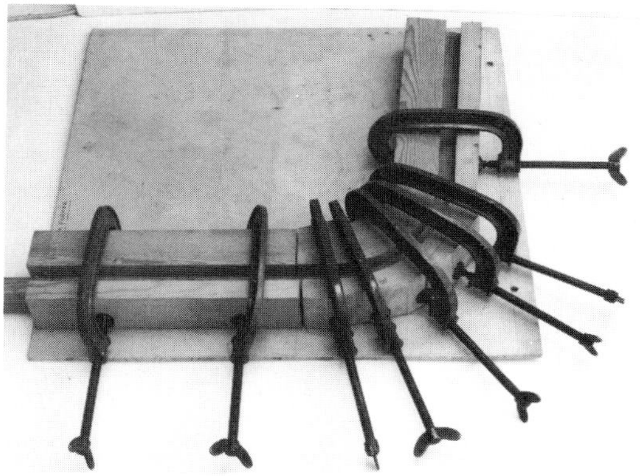

Plate 5 Arm/back stile bend in a former under pressure

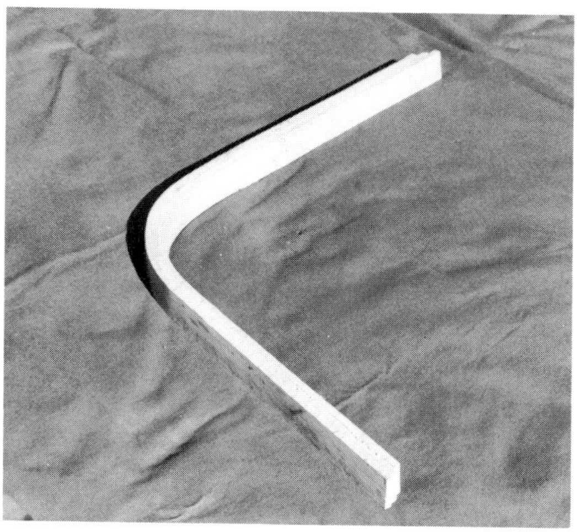

Plate 6 The completed arm/back stile

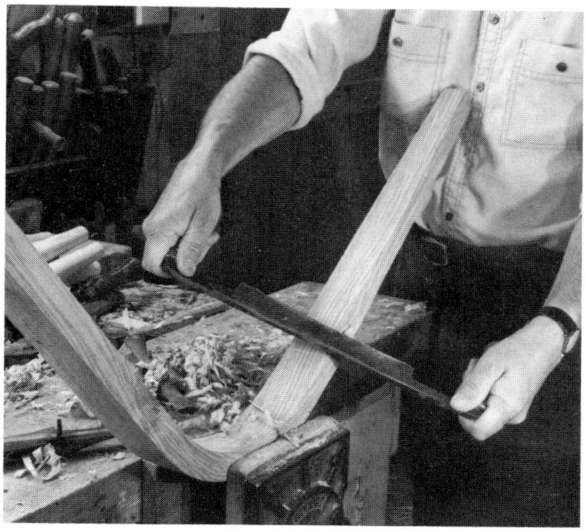

Plate 7 Shaping the arm/back stile with a draw knife

(hot and sunny). The pieces were removed from the former [form], glued together with a waterproof adhesive, replaced in the former [form] and left under pressure for a further 24 hours. The result was a curved component of 2 × 1½in section. A second arm was made in the same way, then both were shaped with draw-knife and spoke-shave as illustrated. See Diagram Four for details of this method and of the former required.

Next, the comb or cresting rail was cut to shape. This not only has a slight curve along its length but is also thicker at its two outward ends than it is at its centre and in addition it tapers across its width. The sections given in Diagram Four will help in understanding this, but in essence, provided the ends of the comb match up with the uprising back stiles the remainder of the shape does not need to follow exactly that shown; aim instead to obtain a pleasing shape to the comb to satisfy your own taste.

The lower edge of the comb has a total of nine holes drilled into it. All are ½in in diameter, seven of them for the back sticks, with the two end ones to accommodate the back stile joints. These are dowel joints, the dowel inserted into the end of the stile and left extra long for entry into the comb. The extra length helps strengthen the short grain in the area of the joint and ensures that a proportion of the dowel passes through this

DIAGRAM FOUR

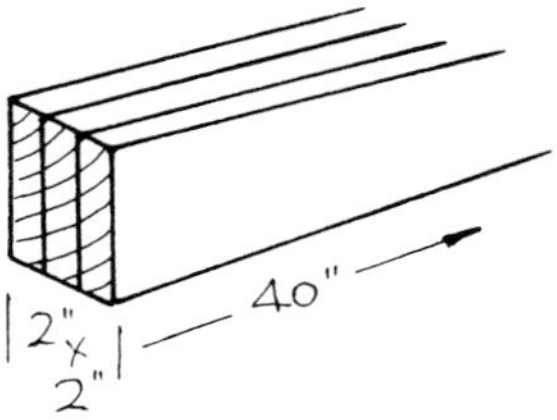

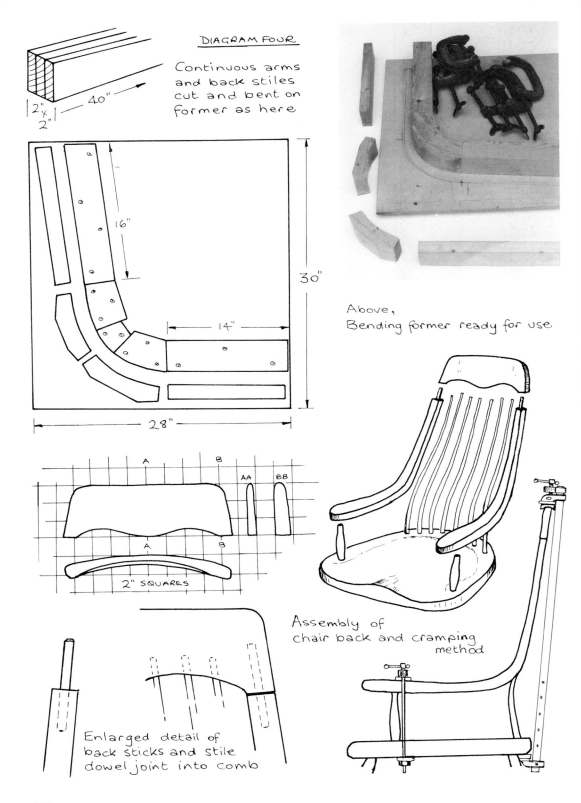

Continuous arms and back stiles cut and bent on former as here

Above, Bending former ready for use

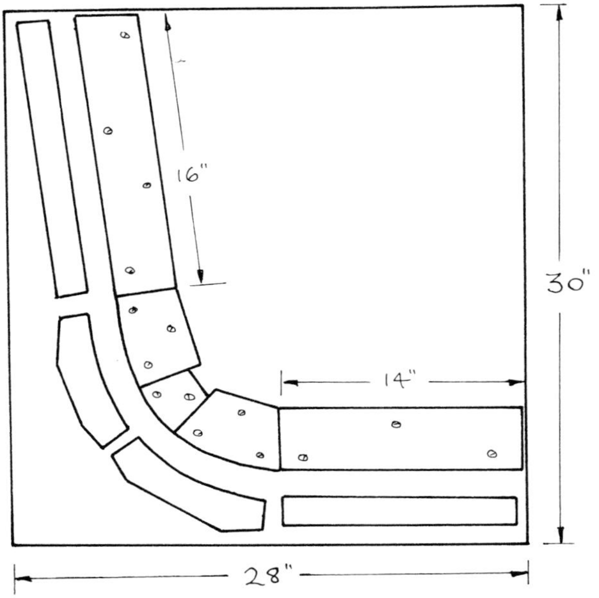

Assembly of chair back and cramping method

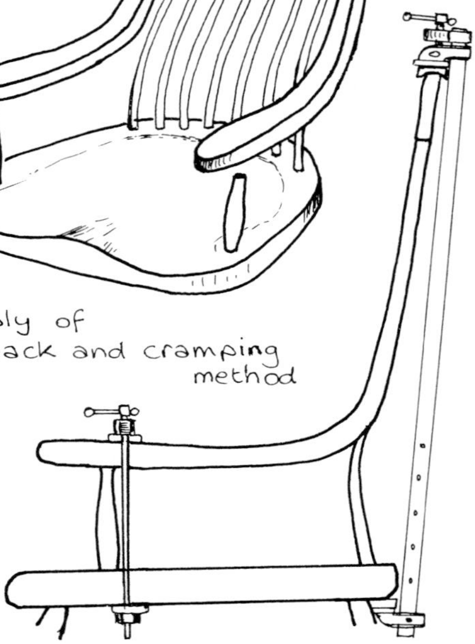

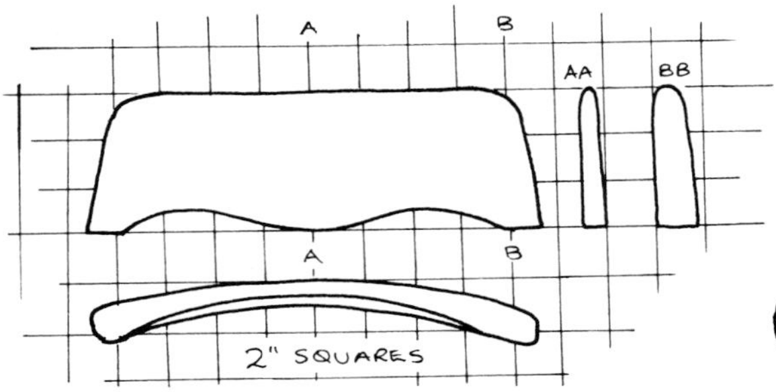

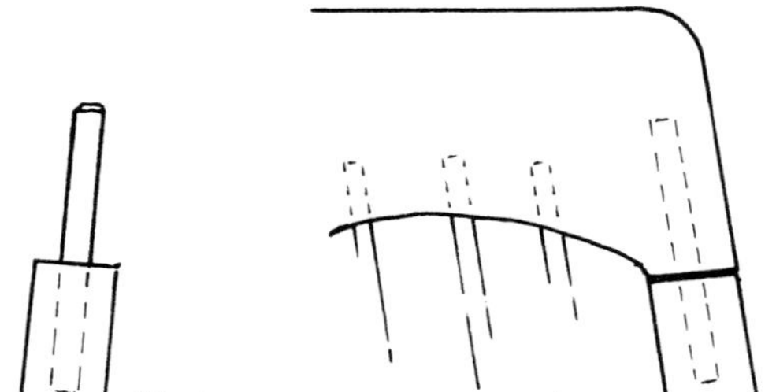

Enlarged detail of back sticks and stile dowel joint into comb

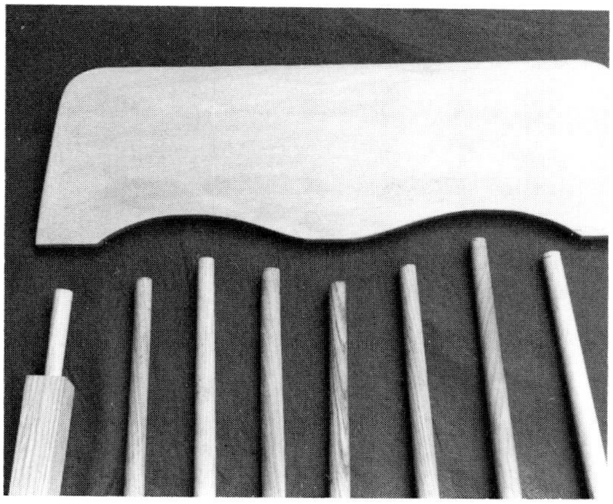

Plate 8 Back stile and back sticks ready for jointing into the comb

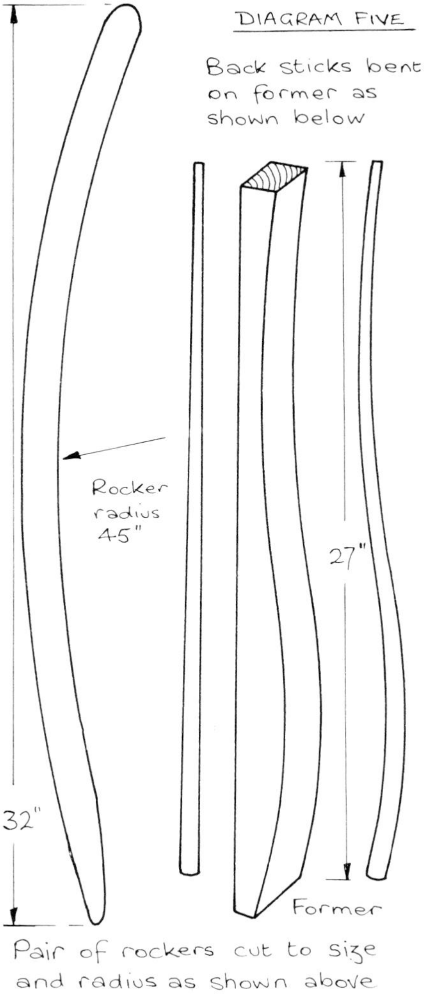

area and into an area of greater strength. Special attention should be given to the jointing surfaces between comb and stiles; their shoulders should be a close fit. Any gap here would not only spoil the chair's appearance it could also affect the strength of the joint.

The chair illustrated had initials carved into the comb and where this is to be done it is best carried out before assembly.

The seven tapered back sticks, already cut to size, require shaping to the curve designed to fit more closely to the back of the sitter. The shape is determined largely by the hollow of the human lumbar region and, although this varies individually, a compromise figure of 9in above the seat for the centre of the shallow radius curve was duly arrived at. A former [form] was made as shown in Diagram Five and after 30 minutes in the steam box the back sticks were bent on to the former [form] and restrained under pressure. The former [form] made accommodates four sticks so the process was repeated. After three days the sticks were removed and, as the steam raises the grain of the wood appreciably, each one had to be sanded smooth again. Note that final stick lengths vary in accordance with the lower contours of the comb.

A dry run of the prepared components was carried out and, when it was seen that everything would go together satisfactorily, legs and stretchers were glued into their respective sockets and the back assembly begun. First, the arm stumps were glued and wedged into the seat, and the back sticks placed into their socket holes. The back stile dowels were then inserted into their holes in the comb and the arms brought down on to the arm stumps, with the ends of the back sticks manipulated into their socket holes simultaneously. With the shoulder of the back stiles in close contact with the underside edge of the comb, and after making sure that the arm stumps were entered up into the arms to their full depth, sash cramps [clamps] were used to keep these joints under pressure until the glue had set. It is important to protect the wood against the hard edges of the sash cramps [clamps] during this time and not to over-tighten the back cramps [clamps] as there is a deal of springiness in the construction which is working against

Plate 9 The continuous line of comb and back stile

the action of the cramps [clamps] while they are in place.

When the glue had set the cramps [clamps] were removed and the area around the back stile and comb joint was smoothed into a continuous line. Then the whole chair was sanded smooth, rockers were fitted and the chair was ready for finishing. Although suitable for a clear-wax finish, the chair was required to match existing furniture in the room where it was to be used. Accordingly, it was stained with a proprietary [commercial] rosewood stain, the colour, and the wood, sealed with two coats of sanding sealer each rubbed down with fine-grain wire wool and finally wax polished.

MATERIALS REQUIREMENTS LIST. (CUTTING LIST IN INCHES)

No.	PURPOSE	MATERIAL	INITIAL SIZES		
1	SEAT	ELM	20 × 20 × 2	SHAPED	
4	LEGS	ASH	15 × 1¾ × 1¾	ROUNDED	
2	STRETCHERS	"	20 × 1½ × 1½	"	
2	ROCKERS	"	33 × 5 × 1½		
2	ARM/BACKSTILES	"	40 × 2 × 2	SAWN TO MAKE 2 × ½ FOR LAMINATING	
2	ARM STUMPS	"	12 × 1½ × 1½	ROUNDED	
7	BACK STICKS	"	28 × ⅞ × ⅞	" AND BENT	
1	COMB	"	18 × 6 × 2	SHAPED	

Appendix and Bibliography

SUPPLIERS OF SAWN HARDWOODS IN BRITAIN AND THE USA

The addresses given are of those timber merchants [lumber dealers] who have indicated that they will supply small quantities of good-quality hardwoods to the amateur and small professional woodworkers.

Both lists which follow are of necessity incomplete; there are certainly many more sources of supply than those given here and readers are advised to seek out their best local supplier. The British list consists of those timber merchants [lumber dealers] with whom I deal personally together with some who are regular advertisers in *Woodworker* magazine and some members of the Home Timber Merchants Association. The American list is a mere hint at a much more comprehensive one compiled by *Fine Woodworking* magazine and from which I have given only the first alphabetically for each state.

SOURCES OF SAWN TIMBER IN BRITAIN

Northern England
John Boddy & Son Ltd, Riverside Sawmills, Boroughbridge, Yorkshire
Duffield & Sons Ltd, Clencairn Mill, Heads Nook, Near Carlisle
Luke Smalley Ltd, Clitheroe, Lancashire
Midlands
Bromyard Sawmills Ltd, Bromyard, Herefordshire
Midland Forestry Ltd, Earlswood, Solihull, West Midlands
Henry Venables Ltd, Doxey Road, Stafford, Staffordshire
South-East England
F. E. Cordy Ltd, Lingwood, Norwich, Norfolk
Timberline, Morley Road, Tonbridge, Kent
Wheelers Ltd, Sudbury, Suffolk
London Area
General Woodwork Supplies, Stoke Newington High Street, London N16
Home Counties Hardwoods, Near Camberley, Surrey
South-West England
The Bathurst Estate, Coates, Cirencester, Gloucestershire
Talewater Sawmill Ltd, Talaton, Near Exeter, Devon
Treework Services Ltd, Church Town, Backwell, Near Bristol
Wales
Boys & Boden Ltd, Welshpool, Powys
Llangadock Sawmills, Llangadock, Dyfed
Scotland
Brownlee & Co Ltd, Graigentinny Avenue North, Edinburgh
Northern Ireland
Ballycassidy Sawmills Ltd, Enniskillen, Co Fermanagh, Northern Ireland

SOURCES OF SAWN TIMBER (LUMBER) IN THE USA

Alabama: Dilworth Lumber Co, 415 Church Street, N.W. Huntsville. 35804
Alaska: Hardwoods Inc, 1940, Spar Ave, Anchorage. 99501
Arizona: Austin Hardwoods, 2045, N. Forbes, 102-A, Tucson. 86705
California: Robert M. Albrecht, 18701, Parthenia Street, Northridge. 91324
Colorado: Bill Collins Hardwoods, 500, W. Wesley Ave, Denver. 80223
Connecticut: General Woodcraft, 100 Blinman Street, New London. 06320
Delaware: Shields Lumber & Coal Co, Kennett Pike, Greenville. 19807
Florida: R. W. Haley Lumber Co, 5517, Mossy Top Way, Tallahassee. 32303
Georgia: Atlanta Hardwood Corp, Box 39038, Atlanta. 30318
Illinois: Atlas Furniture Co, 1133, Railroad Ave, Rockford. 61108
Indiana: Cash & Carry Lumber Co, State Route, 32, Box 427, Daleville. 47334
Iowa: Jack Becker, Rte 2, Dyersville. 52040
Kansas: The Wood Works, 7525 W. 80th St, Overland Park. 66204
Kentucky: Bob Morgan Woodworking Supplies, 1123, Bardstown Road, Louisville. 40204
Louisiana: Kent Courtney, 1413 Texas Ave, Alexandria. 71301
Maryland: Braddock Design & Woodworks, 6, East Street, Frederick. 21701

Massachusetts: Albany Street Workshop, 533, Albany St, Boston. 02118
Michigan: Armstong Millworks, 3039, W. Highland Road, Highland. 48031
Minnesota: Jones Lumber Corp, 722 Kasota Circle, Minneapolis. 55414
Mississippi: Anderson-Tully Lumber Co, Box 38, Vicksburg. 39180
Missouri: Cedar Park Manufacturing Co, Box 593, Mercer. 64661
Montana: O'Neil Lumber Co, 424, Main Street, Kalispell. 59901
Nebraska: Midwest Woodworkers Supply, 13209 E. St., Omaha. 68137
New Hampshire: Wholesale Forest Products, Box 45, Claremont. 03743
New Jersey: Centre Lumber Co, 85, Fulton St, Box 2242, Paterson. 07509
New Mexico: Frank Paxton Lumber Co, 1909 Bellamah Ave, N.W. Albuquerque. 87125
New York: Maurice L. Condon Co, Inc, 248 Ferris Ave, White Plains, New York. 10603
North Carolina: Pete Armstrong Veneer, 2419, Ashford Circle, High Point. 27261
Ohio: American Woodcrafters, Box 919, 1025 S. Roosevelt, Piqua. 45356
Oklahoma: Paxton Beautiful Woods, 1539 St. Yale, Tulsa. 74112
Oregon: Lachlan/Docherty, 517 N. Kutch, Box 397, Carlton. 97111
Pennsylvania: Amaranth Gallery and Workshop, 2500–2502 N. Lawrence St, Philadelphia. 19133
Rhode Island: Allied Plywood, 60, Shipyard St, Providence. 02905
Tennessee: Hardwoods of Memphis, Box 12449, Memphis. 38112
Texas: Alamo Hardwoods, 1, Fredricksburg Road, San Antonio. 78201
Utah: Fremont Lumber Co, 3149 St State St, Salt Lake City. 84115
Vermont: Michael K. Biddy, Box 424, Shaftesbury. 05262
Virginia: Al-San Lumber Co, 4006, Killam Ave, Norfolk. 23508
Washington: Hammond Ashley Associates, 19825 Des Moines Way St, Seattle. 98148
West Virginia: Sunshine Sawmill, Tenick. 24966
Wisconsin: The Board Store, Box 205, Bangor. 54614

SUPPLIERS OF CABINET FITTINGS AND MISCELLANEOUS ITEMS

BRITAIN

Classical Brass West Road, Westcliff on Sea, Essex
Brass fittings, antique reproductions, etc
Woodfit Ltd Kem Mill, Chorley, Lancashire
Cabinet fittings and sundries
Ash Timber Co Ltd Cheetham Hill Road, Manchester 8
Hardware, woodscrews, adhesives, etc
Grenville Airport House, Purley Way, Croydon, Greater London
Clock parts, movements and all accessories
John Wood 108 Chorley Road, Westhoughton, Bolton, Lancashire
Rocking-horse accessories, horse-hair manes, bridles, etc
'And-So-To-Bed' 60/62 West Street, Sowerby Bridge, Halifax, West Yorkshire
Four-poster bed drapes and mattresses to measure
F. T. Morrell & Co Ltd Mill Lane, Woodley Stockport, Greater Manchester
Finishing materials and sundries, wood stains and polishes, etc, adhesives
Mulberry Bush 25 Trafalgar Street, Brighton, Sussex
Doll's house accessories, sae for samplers/catalogues
John Myland Ltd 80 Norwood High Street, London SE27
Finishing materials, French polish, woodstains, etc

UNITED STATES OF AMERICA

Woodcraft Supply Corp 313 Montvale Avenue, Woburn, Massachusetts. 01888
Furniture fittings, finishing materials, adhesives, etc
Albert Constantine & Son Inc 2050 Eastchester Road, Bronx, New York. 10461
Furniture fittings, finishing materials, etc

BIBLIOGRAPHY

Edlin, Herbert L., *What Wood is That?* (Stobart & Son, 1977)
Gloag, John, *A Short Dictionary of Furniture* (George Allen & Unwin, 1952; revised 1969)
Gottshall, F. H., *Reproducing Antique Furniture* (Allen & Unwin, 1971; Crown [New York])
Hayward, Charles, *Period Furniture Designs* (Evans Bros, 1968)
—— *Staining and Polishing* (Evans Bros, 1962; Drake [New York])
Joyce, Ernest, *The Technique of Furniture Making* (Batsford, 1970; 2nd ed reprinted 1978)
Pain, Frank, *Practical Woodturning* (Evans Bros, 1957)
Taylor, V. J., *The Construction of Period Country Furniture* (Stobart & Son, 1978)
Turner & Stevens, *Solid and Laminated Wood Bending* (HM Stationery Office, 1948)

Index

Numbers in *italic* refer to illustrations